Digital Communication and Media Linguistics

This textbook offers an interdisciplinary, comprehensive, and state-of-the-art overview of the media linguistics approaches to explain and understand digital communication and multimodality. Linking the fields of communication studies, applied linguistics, and journalism, it grounds communication practices in a deep understanding of the social and societal implications of language use in digital media. The tools to analyze multimodal texts are examined in light of the advantages and constraints that different communication modes pose, both individually and in combination. Aimed at upper-level undergraduates and graduates in applied linguistics, communication and media studies, including journalism and PR, this textbook contains case studies and professional examples highlighting the interplay between language use and digital communication and encouraging the reader to reflect on the themes covered, and put the acquired knowledge into practice. Online resources for students include videos, writing techniques, a guide to multimodal texts analysis, additional case studies, and a glossary.

ALEKSANDRA GNACH is Professor of Media Linguistics at ZHAW Zurich University of Applied Sciences, Switzerland. Her areas of interest include the use of social media at the interface between public and private communication and the production and use of new media formats (VR, AR, XR) in public communication. She is the co-founder of the IAM MediaLab, a participatory platform that brings together professionals and scholars from different fields to actively engage in the challenges of digital transformation.

WIBKE WEBER is Professor of Media Linguistics at ZHAW Zurich University of Applied Sciences, Switzerland. Her research focuses on visual semiotics, image analysis, digital storytelling, data visualization, information design, multimodality, and virtual reality, and she has published several books and journal articles in all these areas. She has previously worked as a journalist in public and private media companies.

MARTIN ENGEBRETSEN is Professor of Language and Communication at University of Agder, Norway. His research interests include visual and multimodal communication, rhetorics, discourse analysis, digital communication, and journalism. He has published numerous books and journal articles at the intersection of linguistics and media studies. Prior to becoming an academic, he worked as a newspaper journalist.

DANIEL PERRIN is Professor of Applied Linguistics and Vice President at ZHAW Zurich University of Applied Sciences, Switzerland. His research focuses on text production in professional settings. Before starting his academic career, he worked as a journalist and writing coach and is still engaged in training and coaching media and communication professionals as well as leaders in education, economy, and politics in the framework of transdisciplinary projects.

"Highly instructive and very readable, this book provides a clear overview of the broad field of public digital communication. It successfully bridges theory and practice by presenting research approaches from various disciplines as well as useful tools and methods for multimodal analysis."
Professor Christa Dürscheid, University of Zurich

"The go-to resource for anyone doing research in digital communication! Combining selected theoretical concepts and illustrative analyses using diverse research methods, this book provides a modern understanding of today's mediatized world to professionals and students alike."
Professor Judith Bridges, University of South Florida

Digital Communication and Media Linguistics

WITH CASE STUDIES IN JOURNALISM, PR, AND COMMUNITY COMMUNICATION

ALEKSANDRA GNACH
Zurich University of Applied Sciences

WIBKE WEBER
Zurich University of Applied Sciences

MARTIN ENGEBRETSEN
University of Agder, Norway

DANIEL PERRIN
Zurich University of Applied Sciences

CAMBRIDGE
UNIVERSITY PRESS

CAMBRIDGE
UNIVERSITY PRESS

University Printing House, Cambridge CB2 8BS, United Kingdom

One Liberty Plaza, 20th Floor, New York, NY 10006, USA

477 Williamstown Road, Port Melbourne, VIC 3207, Australia

314–321, 3rd Floor, Plot 3, Splendor Forum, Jasola District Centre, New Delhi – 110025, India

103 Penang Road, #05-06/07, Visioncrest Commercial, Singapore 238467

Cambridge University Press is part of the University of Cambridge.

It furthers the University's mission by disseminating knowledge in the pursuit of education, learning, and research at the highest international levels of excellence.

www.cambridge.org
Information on this title: www.cambridge.org/highereducation/isbn/9781108490191
DOI: 10.1017/9781108780445

First published 2023

Printed in Great Britain by Ashford Colour Press Ltd.

A catalogue record for this publication is available from the British Library.

Library of Congress Cataloging-in-Publication Data
Names: Gnach, Aleksandra, author. | Weber, Wibke, 1965– author. |
    Engebretsen, Martin, 1961– author. | Perrin, Daniel, 1961– author.
Title: Digital communication and media linguistics : with case studies in
    journalism, PR, and community communication / Aleksandra Gnach, Wibke
    Weber, Martin Engebretsen, Daniel Perrin.
Description: Cambridge; New York, NY: Cambridge University Press, 2022. |
    Includes bibliographical references and index.
Identifiers: LCCN 2022010933 (print) | LCCN 2022010934 (ebook) | ISBN
    9781108490191 (hardback) | ISBN 9781108780445 (ebook)
Subjects: LCSH: Mass media and language. | Digital media. | BISAC: LANGUAGE
    ARTS & DISCIPLINES / Linguistics / General | LCGFT: Textbooks.
Classification: LCC P96.L34 G58 2022 (print) | LCC P96.L34 (ebook) | DDC
    302.2301/4–dc23/eng/20220713
LC record available at https://lccn.loc.gov/2022010933
LC ebook record available at https://lccn.loc.gov/2022010934

ISBN 978-1-108-49019-1 Hardback
ISBN 978-1-108-74827-8 Paperback

Additional resources for this publication at www.cambridge.org/digitalcommunication.

Contents

4 Professional Context: Journalism, PR, and Community Communication

5 Doing Media Linguistic Research

6 Doing Media Linguistic Analysis

7 Case Studies

Figures

Tables

Acknowledgments

We love texts, we love images, we love communication. Our passion for multimodal communication and digital media has resulted in this book. Many students, colleagues, and friends have contributed to the book with stimulating discussions, challenging commentaries, or ideas for real-world examples and case studies.

We want to express our enormous gratitude to our former colleague Carmel Widmer-O'Riordan for her substantial help. She was the first reader and reviewer of most chapters. She checked grammar and spelling with care, gave us useful feedback on our writing, and provided meaningful feedback on the content. We thank our supportive team based at the School of Applied Linguistics at the ZHAW Zurich University of Applied Sciences: Deborah Harzenmoser for her administrative support and Valery Wyss for checking inconsistencies in quotations, references, and formatting. We would not have made it through the final stages without the invaluable help of Verena Lechner. She drew the many subchapters together into a coherent manuscript, took care of the illustrations and pictures, and checked the copyrights. We were lucky to have the support of such a fantastic team.

Acknowledgement is also due to the copyright holders for their kind permission to reuse their material in this book, and to the authors mentioned in the Further Reading sections for their inspiring work. We are grateful to our colleague Frank-Peter Schilling (ZHAW) for reviewing the chapter on algorithmic culture, and we are grateful to the many other (anonymous) reviewers for the time they invested in reading the chapters and providing constructive feedback. Their commentaries helped us to further develop and refine the manuscript and bring it to its final form. A special thanks goes to the staff of Cambridge University Press for their assistance along the way.

Finally, a big thank you to our families and partners for supporting us throughout with love, encouragement, and good food. Writing this textbook together was an insightful and valuable experience that will advance and enrich our teaching of media linguistics and digital communication – to our students' benefit.

Aleksandra Gnach, Wibke Weber, Martin Engebretsen, and Daniel Perrin

Preface

Media are the communication channels through which we disseminate and exchange information on a daily basis. Over the last twenty years, digital media have hugely impacted our highly mediatized world, and even transformed public communication, a domain traditionally dominated by journalists and communication professionals. Nowadays, personal opinions shared on social media compete with journalistic news, political statements, marketing content, influencer posts, fake news, and social bot communication. Furthermore, public communication has become increasingly participatory, especially on social media, where individuals and interest groups are reframing, remixing, and reshaping media content while sharing it within networks and communities.

As a result, media linguistics – a discipline that lies at the intersection of applied linguistics, media studies, and communication research – has expanded its focus to include not only traditional media (i.e., TV, radio, and print media) but also the new media such as social media platforms.

The fundamental changes that come with the digitalization of communication – the multitude of different actors in the networked public sphere, and the diversification of communication formats and modes – influence the work and self-understanding of communication practitioners. Therefore, this textbook wants to help students of applied linguistics, communication and media studies, and practitioners in related fields to (a) refine their theoretical knowledge so that they can understand participants' roles, reflect on professional norms, and contextualize their actions, (b) familiarize themselves with the methods and tools required to manage the complexity of the interplay between digitalization and public communication, and (c) respond to new technology and the implications that these have on communications strategies and routines.

From a media linguistic viewpoint, language functions both as a display of mental and social structures and processes and as a means to construct and change social reality. Therefore, by investigating language use we can draw conclusions about human actors, technology, social context, and the interplay between these elements.

In digital communication, however, language rarely appears in isolation. Rather, it intersects with other semiotic modes such as images, sound, or layout. Media linguistics has long taken into account that meaning making in this multimodal environment is not a matter of simple addition, but of the interaction and integration of all the modes involved. Thus, media linguistic approaches foster detailed analytical descriptions of multimodal meaning potentials, connect these to their social contexts, and give insights into technology's semiotic work.

In our effort to discuss media linguistics in the context of digital communication, we had to rigorously select exemplary theories, methods, and media. Some topics, such as the analysis of videos, quantitative methods of text mining, or reception analysis, have only been touched upon, but we made sure to direct readers to the relevant publications in the Further Reading section at the end of each chapter. Additionally, this textbook will be accompanied by online resources, including a video explaining what media linguistics is, case studies in the fast-developing field of public digital communication, as well as writing techniques and exercises.

Textbook's Key Features

- Explores how the interplay of language and digital communication can be understood and explained through media linguistic approaches, combining linguistic, semiotic, and sociological perspectives. By doing so, it situates the phenomenon of digital communication in a broader context and links it with offline realities;
- Discusses real-world issues related to the interplay of language and digital communication and highlights the current complexity of digital communication through emergent paradigms (e.g., algorithmic culture);
- Enables the readers to ground their communication practices in a profound understanding of the social and societal implications of language use in digital media. This is crucial as issues raised in relation to digital communication have implications not only for communication professionals but also for society at large;
- Provides an overview of the methodologies and tools to analyze multimodal texts in light of the advantages and constraints that different communication modes pose, both individually and in combination;
- Includes pedagogical features such as chapter previews, learning objectives, activities, list of key terms, chapter summaries, and further reading to encourage readers to reflect on the themes covered, expand their newly acquired knowledge, and put it into practice.

Book Organization and Chapter Overview

Most of the chapters in the book offer a stand-alone reading experience, meaning that they can be read and worked through independently and combined individually.

Chapters 1 to 4 provide fundamental theories and concepts crucial for understanding and contextualizing public digital communication. Furthermore, the chapters help practitioners better assess the changing nature of their professional fields and gain a broader perspective on their daily work.

Chapter 1 introduces basic concepts and critical theories, which are the foundation of this textbook. We first outline the implications of digital communication for our societies by explaining how technological developments affect social realities and vice versa. Then, since digital communication is inextricably interlinked with media, we zoom in on core theories of new media that help the reader understand what is "new" about them and why grasping this "newness" matters. Finally, we outline the discipline of media linguistics and explain how media linguistics can help to make digital media and digital communication more tangible. We focus on three key terms crucial for understanding public digital communication: multimodality, media convergence, and mediatization.

Chapter 2 situates public digital communication in a broader theoretical context. In this chapter, we discuss how the interplay between different societal factors and new technologies fosters a new form of social organization that revolves around the idea of a network. We first explain the implications for public communication when networks are the dominant organizational form. We then shift the focus to social media and explain their role in building and maintaining social networks. The chapter concludes by discussing the influence of algorithms on socialities in a digital society.

Chapter 3 provides the practical context to public digital communication by introducing verbal, visual, and multimodal communication as social practices. In this chapter, we first shed light on the role of writing in the digital age and explore the media linguistic mindset required in rapidly changing digital environments. Then, we introduce social semiotics, an approach to multimodal communication that helps understand how people communicate by combining different modes – e.g., words, images, typography, and layout – into a meaningful whole.

Chapter 4 focuses on the professional context of public digital communication and elaborates on the implications of digitalization for journalism, public relations, and community communication. In this chapter, we provide an insight into the current developments in these fields and an overview of the novel forms and formats of digital communication. We discuss the daily work in journalism and PR and present the literacies and skills needed for writing and producing multimodal content in a digital environment. Finally, we address the ethical challenges that arise because of rapid changes in a digitalized world.

Chapters 5 to 7 aim to enable readers to design research projects on digital communication by outlining research frameworks and introducing methods for conducting linguistic, visual, and multimodal analyses.

Chapter 5 introduces research frameworks that illustrate the role of applied research in identifying problems in society and professions, and its contribution to providing solutions. We explain why the combination of linguistic and ethnographic frameworks is beneficial for finding out what people actually do when interacting in the context of digital media.

Chapter 6 takes the readers from the theoretical frameworks to the research methods applied in these frameworks. We introduce methodological approaches of linguistic, visual, and multimodal analyses and explain how quantitative and qualitative methods can be combined to understand digital communication from a process and a product perspective.

Chapter 7 illustrates the application of the linguistic frameworks and multimodal analysis methods with practical cases from journalism, PR, and community communication. The case studies bring together the perspectives of practitioners and academics and give both tools to examine digital communication processes and products critically.

Chapter 8 offers an outlook on future developments of public digital communication by exploring the implications of artificial intelligence for communication practices and the relationship between human and nonhuman actors. We highlight where communication professions might be headed, outline the challenges facing researchers and practitioners, and explain how media linguistics helps comprehend the dynamics of digital culture.

By combining theoretical reflections with case studies in journalism, PR, and community communication, the book explicitly targets students in programs related to applied linguistics, communication and media studies, including journalism and PR. However, students in other communication fields and practitioners interested in theory and analysis will also find the book relevant and accessible.

1 Starting Point: Digital Society and Media Linguistics

PREVIEW

Where do you read the news? And what sources do you consult before voting in an election or a referendum? Most likely, the answer is online. Digital communication has been playing an increasingly influential role in political contests, mass protests, revolutions, and regime changes worldwide, even when the sources on these issues are unreliable. The Global Inventory of Organised Social Media Manipulation reported evidence of organized social media manipulation campaigns which have taken place in 70 countries in 2019, up from 48 countries in 2018 and 28 countries in 2017, with Facebook remaining the no. 1 platform for these campaigns (Bradshaw & Howard, 2019).

Media and communication influence, shape, and change our societies. Therefore, this first chapter aims to explain the implications of digital communication for our societies and the relationship between media, technology, and society. It also discusses the discipline of media linguistics in the context of digital communication.

First, we introduce the concept of society from a sociological perspective. Then we discuss how societies change as a result of the effects technological developments (such as the Internet) have on them, and vice versa. We illustrate this interplay with a description of digital divides.

In order to explain the significance and changes of public communication in a digital society, we zoom in on the media landscape and explicate the difference between new media and old (or traditional) media. We pay particular attention to the ideas of Marshall McLuhan, as his work remains a cornerstone when studying the relationship between media, technology, and society.

We then explain the relationship between old and new media from a media linguistic perspective by outlining what this discipline covers, its research foci, and the three fundamental key terms in this discipline as well as in this textbook: multimodality, media convergence, and mediatization.

Learning Objectives

By the end of this chapter, you should be able to

- describe the relationship between individuals and society
- explain the major theories on the relationship between technology and society
- discuss why societies are changing
- summarize the key characteristics of new media
- describe the relationship between old and new media
- sketch what media linguistics is about
- map media convergence from four different perspectives
- explain the concept of mediatization.

1.1 Digital Society

Digital communication is, in contrast to analog communication modes, rather fluid. It moves across space and time, overcomes social and geographical boundaries and its contents can be constantly edited and remixed. Digital communication also offers low-threshold tools for the creation of content, which makes **public communication** increasingly participatory. Therefore, new communication models see the public not simply as consumers of preconstructed messages, but as individuals who are shaping, sharing, reframing, remixing, and co-constructing media content. These individuals are not isolated but act within communities and networks, which allow them to spread, share, and create content well beyond their immediate geographic proximity. In that sense, digital communication potentially enables new or transformed social roles and relationships which have the potential to change the relationship between political authority, the economy, mass media, and the public. Scholars all over the world agree that we are on the way to becoming – or that we already are – a new type of **society**. Depending on the perspective, this society is called a post-industrial society, an information society, or a **network society**, to name but a few of the terms used. Following the argumentation of Simon Lindgren (2018), we refer to it as a **digital society** in the sense that we are in an era where our lives, our relationships, our culture, and our **sociality** are affected throughout by digital processes.

1.1.1 Society and Social Structures

Each of us is part of a society, which is generally defined as a group of people with different characteristics who lead interconnected lives and interact directly or indirectly as social actors. Sociology understands social actors as individuals who have the capacity to shape their world in a variety of ways by reflecting on their situation and by the choices available to them at any given time.

Each society has properties of its own and is held together by structures. Individuals perceive these as given structures that cannot easily be changed. Émile Durkheim, a classic sociologist, illustrates the influence of structures as follows:

> When I perform my duties as a brother, a husband or a citizen and carry out the commitments I have entered into, I fulfill obligations which are defined in law and custom and which are external to myself and my actions. Even when they conform to my own sentiments and when I feel their reality within me, that reality does not cease to be objective, for it is not I who have prescribed these duties; I have received them through education.

> (Durkheim, 1895/1982: 50)

Durkheim describes something we all know from our own experience: when interacting with others or doing certain things, we do not always do it because we want to, but rather because we somehow know that we are expected to behave in a particular manner. Durkheim calls the phenomena which make us act in specific ways "faits sociaux" – social facts. Social facts become visible as customs, language use, morals, values, religious beliefs, fashions, rituals, and other rules that influence social life. We can consider social facts to be part of **social structures**, the social institutions and patterns of institutionalized relationships that define our society and enable or constrict what we do daily.

It is helpful to think about social structures as operating on three levels within a given society: the macro, the meso, and the micro level (Figure 1.1).

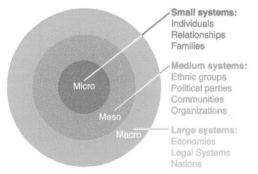

Figure 1.1 Social structures operate on different levels. © 2021 Verena Elisabeth Lechner. Used with permission.

At the macro level, we find patterns of institutionalized relationships, like politics, the economy, education, religion, or the law. They manifest as institutions which are interrelated and interdependent. Together these institutions compose the overarching social structure of a society and organize people into distinct relationships and social roles – such as husband or citizen – as described above. Because institutionalized relationships are typically hierarchical, they lead to power differentials. In many societies, for example, a husband is seen as the head of a household. His social role allows him to decide on how a family spends money or whether family members are allowed to do certain things – or not.

At the meso level, we find structures like network ties between larger groups of individuals or between organizations. These networks are also a manifestation of social stratification. Social stratification refers to a society's categorization of its people into levels of socioeconomic ranks, based on factors like income, race, wealth, education, or power. These factors are of different relevance in different types of societies. In most societies, stratification correlates with the economic system and is therefore based on wealth and income. Parents belonging to the upper class, for example, can afford expensive private schools and tutors, which makes their children more likely to study at an Ivy League university. Graduating from such a university in combination with relationships built during the time there is the ideal prerequisite for a successful career and the associated economic advancement.

Sociologists distinguish between two types of stratification systems, which reflect and foster specific values and influence an individual's behaviors and beliefs. Closed systems – like the Indian caste system – allow almost no change in social position. A person born into a caste has no opportunity for moving into another caste. Open systems, on the contrary, permit movement and interaction between layers, as they are mostly based on achievement. In an open system, a person with parents from a lower class can move to a higher class, through education, economic success, or relationships with people in another class, for example.

At the micro level, social structure manifests in the forms of norms and customs which influence people's everyday interactions. We perceive social structure at this level in the way it shapes our interactions with other individuals and within groups like a family or a neighborhood. The structure also becomes visible in the way institutionalized ideas about aspects like gender or race shape these interactions. An example is discrimination, the unequal treatment based on group membership.

Nowadays, social science also takes global structures such as international organizations, worldwide travel, communication, or economic relations between continents and countries into account.

Social scientists have long debated whether the social structures in Figure 1.1 are the primary means of shaping societies, or whether **agency** – individuals' capacity to act independently and make free choices – is more influential. Structuralists believe individuals are controlled by structures, while those who favor individualist approaches believe agency is the primary influence.

Anthony Giddens, one of the most influential voices in contemporary social theory, reconciled this dichotomy in his theory of structuration (1984). Giddens argues that sociologists should not see individual agency and social structures as being opposed to one another. He claims that just as structures influence an individual's autonomy, they are built, maintained, and adapted through agency. Therefore, social structures are always reproduced or altered by agents and their practices, which are conducted under certain circumstances. Thus, society is reproduced or transformed in conscious practices through every social encounter.

EXAMPLE

Imagine working as a movie producer in Hollywood. You are about to launch the production of a medical drama. Of course, the job comes with many responsibilities, like arranging the finances, hiring writers, a director, and essential team members.

Your project is strongly influenced by the social structures in which it is embedded. The legal system determines your hiring choices. For instance, you cannot hire anyone without a working permit, which excludes a whole range of people from different nationalities. Furthermore, you have access only to candidates whose details are already in your company's file or who can visit and read the website where you advertise the jobs – this is where technology and education come into play.

Moreover, your choices are influenced by cultural norms, the values of the organization you are working for, and the ideas and preferences of the community involved in producing films in Hollywood. The plot of your drama, how each character acts and talks, and how roles are cast reflect those values, norms, and preferences. Are the doctors men or women? What skin color do they have? What challenges do they face in their lives, professionally and personally? How do they live their sexuality? Is that even an issue in your drama, is it allowed to be?

The example of *Grey's Anatomy*, an American medical drama television series, illustrates how far-reaching the consequences of a producer's decisions can be. While the show focuses on the fictional lives of surgical interns and residents, each episode also includes an abundance of social and medical concerns encountered by the hospital's staff. Since its launch in 2005, *Grey's Anatomy* has routinely drawn an audience of around 20 million viewers. As a result, it is not just one of the longest-running dramas in television history; it is also considered one of the most influential. Countless scientific studies document the series' impact on gender equality,

feminism, sexuality, patient behavior, the medical profession, and social issues
dominant in the United States.

This example shows that the seemingly profane choices of a film producer can
have quite an impact on our attitudes and behavior. The decisions of Shonda Rhimes,
who created *Grey's Anatomy*, challenged several stereotypes, and changed many
people's views on social realities and their choices in specific situations. Therefore,
the series had an undeniable impact on social reality.

If you are interested in the interplay of television and social realities or in popular
culture, you might like the book *How to Watch Television*. There you find also a
chapter on *Grey's Anatomy*: "Grey's Anatomy: Feminism" (Levine, 2020).

Most of the agent's practices take place at the level of "practical consciousness" (Giddens, 1984), where we act without reflecting on it. Practical consciousness is informed
by mutual knowledge – taken for granted and often tacit knowledge about how to act –
which is based around rules and norms about the right and wrong way of doing things
and fulfilling social roles. However, individuals sometimes operate at the level of "discursive consciousness," which is when we reflect on how we used to do things and decide
how we want to do them now. Structuration theory argues that individuals always have
agency and knowledge, and actively co-create or alter their relationships and their social
reality.

According to Giddens (1984), social structure consists of two dimensions: first, the
rules implicated when social systems are reproduced or altered; second, resources –
symbolic and others – that people can draw upon while doing things in society. Rules
are general routines that individuals or organizations follow in accomplishing goals.
They indicate how something ought to be done or what we consider as good or bad.
Resources, on the other hand, are attributes or material goods that can be used to perform or influence practices and interactions with others. An agent's capacity to carry out
practices is influenced by access to resources, and practices, on the other hand, create
and recreate rules and resources in social practice.

Following this logic, we can see media – such as newspapers, television – as symbolic
structures, because they are products of social interactions between people. At the same
time, media enable and shape the behavior and interactions of people and, therefore, our
perceptions of social realities. In technologically developed societies, people make sense
of their lives and their place in society through their relationships with media. British
soap operas such as *EastEnders* or *Coronation Street*, for example, are built around the
idea of relationships and strong families, with each character having a place in the community. This allows us to see how people behave in different social roles and can shape
our thinking about what it means to be a woman, a family, or a couple. News coverage,
on the other hand, strongly determines which topics we deal with and which remain

below our radar. This has consequences for the way we perceive the world and interact with it. For example, in 2020, the global headlines were dominated by the COVID-19 global pandemic. Once its potential for extensive infection and the consequences for the health system were understood, the national media turned their focus inwards; on protecting citizens. During this time, at least 1 million people were affected by conflicts or natural disasters. For them, COVID-19 was an additional threat to a host of others – from the global climate crisis to deadly diseases, the unavailability of food and clean water, as well as conflict and violence. Unfortunately, these issues have hardly been covered by the media. The lack of public attention had far-reaching consequences, for example in terms of insufficient humanitarian aid (CARE, 2020).

1.1.2 Social Change and Technology

Social change has many varied causes, four of which are mainly recognized by sociologists: (a) **technology**, (b) social institutions, (c) population, and (d) the environment. All of these areas are interrelated; therefore, a change in one area can initiate changes in all of them.

An illustration of this process is the impact of the invention of the book press on societies. The invention of printing by the the German inventor, printer, publisher, and goldsmith Johannes Gutenberg in 1455 made it possible to print books in higher numbers and for them to be more affordable to a wider public, leading to the democratization of information. Before then, most people could not read and had no reason to learn this skill. Therefore, knowledge was primarily limited to what a person experienced in their lifetime and their immediate surroundings, or to what they heard from others, such as travelers or older people with more life experience.

Books led to a shift from a culture of talking to a culture of **writing**, which had an impact on social institutions; for example, the role of elders as experts. The world was not perceived through their lens anymore; new worldviews and ideas could spread more quickly. The culture of writing also led to the introduction of schools – new social institutions – later even to obligatory schooling, which meant that parents were obliged to send their children to school rather than going to work and contributing to the family income. Over time, this led to a decrease in the number of children that each household had.

The increase and distribution of knowledge has facilitated advances in agriculture, science, and medicine, which have enabled more people to survive and have longer life spans. Population growth, in turn, has impacted the size of the world's population (expected to reach 9 billion before 2050), and we are all grappling with the devastating effect that this has had on the environment all over the world. The interplay of technology and social change inevitably leads to the question of whether technology determines society or is rather determined by society, whereby the term *technology* commonly refers to methods, systems, or machines, which are the result of creative applications of scientific knowledge which serve human needs, and used for accomplishing tasks in the areas of communication, transportation, learning, manufacturing, securing data, scaling businesses, and many more.

There are different views on the relationship between society and technology. Opinions vary on what causes technology to change in specific ways, and on what impact technology has on people. The most dominant theories on the relationship between technology and society are determinism, instrumentalism, substantivism, and social constructivism.

Determinism encompasses two polar opposites. Technological determinism claims that technology develops independently from society; and that when a new technology is taken up and used, it has potent effects on societies. Social determinism, on the other hand, assumes that it is society that drives the evolution of technology. From this point of view, cultural beliefs, values, and social customs determine the use of technology and its impact on society.

Instrumentalism approaches consider technology as a neutral tool. From this perspective, the use of technology reflects the needs, goals, and values of a society, but also its problems and limitations. Therefore, technology does not influence society but is instead used by people for different purposes, which might be good or bad – measured by the standards of society.

Substantivism argues that technology is ruled by its own logic. It influences how society develops because it impacts the political systems, culture, and social structure. From this point of view, technology has its own values, which can be good or bad, and people cannot control the impact of technology on society.

Social constructivism argues that technological development is shaped by a wide variety of social, cultural, economic, and political factors, and by existing technology itself. Technological outcomes, therefore, must be seen as the products of a complex interplay of those various factors, which means that different societies and different people use and develop technologies differently. Emerging technological artifacts and their use influence subsequent technologies, leading to different directions and new artifacts. Seen from this viewpoint, technologies are taken up and used because they are perceived to achieve particular human purposes or to serve the interests of individuals and social groups.

Following social constructivism approaches (e.g., Bijker, 1995; Bijker, Hughes & Pinch, 1987), we can conclude that the plurality and heterogeneity of societies lead to a plurality and heterogeneity of technological applications and outcomes. While some might be considered useful because they improve a particular social world, others may be seen as problematic or destructive.

1.1.3 Sociability in a Digital Society

At the beginning of this chapter, we learned that societies are held together by structures in relation to how people do things: form an identity, design their lives, or interact with others. Societies are usually classified according to their development and use of technology. For most of human history, people lived in preindustrial societies characterized by minimal, simple technology and low production of goods. After the industrial revolution, many societies became based on mechanized labor, which made economies a dominant factor with far-reaching implications for all areas of social life. In a digital society, technological outcomes like the Internet and mobile devices allow us to act and interact in partially new ways. Our sociality is structured and predominantly driven by digital communication, digital processes, and immaterial goods like downloadable music, mobile apps, or various services (Coyle, 1998).

Digital communication shapes people's relationship with the world, while at the same time putting constraints on what can be said, done, or achieved. The Internet and mobile devices link different parts of the world and connect people with different opinions and cultural backgrounds. Digital communication, therefore, expands people's local experiences and social world. These developments initiate significant changes, which may be associated with globalization and new forms of social organization, or, as Eugenia Siapera puts it, "The internet's time, which is timeless and always-on, increasingly becomes the global time. The internet's space, which is a **space of flows** rather than of territories, increasingly becomes the dominant form of spatial organization" (Siapera, 2018, p. 70).

The sociologist Barry Wellman (2001) coined the term **networked individualism** to describe the new form of sociability emerging in digital societies. In his view, networked individualism is increasingly replacing the classical model of social arrangements formed around hierarchical and firmly connected social institutions – like households or village communities – with networks of locally and globally connected individuals. These loosely tied virtual networks do not displace classical networks but connect them: "physical space and cyberspace interpenetrate as people actively surf their networks online and offline" (Wellman, 2001, p. 248).

Although the shift to networked individualism started before the advent of the Internet, it has been fostered by digital communication. The spread of the Internet but also the evolution of wireless connections and the establishment of innovative interaction patterns in digital environments have changed the way people interact with each other. The "networked operating system" (Rainie & Wellman, 2012), fostered by digital social networks, offers people new ways to solve problems and meet social needs but also requires them to develop new skills. People can no longer passively let communities like a village or neighborhood take care of them, but they must actively network and connect with others. Networked individuals have partial membership in multiple networks rather than permanent membership in settled groups. They create communities around themselves and their interests: online, through personal connections, or a mix of both. The individuals and the connecting networks become the actors of social change.

Networked individualism points to one of the most fundamental shifts in society: the shift from a hierarchically and geographically restricted group or community organization to one that revolves around networks established by individuals based on their shared background and interests, mostly independent of geographical and social boundaries.

1.1.4 Digital Divide

While the Internet may enable some people to be better connected, educated, informed, and more politically active, it might raise barriers for others. The term **digital divide** describes the discrepancy between those who, for technical, political, social, geographic, or economic reasons, have both access to and the capability to use information and communication technologies (ICTs), and those who do not.

Digital divides exist at different levels: within countries and between countries, between rural and urban populations, between generations, as well as between ethnic groups, or between men and women. Such divides are not independent phenomena. They can be understood only in the context of broader geographical, social, and economic divides, linked to factors like education, income, or stratification systems in a society.

In the early days of the Internet, the digital divide was mainly understood as the division between those who had access to the ICTs and those who did not. This first-level digital divide, which depends on physical access, is becoming less relevant as more and more people have access to the Internet and use it regularly. Nowadays, divisions develop along the lines of social stratification. This trend is addressed as the second-level digital divide or social access.

Wilson (2004) defines four components of social access: financial access, which determines whether an individual or a social group can afford to be connected; cognitive access, which indicates whether people are trained to use hardware and software, and to understand, use, and judge information in multiple formats from a wide range of sources (Section 4.2); content access, which characterizes whether there is sufficient material available to fulfill people's needs; and political access, which takes into consideration whether users have an influence on the institutions regulating the technologies they use.

The presence or absence of physical and social access has political and societal consequences, as a large part of vital information and services are online. In order to be able to play an active part in society and fulfill their roles in critical and responsible ways, citizens need to be educated and informed. People without access are systematically excluded from participation. This is particularly worrying because studies indicate that digital divides propound preexisting inequalities and therefore can be regarded as a fundamental aspect of social inequity. Scholars stress that strategies for overcoming digital divides must include elements like regulatory frameworks, financial support, education, and other sociocultural conditions (Ragnedda & Muschert, 2013).

The dependence on internet access and changes in digital communication during the COVID-19 global pandemic accentuate the importance of implementing strategies for overcoming digital divides.

The pandemic has changed people's digital communication and their use of digital media. With fewer opportunities to share time in person, people depended on voice and video calls, messaging, and social media to remain socially connected. Furthermore, more businesses and governments moved their operations and services online to limit physical interaction and contain the spread of the virus. In addition, countries around the globe have had to go into lockdown, leading to widespread school closures, which require remote education settings. The 2020 report of UNCTAD, the United Nations Conference on Trade and Development, states, that "the coronavirus speeds up the transition to a digital economy while exposing the digital gap between countries and societies" (UNCTAD, 2020). The pandemic has accelerated the uptake of digital solutions, tools, and services, speeding up the global digital transformation and strengthening the market positions of a few mega-digital platforms. They have benefitted from the shift of many activities to the digital space and their ability to extract, control, and analyze data and transform it into **artificial intelligence** (AI) solutions that can be monetized (Section 2.1.2).

When in-person interaction is restricted, less tech-savvy people are more likely to become disconnected from their social environments, from services, and vital information. People who lack the skills to choose, download, and use digital applications struggle to access virtual services, like arranging a vaccination appointment, and miss out on social activities, like throwing a virtual Christmas party (Nguyen et al., 2020).

The shift to remote education during the pandemic has led to inequalities in access to learning, with already disadvantaged children being most affected. In the UK, for example, inadequate access to devices was less of a concern in private schools, while more deprived schools reported challenges for some pupils (Coleman, 2021). Scholars fear that the rising use of digital remote education practices may have led to increased digital divides due to limited access to the Internet and devices and inequalities concerning digital skills, parental support, teacher skills, and the learning environment.

ACTIVITY

Do you consider yourself a networked individual? Write a blog post that justifies your response and illustrate your justification with examples from your private and professional life. Point out the advantages and disadvantages of being part of different networks and explain the effects of digital divides on networked individualism.

1.2 New Media

"The medium is the message." This is the provocative thesis of the Canadian media theorist and philosopher Marshall McLuhan. It was actually meant to be the title of his new book. The typesetter, however, confused the letters *e* and *a*, so the title on the cover was "The Medium Is the Massage" (McLuhan & Fiore, 1967). When Marshall McLuhan saw the typo, he is said to have exclaimed enthusiastically, "'Leave it alone! It's great, and right on target!'" (McLuhan, n.d.) Why McLuhan was so happy about this typing error will be explained in Section 1.2.3. First, we examine the questions: What are media and what is "new" about new media?

The term *media* is complex because of its many layers of meaning and its different use in various academic, economic, and societal contexts. *Media* can stand for institutions and enterprises (media outlets, news organizations, broadcasting stations, streaming services, etc.). It can also stand for their channels (e.g., print media, radio and television programs, video-sharing platforms, social media platforms); for the material form of the products (newspapers, podcasts, videos, books, films, etc.); or the physical "containers," that is, the physical devices used for production, distribution, and consumption of media content (paper, television set, mobile device, computer). Sometimes *media* is used to describe the various forms and genres of the media products (news, novels, science fiction movies, press releases, newsletters, etc.). When we talk about *new media*, we take these various facets into consideration and use the term in a holistic sense, which means that all these facets are intimately interwoven and contribute to the whole: an epochal turning point that affects all aspects of how we use media to communicate.

The term *new* carries a strong connotation of being better than the old, being innovative, cutting-edge, progressive, groundbreaking, or even revolutionary. However, this is not the notion of new we refer to in this context. We understand new media more as a continuation of certain media traditions, since new media did not arise from a vacuum, but have a past. New media always define themselves in relationship to earlier media forms; new technology can remediate an older medium. **Remediation** means that every medium is in a continuous interplay with older media by imitating, highlighting, incorporating, refashioning, or even absorbing them (Bolter & Gruisin, 2000). For example, the telephone has evolved from a large wooden wall telephone in the early twentieth century into today's multifunctional, mobile computing device with camera, video, music, gaming, voice assistant, and other multimedia features (Figures 1.2 and 1.3). But mobile phones still show a relationship to their predecessor as they fulfill their original purpose of allowing one person to call another and converse, no matter what the distance is between them. Therefore, if we want to understand what is really new about new media, we have to go back to media history.

Figure 1.2 Bell on the telephone in New York (calling Chicago) in 1892. From "Alexander Graham Bell at the opening of the long-distance line from New York to Chicago," 1892. Prints and Photographs Division, Library of Congress. Reproduction Number LC-G9-Z2-28608-B. (Retrieved January 27, 2020, from www.americaslibrary.gov/jb/recon/jb_recon_telephone_1_e.html). In the public domain.

1.2.1 What Does New Media Mean?

The old media world, also known as the era of legacy media, encompasses print media such as books, newspapers, or magazines, but also photos, films, television and radio, videotapes – all based on analog technology. These media products are the outcome of mass production; they are produced and distributed by media industries and organizations, and controlled and regulated by media authorities, the state, or the market. On the reception side, there are the consumers, who receive and consume these products in a more or less passive way – passive because it is difficult to copy analog products, to interact with them or even share or customize their content. The typical communication model of old media is one-to-many (see Table 1.1). When new media appeared, old media was often characterized as *push media*, where messages were delivered to the consumers whether they sought them or not, while new media was called *pull media*, where the consumers had to seek out information on a specific topic (Jenkins, 2006, p. 213).

Figure 1.3 Various mobile devices and virtual reality (VR) glasses. Yagi Studio, Collection: Photodisc, Getty Images.

The term *new media* appeared in the late 1980s when the media landscape began to change in such a radical way that we can speak of a "new era" (Manovich, 2001, pp. 21–26). It was a shift from analog to digital media triggered by new telecommunication and information technologies. Examples of new media are websites, social media platforms, computer games, digital videos, images and audios, augmented and virtual reality. In the wake of this shift, the production, distribution, and use of images has grown tremendously and communication, which until then had been dominated by the printed word, has become multimodal, with a strong focus on visuals (Sections 3.2, 3.3).

New media content is produced and shared by very many people – by media companies as well as by nonprofessionals. The control over these media, therefore, lies not only in the hands of the media industries, news organizations or authorities, but also in the hands of the consumers. The consumers are now becoming so-called *prosumers,* who have the power to both create and consume the media products by (re)producing, (re)mixing, (re)contextualizing, and sharing the content. The typical communication model of new media is many-to-many. New media are also called online media. The term *online* refers to the Internet.

TABLE 1.1 THE MAIN DIFFERENCES BETWEEN OLD AND NEW MEDIA

	Old media	New media
Technology	analog	digital
Examples	books, newspapers, magazines, television, radio, video tapes	websites, social network sites, computer games, video sharing platforms, blogs, virtual worlds
Production	media companies and organizations	media companies, nonprofessionals
Control and regulation	media authorities, the state, the market	media industries, news organizations, authorities, platform providers, consumers
Reception	in a more or less passive way	prosumers (producers and consumers)
Communication model	one-to-many	many-to-many

Lev Manovich, a digital culture theorist, describes new media from several perspectives. From a technological viewpoint, he defines new media as "the cultural objects which use digital computer technology for distribution and exhibition. ... Other cultural objects which use computing for production and storage but not for final distribution – television programs, feature films, magazines, books and other paper-based publications, etc. – are not new media" (Manovich, 2003, p. 16–17). He critically observed that the problem with this definition is that it has to be revised every few years, as the digital culture is constantly developing and changing and the term *new media* will lose its relevance and specificity (Manovich, 2003, p. 17). Like photography, telephone, or television, every new medium has been *new* at some point in history. Manovich, therefore, proposes a focus on the specific aesthetic techniques and ideological implications that evolve with a new technology. Aesthetic techniques are, for example, the animation of images, or split screens to show actions that occur simultaneously.

From an ideological viewpoint, questions arise such as whether new media enable us to simulate something that either could not be represented before or does not exist, as is the case with virtual reality; whether new media allow for more democracy; or whether technology determines society (Section 1.1.2). In order to fully understand new media, Manovich recommends analyzing the history of technology in correlation with social, political, and economic histories of the modern period. He also describes new media "as the mix between existing cultural conventions and the conventions of software"

(Manovich, 2003, p. 18) and has predicted hybrid products that – at the beginning of the 2000s – might have sounded strange but are now standard and no longer new: media products such as clickable maps, navigable financial data, or animated visuals.

To sum up: Rather than understanding new media only from the perspective of technology, media scholars like Lev Manovich propose various approaches to defining new media: political, economic, social, and aesthetic. Moreover, the term *new media* should be understood in its historical context. Even though the term remains problematic because it suggests something novel, many scholars continue to use it, as it has become established in media studies.

1.2.2 Characteristics of New Media

A smartphone is considered a new medium, but younger people might wonder what is new about smartphones. Let us take a closer look at some of the defining characteristics of new media. The term *new* indicates a wide range of changes in the production process of media content, media products, and the use and reception of media. Lister et al. (2009, pp. 13–44) describe six key characteristics that define new media: **digital**, **hypertextual**, **interactive**, **virtual**, **simulated**, and **networked**. Since we have devoted a separate subchapter to the network society, we will only briefly summarize what the term *networked* implies (Section 2.1).

Networked: While old media can be viewed as mass media, new media are described as networked media or network societies where audiences are not seen as information consumers, but as active participants who produce, control, own, and share media content, turning public communication into a **participatory culture**. Networked media are thus decentralized forms of mass media. The World Wide Web or social media platforms are examples of networked media, which are themselves part of a huge, global network, the Internet. Networked media are crucial for the development of network societies. The network society is determined by the concept of space of flows with **time-space-compression**, meaning that (a) things can happen faster because time is compressed and (b) geographical borders and national states are disappearing in terms of trade. It is a de-territorialized, **weightless economy** connected through global nodes and hubs, trading with immaterial goods: data, information, knowledge, and services. These structural changes in societies and economies epitomize the shift from modernity to postmodernity and from an industrial age of manufacturing to a postindustrial age of information technology and digitalization.

Digital: When it comes to digital, we have to distinguish between digitization and digitalization. The term *digitization* refers to digital technologies and describes the process of converting analog signals into digital forms. The analog information – the media text – is then encoded into numerical values: the binary code of 0 and 1. All computers and mobile devices, therefore, run on ones and zeros and all information is converted into 0 and 1. The results of digitization are files that consist of strings of bits and bytes. A bit is a binary digit (0 or 1) and the smallest unit of storage. One byte is a collection of 8 bits. Once the information is digitized, it can easily be read, processed, and searched by computers as well as edited, stored, and distributed. The functioning of digital media is based on algorithms. An **algorithm** is a mathematical process that consists of a set of step-by-step instructions in order to solve a problem or perform a task. Algorithms are used for calculation and data processing, but also for searching or sorting of data. For example, for a search query on the Web, algorithms decide which websites are considered relevant for a search query and in what order the results are presented (Chapter 8).

While digitization emphasizes technology, digitalization refers to adopting and using digital technologies in business and society as well as in private and public communication. The term *digitalization* also refers to the ongoing changes to societal and individual activities that follow from the use of digital technologies, as well as their resulting effects and consequences. A consequence of the shift from analog to digital media is that information is dematerialized and separated from its former physical container. Different media can now be merged into new formats and genres. We can read a book on a mobile device, watch TV on a computer, or animate photos with apps and share them on **social media**. This merging of old and new media is called **media convergence** (Section 1.3.3). Media convergence takes place in several areas and refers not only to the fusion of different kinds of media content – with technology being the basic prerequisite for any kind of convergence. According to the media scholar Henry Jenkins, media convergence is "the flow of content across multiple media platforms, the cooperation between multiple media industries, and the migratory behavior of media audiences who will go almost anywhere in search of the kinds of entertainment experiences they want" (Jenkins, 2006, p. 2). Digitalization also allows for a nonlinear, interactive use of the media text and for data storage and management in clouds (a network of remote servers), which make data accessible at anytime from anywhere and at very high speeds. Digitalization also makes manipulation of media texts possible, particularly of images: from photoshopping, which refers to any kind of digital editing of photos, to deepfake video technology. Deepfake technology uses *artificial intelligence* algorithms to turn a person in an existing image, audio recording, or video into somebody else and have them do or say things that never happened.

Hypertextual: *Hyper* comes from the Greek word meaning "beyond" or "over." A hypertext is, therefore, a textual structure that goes beyond the borders of a single text unit. It is a network of linked information elements (nodes): a text with links to other texts. The links are called hyperlinks. By clicking on the hyperlinks or touching the screen, the users can choose their own path through the hypertext to access information (Figure 1.4). Hypertext technology can be used to connect one text to other texts, or to organize the content that normally would be structured linearly in one single text, into a network

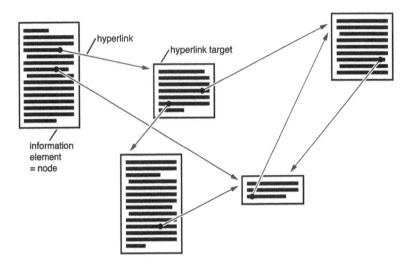

hyperlink

hyperlink target

information
element
= node

Figure 1.4 Hypertextual structure. © 2021 Verena Elisabeth Lechner. Used with permission.

or a hierarchy of smaller, interlinked, text units. **Hypermedia** extends the concept of hypertext by including images, audio, video, and multisensory combinations. In the era of new media, hypertexts and hypermedia are interactive, nonlinear, and networked systems which question the traditional notion of text as a linear and stable product.

The terms *hypertext* and *hypermedia* were coined by Theodor Holm Nelson in the 1960s – long before the term *multimedia* gained significance and ubiquitousness in the 1990s. Nelson, a philosopher and pioneer of information technology, wrote in his book *Literary Machines*:

> By now the word "hypertext" has become generally accepted for branching and responding text; but the corresponding word, "hypermedia," meaning complexes of branching and responding graphics, movies and sound – as well as text – is much less used. Instead, they use the strange phrase "interactive multimedia" – four syllables longer, and not expressing the idea that it extends hypertext.
>
> (Nelson, 1993, erratum; and a note on the term *interactive media*)

The concept of hypertext, however, was already anticipated in 1945 by the engineer Vannevar Bush. In his visionary essay "As We May Think," he proposed an electromechanical system called *memex*, a kind of workstation that enables people to index and retrieve documents. "A memex is a device in which an individual stores all his books, records, and communications, and which is mechanized so that it may be consulted with exceeding speed and flexibility. It is an enlarged intimate supplement to his memory" (Bush, 1945). The hypertextual structure corresponds to the way the human mind operates, namely by association; Bush wrote: "Wholly new forms of encyclopedias will appear, ready made with a mesh of associative trails running through them, ready to be dropped into the memex and there amplified" (Bush, 1945).

Bush's concept of hypertext inspired Nelson to set up the hypertext project *Xanadu*. Nelson had a vision of a worldwide operation network of billions of open accessible documents interlinked in a nonsequential way. He called this huge electronic network of documents a "docuverse." This, of course, seemed absurd in the 1960s, because software was not advanced enough at that time (Wolf, 1995). The Xanadu project dealt with questions such as how to link to evolving documents, how to track changes to a document, how to organize archival storage, how to organize the physical storage of a universe of discourse (Heiser, 2015, p. 54). The idea behind this project was to facilitate nonsequential reading and writing and to create new methods of storage and retrieval. The ambitious project ran for decades until 2014 when, finally, OpenXanadu was released. With Xanadu, Nelson foresaw a new way of knowledge organization: a hypertextual environment in the form of the universal knowledge repository we now know as the World Wide Web. Hypertext and hypermedia are closely connected to the next term: *interactive*.

Interactive: Interactivity is another key feature of new media which addresses the user's engagement with the media text. Interactive media require not only a passive viewer – as is the case in old media when looking at a photo or watching a film – but also an active user who interacts with computer software, webpages, or hypertexts. While interactivity describes the quality of being (inter)active, interaction refers to the communication process. McMillan distinguishes between three traditions of interactivity research: human-to-human interaction, human-to-documents interaction, and human-to-system (human–computer) interaction (McMillan, 2006). Within these traditions, interaction and interactivity are defined differently.

From a computer-technical point of view, the focus is on tools and technical features that enable interaction. The lowest level of interactivity starts with object interactivity. "When a user 'clicks' on the object, there is some form of audio-visual response" (Sims, 1997). A medium level of interactivity is given when the user has the option of manipulating something; for instance, zooming, filtering, or selecting objects. A high level of interactivity is reached when users can influence or even change the content as co-authors. Immersive virtual interactivity, which is the highest level, provides a virtual environment in which the user is fully immersed in a computer-generated world and can explore and interact with objects in this virtual world. From the point of view of interaction design, the user-friendly design of the interaction between users and digital interfaces plays a key role (e.g., Crawford, 2002; Heeter, 1989; 2000; McMillan, 2006; Shneiderman et al., 2017). From a sociological point of view, particular emphasis is placed on the dialogue-like communication process, with the computer as a dialog partner. Kiousis (2002, p. 372) defines interactivity "as the degree to which a communication technology can create a mediated environment in which participants can communicate (one-to-one, one-to-many, and many-to-many), both synchronously and asynchronously, and participate in reciprocal message exchanges (third-order dependency)."

Virtual: Like interactive, virtual is also a shifting concept. Virtual can carry a sense of only existing online and being connected to the online world. As such it is a feature of a networked and technologically imbued society in which everyday activities are simulated digitally: we shop online, teach online, communicate online, or meet friends in virtual rooms. The concept of virtuality here suggests that it is not the opposite of real but an alternative reality that also belongs to reality. In this sense, the philosopher Gilles Deleuze defined virtual as a part of the real. In the digital age, we are used to seamlessly switching back and forth between these different kinds of reality (Deleuze, 1988; Lister et al., 2009, p. 37; Smith & Protevi, 2020).

When it comes to digital technologies, virtual is closely related to virtual reality (VR). In contrast to a 2D text-based environment where users navigate through linked documents, the virtual world is a digitally created environment in 3D. This three-dimensional and computer-generated environment offers users the experience of spatial exploration – a feeling of "being there," just like in a real world. By performing actions in this environment, the user – equipped with a VR headset and motion controllers – becomes part of the virtual reality that we call immersion. Of course, immersion is not a new phenomenon: narrative immersion can also happen with old media when reading a book, listening to music, or watching a movie. The difference is that this narrative immersion is now enhanced by technology. In the new media world, immersion refers to a "technologically induced phenomenon, the experience of being surrounded by data" (Ryan, 2015, p. 61). It is a spatial dimension of immersion that now emerges from the interaction between narration and technology.

One way to explain the difference between real and virtual is the "Reality–Virtuality Continuum" developed by Milgram and Kishino (1994). They propose thinking of the real and virtual environment "as lying at opposite ends of a continuum" (Figure 1.5).

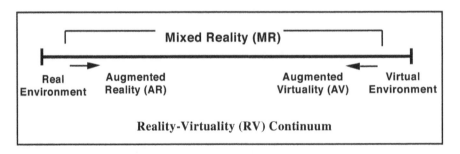

Figure 1.5 Simplified representation of a reality–virtuality continuum. From "Augmented reality: A class of displays on the reality-virtuality continuum," by P. Milgram, H. Takemura, A. Utsumi, and F. Kishino, 1995, *Telemanipulator and telepresence technologies*, SPIE 2351, 282–292. https://doi .org/10.1117/12.197321. © 1995 SPIE. Reprinted with permission.

The *real environment* is defined as an environment with real objects, including whatever might be observed when viewing a real-world scene either directly in person, or via some sort of a display. The *virtual environment*, namely VR, is defined as an environment "in which the participant-observer is totally immersed in, and able to interact with, a completely synthetic world" (Milgram & Kishino, 1994, p. 1321). This synthetic world may imitate or simulate real-world environments or even go beyond reality "by creating a world in which the physical laws ordinarily governing space, time, mechanics, material properties, etc. no longer hold" (p. 1321). Mixed reality (MR) merges the real and the virtual environment with the subcategories augmented reality (AR) and augmented virtuality (AV). From the technological point of view, VR is a simulated reality, which is the next key characteristic of new media.

Simulated: Simulating means making like, imitating, copying, or representing something. Simulation is not a phenomenon exclusive to the new media era. Computing technologies, however, have greatly expanded the possibilities of simulation so that simulations are now applied in various fields and disciplines like engineering, health care, ergonomics, finance, military training, aeronautics, geography, meteorology, or education. In the technological sense, a simulation can be defined as "a mathematical or algorithmic model, combined with a set of initial conditions, that allows prediction and visualization as time unfolds" (Seiden, 1997, p. 168). The aim of simulation is to gain insights into a system that does not yet exist, to explore a situation that is too risky to engage with, to change conditions underlying a system, identify possible errors, explore potential effects, or predict and visualize future scenarios. Video games or VR can also be platforms for simulations.

When it comes to gaming, simulation sometimes connotes something fictitious, artificial, or even counterfeit, such as in video games that imitate a fictional world. But we have to keep in mind that video games are real media artifacts, because they exist, and simulations in video games offer real experiences. We can therefore argue that simulations are "things in their own right," "they exist, and are experienced within the real world which they augment" (Lister et al., 2009, p. 44).

The French philosopher Jean Baudrillard, a critic of contemporary society and consumer culture, goes one step further and broadens the term *simulation* to include media and consumer behavior. In his provocative book *Simulacra and Simulation* (1994), he states that our society relies so much on models or simulations that we have lost the ability to comprehend the distinction between reality and a simulation of reality. He called this status *hyperreality*. "Simulation is no longer that of a territory, a referential being, or a substance. It is the generation by models of a real without origin or reality: a hyperreal" (Baudrillard, 1994, p. 1). Baudrillard argues that a postmodern society is organized around simulation; that is, "by cultural modes of representation that 'simulate' reality as in television, computer cyberspace, and virtual reality" (Kellner, 2019). It is a society where only simulacra exist. Simulacra are representations or models, like photos, videos, or computer games, that gradually lose any connection to the original, to the point where they replace and even become more real than reality itself. Baudrillard takes Disneyland and other theme parks as an example of hyperreality. According to him, digital technologies create experiences that are so intense and engaging that they supersede real life. Consequently, only the hyperreal remains and determines our thoughts and behavior (Kellner, 2019). Like many other theorists and philosophers, Baudrillard was influenced by McLuhan's media theory, which we will deal with in the next section.

1.2.3 The Medium Is the Message

The Canadian philosopher Marshall McLuhan was one of the first to address the fundamental changes caused by media by asking about the impact that media technologies might have on society. His famous statement "The medium is the message," formulated in 1964, captures the idea that the importance of the medium does not lie in its content but in the form of the medium itself. "The medium is the message because it is the medium that shapes and controls the scale and form of human association and action" (McLuhan, 1994, p. 20). This notion of medium was visionary because contemporary media theories framed technologies and media as neutral containers that serve only one purpose: to transport content. In contrast, McLuhan was interested in how each medium affects human perception and behavior.

One of his famous theses is that media are extensions and amputations of the human senses and bodies. For example, a bicycle or a car can be considered an extension of the foot, the telephone as an extension of the voice, the book as an extension of the eye, and the computer as an extension of the human brain. Conversely, every technological extension has the effect of amputating other extensions, which results in the loss of skills; for example, writing or memorizing. These extensions cause substantial changes in people who use these media, and they transform their environment. As long as people are immersed in the technological environment, they remain "as unaware of the psychic and social effects of [their] new technology as a fish of the water it swims in" (McLuhan, 1969; McLuhan & Fiore, 1968, p. 175). What McLuhan wanted to point out was that using media has an effect on our senses; they *massage* our entire sensory apparatus. That is why McLuhan was so happy about this typing error because the title of his book *The Medium Is the Massage* exactly expresses this idea.

The idea of remediation, mentioned earlier in this chapter, is rooted in McLuhan's media theory. He stated that the "'content' of any medium is always another medium" (McLuhan, 1994, p. 19). This idea was taken up and redefined by David Bolter and Richard Grusin in their book *Remediation: Understanding New Media*. "[A] medium is that which remediates. It is that which appropriates the techniques, forms, and social significance of other media and attempts to rival or refashion them in the name of the real" (Bolter & Grusin, 2000, p. 65). For example, silent movies were inspired by theater conventions, early photography by painting; computer games by film animation techniques. VR remediates cinematography techniques; speech recognition is based on oral language use.

Mediatization, sometimes also called mediation, is another concept that draws upon McLuhan's theory. Mediatization describes the process "whereby society to an increasing degree is submitted to, or becomes dependent on, the media and their logic" (Hjarvard, 2008, p. 113; Section 1.3.4).

McLuhan's theory has often been revisited. One critic is Raymond Williams, media theorist and one of the founding fathers of cultural studies. Where Williams differed from his predecessor was in placing media in the larger sociocultural and economic dimensions rather than merely the technological dimension. He criticized McLuhan for overemphasizing the technological dimension of media and neglecting human agency: "It is an apparently sophisticated technological determinism which has the significant effect of indicating a social and cultural determinism: a determinism, that is to say, which ratifies the society and culture we now have, and especially its most powerful internal directions" (Williams, 1974, p. 127). Nevertheless, McLuhan's theory of media as extensions of the human senses was revived with the advent of the new media era in the 1990s. In the light of cybertechnology, cyberculture, VR, and AI, his theses are worth revisiting. Reading McLuhan challenges us to reconsider the relationship between human and machine and to take into account that computers may have an agency, too (Section 8.4).

ACTIVITY

Describe in the form of a timeline the media history of your family from the oldest to the youngest family member.

(a) Which media did your grandparents use? How did they use them in everyday life and which social or cultural role did these media play? Do these media still exist or have they been replaced by others? How has media consumption changed?
(b) Note down the strengths, challenges, or risks of the media used.
(c) Discuss the findings with your classmates.

1.3 Media Linguistics

More than half a century later, after McLuhan's provocative but also influential ideas, the media environment has become as natural to us as running water or electricity. A life without media is therefore hard to imagine. If we don't know something, for example

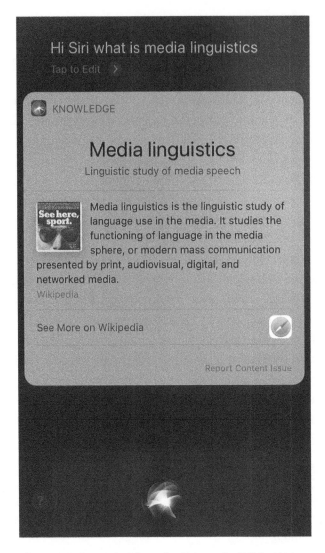

Figure 1.6 Screenshot from the Siri app, by Wibke Weber.

what **media linguistics** is about, we reach for our smartphones and ask, "Hey Siri, what is media linguistics?" (Figure 1.6).

Siri's answer is not bad for a start; it gives us a first inkling of what media linguistics is. But to better understand what constitutes media linguistics, we have to take a closer look at this discipline, its research foci, methods, and key terms.

1.3.1 What Is Media Linguistics?

Media linguistics is a subdiscipline of **applied linguistics** and lies at the intersection of applied linguistics, media and communication studies, and cultural studies. Applied linguistics deals with the practical problems related to language use in real-life situations such as occur in the media, in working life, or in an educational context. Media linguistics overlaps with media studies, communication studies, and cultural studies to the extent that all of these disciplines investigate public communication and its products, production and reception contexts as well as the cultural environment that influences this communication. In contrast to media linguistics, however, media studies place a stronger focus on the investigation of media systems, media economics, media politics, media theory, media history, or media design. Media linguistics also shares some common ground with communication studies and cultural studies, as they all employ concepts and terms such as media convergence and mediatization. Furthermore, media linguistics makes use of methods and **research frameworks** from these disciplines by adapting them for its purposes; for example, linguistic ethnography or computer-mediated discourse analysis (Section 5.1).

Media are at the core of media linguistics, because the discipline focuses on public communication which occurs through media (Luginbühl, 2015; Schmitz 2015). As we have seen in Section 1.2, the term *medium* is a complex one because of its multiple meanings. It can stand for technical devices, media institutions, channels, or products. In order to determine the scope of media linguistics more precisely, definitions of media linguistics usually emphasize the idea of a medium serving as a technical device used to produce, transmit, or store information. In other words, media linguistics focuses on mediated public communication which excludes the investigation of physical face-to-face communication and private communication. Mediated communication involves the use of any technical medium. This can be an analog device like paper or pencil or a digital device like a computer or smartphone, with modern media linguistics placing a strong emphasis on the latter. When communication occurs through the use of electronic devices, we speak of computer-mediated communication (CMC).

Initially, media linguistics studied language and language use in mass media, mainly in journalistic products from newspapers, radio, and television. With the advent of digital technologies and the Internet, media linguistics has broadened its focus to digital media products and communication formats. The subject of research has expanded too, from texts in journalism to multimodal products in the various fields of public communication: public relations, advertising, social media, and interactive media (e.g., video games or VR). Since language rarely appears in isolation in analog and digital media but intersects with other forms of expression, such as still or moving images, sound, or layout – what we call **modes** – media linguistics now also takes into account these other modes and their interplay as well as the various genres and aesthetics.

On the Internet, the lines between public communication and interpersonal communication become blurred. This becomes obvious, for example, when people comment on Instagram posts of a media provider or discuss posts with each other. One could argue that social media communication functions as a bridge between private and public communication, as social media platforms allow actors to choose audience size and degree of privacy (Chapter 2). Where access and availability, affordability, and **media literacy** exist, different actors – and not only media professionals – are able to communicate publicly, one-to-one, one-to-many, and many-to-many. By media literacy, we understand a set of skills that we actively use when we access, analyze, evaluate, create, interpret, reflect on, and interact with media. Media literacy is necessary to participate in a digital society (Section 4.2).

While in the beginnings of media linguistics *media products* were the main object of research, the research focus has now shifted from examining products to investigating the whole process of communication: the *product* and the processes of *production* and *reception*, including all social actors and practices contributing to and thus shaping public discourse (e.g., Engebretsen, Weber & Kennedy, 2018; Gnach, 2018; Gnach & Powell, 2014; Perrin, 2013, 2011a; Thurlow & Mroczek, 2011; Zampa, 2017). Examples of research in this area examine subjects such as how a topic is presented and discussed on different platforms at a given point in time (synchronic approach); how writing has changed over time through new media technologies (diachronic approach); which new genres are emerging due to the effects of media convergence; how the production processes of news reports have changed since the "online first" mantra (or even "mobile first" mantra) has begun to prevail in newsrooms; what corporate social media practices look like; or which reception patterns can be identified in online communities.

The methods used in media linguistics are as multilayered as its research field. Researchers make use of methods from **linguistics**, social sciences, communication and media studies, and cultural studies, depending on the object of investigation. For example, when using linguistic ethnography approaches, media linguistics asks about language practices in professions, particularly in journalism and PR, and how these professional communities develop and experience their own linguistic practices, while multimodal analysis focuses on the systematic description of the **meaning potentials** of a media product. We will give a deeper insight into the media linguistic toolbox in Chapters 5, 6, and online (www.cambridge.org/digitalcommunication).

Besides these theoretical outlines, media linguistics also deals with the more practical aspects of communication output. Based on empirical findings from research studies, it offers recommendations for media professionals on how media products can be produced and designed to match the specific features of the medium or genre used and the expectations of specific audiences. For example, how to write a conversation with chatbots in order to inform or instruct the stakeholders of a company about a specific topic (Figure 1.7). A bot is a software application that performs an automated task such as simulating a conversation via text or voice commands.

To return to Siri's answer to the question of what media linguistics is, we can now define the term more precisely. Media linguistics examines how language is used in the

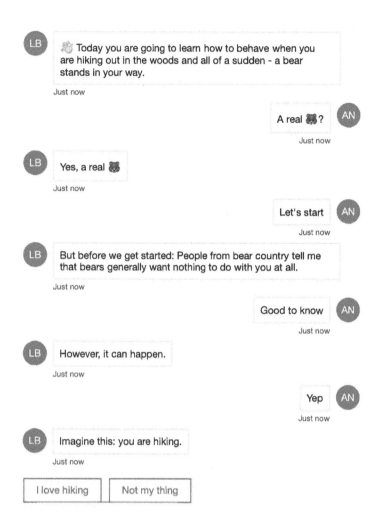

Figure 1.7 Conversation with a chatbot. From "Conversational Interfaces – Workshop with Pascal Rosenberger, co-founder and co-managing director of eggheads.ai," 2020, October 22, IAM MediaLab Workshop. Screenshot by Wibke Weber; icons: Ricardo Farina Mora, used with permission. © 2020 eggheads GmbH. Used with permission.

media and mediated public communication. The term *medium* here refers primarily to the technical means used for the production, storage, reproduction, and transmission of language – which can be, for instance, a computer, a smartphone, a newspaper, or a TV. *Public* means that communication is potentially accessible to everyone. A typical example of public communication is mass communication through media such as newspapers, television, radio, or websites. The counterpart of public communication is interpersonal communication; for example, telephone conversations or WhatsApp-chats between two or more people, the content of which is not intended for the public. Communication on the Internet can be seen as a bridge between public and private communication, as **social networks** allow individuals or institutions to choose to which audiences they wish to send their information.

Media linguistics examines not only multimodal communication in mass media, but also that of companies and institutions as well as noninstitutionalized actors who take part in mediated public communication; e.g., bloggers or exponents of social movements. It studies language and other modes in interactions with digital interfaces such as intelligent virtual assistants and chatbots. Furthermore, media linguistics is concerned with the analysis of multimodal products, their production processes, and their effects on the respective target groups. Studies in media linguistics are therefore interested in investigating and bridging the micro with the macro level of the field: the multimodal media products and interpersonal and publicly accessible media communication (micro level) and the effects of communication on sociocultural processes such as the extent to which language in combination with other modes can bring about cultural, political, or social changes (macro level).

Three phenomena have contributed to the fact that media linguistics has developed into a very dynamic field: **multimodality**, media convergence, and mediatization. The terms highlight the central role mediated communication plays in society.

1.3.2 Multimodality

Language materialized as written or spoken text rarely appears as a single mode in the media. Therefore, media linguistics looks not only at language (verbal mode) but also at other modes, their meanings potentials and the multimodal interplay. Other modes are still and moving images (visual mode), sound and music (aural mode), or layout and color (visual mode with a focus on design). The concept of multimodality, that is, the approach to text and communication that goes beyond language, therefore, has become a central approach to the study of communication in media linguistics and will be discussed separately in Section 3.3.

1.3.3 Media Convergence

The general idea behind convergence is that previously distinct things come together and merge into a unified new whole. Jenkins (2006, p. 2) describes convergence culture as "the flow of content across multiple media platforms, the cooperation between multiple media industries, and the migratory behavior of media audiences who will go almost anywhere in search of the kinds of entertainment experiences they want." Starting from the literature that has grown around this topic (dal Zotto & Lugmayr, 2016; Jenkins, 2006; Wirth, 2006), we describe media convergence from four perspectives that are relevant to our context: technological, economic, sociocultural, and content convergence.

First, technological convergence describes the process through which two or more technologies that were previously separate merge into a single technology or system so that the users are able to access media content through one device. In the old media world, telephone, newspapers, radio, and television were distinct media. In the new media world, we need only one electronic device to read newspapers, listen to music, watch videos, make phone calls, and browse through the World Wide Web. This is essentially what is known as media convergence; more precisely, *technological media convergence*. Technological media convergence allows us to act as producers, consumers, and distributors. Using the same device, we can text or dictate messages, take photos and videos, and edit them; we can upload our own media products to platforms and share them with friends; we can like and comment on images and texts, thus enabling us to participate in media discourses. Technology is an important trigger for media convergence, and, often, the definition of media convergence is reduced to this technological aspect. However, it would be too simplistic to understand media convergence primarily as a technological process.

Second, technological convergence leads to *economic convergence*: a concentration in the media industry. This describes the merging of formerly separate branches of the media industry into giant media players or conglomerates; that is, an increasingly smaller number of media groups owns and controls different kinds of services (e.g., internet access, television, and telephone) or media (e.g., television, radio, newspapers, magazines, and books). Economic media convergence has also changed the nature of media companies. Apple Inc, which once started as a manufacturer of personal computers, now operates one of the largest digital media stores offering music, apps, TV, and films.

Third, the *sociocultural* aspect of media convergence emerges with the rise of social media and networking platforms. It starts from the premise that "[c]onvergence occurs within the brains of individual consumers and through their social interactions with others" (Jenkins, 2006, p. 4). Sociocultural convergence therefore asks how we influence our culture by interacting with each other, learning, working, and communicating with people in various ways – from one-to-one, one-to-many, and many-to-many. Media audiences play a pivotal role in creating and distributing content. The roles of producers and consumers/users that were traditionally separated in the old media world now merge into the hybrid terms *prosumers* and *produsers*, thus leading to increased audience participation, user-generated content, and collective intelligence. A good example of this participatory culture is the online video-sharing platform YouTube. It allows anyone worldwide to view, upload, rate, share, and comment on videos. These communicative practices create and influence cultural trends.

Fourth, media convergence has led to a variety of new media formats, genres, narrative techniques, and thus to new media aesthetics. These phenomena at the content level are referred to as content convergence. One form of content convergence is transmedia storytelling in which a story or components of a story are told across multiple platforms and formats. The term was coined by Jenkins (2006), who describes the ideal form of transmedia storytelling as a narrative process in which "each medium does what it does best – so that a story might be introduced in a film, expanded through television, novels, and comics; its world might be explored through game play or experienced as an amusement park attraction" (Jenkins, 2006, p. 96). Since it is becoming increasingly difficult to reach large masses of consumers through a single medium or channel, transmedia storytelling reacts to the media behavior of the target groups by adapting the content for different channels. This, in turn, has implications for the production process. Media professionals can no longer focus on just one medium (writing stories for a newspaper; producing news for the radio) but need a basic knowledge of the various other media channels, genres, and modes. We will come back to the implications of media convergence for journalism and PR in Chapter 4. Furthermore, this shift in focus requires a willingness to communicate with the target groups and listen to what the audience is discussing. Monitoring these discussions can lead to generating new stories, spotting trends in a specific community, or creating engaging content.

With media convergence, boundaries that were once clearly set are now blurring. As a result, new questions are being posed such as, for example, who is a journalist and who is not; is it possible to present real facts and news in a VR setting and what effect does the use of VR have on the credibility of journalism; how is media aesthetics changing through the use of multilayered images when it comes to, for instance, AR; how does the use of animation – which may suggest a kind of fiction – change the perception of fact-based documentaries; what does it mean for the communication strategy of a company when employees blog about their work and thus become public influencers? These challenging questions show that media convergence is not an end point but an open ongoing process.

1.3.4 Mediatization

Our life is permeated by the media. A critical look at our daily routines reveals that we constantly use media to, for example, get in touch with friends, organize our appointments, do online banking, meet colleagues in virtual rooms, track our fitness, check our home remotely, shop, play games, or keep up to date with what is happening in the local community or in the world. We watch videos while commuting to work, listen to music while driving, chat online with friends during dinner, and send text messages during class. Media are accessible everywhere 24 hours a day; they can bridge spatial and temporal distances; simulate future scenarios; enable us to immerse in fictional worlds; and can even become a substitute for social relationships (Section 2.3). If, therefore, media play such a central role in our everyday life – what Couldry and Hepp (2013, p. 193) call "a basic reference point for children, friends, family, and work" – then media can no longer be considered separate from cultural and other social institutions (Hjarvard, 2008, p. 105). The concept of mediatization thus describes the interrelationship between the change in media and communication and the change in culture and society (Hepp, 2020, pp. 3–4). It is concerned with the "molding forces of media," which means that media have the ability to mold and shape how we communicate – with communication being understood as a sociocultural practice (Hepp, 2020, p. 4).

There are two parallel lines in mediatization research: the *institutionalist* and the *social-constructivist* traditions (Section 1.1). Scholars who represent the former argue that mediatization means that our culture is dependent not only on media but also on their logic. Media logic refers to the underlying conceptual logic in terms of production routines, decision-making, formats, dramaturgies, narrative forms, visualizations, aesthetic styles, or materiality of the media. Furthermore, media logic can refer to the institutional and technological ways in which media operate. The question here is the extent to which media, that themselves have become more or less a social institution with its own norms and rules, influence other social and cultural institutions such as politics, religion, or family. In other words, other institutions become increasingly mediatized so that they have to adapt to the logic of the media. When people use mass media as the main source of political information, media shape people's perception of political debates and politicians. Strömbäck (2008) concludes that the important question is no longer about the independence of the media from politics and society but about the independence of politics and society from the media.

Other researchers belonging to the social-constructivist tradition do not go that far. They focus less on media as the powerful center of our culture, but discuss mediatization as "a concept that signals a historical transformation in how the media have become more important for the workings of different social and cultural spheres or fields" (Ampuja, Koivisto & Väliverronen, 2014, p. 118). Krotz (2009), for instance, views mediatization and other processes such as globalization, individualization, and commercialization as metaprocesses, which he defines as long-term and culture-crossing changes. According to him, mediatization reaches far back to the history of humanity, since communication is a basic practice that allows people to create meaning and construct reality. Mediatization here foregrounds "the process of a communicative construction of socio cultural reality and analyzes the status of various media within that process" (Couldry & Hepp, 2013, p. 196). Researchers therefore investigate the extent to which social practices change when they are intertwined with media by taking into account the specificities of the different media – their molding force (Hepp, 2012).

To return to media linguistics, we can conclude that mediatization is a concept that can be studied from multidisciplinary perspectives: media studies, communication studies, cultural studies, and media linguistics. Mediatization falls into the realm of media linguistics insofar as it deals with mediated communication and how this communication is influenced and shaped by media – because language and other semiotic modes always constitute social reality. Mediatization therefore offers a theoretical bedrock for media linguistic research and anchors language and other modes in a sociocultural context. In this respect, media linguistics contributes to the development of the concept of mediatization by examining the changes in language use; the affordances of media and modes; the dynamic field of genres; and the act of communicating (writing, blogging, visualizing, taking pictures and sharing them, etc.) as a social meaning-making practice that shapes our culture and society.

ACTIVITY

Keep a diary of your media consumption during the period of one day: from getting up to going to bed. How much time do you devote to this activity? Find rooms or situations that are free of media and describe how these situations feel compared to your daily media routine.

Key Terms

agency, algorithm, applied linguistics, artificial intelligence, digital, digital divide, digital society, hypermedia, hypertextual, interactive, linguistics, meaning potentials, media convergence, media linguistics, media literacy, mediatization, modes, multimodality, networked, networked individualism, network society, participatory culture, public communication, remediation, research framework, simulated, social change, social media, social network, social structures, sociality, society, space of flows, technology, time-space-compression, virtual, weightless economy, writing

Chapter Summary

- Each society has unique traits and characteristics, and is held together by social structures that operate at different levels, limiting or enabling what individuals can do on a day-to-day basis, how they perform their social roles, and how they shape their lives.

- Technology is a significant factor in social change and, although each society develops it and uses it differently, technological influences such as digitalization happen at a global level.

- We can argue that Western societies are digital societies, where digital media and digital communication shape people's relationship with each other and the world. While this development enables some people to be better connected, educated, informed, and more politically active, it raises barriers for others.

- Key characteristics of new media are: digital, interactive, hypertextual, virtual, simulated, and networked. Understanding new media is a prerequisite to fully appreciating (a) our digitalized culture: how we communicate, learn and work with media and what value we accord them in our lives; (b) media linguistics, since media linguistics seeks to identify and solve real-world problems of communication and language use by examining how language and other forms of expression are used in the media. Media linguistics lies at the interface of applied linguistics, communication and media studies, and cultural studies.

- Three terms are at the heart of media linguistics: multimodality, media convergence, and mediatization. Multimodality is the approach to text and communication that goes beyond language and refers to the semiotic interplay of various modes; for instance, images, sounds, layout, or gestures. Media convergence is primarily understood as the merging of distinct technologies. In addition to this technological convergence, media convergence can also be described on an economic, sociocultural and content level. Mediatization is a concept that seeks to capture the changes in our everyday life and in our communicative practices brought about by media; that is, the relationship between changes in communication and changes in culture and society.

Further Reading

Digital Society

The chapter "Digital society" in Lindgren (2018) explains the concept of digital society and puts it in its technological, social, and historical context.

Rainie and Wellman (2012) show vividly how digital communication impacts our socialities. The authors combine extensive statistical analyses with in-depth qualitative research and personal anecdotes.

The edited volume of Ragnedda and Muschert (2013) explains the concept of digital divide against the background of classical sociological theories of inequality, and provides a comparative analysis of inequality and the stratification of the global digital sphere.

The article "Changes in digital communication during the COVID-19 global pandemic: Implications for digital inequality and future research," by Nguyen et al. (2020), addresses how the pandemic has changed people's use of digital communication methods, and how inequalities in the use of these methods may arise.

The chapter "The economic foundation of the information age" in Miller (2020) shows how and why nationally based economies changed into globalized forms of production where intangible or "weightless" goods and intellectual property are dominant.

New Media

The textbook *New media: A critical introduction* (Lister et al., 2009) provides a comprehensive introduction to media theories as well as the culture, history, and technologies of new media and is especially written for students.

E. Siapera's *Understanding new media* (2018) can be read as a guide to exploring new media. It covers a wide variety of topics from the political economy of new media to new media uses and abuses, to social media and socialities. The book contains pedagogical features to motivate students to delve deeper into the topics covered.

Media Linguistics

If you are interested in state-of-the-art research in media linguistics, the *Routledge handbook of language and media* (Cotter & Perrin, 2018) provides a comprehensive overview. It analyzes both language theory and practice and investigates mediated language use in public communication, organizations, journalism, and social media.

In order to keep up to date with media linguistics, take a look at the *Journal for Media Linguistics* (jfml, https://jfml.org). This publication informs about studies and current trends that are related to theoretical, empirical, and methodological questions.

Another journal is the *Journal of Computer-Mediated Communication* (*JCMC*) which focuses on social science research on communicating with computer-based media technologies but includes work from other disciplines such as communication, business, education, political science, sociology, psychology, media studies, or information science. https://academic.oup.com/jcmc/.

2 Theoretical Context: Understanding Public Digital Communication

PREVIEW

In the section on network theories, we discuss how the interplay between different societal factors and new technologies fosters a new form of social organization, which is no longer based on the individual or the traditional community but revolves around the idea of a network. The section first explains the idea of the network society along with the concepts of timeless time, the space of flows, and the weightless economy. It then presents the leading theories on network societies.

In the section on public communication, we discuss the effects of the increasing fusion of national public spheres with global information flows on public communication and explain two opposing developments: the participatory character of public communication and its restriction through economic interests and algorithmic processes.

In the last section, you learn more about the concept of network sociality. This concept is based on the assumption that networks and not communities are the dominant organizational form in a digital society. After defining social media and explaining its role in building and maintaining networks, the term *social capital* is introduced, which helps to understand networking motivation. The chapter ends with a reflection on the influence of algorithms on our socialities.

Learning Objectives

By the end of this chapter, you should be able to

- explain the concept of the network society in connection with the concept of the space of flows
- discuss the change of power distribution through the transition from the industrial to the digital age
- outline the implications of networked individualism on daily lives
- discuss the concept of the public sphere in relation to mass media and social media
- explain the idea of networked publics
- explain the concept of network sociality
- define social media and describe their role in relation to socialities
- explain the role of weak ties and strong ties in the context of social capital.

2.1 Network Theories

In 2014, Facebook users were asked to participate in a quiz in order to determine their personality type. The Facebook app hosting the quiz collected data of all participants as well as the public data of their friends. According to Facebook, data of up to 85 million people were harvested in this way. The media and some former employees of Cambridge Analytica, a British political consulting firm, claim that the company used these data to assemble psychological profiles of people in the United States. These profiles were then used to target voters with custom-made campaign ads in order to influence voting behavior during the 2016 election.

This example illustrates some of the challenges of digital communication in networks: questions of privacy, data ownership, and business models which incentivize the use of personal data with a potential to manipulate human behavior on a massive scale, as well as the growth of new power brokers who own data or social media platforms.

2.1.1 From the Industrial to the Digital Age

Following the theoretical stance of social constructivism (Section 1.1), which assumes a co-constructive relationship between technology and social realities, we can conclude that the use of new technologies can be associated with new forms of social organization.

Urbanization, the rise of fast and efficient forms of transportation, and an increasing volume and speed of communication between 1450 and 1800 led to a shift from an agrarian to an industrial society, where technology was predominantly used to enable the mass production of goods through a division of labor. Sociology associates these developments with the rise of capitalism, the growth of mass production and trade, and the increasing complexity of industrialized processes, sometimes referred to as industrialism.

The term *industrialism* describes a social and economic system in which manufacturing industries are prevalent. Industrialism was fueled by the exploitation of new forms of energy with the ultimate goal of maximizing output and economic growth. Mainly, the economy in industrialism aimed at producing a maximum turnover of goods at lower cost. In the industrial age, social power was mostly accumulated through ownership of tangible property: land, resources, machinery, and commodities.

The rise of information and digital communication technologies after World War II led to a new technological paradigm that marked the transition from an industrial age to an information age. This new paradigm is connected with the information revolution, a prerequisite of the digital society. The information age is characterized by the growing importance of knowledge, information, and communication in a globalized world. Human labor is increasingly involved in the production of immaterial goods in the so-called weightless economy.

2.1.2 Weightless Economy and New Forms of Capitalism

Scholars (e.g., Coyle, 1998; Quah, 1999) use the term *weightless economy* to describe a postindustrial economy that relies on information technology and telecommunications to produce a high-value output of exchangeable information, knowledge, or services. These immaterial goods can be delivered to large numbers of customers across vast distances. They can be produced with limited resources and without the help of physical labor. A vital concern of the weightless economy is how to protect intellectual property without, at the same time, creating socially harmful monopolies.

An example of how the weightless economy changed the economic system is the music industry. Record labels manufacture only small numbers of vinyl records or CDs, which need to be moved to warehouses and stores; they stream most of their products instead. Although an artist still needs the same amount of time to produce an album, the distribution through streaming services like Spotify is practically instantaneous, regardless of whether that album is sold to one customer or thousands of them. Thanks to the possibility of streaming, the record label has fewer production and distribution costs and can, therefore, make more profit. Besides, its profit increases with every unit sold, as selling each additional unit costs almost nothing. That is the case for all virtual goods: any number of copies of songs, books, or software can be provided without a shortage of supply or increase in costs.

One of the consequences of the weightless economy is that it permits suppliers to offer products and services to a large potential customer base with relatively low barriers to entry. Anyone who can code, for example, can create a software application and sell it globally. Although developing and distributing an app is not free, the costs are low in comparison to those involved in establishing a new factory. Companies in the weightless economy, therefore, can achieve almost limitless growth and profitability. That is especially the case when their product or service, like a piece of software or service such as a search engine, has no competitors – as we can see from the example of Microsoft's Windows operating system or Google's search engine. Success in the weightless economy is strongly related to data access and the ability to combine specific pieces of information. This leads to a new form of capitalism based on data and knowledge. The power in societies shifts to those who own, control, and can utilize information during the digital age. With the rise of digital communication, information industries have become a powerful economic and social force in societies.

Shoshana Zuboff (2015, 2019) coined the term **surveillance capitalism** to describe a process where companies like Google, Amazon, Facebook, or Apple collect data on our online behaviors (e.g., likes, searches, shares, purchases) in order to use them for commercial purposes – like targeted information and marketing, or the development of products and services.

Not only do such companies collect user data, but they also sell it to data brokers who compile detailed profiles on billions of individuals. Such profiles comprise factors like age, race, sex, education level, political stance, fitness level, marital status, shopping habits, health issues, holiday plans, and more. Newly available data sources, like wearables, smart speakers, or smart home devices, have dramatically increased the quantity and variety of data available. The application of **machine learning** and artificial intelligence (Chapter 8) allows the use of this data to predict products, services, and future markets. That is where surveillance capitalism's profits primarily derive from, because the more predictive a product is, the higher the volume of its sales.

2.1.3 Space of Flows

The developments described above are made possible through digital communication. Digital communication connects locations that are geographically distant as if they were right next to one another and enables them to communicate without delay as if they were in the same place. Scholars refer to this phenomenon as time-space-compression, meaning that things can happen faster because time is compressed. At the same time, they can happen across larger distances because space is compressed.

The Spanish philosopher and sociologist Manuel Castells (1989) argues that next to the physical space, which is characterized by geographical and political boundaries, a new kind of space is emerging: the space of flows. This globalized sphere consists of communication, people, and goods with largely unrestricted mobility. The space of flows is the space of free-flowing capital and real-time communication. It allows multinational corporations, for example, to coordinate production, investment, and communication strategies on a global scale.

Castells sees the space of flows produced through local nodes and hubs, such as corporate offices, co-working spaces, or airports, which are often separated from the rest of a city but connected to nodes in other metropoles. These "real virtual spaces" become essential places in the space of flows, where elite knowledge workers mine and exchange the information necessary to run global enterprises. The effects of the space of flows are materially and socially uneven. For example, the data cable capacity in financial districts like Manhattan surpasses the whole continent of Africa (Fukui et al., 2019). Also, the unrestricted mobility applies only to particular groups of people. While international business people, politicians, and the wealthy can move across the globe almost without restriction, others, such as refugees, the unskilled, or the poor, tend to be restricted in their ability to cross social and geographical boundaries. Some scholars argue that the timeless and globally connected economy has led to the rise of a new super-elite whose members are becoming a transglobal community of peers who have more in common with one another than with their fellow citizens.

Owing to the time-space-compression, companies and corporations become de-territorialized networks of economic nodes. They seek urban centers whose social and technological affordances enable interactivity among mobile elites, and their organization begins to resemble the architecture of digital communication technologies that make their global expansion possible. In that respect, the networking logic substantially modifies the operation and outcomes in potentially all dominant societal processes: production, consumption, power, culture, and experience. Some scholars, therefore, argue that we are living in a network society.

2.1.4 The Network Society

Some sociologists describe the society at the beginning of the twenty-first century as a network society. They refer to the result of the social upheavals caused by digitization, which lead to not only technological and economic change, but also social changes; for example, in the way people communicate, organize themselves, or shape their relationships. The term *network society* (nettsamfunn) was introduced by the Norwegian Stein Braten in his book *Modeller av menneske og samfunn* (1981). Later it was used in Dutch by Jan van Dijk in his book *The Network Society* (2006b) (Dutch original: *De Netwerkmaatschappij* (1991)) and by Manuel Castells in his trilogy *The Information Age: Economy, Society, and Culture* (1996, 1997, 1998).

Van Dijk defines the network society as: "a modern type of society with an infrastructure of social and media networks that characterizes its mode of organization at every level: individuals, community/organizational and societal. Increasingly, these networks link every unit or part of this society" (2006a, p. 24). In his opinion the network society increasingly organizes its relationships in computer-mediated networks, which gradually replace or complement the social networks of face-to-face communication.

Castells has developed a social theory of networks in connection to societies. He defines the network society as "a society whose social structure is made up of networks powered by micro-electronics-based information and communication technologies" (2004, p. 3). While a networking form of social organization has always existed, Castells argues that contemporary information technology provides the basis for its pervasive expansion throughout the social structure. One reason for this, in his view, is that the hierarchical one-way flow of information, such as mass communication, has been replaced by communication in horizontal networks and by many-to-many communication.

A network, in this perspective, is a decentralized system of nodes through which communication can occur. Every node is necessary for the system to function, but not all nodes are equally important. Networks have an open-ended structure and can contract or expand. The multidirectional communication within a network takes place via nodes and is not restricted by time and space. The process of managing communication within the networks in a network society is performed through digital communication structures; such as smartphones, computers, or the Internet. Societies or organizations, therefore, no longer have to be connected to a specific geographical or political space, like a country, but to the space of communication and information flows, the space of flows. New technologies decentralize communication and increase the efficiency of networks compared to hierarchical and bureaucratic structures in industrial societies. The networks are highly efficient because they are good at managing complexity; they are highly dynamic and innovative and adapt very quickly to new social conditions.

In the view of some scholars, the rise of the network society has the potential to change the relationship between organizations, political authority, mass media, and the public, as the access to networks is not dominated by one powerful social group. Furthermore, digital communication creates opportunities for the mobilization of collective action as well as the creation and coordination of social movements around the world. A prominent example is cyberactivism, demonstrated by antiwar, anti-globalization, and global justice or political movements like the Arab Spring. In Castells' opinion, the network structure ultimately leads to a more connected and open-minded global society, because digital communication allows people to create social networks that allow the exchange of different cultural and ideological worldviews.

Other scholars (e.g., Bauman, 1998, 2005; Webster, 2005) argue that this view is too idealistic and utopian and too firmly based on technological determinism. It also tends to put too much emphasis on the influence of technology on social relations and not enough on how humans shape and reshape networks. Nonetheless, Castells' theories are influential, as they paved the way for many others to study the interplay of technology and social structures.

ACTIVITY

Do you agree with the statement below? Justify your answer in two to three sentences.

"The ongoing transformation of communication technology in the digital age extends the reach of communication media to all domains of social life in a network that is at the same time global and local, generic and customized."

2.2 Digitalization and Public Communication

In 2019, Twitter declared that rule-breaking tweets made by influential politicians would in future be hidden behind a warning but left online "in the public interest." Although journalists labeled this the "Trump rule," it soon became clear that Donald Trump's tweets, though often considered racist and not always truthful by the media, were not affected by this new Twitter policy. Indeed, Twitter even declared that his tweets did not violate its policies. In 2020, shortly before the end of Trump's term in office, Twitter, Facebook, Instagram, and Snapchat blocked his social media accounts. Twitter justified its decision as follows: "After close review of recent Tweets from the @realDonaldTrump account and the context around them – specifically how they are being received and interpreted on and off Twitter – we have permanently suspended the account due to the risk of further incitement of violence" (Twitter Inc. 2020).

If the Internet can be a considered a democratic platform where everyone is able to contribute to public communication, how is this affected when someone is banned from using it? Should public figures and private users be treated differently? How much say do social media platforms have? In order to understand the issue and its implications more completely, we need to look at public communication in a wider context.

The term *public communication* refers to communication intended for public consumption or distribution. From a process perspective, public communication shapes decisions that institute and reinstitute social order, a particular system of social structures and institutions in a society, and therefore shapes social reality. Public communication takes place in the **public sphere**, the social space where different opinions are expressed, ideas regarding public affairs exchanged, discussed, and ultimately, where collective solutions are developed communicatively. The public sphere can emerge when citizens gather, for example, in a town hall meeting or a demonstration. It can also be constituted through media or communication infrastructure. Therefore, the public sphere goes beyond space and includes all communication channels through which information can be exchanged, opinions expressed, and discussed. The concept of a public sphere is a useful starting point for reflections on public communication in a digital society.

2.2.1 The Ideal of a Public Sphere

Media studies usually take the German sociologist Jürgen Habermas' theory as a starting point for reflections about the public sphere. His historical study *The Structural Transformation of the Public Sphere* (Habermas, 1989), first published in German in 1962 and translated into English in 1989, is commonly seen as the first attempt to classify the formation of public opinion and the legitimization of state and democracy in postwar Western societies.

Habermas locates the emergence of the public sphere in parts of eighteenth-century Europe. Before that, he argues, feudalism's structure did not allow a distinction between the public and the private; between the state and society. In his historical analysis of democratic societies, Habermas describes how citizens left their private space to discuss political issues in public spaces like coffee houses, salons, or literary societies. The public sphere appeared initially as the bourgeois public sphere, related to the emergence of a middle class with the time, money, and education to engage in political and social debates. According to Habermas, the public sphere is a neutral social space, ideally separate from the state and the economy. There, citizens engage in debates about issues important to social life. Their discussions inform public opinion and attitudes, which can either support or challenge the state's operations and impact state decisions.

Habermas argues that with the growth of mass media at the beginning of the twentieth century, the civil public sphere was replaced by a commercial mass media public sphere, where different actors, like the state or representatives of civic and commercial interests, started to dominate public communication. Furthermore, media corporations' commercial power allowed them to influence the public sphere and public opinion significantly. This led Habermas to the critique that the pursuit of profit by media corporations had turned public discourse into a product to be sold back to consumers rather than communicated back to members of the public.

In an ideal public sphere, the media are a facilitator of democracy. They provide a communicative infrastructure that allows the free exchange of information and ideas, discussion of issues of public concern, the formation of public opinion, and its transmission to the state. Furthermore, they provide the public with equal access to information and equal opportunities for participation in debates. They additionally make authorities accountable for their actions through communication in the public sphere. Habermas, therefore, regarded a free and unrestricted media system as a fundamental basis for citizens to inform themselves, discuss issues, and build public opinion (Habermas, 1996, 2006).

Habermas' concept of the public sphere has been extensively discussed and criticized in academic literature (see, e.g., Calhoun, 1992; Downey and Fenton, 2003; Warner, 2005). Nancy Fraser (1990) and Chantal Mouffe (2000), for example, pointed out that

Habermas overlooked the issues of women or minorities within the political sphere. In his later works (1992, 1998), Habermas accepted the importance of counterpublics for the public sphere and the necessity to include all kinds of societal actors. He also acknowledged the importance of the mass media in constructing the public sphere (Habermas, 1996, 2006).

Habermas' updated definition takes into account the network character of communication and multiple publics, and is therefore valid for public communication in a digital society. Habermas defines the public sphere as "A network for communicating information and points of view (i.e., opinions expressing affirmative or negative attitudes); the streams of communication are, in the process, filtered and synthesized in such a way that they coalesce into bundles of topically specified public opinions" (1996, p. 360).

2.2.2 Networked Publics

The idea of a single, coherent, central public sphere, where individuals come together, put aside their differences, and participate as equals proved to be an unattainable ideal from the very beginning. However, the rise of digital technologies, the Internet, and **social network sites (SNSs)** have made it even more challenging to achieve. The increasing fusion of national public spheres with global information flows has led to the formation of a multitude of parallel, fluid sub-publics that constitute the public sphere.

The "cultural anthropologist" Mizuko Ito coined the term **networked publics** to "reference a linked set of social, cultural, and technological developments that have accompanied the growing engagement with digitally networked media" (2008, p. 2). The media scholar danah boyd (2011, p. 39) further developed this notion of networked publics by stating that "networked publics are publics that are restructured by networked technologies ... they are simultaneously (1) the space constructed through networked technologies and (2) the imagined collective that emerges as a result of the intersection of people, technology, and practice ... . They allow people to gather for social, cultural, and civic purposes, and they help them connect with a world beyond their close friends and family." For boyd, networked publics are spaces constructed through digital technologies and imagined communities (Section 4.3.3). Digital technologies change the information flows and reorganize how people interact – with information and with each other. Boyd describes three interconnected dynamics of digital platforms: largely invisible audiences, the collapsing social context, and, as a result, the blurring between what is public and what is private. These dynamics regulate the structure of networked publics, enable new practices, and shape the interactions that can occur.

When individuals or organizations communicate on social media, they do not know exactly who sees the content posted, as algorithmic processes determine in no small part who sees which content and when they see it. Authors therefore imagine their audiences; they create mental concepts to determine what content is appropriate and relevant and how to design it. Furthermore, the multitude of online platforms, like Facebook, Snapchat, or Twitter, all have their separate affordances, possibilities, rules, and communication cultures. Thus, while engaging with networked publics, actors need to adjust their communication and interaction practices according to the general principles of online communication and then change them again depending on the rules and norms of a specific online environment and imagined audience.

When interacting with others, people adapt their communication to the social context of the communication situation. We talk about different topics with different people, use a different vocabulary, and generally behave differently in different communication situations – for example, during a night out with friends or at a business meeting. Social network sites make it challenging to keep our audiences segregated and, therefore, our social contexts may collapse. Marwick and boyd (2011) describe context collapse as the flattening of multiple audiences into a single context. As a consequence, individuals must meet the expectations of multiple and diverse audiences simultaneously – for example, work colleagues and close friends who are both followers on Twitter. Studies differentiate between two main types of imagined audiences on social media: an abstract imagined audience, which is general and vague, and a target imagined audience, which is more specific and comprises personal, communal, and professional ties (Litt & Hargittai, 2016). In the latter case, social media users often create in their minds an "ideal audience" (Marwick & boyd, 2011), such as people with whom they share common interests, sense of humor, political opinions, or concerns.

As a consequence of the difficulties of keeping audiences apart, the boundaries between public and private become blurred. Accordingly, social media users sometimes perceive the audience described above rather as a form of "public surveillance" (Nissenbaum, 2004) – a vast, uncontrollable audience which is a threat to one's privacy. Alice Marwick and danah boyd conclude that personal publics on social media challenge users to "maintain an equilibrium between a contextual social norm of personal authenticity that encourages information-sharing and **phatic communication** (the oft-cited 'what I had for breakfast') with the need to keep information private, or at least concealed from certain audiences" (Marwick & boyd, 2011, p. 124).

Despite networked publics, the media and the patterns of media use and consumption have not changed completely. We still consume media products in a relatively passive, noncreative way. Also, the classic mass media communication model where one, or a few, speak to many is still predominant in our societies. However, what has changed is how people today are "networked and mobilized with and through media" (Ito, 2008, p. 2). To consider the digitalization of public communication, scholars introduced the concept of a **networked public sphere** defined as a "transnational online space in which networked publics engage in public discourse, social discussion, and political debate, and which are arguably less subject to censorship and control and potentially open to wider democratic participation and dialogue than in the traditional public sphere dominated by the mass media" (Chandler & Munday, 2016).

2.2.3 Public Communication in a Networked Public Sphere

The Internet has changed public communication and, therefore, the public sphere. Digital media offer the means for self-presentation and the opportunity to share ideas, thoughts, and opinions within networked publics and, consequently, a many-to-many-communication flow which allows more freedom of expression and supports an interactive dialogue between all kinds of actors – institutions, organizations, individuals, and the mass media. This has raised the expectation that public digital communication might improve political participation and democratic decision-making processes as political elites distribute information to non-elites, but "consumers" of (political) information can also be "producers" of (political) information (Rheingold, 2000). Social media, for example, has the potential to change the relationship between political authority, mass media, and the public, by providing means for collaboration and expression of opinions or concerns (Castells, 2007; Rheingold, 2000). Social media platforms are used for organizing and implementing collective activities, promoting a sense of community and collective identity among groups, establishing connections with different social movements, and publicizing causes to gain support from the global community.

However, many scholars regard the prominence of connective technologies in a digital society as a threat to individual freedom of speech and transparent public communication. Scholars argue that the Internet reproduces existing inequalities by widening the digital divide (Section 1.1) and creating a participation divide (Hargittai & Walejko, 2008; van Dijk, 2006a). The fact that providers of social media platforms and search engines are driven by economic interests affects the quality of public communication (van Dijk, 2006a). This tendency becomes even more marked as the logic of technological infrastructures with its algorithms shapes what and how something can be communicatively expressed, and who gets which information at which point in time (Chapter 8).

Several scholars have pointed out that the digitalization of public communication calls for a reconceptualization of the public sphere as a result of multiple connections and interrelations of publics, enabled and constrained by technological features (e.g., Castells, 1996; Benkler, 2006; Friedland et al., 2006). While classical concepts of the public sphere emphasize the role of mass media, the concept of a networked public sphere takes into account digital communication with Its different actors, modes, channels, and forms of interaction (Kaiser et al., 2017).

In a digital society, the mass media system is complemented by, and interconnected with, a new form of socialized communication, which Castells (2007) calls "mass self-communication." According to Castells, mass self-communication is mass communication because, on the one hand, it potentially reaches a global audience through networks and an internet connection. On the other hand, it is self-communication because it is "self-generated in content, self-directed in emission, and self-selected in reception by many that communicate with many" (Castells, 2007, p. 248).

The ethnographer Daniel Miller and his research team (Miller et al., 2016) see the key to understanding the consequences of communication in social networks in the concept of **scalable sociality**. The authors model social networks, such as Facebook or Twitter, as an extension of the continuum on the scale between private and public media. Social networks restrict the distribution of public messages to a defined group. Other networks, such as WhatsApp, extend one-to-one communication by allowing groups to be set up, thereby increasing the reach of information. Social networks, therefore, allow actors to choose audience size and level of privacy. Individuals or institutions can choose which audiences they send information to, or with whom they interact.

In social networks, information is not only distributed but also supplemented, changed, or placed in new contexts. Henry Jenkins (Jenkins et al., 2012) coined the term *participatory culture* to describe public communication, which sees the public not merely as consumers of preconstructed messages but as people who are shaping, sharing, reframing, and remixing media content within larger communities and networks. As the concept has evolved, it now refers to a range of different groups – communities, companies, or organizations – deploying media production and distribution to serve their collective interests. The discourses within and between networks both mirror and influence social reality. Furthermore, their processes of meaning-making, by combining new information with existing knowledge, can become drivers of social change.

Mass media also use social networks to disseminate their content and interact with their audiences. This leads to a mix of vertical and horizontal modes of communication, because mass media content is, in turn, shared by individuals and institutions and, thus, recontextualized, and then discussed in networks or communities. In these linguistic interactions, new meanings are constructed by combining new information with existing culturally and regionally shaped knowledge. The intertwining of the mass media system with communication in social networks potentially offers an unlimited variety of information and mostly free access to all communication flows. Owing to their engagement on social media, audiences can potentially be exposed to more and more diverse content. Articles can be read free of charge, podcasts with news programs can be called up practically without restriction and are an addition to the linear range of traditional mass media. Castells (2007) claims that mass self-communication enables infinite diversity as the communication flows construct and reconstruct the global and local production of meaning in the public mind.

However, the participatory character of public communication is constrained and influenced by algorithmic processes. The amount of information produced on the web exceeds our capacity to consume it. Users' attention has become one of the most valuable resources of the digital age. Optimizing the experience of internet users therefore plays a key role in the business model of many companies which adopt algorithmic strategies to filter information to which we are exposed, which affect opinion formation and its dynamics. Eli Pariser (2011) introduced the term **filter bubble** to describe a concept where website algorithms selectively guess what information a user would like to see based on personal information like location, click behavior, and search history. A filter bubble can result in users being less exposed to contradictory viewpoints. This development is socially relevant insofar as the audience increasingly consumes news via social networks. By limiting people's exposure to new and diverse information, the bubble effect may have negative implications for public discourse. The effects are sometimes estimated to be so strong that the term *echo chamber* has been established in discourses on the subject in order to describe communication spaces in which the information that corresponds to the user's attitudes echoes particularly loudly.

Additionally, targeted political campaigns on social media can deliver different arguments to different groups of voters, so no two people may ever see the same set of adverts or arguments. These new dynamics of persuasion and surveillance, fueled by surveillance capitalism (Section 2.1.2), can take political campaigning from being a public process to being a private, personalized affair. Furthermore, in public discourses in the digital era, the opinions and statements of amateurs can achieve the same legitimacy as those of traditional media, communication professionals, and experts. The fact that anyone is free to publish content means that a great deal of information reaching the public abbreviates, distorts, or misrepresents a particular factual situation. When disinformation is intentional and targeted, it is referred to as fake news (Ireton & Posetti, 2018).

The Internet may be ideologically "neutral," but its continually evolving technologies and platforms shape the dynamics of public communication. As long as channels are public, they can be monitored: by the platforms themselves, by scholars, authorities, or the media. The situation is different for closed groups or messenger apps like WhatsApp, Telegram, or WeChat, which have an enormous reach. On Telegram, up to 200,000 people can join a group. For Telegram channels, where only a channel creator can write messages, the number of participants is unlimited. Such features make messaging apps a perfect meeting place for extremist groups that are not tolerated elsewhere (Ebner, 2020). The phenomenon of sharing content through private channels is referred to as **dark social** (see, e.g., Boccia et al., 2021). In dark social, the threshold for entry into very active groups is low. Such groups are well networked; they share their contributions very frequently. Thus, one can quickly end up in a network with a closed worldview that is fundamentally characterized by misinformation. The private nature of the exchanges also means that there is no contradiction or corrective information available.

There is a variety of platform operators' efforts to solve the problems of misinformation on their platforms. Simultaneously, politicians and the judiciary systems are increasingly addressing these issues at different levels; for example, through demands to regulate platforms and their use of algorithms. The movement toward encrypted, non-public areas of the Internet complicates any approaches to solutions and shows that the question of competencies and responsibility in the networked public sphere is far from being resolved. As a consequence, one of the biggest challenges for media and communication experts is to redefine their roles and responsibilities in public communication and the networked public sphere (Chapter 4).

ACTIVITY

Does Twitter's practice of hiding rule-breaking tweets by influential politicians behind a warning while at the same time leaving them online contribute to Habermas' ideal of the public sphere? Provide arguments for your answer.

2.3 Sociality and Social Media

When you type the keyword "networking" in a search engine, thousands of results come up, most of them related to the terms *social media* and *career*. Networking has become a crucial skill in a society that is characterized by a shift away from geographical proximity toward de-territorialized networks created and maintained through digital communication. The changes introduced by new media indicate a new form of sociality, one that replaces long-lasting bonds and belongs with temporary, and often instrumental, relationships. The building of diverse and wide-ranging network connections is closely linked to communicative structures and the dynamics of social media.

2.3.1 Network Sociality

As we have seen in the previous section on network theories, the digital society is characterized by networks – as structures of digital connectivity, and as a practice of making social ties, which can be private, professional, or, as we will see later in this chapter, somewhere in between. The shift from location-based communities to technologically based networks implies new forms of sociality.

The term *sociality* refers to the ability and need of people to form social ties. In their recent anthropological work, Nicholas J. Long and Henrietta L. Moore conceptualize human sociality as a "dynamic relational matrix within which human subjects are constantly interacting in ways that are co-productive, continually plastic, and malleable, and through which they come to know the world they live in and find their purpose and meaning within it" (Long & Moore, 2012, p. 41). New media reorder this matrix as they enable new forms of connections between people and the ways they orientate toward each other.

Following Castell's notion of network society and Wellman's concept of networked individualism (Section 2.1), Andreas Wittel (2001) introduced the term **network social-ity** to describe the social implications of a shift from communities to networks. He argues that flexible and uncertain working conditions in the network society and its relation to space in the form of space of flows (Section 2.1) has undermined the basis for community and, therefore, substantially changed our sociality. While community sociality was based on face-to-face interaction, long-lasting and close relationships, a sense of belonging as well as common history and narratives, network sociality consists of social relations which are not based on mutual experience or shared history, but primarily on an exchange of information.

According to Wittel, relations between people in a network sociality are brief but intense. Strangers bond quickly but also drift apart promptly, as geographically dispersed groups of professionals assemble and disassemble. Social connections are mostly compressed in acts of "catching up." As relationships are not based on a common and shared history, the brief interactions that make up private and professional lives foreground the exchange of information rather than shared experiences or continuous narratives. Furthermore, in the context of network sociality, the distinction between private and professional life becomes blurred. Parties become network opportunities, colleagues become friends, and people work in coffee shops, at home, or on holiday. Because social ties in this form of sociality need to be continuously formed and maintained, communication and presence within networks gain importance.

Wittel developed his concept of network sociality before smartphones and social media became a central part of our lives. Since then, society has become not only more networked but also more mobile. While people increasingly move and travel long distances, building and maintaining social ties despite physical absence has become an additional challenge for networking.

Christian Licoppe (2004) introduced the concept of **connected presence** to describe relationships in which physically absent parties achieve presence through digital communication. His ethnographical research showed that a large part of interactions on mobile devices consists of phatic communicative gestures. The term *phatic communication* was introduced by the ethnographer Bronislaw Malinowski (1923). It refers to the verbal or nonverbal communication that has a social rather than an informative function. In digital communication, messages are often used to share feelings or establish a mood of sociability rather than to communicate information or ideas. People maintain connection despite physical absence by updating each other through short messages, expressing emotions and feelings, and informing each other about what is going on during any given day. These quasi-continuous exchanges through digital communication tools lead to a blurring of the concepts of presence and absence.

Nowadays, social network sites help decontextualized and mobile individuals to construct and maintain social relations in the context of networked sociality and to replace shared biographies with information exchange as a basis for communication. Social media allow us to maintain a continuous communicative social presence which requires relatively small time investments. "Catching up" through status updates, messages, comments, shares, and likes is supported by easy-to-use technology that can be accessed independent of time and location.

2.3.2 Social Media

The term *social media* mainly refers to web-based platforms and mobile applications that promote social interaction and allow the creation of content that can be liked, commented on, or shared. The base of social media is users who have accounts or profiles composed of personal information in different modes; for example, picture and text. Social media users can "friend" or follow each other. By doing so, they connect, interact, and build social networks on one or several social network sites like Instagram, Facebook, or Twitter. These networks consist, as do all networks, of nodes, ties, and flows. Nodes on social media represent the profiles of people or companies, ties stand for the way they are connected, and flows refer to communication content that builds and maintains their connections.

In the early stages of social media, the terminology to describe the new phenomenon was unsystematic and varied. The terms *social media*, *social network sites*, *online social networks*, or *social networks* were often used as synonyms to refer to a broad and diffuse range of sites and services. Nowadays, scholars mostly use social media as an umbrella term for social network sites, which allow social interaction and the sharing and co-creation of content. In contrast, the term **social network** is used to refer to a web of social relations that exists both online and in the real world.

boyd and Ellison (2007) were among the first to systemize the concepts around social media. They defined social network sites as "web-based services that allow individuals to (1) construct a public or semi-public profile within a bounded system, (2) articulate a list of other users with whom they share a connection, and (3) view and traverse their list of connections and those made by others within the system" (boyd & Ellison, 2007).

Since the social and technical landscape of social media has undergone dramatic changes over the years, boyd and Ellison revised their definition in 2013. Their new definition, named definition 2.0 by the authors, describes a social network site as "a networked communication platform in which participants (a) have uniquely identifiable profiles that consist of user-supplied content, content provided by other users, and/or system-provided data; (b) can publicly articulate connections that can be viewed and traversed by others; and (c) can consume, produce, and/or interact with streams of user-generated content provided by their connections on the site" (Ellison & boyd, 2013). This updated definition takes into account the development of social network sites from profile-centric to media-centric, as well as the growing importance of communication and information sharing.

Today, most social network sites are organized around a feed of content, which is fed by updates from people and groups followed by a user, news media, or organizations. This aggregated collection of multimodal content serves as a starting point for activities on the social network site itself, on other social sites, or on the web. As social media content can be enriched with links, or features like hashtags or mentions, it makes it the perfect starting point for communication, for finding new content and for content sharing.

The choice of networking sites depends on age, geographical location, cultural background, and the preferences of peers, since one reason for being present on social media is the possibility of communicating with friends, acquaintances, and potentially interesting private and professional connections. Social media allows users to determine audience size and the privacy of content, a fact Miller et al. (2016) refer to as scalable sociality (Section 2.1). Recent research shows that different social media platforms play different roles in people's lives. While WhatsApp and Snapchat are mostly used for maintaining a continued, synchronous co-presence through a frequent exchange of updates with closely related people, platforms like Facebook are used for staging identities, getting and sharing information, and networking with weaker ties (see, e.g., Karapanos, Teixeira & Gouveia, 2016; Katz & Crocker, 2015).

This points us toward the reasons why we use social media. Social media profiles and our interactions on social media platforms allow us to access and share content but also to stay connected with others and to build and maintain relationships on different levels.

2.3.3 The Power of Weak Ties

As we have seen in this chapter so far, networked sociality emphasizes fast-paced, fleeting, and instrumental encounters with a broad set of contacts. Therefore networking – the creation and maintenance of an extensive social network of people with different connections, backgrounds, and information – is gaining importance.

People within social networks are connected in different ways. Some of them have close and intense relationships, while others know about each other only because they are friends of friends or because their names became known in a particular context. Mark Granovetter, one of the pioneers of social network theory, introduced the distinction between strong and weak ties to describe two different types of connections between people (1973, 1983). He defines the strength of the ties through a combination of the amount of time spent together, the emotional intensity invested in the relationship, and the degree of intimacy and reciprocity between individuals. Strong ties are characterized as requiring a greater time investment, and by higher social similarities. They are also indicative of a deep connectedness; for example, between family members, friends, or colleagues. Weak ties, on the other hand, are characterized by a lower level of time-sharing and less resemblance between the people connected, who are just acquaintances, or people with a common professional or cultural background. The strength of the ties can substantially affect interactions, professional success, and personal well-being.

In his ethnographic study, Granovetter (1973) discovered that vital information for new hire options came from acquaintances rather than family or close friends. Furthermore, his research showed that people with weak ties find jobs that not only are not visible to the rest of the tight network, but also come with higher compensation and satisfaction. This is especially true for higher-educated workers, because a large number of jobs in this segment are found through referrals.

Granovetter attributes the advantage of weak ties to the fact that information transmitted through strong ties tends to be redundant, as socially close individuals share similar interests and knowledge and spend time in the same places. Weak ties, on the other hand, connect individuals who have less in common, including contacts and access to information. Weak ties, therefore, function as bridges that connect otherwise disparate groups of individuals. They allow information to move rapidly and widely in a network, across social and geographical boundaries.

2.3.4 Social Capital

Granovetter's "strength of weak ties" theory is closely related to the notion of bridging and bonding social capital. The term **social capital** describes the influence of relationships on the kind of advantages people enjoy because of their connection with others. Bourdieu and Wacquant (1992, p. 119) define social capital as "the sum of the resources, actual or virtual, that accrue to an individual or a group by virtue of possessing a durable network of more or less institutionalized relationships of mutual acquaintance and recognition." While bonding social capital exists *within* close social groups, bridging social capital exists *between* social groups that are connected with "weak ties" – acquaintances, work contacts, or friends of friends (Putnam, 2000).

Social capital has been approached from many different theoretical perspectives, and these disagree on its source, form, and consequences (see, e.g., Bourdieu, 2018; Coleman, 2009; Putnam, 2000). For a better understanding of the concept, it is useful to examine how it functions at different levels: from individuals to groups through to societies.

On an individual level, social relationships can give us access to benefits and resources which influence other forms of capital – like human capital (in the form of education and knowledge) or economic capital (like savings or access to loans). If your neighbor is a car mechanic, for example, they can fix your car for free in exchange for other services, or in exchange for a potential future favor. They can also give you access to valuable information: teach you how to fix small problems yourself or recommend other reliable mechanics. Putnam (2000, p. 318) argues that, especially for people who have little economic and human capital, social capital becomes essential to their welfare.

The examples at the individual level are also relevant for the group level, since individuals interact with others and form relationships. A person who has good standing in a group can use their social capital to request assistance from members of that group. Making the association with the group visible to others, for example through connecting on social media, can open up otherwise unavailable opportunities. In a professional context, a higher number of promotions and salary increases are examples of benefits for individuals with social capital.

At the societal level, social capital is associated with phenomena like lower crime rates, association membership, or voluntary activities. Examples of social capital on this level are returning a lost item to a stranger, loaning something without a contract, giving up one's seat on public transport for someone in need, or any other beneficial interaction between strangers.

Scholars from different disciplines observe an erosion of social capital in individualistic Western societies, which stress the needs of the individual over the needs of the group as a whole. They claim that, compared with previous generations, fewer people get involved in social activities and do fewer things together. Putman (2000) uses the metaphor of bowling to illustrate this development: although more Americans are bowling today than ever before, he argues, fewer of them are bowling in leagues. He attributes this social disengagement and the associated loss of social capital to new technologies, as people are spending more and more time in the office, commuting to work and watching TV.

Putman (2000) has put forward the argument that watching television occupies our time and, as a consequence, disrupts our opportunities for the formation of social capital. The time we spend watching television is time lost for socializing, for meeting people and forming relationships. Digital communication seems to have the opposite effect. In their widely cited study, Wellman et al. (2001) have found that the Internet supports our relationships with friends and family and increases participatory capital – the involvement in politics and voluntary activities.

Examining the relationship between social capital and social network sites, Ellison et al. (2007) found that the use of Facebook increased both bonding and bridging capital, as well as the ability to hold on to social capital despite less frequent face-to-face contacts. The study shows furthermore that interactions on Facebook increase bridging social capital rather than bonding social capital. These findings are in line with those of Donath and boyd (2004), who argue that social network sites multiply and strengthen the weak ties in networks. The authors show that the effects on social capital are interlinked with the technical features of social media platforms, which allow an effortless communication with people we know only superficially and do not apply to the Internet as such.

2.3.5 Algorithmic Socialities

While social media facilitates building and maintaining social ties, socializing via SNS becomes increasingly dependent upon an infrastructure provided by companies like Facebook or Twitter. Furthermore, people interacting on social media create storable and sortable data sets about themselves, their network, and their social lives. Photos, events, and pages are merged with other information such as the relationships to friends, the content we like or share, and photos that we tag. Our "social graph" – the global network of linkages between all individuals within a system (Fitzpatrick & Recordon, 2007) – becomes a valuable economic resource.

Social media platforms provide open application programming interfaces (APIs) and other technologies that enable third parties to integrate the social graph from their platforms into other tools and sites, like TripAdvisor, Yelp, or Spotify. TripAdvisor, for example, leverages Facebook's social graph to ensure that when people are looking at hotel reviews, the reviews posted by their social connections appear right at the top (CBS Interactive Inc., 2010).

In their reflections on the interplay of social media with socialities, Ellison and boyd describe how the social graph rose in significance when companies started using it in combination with algorithms to recommend personalized content, contacts, and provide targeted advertisements. While marketers use the social graph for advertising purposes, media companies use it to shape the flow of information (Ellison & boyd, 2013).

We are only at the beginning of understanding how algorithms affect social life, our relationships, and the production and dissemination of knowledge. The example of Cambridge Analytica in Section 2.1 shows that combining sensitive information from social media profiles can lead to massive misuse and manipulation. Not only are algorithms technological features that translate content, actions, and interactions into data points that can be related to each other in endless combinations, but they also shape our discursive and social practices and, thus, the structure of our societies.

ACTIVITY

Have a look at your social media profiles. Which of your contacts would you categorize as weak ties and which as strong ties? Describe how you use social media to interact with these two types of connections (a paragraph for each one). Dedicate the third paragraph to reflecting on how these interactions affect your social capital.

Key Terms

connected presence, dark social, filter bubble, machine learning, network sociality, networked publics, networked public sphere, phatic communication, public sphere, scalable sociality, social capital, social network sites (SNS), surveillance capitalism

Chapter Summary

- The network society is a social order embodying a logic that is characterized by digital communication, a time-space-compression, and the space of flows.

- In contrast to the social organization of industrial societies, the network society is determined by de-territorialized networks of economic nodes that are held together through digital communication.

- In a network society, the mass media system is complemented by, and interconnected with, communication on SNS and the Internet. As a result, public communication can potentially become increasingly participatory. However, unrestricted and free access to information is restricted by algorithms and the mechanisms of surveillance capitalism.

- The Internet may be ideologically "neutral," but its continually evolving technologies and platforms shape the dynamics of public communication. Every second, endless communication flows construct and reconstruct the global and local production of meaning in the public mind. However, this diversity is constricted, for example, by algorithms which can limit people's exposure to new and diverse information.

- Additionally, targeted political campaigns on social media can deliver different arguments to different groups of voters, so no two people may ever see the same set of adverts or arguments.

- These developments, together with the movement of publics toward encrypted, non-public areas of the Internet show that the question of competencies and responsibility in the networked public sphere is far from being resolved.

- Sociality on social media is supported by technological features that enable not only a quick and effortless exchange of information but also phatic communication in the form of pictures, emojis, memes, or likes.

- People use different SNS for diverse purposes, such as maintaining strong ties with a narrow circle of people who are already close, or networking with weak ties. Social relationships created and maintained through social media influence individual social capital.

- Social capital arises and becomes tangible in social interaction and provides people with benefits like useful information and future opportunities. The interactions on social media create storable and sortable data, which is increasingly used for commercial purposes.

Further Reading

Network Theories

The textbook *The network society* (Barney, 2004) provides undergraduate students with an accessible resource for a thoughtful engagement with the concept of the network society.

The weightless world: strategies for managing the digital economy (Coyle, 1998) provides a comprehensive introduction to the idea of the weightless economy and addresses problems like economic inequity and unemployment.

Digitalization and Public Communication

The chapter "What happened to the public sphere? The networked public sphere and public opinion formation," by Kaiser et al. (2017), introduces the concepts of public sphere, public opinion, and networked publics and explains their role in shaping democracies.

Sociality and Social Media

IF ... THEN: Algorithmic power and politics (Bucher, 2018) critically discusses the socio-technical aspects of algorithmic power and offers a theoretical framework for understanding the relationship between algorithms, politics, and new media.

Achieving success through social capital: Tapping the hidden resources in your personal and business networks (Baker, 2000) shows the concrete benefits of social capital through examples from private and professional contexts.

3 Practical Context: From Writing to Multimodal Communication

PREVIEW

From the earliest cuneiform scribes of Mesopotamia to the best-selling authors of today, most people who use words in their work would probably agree that, as novelist Margaret Atwood has said, "A word after a word after a word is power" (Lang & Raymont, 2019). This chapter is about the power of words and images. It introduces basic concepts that are pivotal in verbal, visual, and multimodal communication. We begin with the role of writing in the digital age and explore the media linguistic mindset that is required in rapidly changing digital environments. Then, we present a set of sixteen key practices of focused writing and writing-by-the way (Section 3.1.3) in the newsroom and beyond.

The second section of the chapter covers theoretical concepts of visual communication. We address different approaches to reading images. One pivotal approach is social semiotics – a grand theory that can be applied to all kinds of semiotic material used for communication: verbal texts, sounds, gestures, or images. We will complement this approach with concepts from other semiotic traditions as well as rhetorical and critical theories about images and their effects on the users.

When it comes to multimodal communication, we ask: What semiotic work is carried out by words, images, typography, and layout? How do these components combine into a coherent meaningful whole? We discuss the concept of multimodality and related key terms. The main message of the chapter is that all forms of human communication are multimodal.

Learning Objectives

By the end of this chapter, you will be able to

- discuss the social practice of writing
- compare the practices of focused writing and writing-by-the-way
- explain the relevance of writing and its investigation in the digital age
- explain the social semiotic approach and its three metafunctions
- understand how to uncover the hidden meanings of visual representations
- understand the concept of multimodality
- describe the technique of information linking that is relevant to multimodal cohesion
- reflect on the power of texts and images.

3.1 Writing

Whatever the language and script system, people harness the power of writing to store, process, and share thoughts. It is not surprising that some scholars consider writing the mother of all the power of media. For H. G. Wells, for example, writing "made the growth of states larger than the old city states possible. It made a continuous historical consciousness possible. The command of the priest or king and his seal could go far beyond his sight and voice and could survive his death" (Wells, 1922, p. 41).

Today, new forms of writing foster social change. This section thus is about the social relevance of writing. It first outlines the development from handwriting to **digital writing**. Then, we discuss writing practices in multimodal and multimedia environments and explore the mindsets such environments require. We conclude by looking at ways in which we can investigate digital writing and improve its fitness for specific communicational needs.

3.1.1 The Relevance of Writing in the Digital Age

Public and corporate media are becoming user interfaces for content management systems, for databases of facts and fakes, and for multimodal public storytelling (Perrin & Zampa, 2018). At the same time, social media and mass media are getting thoroughly intertwined (Haapanen & Perrin, 2018). For example, potentially attractive utterances made by potentially attractive people in social media are quoted in mass media and vice versa – which results in a helix movement of **linguistic recycling** with increasing audience reach, as can be seen via the visual representation of this in Figure 3.1.

Figure 3.1 visualizes the dynamics of linguistic recycling in public discourse. In social media posts, we reach our audience with our crispy utterances or crunchy quotes from attractive agents such as influencers or rhetorically strong politicians. Their role and image in social media networks, as well as the wording of their utterance, may be much more

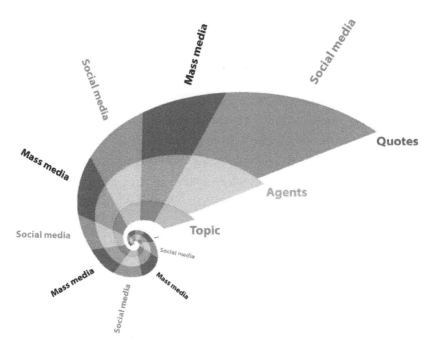

Figure 3.1 The quoting helix of public discourse. From "Media and quoting: Understanding the purposes, roles, and processes of quoting and social media," by L. Haapanen and D. Perrin, in C. Cotter and D. Perrin (eds.), *Handbook of language and media* (p. 438), London: Routledge, 2018. © 2018 Daniel Perrin. Adapted with permission.

important than the topic they talk about when it comes to making decisions in newsrooms to further spread the quote through mass media. Once amplified by mass media, the quotes are taken up by social media again, but on a much broader basis now – and so on.

Such developments are unstoppable, just as when communication markets switched from black-and-white to color photography, from silent movies to sound films, from letters to email, from landline to mobile connections, and from mass media to social media. In all of these – and many more – cases of technology-driven media development, new media have emerged, raised people's attention, and increased users' demand. In many cases, the old media and their specific ways of writing have not totally disappeared but were pushed into niches, as has happened with cinema defying Netflix's rapid growth.

The research on professional practice in newsrooms (e.g., Brannon, 2008; Catenaccio, et al., 2011; Huan, 2018, p. 69; Jacobs, 2018; Quinn, 2005; Tunstall, 2009) has been exemplified in three key competences: writing on all channels, working in teams (e.g., Perrin, 2011a), and finding emergent solutions (e.g., Perrin, 2012). The first of these three competences is what this chapter focuses on: writing in today's digital environments, exploiting all the available channels and semiotic systems.

By writing, we mean the practice of producing complex verbal signs such as words, sentences, and texts. The verbal signs are embedded in – and interact with – nonverbal semiotic environments, such as acoustical and optical, but also olfactory, gustatory, and tactile contexts. The practice of writing is oriented toward storing, processing, and/or sharing its products. In other words, we write memos on post-its not to forget what to buy on our way home (mnemotechnical writing); we jot down words and rearrange them to develop ideas (epistemic writing); and we type messages and blog posts to share our thoughts with others in different places and moments of time (communicative writing).

Like all human practices, writing includes cognitive, material, and social aspects. It both affects and is affected by its environments and changes with cultures and societies (Perrin, 2021). Writing today is characterized by recent developments that seem to be novel at first sight. An example is replacing the word you by the letter u. Such phenomena have been termed **heterography** "the deployment of literacy techniques and instruments in ways that do not respond to institutional orthographic norms, but that nevertheless are not completely chaotic, even if such chaos appears to be the most conspicuous feature" (Blommaert, 2010, p. 87).

On closer consideration, however, heterography has always preceded eras of standardization of written languages. This becomes clear when we remember that early Greek and Latin used to be written without any spaces or blanks between the words – withoutanyspacesorblanksbetweenthewords. This *scriptio continua* (continuous script) was the only way to write until some innovative writers started to separate words from each other. In doing so, they introduced a fundamental difference between spoken and written language: When speaking, we normally do not pause between the words; when writing, we now do in most scripts and languages (Saenger, 1997).

So far, in a nutshell, for the development of structural micro characteristics of scripts and writing. However, on a macro plan, the social relevance and everyday practices of writing itself are about to change fundamentally – a development that has long been underestimated (Brand, 2016). People now spend more time writing than reading, both in their leisure time and at work. If they read, they do it to foster subsequent or parallel writing. Brand has referred to this as "writing emerges as a dominant form of labour" (Brand 2016, personal communication), meaning that the way we write becomes a key practice throughout our professional and labor fields. For many huge organizations such as Facebook or Al Jazeera, **multimodal texts** are the only product. And for most organizations, communicating with their stakeholders through multimodal text is a key success factor. Literacy and writing have become a key factor of economic production and competition.

3.1.2 From Handwriting to Digital Writing

Across cultures and societies, until fairly recently writing was a privilege of scholars, often attached to their religious and political power. Writing was exclusive on three levels: on a material level, it was as expensive as the hand-crafted parchment and ink it required; on a mental level, it was an art taught to an educational elite only; on a social level, it was used by powerful people who could afford to buy parchment and paying professional scriptors to spread their word, their goals, their framing of the world. Access to that written knowledge in turn was limited to privileged readers.

When the printing press and affordable paper finally allowed for the mass reproduction of written texts, literacy first spread in the form of reading, not writing. Masses of people started to read, whereas still only a narrow elite was able to and in the position to write and have their words printed. This means that written communication was a top-down enterprise, managed by powerful people and influential institutions. In many areas, municipalities employed professional writers who could be hired by citizens when, for example, legal documents, business contracts, or love letters had to be put down on paper.

Social landmarks of literacy history (Figure 3.2) include the rise of modern cities and their record-keeping bureaucracies, industrialization and trade communication, the development of efficient postal networks, the adoption of systematic schooling, and the shift toward knowledge-based economies. Since the mid-nineteenth century, the number of people able to read and write has risen from 10 percent to more than 80 percent globally (Lillis, 2013, p. 75). The current global adult literacy rate is 86 percent, with a male and female literacy rate of 90 and 83 percent respectively.

Three technological revolutions have thoroughly changed the practice of writing. First, the invention of the printing press in 1440 mechanized the mass storage of written text and made it available to multitudes. Second, beginning in 1837, the telegraph electrified written communication and dramatically increased the transmission of written text in global networks. Third, the computer digitalized the processing of all the audible and visible signs and irrevocably welded writing with programming (Ford, 2015) and surveillance (Zuboff, 2020).

The term *digital writing* mirrors the fact that computers treat the signs of all semiotic modes as numbers or digits (itself a metaphor, based on the practice of counting with fingers). Landmarks of digital writing include the invention of the ASCII code representing characters of verbal languages by numbers between 1 and 256; Ted Nelson's concept of hypertext based on Vannevar Bush's "memory extender" (Section 1.2.2); and the unveiling of the first PC, developed by Xerox in 1974 and equipped with a text editor showing print-like formatted texts on screen: What You See Is What You Get, the WYSIWYG principle (e.g., Hepp, 2020).

Since Xerox was not quick enough to realize the potential of digital writing, key engineers and ideas drained off to garage start-ups such as Microsoft, Apple, and Adobe. They have become market drivers of office automation based on digital writing. Much earlier, the practice of writing had coined a metaphor of multimodal semiotic assemblage which is mirrored in terms such as *photoGRAPHY, cinematoGRAPHY,* or *phonoGRAPHY.*

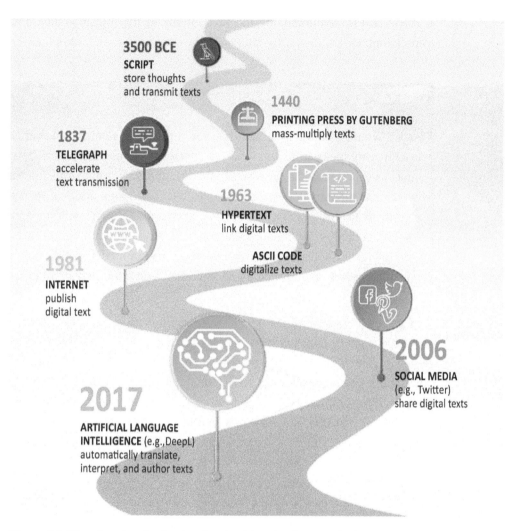

Figure 3.2 Time line showing landmarks of writing development in the context of historical landmarks

With the Internet and social media, digital writing has become the key practice of pro-gramming virtual environments and pro-grammed societies (Rushkoff, 2010).

3.1.3 Routinized Creative Writing on All Channels

Leading professionals have said that since the beginning of media convergence in the newsrooms, the ability to write on all channels will be the key competence and practice in communication businesses of the future (e.g., for an early position, Moser-Wellman et al., 2008). This practice includes all editing at the interface of text, sound, and pictures. Writing has thus become a multimodal practice of encoding semiotic entities that can be edited and shared using a variety of increasingly interconnected media (e.g., Hicks

& Perrin, 2014). Multimodality includes intermodality, transmodality, and processes of transcoding.

EXAMPLE

Award-winning data journalism (see, e.g., https://datajournalismawards.org) usually combines verbal and visual languages (intermodality), goes beyond their limits as experienced so far (transmodality), and often transforms information into complementary codes, e.g., complex data sets into emotional stories and vivid graphics (transcoding). Writing in such a broad understanding succeeds by combining the specific strengths of media, such as print and video mass media, with interactive social media. Writers' awareness of media-specific strengths is more urgently needed in multimodal and multimedia environments than ever before.

Whoever opts for a media item with sound but no images, for example, must know and make clear to their audience why audio information alone conveys the topic in the best way. And whoever includes social media in their professional work in order to build communities needs to be able to benefit from these channels' advantages. Moreover, digital writing gradually develops from the traditional form of purposeful writing, such as writing an editorial, toward a new hybrid form between the linguistic modes of writing and speaking. This calls for some details.

Purposeful writing has long been a key competence of professional life: people sit down at their desk in order to write good texts. They start with a draft, using pen and paper or a computer. Then, they edit their text until they consider it done. Finally, they send it off or publish it, as a carefully designed piece. Unlike speech, purposeful writing is decoupled from traces of fighting with thoughts and words – a close-to-perfect communicational offer of written language. This traditional, purposeful way of producing texts has been termed **focused writing** (Hicks & Perrin, 2014, p. 231).

Digitalization, mediatization, and "glocalization" (Khondker, 2004) – which means that we increasingly interact on global *and* on local levels when, e.g., translating Facebook into minority languages – however, foster new forms of communication that transgress traditional boundaries between speech and text as well as between private, educational, and professional domains. People use micro texts such as Twitter or WhatsApp messages, sound bites, and visual snapshots to synchronize knowledge, share emotions, and maintain identities from everywhere and at all times of the day. This new, ubiquitous, and highly interactive communication activity has been termed **writing-by-the-way** (Hicks & Perrin, 2014, p. 232). For an in-depth example of writing-by-the-way in organizational roles see the case study in the book's online repository (www.cambridge.org/digitalcommunication):

3.1.4 Building Digital Writers' Multimedia Mindset

Multi- and transmodal writing in multimedia environments benefits from a **media linguistic mindset** (Perrin, 2013, p. 69) combining sixteen activity fields (Table 3.1). In all the fields, writers have to constantly respond to the partly contradictory contextual expectations by deciding about, for example, how to collaborate in multimedia newsrooms (activity field of HANDLING SOCIAL ENVIRONMENT) or how to split goals and related tasks across media (activity field of GOAL SETTING). Increasingly, the Internet and social media are integrated throughout the production process, from reading source text to implementing the product.

TABLE 3.1 EXAMPLES OF DECISIONS TO MAKE IN THE ACTIVITY FIELDS OF (CORPORATE) NEWSWRITING

	Key activities of writing ...	... and exemplary decisions for the multimedia mindset
Context	HANDLING SOCIAL ENVIRONMENT	How do I collaborate in multimedia newsrooms?
	HANDLING TOOLS ENVIRONMENT	How do I cope with new, as yet unfamiliar tools?
	HANDLING TASK ENVIRONMENT	How do I update hot items?
	COMPREHENDING THE TASK	What is my task within the cross-media concerto?
	IMPLEMENTING THE PRODUCT	How do I tease and promote my piece on social media?
Function	FINDING THE SOURCES	Which channels do I use to cover which aspects?
	LIMITING THE TOPIC	How do I integrate the sources into my own items?
	TAKING OWN POSITIONS	How do I achieve a unique selling point across media?
	STAGING THE STORY	Which media transformation for which effect?
	ESTABLISHING RELEVANCE	How do I tune audience design across media?
Structure	READING SOURCES	How do I gather linkable sources?
	READING OWN TEXT	How do I navigate through my product so far?
	GOAL SETTING	How do I split goals across media?
	PLANNING	How do I negotiate my workflow?
	CONTROLLING	How can I improve the interplay across media?
	MONITORING	What do I want to achieve across media?

The leftmost column in Table 3.1 shows the three main groups of writing activities: first, those related to contexts such as the social environment; then those related to the function of the emerging text product, such as giving the floor to relevant sources; and finally, those related to the structure of the **text production** process itself, such as reading the relevant sources before and while writing. Whereas the same set of sixteen key activities has been observed in all kinds of newswriting, the decisions in the third column are typical for multimedia writing (Perrin, 2015b, p. 147).

When analyzing this media linguistic mindset in a series of research projects on professional writing since 1996, researchers realized that the sixteen activity fields can be considered constants, whereas their use in decision-making practices depends on drivers such as media technology, organizational culture and development, writers' psychobiographies, and the writing task to be accomplished. In newsrooms, three shifts of realization could be observed, delimiting four stages of digitalization of (corporate) newswriting (Miller et al., 2016; Perrin & Gnach, 2017):

- In the early 1990s, writers started to transfer the focused writing of printed media to the new publication environment of the Internet.
- Around 2000, focused writing for offline and online media was combined with browsing the Internet by-the-way while writing.
- Since 2010 writers have used social media while writing by-the-way to track down topics, find sources, and interact with addressees.
- Towards 2020, this management of stakeholder groups through writing-by-the-way in social media has become dominant in professional writing.

This development changes the demands placed on professional writers. In the past, being a writer often meant to be a lone fighter who completed his or her work in silence before publication; today, those who want to get their message across must have a constant communicative presence on all channels. The resonance of the contributions is measured online; contributions that triggered many comments are rewarded by prominent placement in the user interfaces. Of course, such mechanisms impact the practices of digital writing in public discourse (Haapanen & Perrin, 2018).

Practical measures derived from this analysis include preparing professionals for the close interplay of focused writing and writing-by-the-way. On the societal level, measures include fostering media literacy via primary school to help media users identify fact-based information in bubbles of algorithm-driven relevance construction in the media. Professional writers can only contribute to reasonable decision-making in their contexts if they manage to publish the essential information – and if this essential information is in demand and understood (e.g., Schudson, 2008).

Investigating the multimedia mindset in the newsroom requires close collaboration with practitioners, for example with journalists, video-editors, bloggers, influencers, and other professional and para-professional communicators. Such research "on, for, and with" (Cameron et al., 1992, p. 22) practitioners is called **transdisciplinary research**, since it transgresses the boundaries between academic and nonacademic disciplines (Perrin & Kramsch, 2018). It is oriented toward sustainably solving practical problems, in this case that of writing in digital environments.

How such writing has been investigated and is further developed is explained in Section 4.3.1, on focused writing and writing-by-the-way; Sections 5.1.1 and 5.6.1 on frameworks and methods of linguistic analysis; and in Section 7.1, where we discuss a case study of writing in journalism.

ACTIVITY

How has your writing developed with increasing digitalization? Explain your response on one page by drawing on the above insights about contextual change and the media linguistic mindset and illustrate it with examples from your personal and professional experience.

3.2 Visual Communication

How many images do you consume a day? And have you ever thought about whose perspective is represented in thoses images and why? This section is about the power of images; how images and other visual representations create meaning and how they influence the way we see the world.

3.2.1 The Visual Turn

New media technology always leads to new forms of expression, and thus to changes in what can be said in what way and by whom. The developments of the television medium in the 1960s and the offset press in the 1960s and 1970s are examples of media innovations with great cultural consequences. Images were given more space and greater attention, graphics and layout became important means of communication and new forms of visual storytelling emerged. During the digital revolution, gaining speed in the first half of the 1990s, digital developments – such as the World Wide Web, and later in the 2010s, the smartphone – have taken a new direction. Today, amateurs as well as professionals can produce and distribute advanced visual expressions easily and cheaply. Some scholars talk about this development as a **visual turn** in our culture. This turn, also called pictorial or iconic turn, is about an increased and changed use of visual forms of expression in a number of genres and formats.

According to Kress, we are witnessing "a move from telling the world to showing the world" (2003, p. 140). Moreover, the visual turn is about a rapidly growing professional and academic interest in the uses and effects of these forms of expression. While researchers within the humanities and the social sciences since the 1970s have been keen to discover how verbal language lays the foundation for our understanding of the world, interest is now equally directed toward images and other forms of visual expression (Mitchell, 2005). How do they create meaning, how do they affect us, and how do they shape our culture? To answer these questions, in the next section we will introduce the social semiotic theory as a "grand" theory, which can be applied to all kinds of semiotic material, including visual modes like images, graphics, and color.

3.2.2 A Social Semiotic Approach to Visual Communication

Semiotics is the study of signs and their meanings. A social semiotic approach to human communication focuses on the ways in which meanings are created in the social interplay between human actors, using language in order to achieve certain goals in certain social situations. This approach was first developed by the Australian linguist Michael Halliday (1985). A central idea in **social semiotics** is that any linguistic utterance carries three different categories of meaning: *ideational*, *interpersonal*, and *textual* (Table 3.2). The three categories correlate to three aspects of the social situation: the field (what kind of social activity is going on?), the tenor (who is participating and what is the relationship of the participants?), and the mode (in this context "mode" refers to the linguistic resources for meaning-making that are involved and how they are organized).

TABLE 3.2 THE THREE METAFUNCTIONS

Metafunction	Meaning	Social situation
Ideational	says something about the world	field: what kind of social activity is going on?
interpersonal	constructs certain social relations and roles in the interplay between the participants engaged in the communication	tenor: who is participating and what is the relationship of the participants?
textual (compositional)	organizes the text elements into a coherent message	mode: what semiotic resources are applied and how do they create a coherent text?

This means that any utterance, e.g., a spoken sentence, fulfills three functions: 1. it will say something about the world (ideational meaning), 2. it will construct certain social relations and roles in the interplay between the participants engaged in the communication (interpersonal meaning), 3. it will apply certain linguistic resources in a way that creates a coherent message (textual meaning: according to its Latin origin, textual is used here in the sense of "woven" and refers to the composition of the whole message). These three forms of meaning that an utterance can carry are also refered to as **metafunctions**.

Since the late 1980s, Halliday's social semiotic framework has been applied to semiotic modes other than verbal language; for instance, images or gestures (e.g., Hodge & Kress, 1988; Norris, 2004; O'Toole, 1994). Here, the term *mode* refers to a specific class of meaningful expressions (Section 3.3). *Reading Images: The Grammar of Visual Design* has been a particularly influential book. It was first published in 1996 by two of Halliday's close associates, Gunther Kress and Theo van Leeuwen. In the book, the authors demonstrate how Halliday's theories can inspire the systematic analysis of images and other forms of visual communication concerning their potentials for meaning making. Since that time, Kress and van Leeuwen, as well as many other theorists, have been concerned with the dialectic issue of identifying both the potentials and the *limitations* of the linguistic approach when it comes to understanding the broad spectrum of nonverbal communication (e.g., Machin, 2007). For example, language is organized in time, which means that each word is followed by another, while images are organized in space: they unfold the message in a two-dimensional plane or in a three-dimensional space. This difference affects our understanding and description of the verbal and the visual mode. Yet, the three metafunctions remain a good starting point to consider a number of aspects regarding visual communication.

3.2.3 The Metafunctions

One aspect of *ideational meaning* is the differentiation between a *narrative* and a *conceptual* visual structure. We call it a narrative structure when an image focuses on some kind of action – when something is going on in the picture, giving specific roles to participants, acting in specific physical environments. A narrative structure contains vectors: lines that depart from the participants in the image and represent a process or an action; for instance, gaze could be such a vector or the straight arm pointing into a direction (Figure 3.3a). Other images have a conceptual structure, meaning that they simply show what certain persons, places, or objects look like (Figure 3.3b).

EXAMPLE

Figure 3.3a Narrative structure: The image shows actions – a man and a boy looking at the sky. Vectors are the gazes, the outstretched arm of the man pointing toward the sky, and the telescope. Credit: stevecoleimages, Collection: E+, Getty Images.

Figure 3.3b Conceptual structure. There is no action in the image. It depicts only the concept of the telescope. Credit: bubaone, Collection: DigitalVision Vectors, Getty Images.

Another aspect of ideational meaning is captured by the concept of *coding orientation*: *naturalistic* vs. *abstract*. This explains why we interpret the content of a photo and a line graph very differently. A photo communicates on the basis of a *naturalistic* coding orientation (Figure 3.4), which means that the more it looks like the real world, the more true and realistic we think it is (Kress & van Leeuwen, 2006). That also means that a photo with unclear details due to faded colors or contrasts, or with too vivid colors, can be used intentionally to signal a nonrealistic representation of the world – maybe a dreamlike world or a metaphoric representation. A line graph or a bubble chart, on the other hand, will be regarded as true and realistic if the graphical representation reveals some essential patterns, proportions, structures, or relations as clearly and precisely as possible. That is because it does not communicate according to a naturalistic, but to an *abstract* coding orientation (Figure 3.5).

EXAMPLE

We share the naturalistic coding orientation when looking at photos on a website or watching videos on social media (Figure 3.4). Expressions following an abstract coding orientation (Figure 3.5), typically diagrams and data visualizations (graphs and charts) applying geometric forms like lines, circles and squares, do sometimes need a verbal description to explain the meaning of each shape and color.

Figure 3.4 Naturalistic coding orientation. From "Equinor," by Equinor ASA, n.d. (www.equinor.com/). Screenshot by Martin Engebretsen, August 1, 2018. © Equinor ASA. Reprinted with permission.

PROPORTION OF WOMEN IN THE WORKFORCE
(percentage)

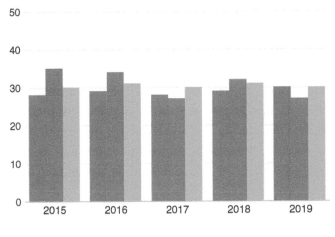

■▋■ In leadership positions

■▋■ Newly hired

▎▋■ Permanent employees

Figure 3.5 Abstract coding orientation. From "Equinor sustainability data hub," by Equinor ASA, n.d. (https://sustainability.equinor.com/#workforce). Screenshot by Martin Engebretsen, November 10, 2020. © Equinor ASA. Reprinted with permission.

Combinations of the two coding orientations are also possible, for instance, in layered representations. In Figure 3.6, the layer in the background represents a naturalistic coding orientation (the landscape), while the layer in the foreground (line graph and bar chart) shows an abstract coding orientation.

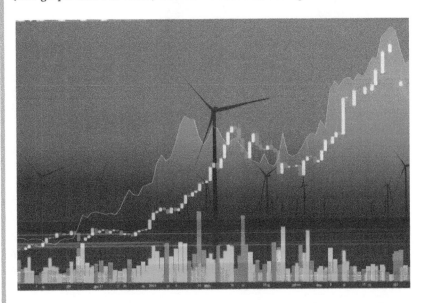

Figure 3.6 Graphic with a combination of a naturalistic and abstract coding orientation: wind turbines on the background of stock charts. Anton Petrus, Collection: Moment, Getty Images.

The difference between a naturalistic and an abstract coding orientation is related to the division between **symbols**, **icons**, and **indexes**, as presented by the philosopher Charles Sanders Peirce in the early twentieth century. According to Peirce (Moore et al., 1984, pp. 49–59), who is regarded as one of the founding fathers of modern semiotics, a symbol (e.g., a word) creates meaning purely through social convention, an icon (e.g., a photo, drawing, or painting) creates meaning through similarity with the object it refers to, and an index (e.g., a footprint, smoke, or a weathervane) creates meaning through causality (Figures 3.7a–c). Which class of signs, then, does the bar graph belong to? That is actually a disputed question. Some scholars say that an abstract data visualization is an index, because it indicates (points at) certain essential characteristics of some other units in the world (Bateman, Wildfeuer & Hiippala 2017, pp. 59–61; Engebretsen 2001). Others say that it can be classified as an icon, because it represents real relationships and properties, and thus works as a model-like or "skeleton-like sketch" of the real world (Stjernfelt 2007, p. 94) and possesses iconicity – albeit to a lower and less obvious degree than a photo.

Considering the difference between photos and handmade drawings, it is useful to draw on the social semiotic category of *interpersonal meaning*. The "social contract" between a viewer and a photographer is that the image reveals what was in front of the

DOG

Figure 3.7a Example of a symbol: the word *dog*

Figure 3.7b Example of an icon: picture of a dog. © 2021 Daniela Hoos. Reprinted with permission.

Figure 3.7c Example of an index: dog tracks. © 2021 Daniela Hoos. Reprinted with permission.

lens at the moment the shutter was pressed. The contract following a drawing is very different; it shows only the aspects and details of the objects that the artist wants to communicate. It is a personal and subjective account of some aspect of the world, be it physical or emotional. A photo and a drawing represent different "ways of showing." While the photo can be regarded as a more realistic representation (despite the fact that digital techniques offer plenty of ways to manipulate images), the drawing will most often carry a stronger visible thumbprint of the sender. Although it does offer ideational meaning, it does so through the eyes, intentions, and feelings of the person drawing, adding interpersonal meaning to the expression (Figure 3.8).

A shared characteristic of photos and drawings is that they offer the viewer a specific social *position* in relation to the depicted object through proximity, angle, or gaze. The position can be close or distant, and it can be low or high. These choices of positions have different potentials for interpersonal meanings, based on our everyday experiences with physical encounters. A close-up will give a feeling of intimacy, while a distance shot has the opposite effect. Likewise, when we look at a person or an object from a top-down angle, we gain a feeling of power and control. The opposite may happen when we look at someone from a position lower than the horizontal one. Maximum equality in the "power balance" is obtained using a horizontal angle, inviting the viewer into the universe of the depicted object on equal terms. A character in a photo can directly look at the viewer, thus demanding something of the viewer, or the gaze of the character can be averted, which Kress and van Leeuwen call an offer (2006, pp. 117–119).

The last of the three metafunctions, which in visual contexts is called the *textual* or *compositional* metafunction, offers concepts to understand how different visual elements

Figure 3.8 Drawing of a dog by Emma Haven, seven years old. © 2020 Emma Haven. Reprinted with permission.

are integrated to constitute a larger whole, where each element plays a specific role and is provided with meaning by other elements in the composition. The concepts related to this metafunction help us describe the organization of any visual structure; for instance, the composition of a photograph. In particular, they help us understand the visual mode of *layout*, meaning the organization of photographs, verbal elements and other visual units on a page or a screen. Some important concepts related to compositional meaning-making are *salience, information value*, and *framing*. Other aspects of compositional meaning will be dealt with in Section 3.3.5.

Salience concerns the ways in which some element – e.g., an image, a title, or a citation – is formed to gain more attention than others, due to its assumed importance. Salience can be provided through, for instance, size, color, contrast, movements, or position. Likewise, an overlapping element will normally be given more attention than the element being overlapped. *Information value* concerns the value given to an element by placing it to the left or to the right, at the top or at the bottom of the page. In our Western text culture, we expect new and exciting information to be placed on the right, while information that we are already familiar with is normally placed on the left. The reason being that we read from left to right, and we need new information to be linked to something we already know. Also, we expect the most important and ideal information to be placed at the top of the page, while less important and more prosaic information is placed at the bottom. Many conventions related to position are slowly fading in the age of computer screens, however, and a growing supply of templates for web design.

Framing is a concept that refers to the techniques for grouping and separating between visual units, indicating that they have, or have not, something in common. Framing is about using framelines or empty space, or establishing contrast though form or color, in order to connect or disconnect visual elements (Jewitt & Oyama, 2001). Framing techniques thus signal which elements in a composition belong together and which do not, and they may help us choose an effective reading path. These techniques are based on insights developed by the Gestalt School of Psychology in the early twentieth century. The Gestalt psychologists – mainly Max Wertheimer, Wolfgang Köhler, and Kurt Koffka – studied human visual perception. They developed the so-called *gestalt laws*. The term *Gestalt* means shape, form, or pattern. The Gestalt laws are a set of organizing principles for describing how people normally group and relate visual elements on the basis of their internal organization: proximity, similarity, continuity, symmetry, etc. (Ware, 2000, pp. 203–213).

3.2.4 Symbolic and Hidden Meanings in Images

An interesting topic in visual theory is that of symbolic meaning in images. An image will always show objects belonging to the physical world, but its meaning potential may go far beyond the depicted motive. The symbolic nature of images has many aspects. The French semiotician Roland Barthes wrote in his classic essay, *The Rhetoric of the Image* (1964/1977), about **denotation and connotation** in images. In his example, an advertisement for Italian food, he shows that in the first layer of meaning, which he calls denotation, the image simply refers to the depicted objects: tomatoes, spaghetti, pasta sauce, an open bag, etc. However, analyzing the second layer of meaning, the connotations of the image, Barthes addresses the ways in which the depicted objects refer to a certain *Italianicity*, playing on popular views of Italian characteristics (Section 6.2.2). Connotations, whether in images or in verbal expressions, thus refer to associations and value judgments shared in a specific culture or community, adding a second layer of meaning to the basic, literal meaning of the expression in question.

Barthes' essay also deals with the differentiation between two possible functions of a photo; namely, the function of documentation and that of illustration. When a photo is used as documentation, as in journalistic reportage, a trial exhibit, or a passport, it is used as evidence of the existence and appearance of certain unique objects or actions. When used as illustration, the photo is meant not as evidence, but as an example of what something *may* look like. Sometimes it is not immediately clear whether an image is meant as documentation or as illustration; e.g., in promotional material for new apartment buildings. When such functional ambiguity appears, it may cause serious misunderstandings and conflicts.

A similar interest in the hidden meanings of images characterizes the theory and the analysis methodology of the German-American art historian Erwin Panofsky. According to Panofsky, classical works of art should be understood and described with respect to their meanings, and not just with a view to their stylistic expression and their relation to historical periods and trends (Panofsky, 1955). Panofsky's **iconology** prescribes a three-step approach to images. On the first level, an examination of the image's *representative* meaning reveals *who* and *what* is depicted (pre-iconographical description). On the second level, an examination of the *iconographic symbolism* of the image reveals how people, objects, and places in an image represent – and possibly comment on – particular cultural values and ideas (iconographical analysis). The iconographic effect requires that the viewer has certain insights into the relevant cultural codes and ways of thinking. The third level of Panofsky's methodology involves an examination of the *iconological symbolism* of the image (iconological interpretation). At this level, one interprets the image in relation to biographical and historical facts, and considers it as an expression of a particular style, era, or art form. This level of analysis can also be called a *symptomatic* level (Section 6.2.3).

A third approach to the symbolic meaning of images sees images as visual *metaphors*. A visual metaphor is meant to be understood not by its denotation, but rather by one or more characteristic features of the depicted object. An arrow can travel silently and swiftly through the air, and thus it can work well in an advertisement for a sporty car. A medieval fortress, or a closed iron fence, can work as a visual metaphor in a political campaign for a more liberal policy on migration issues. When using images metaphorically, we appeal to the imagination and the active interpretation of the viewer. When it works well, such a metaphor will evoke more associations and emotional engagement than a more literal and "prosaic" expression would do (Kjeldsen, 2012).

3.2.5 Visual Culture

In the introduction to this section, we talked about a visual turn in academia and in society in general. *Visual studies*, or *visual culture studies*, is the name of a broad and interdisciplinary field seeking to understand how visual culture – its forms, objects, practices, and consumption – affects modern life (e.g., Mitchell, 1994; Sturken & Cartwright, 2001). This interest is based on the view that our ideas about the world are shaped, communicated, and negotiated through visual representations as much as through verbal expressions. One direction within this field of study is concerned with the ways in which images can lead to, or prevent, social change. In a critical approach to visual studies, it is pointed out how necessary it is to be aware of what perspectives seek to dominate the culture, or parts of it, through different forms of visual expression. Images always represent a "way of looking," a certain perspective on the world – and whose perspective is that (Sontag, 1977; Stocchetti & Kukkonen, 2011)? To gain a critical understanding of the social and political impact of images, one needs to ask questions like these: Who is showing this image to whom, why and with what effects? Who is looking at the image, and why? And also, what is the origin of the image? The contexts of production, distribution, and consumption will always frame the effect of the image, as much as the motive, style, and format of the image itself do (Lister & Wells 2001).

ACTIVITY

Look at the news website you normally use. List what types of images are used there. Which coding orientation is appropriate for communicating which messages? Compare the strengths and weaknesses of the different coding orientations.

3.3 Multimodal Communication

When we go to a news media website to check the latest reports on a breaking story, we mostly encounter words and images. Both are used for meaning-making; that is, to convey a certain message. When we engage in everyday conversation, we combine words with many forms of body language; posture, gestures, mimicry. Our voice alone combines a number of systems for meaning-making; intonation, volume, pitch, not to mention the specific qualities of the voice; soft, rough, hoarse, whispery, etc. All of these aspects of body language – even the way we choose to dress, or how we have our hair cut – contribute to the meaning created in the process of speaking. Similarly, when we communicate through writing, the meanings of the words interact with the semiotic signals afforded by typography and layout. That means that all forms of human communication are multimodal. In digital media, the multimodality of our communicative practices is even more obvious.

3.3.1 What Is Multimodality?

Multimodality is a broader approach to communication that goes beyond language and verbal texts and also involves nonlinguistic resources, e.g., images, sounds, and gestures. When, in studies of human communication, we often tend to distinguish between the various forms of expression, we do so because we are influenced by the traditional division into scientific fields: linguistics, media studies, art history, graphic design, etc. In the real world, and in real communication, the forms of expression are not separated in the same manner. They always work together in a complex, multimodal interplay.

This is one reason why multimodal studies have gained increasing interest in several academic fields since the late 1980s. They deal with textual and interactional issues in ways that appear to be realistic and in accordance with the growing interest in cross-disciplinary activities throughout academia. We can find other reasons in the technological developments that occurred in the same period. For example, new tools for text creation have made it easier to produce multimodal texts that combine words, images, sound, and video, forcing text producers to reflect on how these combinations should be designed and how they affect the processes of meaning-making and communication. In this situation, it is reasonable that eyes are turned toward multimodal communication both in professional text production and in education and research.

When we talk about text in this book, we mean a coherent semiotic unit, meant to communicate a certain message and being the result of interplay between any semiotic modes. The notion of text thus goes beyond verbal language. Such a multimodal, holistic approach to texts, and to other cultural artifacts that carry meaning, demands of us a particular open-mindedness and curiosity. In order to gain insight into the meaning-potentials of a complex textual product, we first need to understand the communicative potentials of each form of expression: what semiotic work can be done by the photograph, or by the layout, the diagram, the words, etc. in the composite text that we are studying? Then, we need to investigate how the different modes work together to shape a meaningful *whole*, similar to what happens when different instruments contribute to the performance of a symphony by an orchestra. We will discuss both these aspects of multimodality, the contribution of the single mode and the semiotic interplay between modes, later in the chapter.

3.3.2 What Is a Mode?

All communication is multimodal, as communication always involves several semiotic modes. The term **mode** refers to a semiotic mode, which means a specific class of meaningful expressions. Each class is characterized by certain material and semiotic characteristics – its *affordances* (Section 3.3.3) – as well as historically shaped conventions of use (Kress, 2010). Modes can be categorized in hierarchies of subordination. The mode of writing consists of the *submodes* of verbal language and typography, as mentioned earlier. Moreover, each mode consists of a set of semiotic resources. For instance, the verbal language has words, phrases, and sentences, all organized by grammatical rules. Looking at typography, the semiotic resources are, for instance, font, boldface, bullet points, indent and space, etc. On the other side of the spectrum, the mode of writing can be integrated with photos and diagrams in the *composite mode* of an infographic, found, for example, in the news media.

Although a core term in the field of multimodality, *mode* is a contested concept that is difficult to define as a clear category (Bateman, Wildfeuer & Hippala, 2017). Among the topics for discussion are the borderlines between *mode* and *medium*: Is video a composite mode, or a medium, carrying a cluster of verbal, visual, and aural modes? It is also controversial whether the meaning potential of a mode is formed mainly by cultural convention or by the unique situation of use. If we look at the issue of conveying meaning, the question arises as to whether a form of expression needs to be able to communicate *meaning* in the traditional sense in order to be called a mode. For instance, music and color cannot communicate meaning in the same sense that words and photographs can. Are they still semiotic modes? Most multimodalists will definitely say *yes*! Bearing this in mind, let us look at some basic terms and concepts of multimodal communication. The terminology springs largely from the discipline known as *social semiotics*, presented in Section 3.2.2.

3.3.3 Different Modes – Different Affordances

Different modes are distinguished by their different sets of **affordances**. In the context of multimodality, the term *affordance* refers to the potentials and limitations characterizing a specific form of expression. A photograph can communicate the surface of an object in a much more detailed way than a string of words can. But it cannot tell how much it weighs, or who owns it. The affordances of a certain mode are shaped by its material qualities, as well as by conventions of use; how the mode has normally been shaped and used through history or in a specific culture.

EXAMPLE

The ways we use and interpret photos in social media today are, for example, very different from the way portrait photography was used and understood in the late nineteenth century, or in the postwar era of snapshots and family albums. The portrait photographs in the nineteenth century, when photography was invented, reflect the aesthetics established in painting: a person or a group of persons sitting against a plain background in a studio. At that time, going to a photo studio was the only way to get a portrait photograph (Figure 3.9). Today, smartphones enable us to take pictures in any situation. We post, like, and share our photos on social media. We edit photos by applying tools to animate elements in photos or using color filters to make photographs aesthetically more appealing (Figure 3.10).

Figure 3.9 Studio portrait depicting a woman standing next to a chair, late nineteenth century. Contributor: Sally Anderson Archive Photos / Alamy Stock Photo.

Figure 3.10 Stock photo showing a group of people taking selfies with their smartphones. LeoPatrizi, Collection: E+, Getty Images

When we become familiar with the affordances of a semiotic mode, we know what kind of discursive work the mode is best suited for, what work it can do under certain conditions, and what work it is not suited for at all. You *can* use an off-shore racing boat for fishing. However, it is not a very effective use of the boat's affordances. In the same manner, images, written language, music, etc. have different affordances, and it is the task of the designer to choose and combine them in a way that serves the communicative purpose.

Modes that are weak on ideational meaning-making, like music or color, may be strong on interpersonal or compositional meaning-making (Section 3.2.3). For example; in graphic design, colors are often used to express difference, with no other intended meaning related to them. Different colors in a graphic may be used to distinguish between different variables or different units. However, readers might associate the colors with ideational meaning all the same, and assume, for instance, that the choice of red, green, or blue implies some kind of political signaling. This may sometimes lead to an over-interpretation of color. For similar reasons, color can lead to misunderstandings in instances of intercultural communication. A certain use of color, in a certain kind of situation, can have one conventionalized meaning in one culture, which is not recognized in a different culture. In China, white will often symbolize death and mourning, while most people in the West will associate the color white with purity and goodness (Figure 3.11).

Figure 3.11 People at a mourning procession in the Fujian province in China, women with white shawls. In China, white is the color of death and mourning. Image Professionals GmbH / Alamy Stock Photo.

3.3.4 Multimodal Interplay

To analyze the semiotic interplay between modes, as they appear in a certain multimodal text, we need to look at several aspects of **discourse**. Various modes bring various discourses into the multimodal interplay. By discourse we mean the production and shaping of meanings and worldviews through the situated use of language or other semiotic resources. In other words, discourse refers to the way we think and talk about the world. It is always linked to a certain perspective, meaning that some aspects of the world are highlighted, while others are ignored. Discourses are expressed in multimodal texts, and they represent the knowledge and thinking of a certain time, a certain culture or a certain social group unified by a common interest. Closely linked to discourse is the term *social practice*. Writing a news report or designing an infographic can be seen as social practices that are influenced by the interest of the producers, by culture, by specific design conventions or professional norms. Social practices are therefore inextricably intertwined with discourses, the two mutually influencing each other.

One aspect of multimodal discourse concerns the direct interplay between two modes; for example, whether one mode dominates the meaning potential of the other mode. Another aspect concerns what role each mode is given in the entirety of the multimodal text, often indicated by its position in the larger composition of modes. The interplay between words and images is given specific attention in multimodal theory and analysis. Sometimes the verbal text visually dominates the page or the screen in question, and also contains the most important information. Other times, the page or screen is dominated by one or more images, and the verbal text has only a subordinate role in the interplay – a so-called image-centric format. How should these text-image formats and their semiotic potential be described? The French semiotician Roland Barthes created the terms *anchorage* and *relay* in order to describe two basic forms of image–text relations (Barthes, 1964/1977). *Anchorage* describes a relation between two modes of expression, where the verbal text restricts and focuses the interpretation of the image. This is often the case where a caption or a title tells us what elements in a photograph we should pay attention to in a specific context. *Relay*, on the other hand, describes a relation where the text says something more and different from what is possible to read from the image. The text *adds* information, as is the case in comic strips, where the text elements tell us what the depicted characters are saying or thinking.

3.3.5 Multimodal Cohesion

The concepts of anchorage and relay can be applied to modes other than verbal language and images. Thus, they steer us into the broader concept of **multimodal cohesion**. Cohesion concerns the mechanisms used to inform the reader that the different elements of a text should be regarded as constituent of a bigger whole, and not as independent fragments of meaning. In studies of verbal texts, we sometimes speak of a red thread running through the text, giving all sentences and paragraphs a specific role and value in the totality of the text. The word *text* itself actually means a "weave of threads," as in *textile*. In studies of multimodal texts, we speak of multimodal cohesion in a similar way. The mechanisms of cohesion, however, are more complex than in verbal texts, since they work both locally, within each mode, and globally, between the modes. According to van Leeuwen (2005), multimodal cohesion can be constructed through four different techniques: *information linking, composition, dialogue,* and *rhythm.* The two forms most applied in multimodal analysis are information linking and composition. As we presented aspects of composition in the Section 3.2.3 (*salience, information value,* and *framing;*), we shall here take a closer look at information linking.

Information linking concerns types of multimodal relations similar to those Barthes named *anchorage* and *relay*. However, van Leeuwen (2005) uses the terms *elaboration* and *extension*. Elaboration and extension refer to relations that may work both ways between two modes. Imagine a photo of a young man with a smiling face (Figures 3.12a–c). Then imagine how different captions create different text–image relations. If the caption says "Tom is happy today," the text and the image basically say the same thing, although the text adds a name. The relation may be called an *elaboration*; more specifically, a *specification*. If the caption says "Tom is happy today, he got the job as head of communications," we may call it an *extension*; more specifically, a *complementation*. But note that the complementation works both ways, as the image, with its detailed information concerning the boy's physical appearance, also complements the information given in the caption. However, if the text says "Tom is sad today," the text and the image not only say different things, but contradict each other. That is a specific form of extension, involving conflicting content, and it is named *contrast* in van Leeuwen's system. When multimodal interplay involves elements of semantic contrast, or *tension*, the reader will have to make an extra effort in order to establish an interpretation that makes the total text meaningful and coherent, despite this contrast. Maybe Tom has a reason to *pretend* to be happy, although he is actually sad? The important questions to ask are always as follows: Why has the text designer, the producer, chosen to combine these modes in exactly this way? What other options exist, and what effect would other choices have had on the content and the user-friendliness of the multimodal text?

In a nutshell, Barthes' term *anchorage* corresponds to the term *elaboration*, which means one mode explains, illustrates, or restates the other mode or specifies it in greater detail by exemplifying it. The relay-relationship of setting out new meanings is equivalent to the term *extension*; that is, one mode provides new information that is not given by the other mode, or one mode can enhance the other mode by qualifying it with

Figure 3.12a Elaboration: "Tom is happy today." (Pexels: dgtportraits.com)

Figure 3.12b Extension: "Tom is happy today, because he got the job as head of communications." (Pexels: dgtportraits.com)

Figure 3.12c Contrast as a specific form of extension: "Tom is sad today." (Pexels: dgtportraits. com)

temporal or spatial information, logical features of cause and effect, result, reason, or by using rhetorical figures (e.g., contrast).

3.3.6 Practicing Multimodal Communication

It is one thing to analyze multimodal communication, applying the appropriate terms and perspectives, but it is another thing to practice it in a conscious and effective way. What are the preconditions for successful multimodal communication?

In the role of a journalist or a communication expert, we first need to decide what the purpose of the communication is, and who we are communicating with in which medium. When the communicative purpose and the target group are identified, it is time to design and produce the multimodal message. The term *design* refers here to the planning stage of the process. What exactly do I want to express, and what modes are best suited to express it? What modes are most accessible to me, with regard to my skills and available tools, and what modes are best suited to fit the needs of my target group? A big photo might catch the attention of the audience, but does it carry the message I want to convey? Does a thirteen-year-old understand a stacked bar graph, or is it better to show the data in a table (Figure 3.13)?

We mentioned *tools*, which is a keyword for the next step in the process; the production of the designed message. In modern multimodal communication, we often need to apply digital tools, both in production and in distribution. We need to be aware that the meaning of a multimodal text is also affected by these technological "helpers." Most tools for text production and visual design are based on templates, which will suggest a set of conventionalized frameworks for the composition. Templates make text production

Figure 3.13 Bar charts and line graphs look clean and tidy, but that does not mean that they are always easy to understand. (Pexels: Lukas Blazek – goumbik).

easy and convenient, and they provide a hint of professionalism for any amateur piece of work. However, templates are always socially shaped too and influence the meaning potentials of the multimodal outputs, which sometimes has ideological implications.

Practicing multimodal communication leads to another term relevant to multimodality theory: **genre**. In its traditional notion, genre means type of text – type, because the text is characterized by certain features and patterns that it has in common with other texts; for instance, commonalities in content, form, structure, or style. In social semiotics and multimodality theory, genre is defined as a set of social practices and actions for achieving a communicative goal. The notion of genre is closely linked to modes and their combination that elicits recognizable multimodal patterns, but also to available tools, the selected medium, social context, communicative purpose, and target group (Bateman, 2008).

We can conclude that whatever modes, tools, and technologies we use to create our multimodal messages, we need to be aware of many things in order to reach our communicative goals. We need to understand and reflect on what combination of modes suits our intentions, our skills, and our target group the best. We need to reflect on what semiotic work we should allocate to each mode, and how to create the right balance between coherence and tension in the multimodal interplay. And, lastly, we need to make sure that our intended meanings are not distorted or weakened in the stage of production, where convenient software and templates may tempt us to take shortcuts to reach our goals.

ACTIVITY

Choose an advertisement of a nongovernmental organization, e.g., Greenpeace or World Wide Fund for Nature (WWF). Describe, in one or two pages, what modes are used and the semiotic work of these modes. How are text and image linked to each other? Are there any tensions in the interplay between modes? Which discourses does the advertisement as a whole relate to – by supporting or opposing them?

Key Terms

affordance, metafunction, denotation and connotation, digital writing, discourse, focused writing, genre, heterography, icon, iconology, index, linguistic recycling, media linguistic mindset, metafunctions, mode, multimodal cohesion, multimodal text, social semiotics, symbol, text production, transdisciplinary research, visual turn, writing-by-the-way

Chapter Summary

- Writing is key for sharing knowledge across space and time, developing organizations, and synchronizing communities. As a social practice that impacts – and is impacted by – the way we live, it has substantially changed with increasing mediatization and digitalization. The ongoing shift from focused writing to writing-by-the-way requires new media linguistic mindsets and skills.

- Having been part of writing throughout its history, phenomena such as linguistic recycling and heterography have become much more important with the rise of writing by-the-way. Research into writing practices, for example in newsrooms, helps reflective practitioners develop their writing as a key competence of multimodal digital communication.

- Social semiotic theory helps us understand how people communicate visually. A central idea in social semiotics is that any semiotic expression carries three categories of meaning: ideational, interpersonal, and compositional. The three metafunctions work as a good starting point to analyze how semiotic resources create meaning.

- Other theoretical concepts for analyzing images are (a) Barthes' semiotic model of the two layers of visual meaning (denotation and connotation) and (b) Panofsky's method of visual interpretation (iconology). Both approaches address the symbolic and metaphorical meanings of images and seek to reveal the hidden social relations and power structures in the images by asking: who is showing this image to whom, why, and with what effects?

- The concept of multimodality goes beyond writing and images. It suggests that communication always involves several semiotic modes. Therefore, all communication is multimodal.

- A mode is a class of expressions that involves a certain set of semiotic resources. Writing, speech, images, sound, and body language are all examples of modes. Modes have different affordances (both potentials and limitations) and they are shaped by their historical application in various social practices.

- Meaning is made by combining several modes into a coherent whole: the multimodal text. The two forms most commonly used to achieve multimodal cohesion are information linking of images and words and composition. Concepts of information linking are elaboration and extension. Concepts of compositional meaning-making are salience, framing, and information value.

Writing

Haapanen and Perrin (2020) investigate "linguistic recycling" in digital environments from complementary angles. As a reader, you learn how and for whom language users – both as individuals and as communities – save resources and create value by quoting and recontextualizing others' utterances while writing what they call "their" texts.

Jakobs and Perrin (2014), in their introduction to the *Mouton de Gruyter handbook of writing and text production*, allow for an inclusive overview of writing and its investigation from complementary perspectives and in different traditions and cultures of research.

Visual Communication

Reading images: The grammar of visual design (Kress & van Leeuwen, 2006) is a basic guide to visual design, its grammar, and how images communicate meaning.

Mitchell (2005) provides profound insights into the theoretical discourses on visual culture to help us better understand the power that pictures and images have on our society. The book is divided into three parts: images, objects, and media.

Multimodal Communication

In *Empirical multimodality research* (2021a), Pflaeging, Wildfeuer, and Bateman foreground the data-driven study of multimodal artifacts and discuss mixed method approaches to investigating a wide range of multimodal artifacts (e.g., corporate logos, advertisements, news texts, movies, video games). Empirical case studies illustrate the state-of-the-art work in the field of multimodality. The implications of these findings are reflected upon to inform further research in multimodality.

Jewitt, Bezemer, and O'Halloran (2016) provide a comprehensive introduction to multimodality by describing key concepts, methods, and various approaches to this discipline. In addition, the authors explain how to set up a multimodal study.

Focusing on multimodality and image-centricity, Stöckl, Caple, and Pflaeging (2020) showcase image-centric practices in contemporary media: magazines, advertising discourse, multimedia storytelling, and social media platforms.

While many scholars have explored multimodality in visual communication, Bouvier and Machin (2013) turn their attention to sound and music and investigate how advertisers use these auditory modes to communicate ideas, attitudes, and identities.

In *The language of colour*, van Leeuwen (2011) presents an overview of the use of colors in everyday life and cultural and historical contexts, and develops a multimodal approach to colors.

Engebretsen's (2012) article on cohesion and tension in multimodal rhetoric explains how the visual and the verbal modes can create different kinds of tension and why a certain level of tension can be a good thing. (The answer is that tensions in the multimodal interplay force the reader to actively "fill in the gaps.")

In a special issue of *Social Semiotics*, edited by Poulsen, Kvåle, and van Leeuwen (2018), researchers in the field of multimodality and social semiotics deal with media as semiotic technology, exploring how social software enables meaning-making and how much social media technology changes semiotic practices.

4 Professional Context: Journalism, PR, and Community Communication

PREVIEW

Red Bull became famous in the early 1980s for their energy drink. Today, powered by its multi-platform media company – Red Bull Media House – the brand has blurred the boundaries between entertainment, marketing, PR, and journalism. Like many other brands, they chose to communicate directly with their target groups, using different media formats, and reporting about topics they want to relate to their product rather than promoting it.

In this chapter, we answer questions such as: How are digital media and digitalization transforming public communication? What is the working framework in which journalism and PR operate? What is journalists' and communication professionals' daily work?

The first part of the chapter covers the impact of digitization on journalism and PR, and how this affects their relationship. We then introduce the concept of attention economomy to elucidate the consequences that the digital financing model has on public communication. Finally, we provide an insight into the recent developments in journalism and PR by presenting novel forms and formats of digital communication, which are at the heart of media linguistic's research.

The second part of the chapter focuses on the concepts of media literacy, digital literacy, visual and visualization literacy, and data literacy, and how these skills translate into journalists' and communication experts' daily job, particularly when faced with the new ethical challenges posed by new digital technologies and tools. We close the chapter by introducing the discipline of ethics in general and with a special focus on media ethics in journalism and PR and digital media ethics.

Learning Objectives

By the end of this section, you will be able to

- give reasons for the changed relationship between journalism and PR in the context of digitalization
- explain the concept of the attention economy and its consequences for the journalism and PR
- define media literacy and list essential skills for media literacy
- give examples of skills needed by communication professionals or journalists working in digital environments
- describe the three major theoretical approaches to ethics
- comment on examples of practices or specific situations that led media practitioners to act unethically.

4.1 Digitalization in Journalism and PR

The Internet has become central for sharing information, for social and political orientation, and for relationship management in business and society. Companies and organizations are no longer dependent on journalistic gatekeepers; they can present their brands and expertise on their online channels and directly interact with stakeholders. The public can easily express opinions online, evaluate brands, products and services, and create content themselves. This boom in digital content has led to competition for attention. In the process, the traditional boundaries between communication producers working in journalism and PR and their intended audiences are becoming blurry.

4.1.1 Digitalization Is Changing the Relationship between Journalism and PR

PR and journalism both contribute to communication in the public sphere. Their overall aim is to make information public. Although journalists and PR professionals have a symbiotic working relationship, they draw on different expertise, work in different roles, and pursue different goals.

The term *public relations* (PR) or corporate communications refers to the **strategic communication** process between organizations and their publics. PR professionals define what information an organization shares in order to direct and manage its public image and build and maintain relationships with its publics. PR practitioners work in their clients' or companies' interests and construct desirable and intentional realities (Bowman, 2021).

Historically, the purpose of journalism has been to gather information, interpret events, act as a watchdog on government, advocate for the reform of specific causes, educate and empower the public as citizens and guide public opinion. Journalists collect facts considered relevant for the public, edit those under the journalistic principles of objectivity, accuracy, balance, and fairness, and disseminate them through media for public discussion. By doing so, they create up-to-date, factual, and publicly relevant realities (Wahl-Jorgensen & Hanitzsch, 2019).

PR practitioners and journalists depend on each other: PR provides journalists with information and suggestions for stories, shaped by how PR professionals would like them to be published. Journalists request information and sources from PR practitioners that may help them develop news and stories for the public. The relationship between PR and journalism has been wildly reflected and studied in academia (see, e.g., Macnamara, 2014; Raupp & Klewes, 2004; White & Hobsbawm, 2007). Since the 1980s, studies have observed a diminishing dependence of PR on journalism and the growth of journalism's dependence on PR. Consequently, journalism is becoming increasingly dependent on and more easily affected by PR agendas and content (Blumler, 2018; Blumler & Gurevitch, 1995; Davis, 2002).

Scholars regard the evolution of digital communication as a mechanism that signaled a changed relationship between journalism and PR. Although PR is still dependent on journalistic media to spread content, digital media and the Internet allow companies and organizations to bypass journalistic gatekeepers and directly communicate with their target groups. New access to markets and new ways to manage and place content have led to an increased global dissemination of information about products, services, and lifestyles. This development goes hand in hand with PR's worldwide growth and professionalization (Pieczka, 2008; Sriramesh & Verčič, 2003; van Ruler, 2015).

At the same time, journalism is facing significant structural changes. On the Internet, a large amount of advertising revenue goes to IT giants like Google or Facebook rather than traditional media. Furthermore, the generation that grew up with free information on the Internet is often unwilling to pay for journalistic content. These developments have led to financial and personnel cutbacks in many news organizations. For the media, especially print media, the digital shift has been highly disruptive, forcing them to move away from paper-based or analog output to digitalization while continuing to safeguard what they can from the previous system, which is still in demand, and meeting much greater competition while doing so (Lloyd & Toogood, 2016).

Attention economy: Organizations, brands, and media companies are not the only ones communicating in the online public sphere: public institutions, bloggers, politicians, business leaders, artists, athletes, and celebrities are all competing for attention in the public sphere. They produce niche content that appeals to subgroups of the general public. The boom in digital content has led to a phenomenon referred to as the attention economy. The term was coined by psychologist and economist Herbert A. Simon (1994), who was one of the first to predict a reversal of the economic relationship between media producers and media consumers. While the amount of information available online is almost endless, consumers' attention is a limited resource. This affects the value placed on each, with that of consumer attention rising and that of online information sinking rapidly. The attention economy is a competitive market. On the Internet, revenue results from continuous consumer attention, measured in clicks, shares, and time invested in consuming content. Individuals and institutions make every effort to be the first to reach audiences in order to command their limited attention span and their time. The attention economy privileges the most provocative views, often using clickbaits – links designed to attract attention, to make audiences click, read, and share content. As a consequence, emotional, polarizing information or even disinformation spreads faster than nuanced content (Hendricks & Vestergaard, 2019; Ryan et al., 2020). As journalism's gatekeeper role is being increasingly challenged, it has become easier for fake news, conspiracy theories, and others forms of biased information to gain public attention.

While the information available online seem to be accessible for free, it is paid for with content generated by users and with personal data. Web-users produce and access a large volume of products – like pictures, blog posts, or YouTube videos. This content, provided free-of-charge, is available to tech giants like Google, Facebook, Amazon, or Apple, who use it to increase their knowledge about their customers. As data-processing techniques are refined, they allow the accumulation of all kinds of data, like past consumption, online comments, or geolocation of smartphones. Through their cross-comparison, interested parties can obtain an increasingly detailed knowledge about individuals and their networks, which can then be used to gain their attention and maximize profits in the attention economy.

Digital products are designed to draw our eye to specific features and then focus our attention on them (Stjernfelt & Lauritzen, 2020; Wu, 2015). The behavioral scientist BJ Fogg (2003) introduced the term *captology* to describe the invisible and manipulative way in which technology can persuade and influence its users. We experience this persuasive technology daily; e.g., through app notifications that demand our attention, the endlessly scrollable Instagram stream, or the auto-play function on Netflix or YouTube where one video flows seamlessly into another. All of these functions are designed to make users spend as much time as possible on a platform. In the attention economy, the design of applications and platforms therefore plays an important role.

EXAMPLE

Corporate engineers, designers, and psychologists use advanced personalized data to predict how the individual user is likely to respond to different temptations (Stejenfelt & Lauritzen, 2020). One example is the like button we all know from Facebook. The platform's co-founder, Sean Parker, has revealed that Facebook was developed out of a desire to maximize the exploitation of users' time and attention. The Facebook like button is designed to give the users "a little dopamine hit," which motivates them to spend more time on the website. "It's a social-validation feedback loop ... exactly the kind of thing that a hacker like myself would come up with because you're exploiting a vulnerability in human psychology" (Solon, 2017).

One reason why we engage so intensely with technology is dopamine, a neurotransmitter that is released in the brain as a reward for an action. Dopamine ensures that we keep doing biologically relevant things, like drinking water when thirsty or – in prehistoric hunter-gatherer societies – keep searching for food so as not to starve. In a social context, positive social stimuli such as a smile, eye contact, or a compliment release dopamine. Dopamine reinforces the behavior that prompted it, which includes interaction on a screen. Text messages, likes, comments, notifications – they all have the potential to release dopamine. The result is a short-term, addictive, dopamine-driven feedback loop. Consequently, we are constantly checking our smartphones to see what notifications we have got. We refresh our e-mails driven by the expectation of new information or scroll the Instagram feed to see what photo comes next.

Scholars and experts increasingly criticize the effects of the attention economy on individuals and society. The digital content organization around dopamine-dosing tools is designed to hook the public, as persuasive interface design leads to digital addiction and negative influences on individuals' well-being. The spread of biased, personalized, and misleading content, on the other hand, contributes to the loss of high-quality information and the polarization of public opinion (Giraldo-Luque et al., 2020; Menczer & Hills, 2020; Pew Research Center, 2018; Stjernfelt & Lauritzen, 2020).

Strategic mediatization: Owing to digitalization and structural changes in both fields, the lines between journalism and PR have become blurred. Brands are moving to a space once occupied by media companies, while media companies are moving into digital marketing. This shift becomes visible in phenomena like **brand journalism** and **native advertising** (Serazio, 2021; Sirrah, 2019b; Voorveld, 2019). These changes are referred to as strategic mediatization: "first the blurring of lines between advertising and editorial content of the media and secondly the media housing of corporations. This media housing involves the production of media content by organizations themselves instead of by traditional media companies" (Tench et al., 2017, p. 32).

More and more companies create content that might be considered journalistic, some even launching newsrooms, and hiring journalists and camera crews to produce content they directly distribute to consumers. This new form of corporate communications that merges the content and formats of PR and journalism is referred to as brand journalism, sometimes also as corporate journalism or corporate media.

EXAMPLE

The global website of Red Bull, an Austrian company internationally known for its energy drinks, offers access to multimedia formats like Red Bull TV – with movies, clips, or shows – and provides articles about topics like Formula 1, athletes, or gaming (www.redbull.com). The attractive and unique content and the collaboration with extreme sports enable an engagement with different target groups, such as sports fans or the gaming community. The brand story is delivered in multifaceted ways across multiple devices and platforms and constructs the brand's essence across conversations with different audiences (Light, 2020; Spayd, 2014).

At the same time, media companies are increasingly running content created by organizations. So-called native advertising refers to the use of paid advertisements that match the look, feel, and function of the media format in which they appear. Unlike conventional ads, native ads appear to be part of the editorial flow. The pioneer most often associated with the development of native advertising is Forbes. In 2010 Forbes offered brands the chance to buy and write sponsored blogs hosted on its news platform. The *New York Times* and the *Washington Post* followed shortly after with their native initiatives (Coddington, 2015, p. 75).

As native advertising is a relatively new format, media companies' deployment strategies are still forming and changing. Untransparent and ill-regulated forms of disclosure make it difficult for the public to identify native ads as commercial content (Amazeen & Wojdynski, 2020). This, in consequence, has potential implications for journalism with regard to transparency, trust, and credibility (Ferrer-Conill at al., 2020; Sirrah, 2019a; Sirrah, 2019b).

To sum up, we can say that digitalization and mediatization changed the relationship between journalism and PR, and the communication forms and power relations in the digital public sphere. Digital and social media have spawned many new communication formats and forms in both journalism and PR. New technological tools like artificial intelligence (AI), virtual reality (VR), augmented reality (AR), and mixed reality (MR), or voice interfaces (VUIs) open up new possibilities, new challenges, and, with it, new research areas for media linguistics (Chapter 8).

The following sections give an overview of the main trends in journalism and PR.

4.1.2 Digitalization in Journalism

As we have seen in the last section, in a digital society, journalism competes in a much broader, global market with content from different actors. Technological developments, like constant access to the Internet or rapidly evolving smartphone apps and social media platforms, enable users to produce media content and access up-to-date information from different sources independent of time and place. Big tech companies control the information flows and the digital business ecosystem, as they own a tremendous amount of data about individuals and their networks, about organizations and corporations. Furthermore, the attention economy mechanisms privilege short and simple content that is easy to process and share.

All these developments have changed the way journalists understand and practice journalism. Media companies create new journalistic experiences and products by using novel methods such as gamification and virtual or augmented reality. Consequently, new forms of journalism have emerged, like multimedia journalism, networked journalism, computational journalism, data-driven journalism, hybrid journalism, and immersive journalism – to mention just a few.

The next sections outline the main trends and provide an outlook on future developments.

Multimedia journalism is what we encounter every day on news websites and social media platforms. It can be defined in two ways (Deuze, 2004, p. 140):

- as news content that is presented as a story package using two or more media formats that complement each other, such as text, images, sound, video clips, graphics (still, animated, or interactive), and other interactice and hypertextual elements with the aim of telling compelling stories (also referred to as multimedia storytelling, digital storytelling, or multimedia reporting).[1]
- as news content that is disseminated via different media platforms, such as a website, social media, radio, television, print newspapers, and magazines.

Both ways are inextricably linked to and triggered by media convergence (Section 1.3.3). An often-cited example of multimedia storytelling is the *New York Times* feature "Snow Fall" (Branch, 2012) – a story about a deadly avalanche in Washington State. The multimedia feature is presented in six chapters with photographs, videos, audios, slide shows, and animated graphics. "Snow Fall" won the 2013 Pulitzer Prize in feature writing because

---

[1] From a media linguistic perspective, we would call this type multimodal storytelling.

of its multimedia experience provided to the users. It is considered a milestone in multi-media storytelling among journalism and scholarly circles (Dowling & Vogan, 2015).

Networked journalism refers to the collaborative process of journalism. It involves the practice of building networks of professionals and amateurs (citizens) in order to find the real stories; it includes technical, editorial, and managerial processes. The emergence of interactive and participatory media and the technologies of the Web 2.0 (the social web) enable the audience to get involved in the news production process; that is, from news gathering to reporting and news sharing. Professional journalists remain essential to news production, even though networked practices have blurred the lines between professionals and audiences (van der Haak, Parks & Castells, 2012). Forms of user-generated content are, for instance, blogs, comments on stories, polls, video, or posts on social media platforms provided by the public (Thurman & Hermida, 2010). Networked journalism focuses on the process, especially on the news-gathering process, rather than the product. An essential skill here is to be able to verify the sources of user-generated content.

Computational journalism can be described as an advanced application of computing, technologies, and software to journalistic practices such as information gathering, organization, evaluation, composition, presentation, and distribution of news. "Computational news gathering and evaluation can utilize tools that find and filter newsworthy information from social media platforms and document caches and that provide guidance on the credibility of content and contributors" (Thurman, 2019). Computational journalism has its roots in computer-assisted reporting. It draws on the disciplines of computer science, social science, and communications and includes subfields such as data-driven journalism (DDJ), immersive journalism (AR/VR), and automated journalism. Automated journalism is defined as the process of using data, algorithms, and AI to automatically generate news stories (Chapter 8).

Data-driven journalism (DDJ) has emerged in the wake of the datafication of society (Section 4.1.3). Datafication means turning aspects of life into quantitative data which has been previously experienced in qualitative, non-numeric forms (Engebretsen, Kennedy & Weber, 2018; Gray & Bounegru, 2021; Mayer-Schoenberger & Cukier, 2013; van Dijck, 2014). It includes an increased accessibility of large amounts of public data and an increased presence of data in journalism with a growing focus on data visualization as an integrated element in journalistic genres (Engebretsen, Kennedy & Weber, 2018). Data journalism has been discussed as "a qualitatively new way of reporting which gains insights about relevant societal trends by analyzing open datasets using (semi-)automatized methods to detect meaningful patterns in data structure" (Rinsdorf & Boers, 2016, p. 1). Gray and Bounegru (2021, p. 16) describe the work of data journalists this way: "[D]ata journalists interrogate official data sources, make and compile their own data, try new visual and interactive formats, reflect on the effects of their work, and make their methods accountable and code re-usable." In short: data journalists gather, organize, analyze, and visualize data in order to tell news stories. DDJ can be understood both as a process – that is, analyzing large data sets and telling stories with data – and as a product, including data visualizations and other textual outputs based on data (Ausserhofer, 2017, p. 4). With data journalism, data visualizations have found their way into newsrooms as a form of visual news reporting, often called data stories.

Hybrid journalism: As a result of a journalism that appears increasingly datafied and networked, we can see a burgeoning field of hybrid forms. These hybrid forms often go beyond the traditional notions of journalism. They cross the boundaries of producers and recipients; facts and fiction; distance and immersion; images, texts, and numbers; and of established disciplines such as literature, arts, film, and animation. Hybrid forms conflate and hybridize showing and telling; visualizing and writing; news reporting and activism; reality and virtuality. They combine subjectivity with objectivity; editorial articles with user comments, information with entertainment and gaming; human knowledge with artificial intelligence; and traditional news writing with machine learning. Along these lines, a plethora of new hybrid products has emerged to present news content; for instance, interactive multimodal features, data visualizations and data stories, exploratory and explanatory graphics, animated simulations, doku games, 360-degree video, immersive storytelling using augmented and virtual reality – forms that are primarily produced to be consumed on smartphones. Hybrid forms can also be found in the production process, when journalists, data scientists, programmers, hackers, designers, or illustrators collaborate in the newsroom. These blends of old and new forms are conceptualized by the term *hybrid journalism*, which is defined as a wider network or assemblage of actors, agencies, genres, and values that intermingle and influence each other (Bucher 2018, p. 144; Chadwick, 2013; Porlezza, 2020). In particular, hybrid systems consisting of human–machine interactions will play a pivotal role in shaping future trends in journalism.

Immersive journalism: More and more news organizations and media companies are experimenting with augmented and virtual reality. In AR, reality prevails and virtual layers enhance the real world. AR can be defined as "a real-time view of information overlaid on a view of the real world" through a display, for instance, on the smartphone. It "superimposes digital content (text, images, animations, etc.) on a user's view of the real world" (Peddie, 2017, p. 20). Unlike VR, you do not need an expensive VR headset and motion controllers, just a smartphone and the news app. Using AR in news coverage can make a news story less abstract. Users can engage with the news by examining 3D-objects from multiple angles; for instance, Apollo 11 and its landing on the moon (Time, 2019) or the model of a mysterious dinosaur skull (The Washington Post, 2018). Thus, AR can "contribute to journalism's dual goals of informing and engaging people" (Aitamurto et al., 2020).

The main difference between AR and VR is that in VR the user is taken out of the real world and fully immersed in a synthetic computer-generated world, whereas AR enhances the real environment by providing additional information (Peddie, 2017, p. 24; Section 1.2.2). The synthetic data-world simulates real-world environments, thus blurring the line between reality and illusion. The brain believes that the virtual experiences are real. The resulting strong immersion arises from the interplay between technology and storytelling. The technology makes it possible to move around and interact in the virtual world, and to feel like you are right in the middle of the virtual event. Instead of being an observer in front of a screen, the user can experience the news from a first-person point of view and in a three-dimensional space. It is an interactive, multimodal experience involving vision, hearing, and touch. In the award-winning VR production *We Wait* (BBC, n.d.), users can experience what it feels like to be a refugee crossing the Mediterranean Sea. The users are involved in the unfolding events instead of just watching a news report. Immersive journalism thus aims at involving the users emotionally in news as if they are taking part in the news event. The goal is to trigger empathy toward the news issue and the people involved and to make the viewers reflect on their opinion of a news topic (De la Peña et al., 2010; Sánchez Laws & Utne, 2019; Slater & Sanchez-Vives, 2016). The bodily experience of virtually delivered news is sometimes referred to as story-living: we virtually "live" in a war scene or a refugee camp. But do we really want this? Do we need virtual reality as an empathy machine in order to better understand what others have experienced in real life? What on the one hand might sound thrilling – to explore another reality, e.g., a visually amazing landscape – could on the other hand have profound psychological effects on individuals if the content is shocking, violent, or scary. As Bailenson (2018, p. 47) explains, "a VR experience is often better understood *not as a media experience, but as an actual experience.*" Virtual reality may be a powerful tool in journalism; however, journalists as well as users must be made aware of the physical (e.g., motion sickness) and psychological risks attached to the experiences of VR content. Besides these ethical challenges, VR raises questions in terms of credibility and authenticity: how can users distinguish between fact-based news and fiction, when the real environment is overlaid with additional information; for instance, in the form of animation? What role does the design of the virtual environment play? What can we say about the authorship of VR scenarios? And how credible is the news presented and experienced in a VR setting?

Credibility, trustworthiness, accountability, accuracy, objectivity vs. subjectivity – these journalistic values call for transparency practices, not only in immersive journalism but also in networked, data-driven, and automated journalism. Transparency means: stating the source or where information comes from, providing access to the raw data, explaining the methodology. Transparency also includes providing information about traceability in the creation of visuals – in order to deliver trustworthy news (Kennedy, Weber & Engebretsen, 2020). The more hybrid, digital, and networked news products become, the more urgent the need for transparency regarding journalistic practices.

Industry leaders, experts, and scholars predict that the next decade will be defined by increasing internet regulation and attempts to re-establish trust in journalism. Journalism will continue to be influenced by AI and **big data** and other new formats, primarily visual and voice-based ones (Newman et al., 2020). Some experts argue that journalism will have to partly reinvent itself and reconnect with its audiences to face the challenges of algorithmic information flows and global power structures in the networked public sphere. Experts and scholars propose solutions like combining journalism, data science, design, and delivering unique, rich content, focusing on contextualizing information and bridging national, local, and intentional perspectives. Especially young people wish for constructive journalism that provides usable information, enabling them to make more informed choices in their daily lives and participate in social and political decision-making processes (Gnach et al., 2020; Tamboer et al., 2020).

4.1.3 Digitalization in PR

In the networked public sphere, organizations are no longer providers of information for journalistic gatekeepers and the mass media; they have become content producers and distributors themselves. Their active participation in public discourse makes organizations and businesses influential social actors who take a stand on publicly relevant issues and influence opinion-forming processes (Verčič & Tkalac Verčič, 2015; Zerfass et al., 2019; Zerfass et al., 2016a).

PR and strategic communication provide an essential link between organizations and the networked public sphere. Communication professionals determine relevant topics in public discourse; for example, through issue management or stakeholder dialogue, and then support the participation of organizations as a whole, along with that of executives, specialists, and employees, in the public sphere. By doing so, they are serving increasingly more channels in even more formats. Communication professionals not only produce content but also contribute to building and maintaining relationships with relevant stakeholders.

The integration of digital technology into all of the private and professional areas of life is leading to fundamental changes in how organizations operate and how they deliver value to stakeholders and society (Bouwman et al., 2018; LLYC, 2016). Scholars and experts in the field of PR acknowledge that a digital transformation not only is a technical process but also involves social and cultural change. They emphasize strategic communication's role in the success of organizations' digital transformation, as the associated changes require communicative accompaniment or even an initiating role led by communication departments (Hirnschal, 2018, Zerfass et al., 2021). Strategic communication is thereby defined as the purposeful use of communication by an organization to fulfill its mission (Hallahan et al., 2008). It is based on strategic communication management, "the attempt to manage the communication of strategic significance with regard to a focal entity" (Zerfass et al., 2018, p. 497).

Literature in this field situates PR's and communications management's tasks and responsibilities on three interconnected and interdependent spheres: society, organization, and communications department (Figure 4.1)

- *At the societal level,* businesses and organizations participate in the change process triggered by digitalization. They are also confronted with new responsibilities. In the networked public sphere, opinions are negotiated on topics relevant to society like the acceptance of technological developments – e.g., AI – or sustainability. PR has a significant impact on public discourse, as organizations and companies frame and evaluate issues through their communication – a role that was previously performed primarily by mass media and journalism (Ingenhoff et al., 2020; Pleil & Helferich, 2020).
- *At the organizational level,* strategic communication accompanies the digital transformation within the organizations. Scholars see the tasks of communication professionals mainly in four areas: participation in corporate and organizational development; consulting of management, executives, and departments within the organizations with a focus on organizational culture; knowledge transfer and enablement; and positioning the organization internally and externally (Rosenberger & Niederhäuser, 2019; Zerfass et al., 2014).
- *At the communications department level,* the main tasks concern the transformation of products and processes in terms of strategy, structure, culture, technology, and competencies. The aims here are to ensure that organizations can communicate within the networked public sphere while using a wide range of new communication channels and formats, and ensure their ability to build and maintain direct

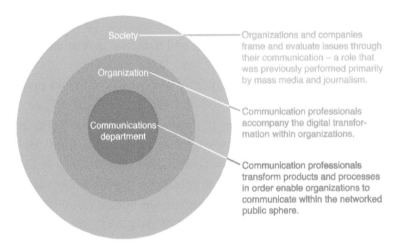

Figure 4.1 Activity spheres of PR and strategic communication. © 2021 Verena Elisabeth Lechner. Used with permission.

communicative relationships with stakeholders. Consequently, the roles of communication departments change from being the voice of an organization to being an
enabler of agile and strategic communicative processes and relationships (Tench
et al., 2017; Verčič & Zerfass, 2016; Zerfass et al., 2014).

Datafication: Our world is increasingly datafied. Datafication refers to the process by
which the practices of subjects and objects are transformed into digital data as more and
more dimensions of social life play out in digital spaces (Schäfer & van Es, 2017; Southerton, 2020). Google searches, online shopping behavior, communication and interactions
through smartphones, picture and video sharing on social media platforms, and communication with voice assistants like Siri or Alexa create unimaginable amounts of data
every day. Not only humans but also devices and appliances connected within the Internet of Things (IoT) collect and produce all kinds of data. Smart buildings, navigation
systems, wearables, or smart home devices exchange data in real time, using embedded
sensors. The systematic and strategic analysis of such massive data sets enables businesses and organizations to predict their stakeholders' needs, opinions, attitudes, and
behavior and adapt their products, services, and communication accordingly. Scholars
and experts, therefore, consider big data a crucial framework condition for strategic communication and PR (Weiner & Kochhar, 2016; Wiencierz & Röttger, 2017; Wiencierz &
Röttger, 2019; Wiesenberg et al., 2017).

Big data refers to a set of practices that involves collecting, processing, and analyzing
large data sets. Big data characteristics are commonly referred to as the four Vs – Volume, Velocity, Variety, and Veracity. The first three of these "four Vs" were proposed by
McAfee and Brynjolfsson (2012). Over time, several other Vs have been proposed; for
example, the V for Value which refers to the fact that, if analyzed effectively, big data can
provide essential knowledge of stakeholders and optimize products and services along
with business and communication processes.

Compared to conventional databases, big data consists of very large, complex, and variable amounts of data that require specific technologies and capabilities for their collection, analysis, and storage (volume). Examplea of high-volume data are Twitter messages
or Instagram posts with a trending hashtag, or all credit card transactions within a country on a specific day. Big data is generated with high-speed (velocity), and analyzing it
in real time holds considerable potential for PR and strategic communications. Up-to-the-
minute insight into discussions on social media, for example, allows agile and targeted
communication and marketing. Big data sets come from a great variety of sources and
are composed of data with diverse formats and structures (variety); e.g., text, videos,
pictures, likes, and shares on social media, or metadata like geolocations. The variety in
data types complicates their processing. Big data comes in different quality from different
sources (veracity), which carries a high degree of uncertainty, especially concerning data

quality, accuracy, and trustworthiness. High-veracity data has many valuable records and therefore contributes in a meaningful way to the overall results. Low-veracity data, on the other hand, contains a high percentage of meaningless data. The non-valuable in these data sets is referred to as noise. An example of a high-veracity data set is data from a controlled scientific experiment. An example of low-veracity data is negative comments on a topic on social media, as long it cannot be verified if the commentators are humans or social bots.

Studies demonstrate the great potential that big data offer PR, strategic communication, and marketing (Wiesenberg & Zerfass, 2016; Zerfass et al., 2016). The variety and velocity of big data, in particular, can create value for communication professionals (Wiencierz & Röttger, 2017). They can use social listening tools on social media, for example, to gather and process the needs, opinions, attitudes, and user behavior of target groups from around the world. By connecting this data with other data sets, the real-time insights from social media analyses can help track an organization's or executive's image for stakeholder identification and segmentation, and identify communication and network potential. Insights gained from big data also allow communication professionals to plan and carry out more individualized communication in marketing, public relations, and internal communication than they have done in the past.

In sum, big data has the potential to enhance all aspects of strategic communication: planning, execution, and evaluation. The more communication practitioners know about their stakeholders, and the networked public sphere's discussions, the more strategic, targeted, authentic, and value-creating PR and strategic communication become. However, big data reveals meaningful information only through systematic and strategic analyses, which require suitable technologies and competencies. Working with big data also requires interdisciplinary approaches and collaboration, and data storage and processing infrastructure. Studies show that only a minority of businesses and organizations make use of big data applications for their communication, as the processing of big data, especially data from social media, represents a challenge for organizations. The reasons are commonly traced to restricted access to application programming interface (APIs) of social media platforms and a lack of methodological expertise.

Shifting preferences toward visual communication: As we communicate less face-to-face and more through devices like computers or smartphones, nonverbal communication features: e.g., hashtags, likes, or emojis, and visual features; e.g., pictures, videos, or graphics, gain importance in digital communication (Adami & Jewitt, 2016; Fahmy et al., 2014). The ongoing mediatization (Section 1.3.4), with its growing digital technologies, platforms, and media, makes visual communication formats predominant in PR (Wiesenberg & Verčič, 2020).

Organizations have been increasing personal and technical capacities to produce multimodal content like online videos or infographics. This development is driven by technology that enables easier use of visuals in digital environments and by stakeholders' expectations. European studies show that PR practitioners perceive visual communication as an increasingly important component of their work (Zerfass et al., 2017; Wiesenberg & Verčič, 2020).

Literature in the field of strategic communications points out that, in order to be successful, visual communication should be approached strategically (Collister & Roberts-Bowman, 2018a; Dhanesh, 2018; Jin et al., 2017). Strategic visual communication management refers to all visual elements' strategic usage to fulfill an organization's goals and purposes and create a unique visual identity (Zerfass at al., 2018). Visual communication does include classical visual content like pictures, graphics, and movies, but also domains like space design or architecture. The production and management of visual communication require specific technical infrastructure, skills, and competencies; for example, measurement routines like eye-tracking, or video analysis (Wiesenberg & Verčič, 2020).

Surveys by communications specialists make evident that there is a significant difference between how important, on the one hand, visual competencies are perceived and yet how negatively practitioners rate their competencies in this field (Zerfass et al., 2017; Wiesenberg & Verčič, 2020).

Shifting preferences from text to voice: Many Android smartphone users say "Ok, Google" to their smartphone as a request to search the web. This so-called voice search, which allows the use of voice commands for Google queries, is only one example of **voice interaction** – the use of voice and natural language for interaction with digital devices. Voice interaction is an umbrella term for different forms of VUIs and the global trend toward more voice-based interactions between humans and technology (Telner, 2021; Zerfass et al., 2021). VUIs are digital systems that enable human-computer interaction through a combination of **natural language processing (NLP)**, automatic speech recognition (ASR), and AI (Section 8.1). Well-known examples of VUIs are digital assistants integrated into smartphones, computers, or smart speakers – such as Siri, Google Assistant, or Alexa – or the use of voice commands for interaction with devices connected within the IoT, like smart TVs or smart voice assistants in cars.

Voice interaction is increasingly replacing other forms of device interactions like typing, clicking, or swiping (Telner, 2021). This development is fueled by rapid technological developments along with legal requirements to ensure accessibility to devices and services to people with disabilities (Lazar at al., 2015). The increased use of VUIs is relevant for PR communication formats. One example of how the increase in voice-based interactions might affect communication formats is voice search.

Research suggests that voice and text search differ in several respects. For example, compared to typed questions, spoken queries tend to be longer, more conversational, and much closer to everyday language (Guy, 2016). Accordingly, communication experts predict that conversational language will constitute the future of search engine optimization (SEO), the process of improving digital content to increase its visibility for relevant searches. The shift toward voice searches means that creators of blogs and websites need to incorporate more conversational language into their sites, present information differently, and integrate more voice content such as podcasts to ensure visibility in search results.

Scholars predict that VUIs will perform gatekeeper functions for corporate communications and marketing (Zerfass et al., 2021). VUIs mostly only provide a single result to queries – in contrast to a text search that offers a list of results that users can scan to find the information they need while also potentially learning other information peripheral to their query. Additionally, mobile device users perform location-based searches more often, such as directions to locations or local businesses' phone numbers. These new technological gatekeeper functions require corporate communications to find new ways to reach their stakeholders.

Voice interaction is also predicted to create new opportunities for more personalized corporate communications. Smart speakers, for example, facilitate the development of new communication formats that enable playful voice interactions and different forms for acoustic branding. Such communication formats can integrate sounds that are difficult to express in words but that evoke strong feelings, like a powerful engine or ocean sounds (Zerfass et al., 2021).

An ethically and legally controversial aspect of this development is voice interaction's potential to reveal critical real-time information about users. Voice interactions provide information on gender, age, personality, health, physical characteristics, and mood (Kröger et al., 2020), and information on the context in which communication happens, based on location services and background noise (Telner, 2021). Such information could enable more targeted and personalized stakeholder segmentation and communication, especially when combined with other data such as the user's past queries, shopping history, or calendar.

Not only is digitization changing the professional fields, it also raises new ethical questions (Section 4.4). In addition, it requires a modified set of media competencies and skills, which we will discuss in the next two sections.

ACTIVITY

Put yourself in the role of a Head of Communications in an international company like Siemens. How would you explain to your team the consequences of the shift to voice interaction for the daily work in your communications department? Which communication areas are particularly affected?

4.2 Why Digital Media Literacy Matters

Digital media enable everyone to send their messages to millions of users. One consequence is that we are flooded with information on our smartphones, tablets, and other mobile devices – information generated by clicks, posts, likes and shares, photos, videos, tweets, e-mails, and text messages. Within this vast amount of digital content, private opinions compete with journalistic news, political statements, marketing messages, influencer posts, alternative facts, fake news, conspiracy theories, and social bot attacks. These various forms of communication are on an equal footing with each other, which leads us to the crucial question: Which information is reliable, which is fake? Is a video with more clicks of higher quality than a video with less reach? How to avoid the filter bubble? If we do not want to get lost in digital media, we need skills beyond being able to write and read messages. We need an understanding of how to access and evaluate information, how to judge the reliability of sources or to spot fake news. In other words, we need digital media literacy. It is the bedrock of our daily private and professional communication.

4.2.1 Media Literacy

Traditionally, literacy has been perceived as linguistic literacy; that is, the ability to read and write, understand and use, reflect on and engage with language. These skills are still crucial to becoming literate. Today, however, the term *literacy* has expanded to include an array of literacies and skills. One literacy that is most relevant in the context of this textbook is media literacy. Media literacy refers to analog and digital media and has been defined in different ways in recent decades (e.g. Carlsson, 2019; Hobbs, 2010; Hobbs, 2019; Livingstone, 2004; Potter, 2021; Rosenbaum et al., 2008;). Most of the definitions agree on the following core elements: access, analyze, evaluate, create, reflect, and act. Hobbs (2010, p. vii) describes digital media literacy "as a constellation of life skills that are necessary for full participation" in digital society. This includes the ability to:

- *Make responsible choices and access information by locating and sharing materials and comprehending information and ideas;*
- *Analyze messages in a variety of forms by identifying the author, purpose and point of view, and evaluating the quality and credibility of the content;*
- *Create content in a variety of forms, making use of language, images, sound, and new digital tools and technologies;*
- *Reflect on one's own conduct and communication behavior by applying social responsibility and ethical principles;*
- *Take social action by working individually and collaboratively to share knowledge and solve problems in the family, workplace and community, and by participating as a member of a community.*

(Hobbs, 2019, pp. vii–viii)

Potter (2021, p. 23) defines media literacy as "a set of perspectives that we actively use when we expose ourselves to the mass media to process and interpret the meaning of the messages we encounter." His definition is built on three key components: 1. skills, 2. knowledge structures, and 3. personal locus. The skills he describes as crucial to media literacy (Table 4.1) mirror the core elements mentioned above.

According to Potter (2021, p. 20), these skills are the tools we use to "create, alter, and update our knowledge structures." By *knowledge structures* – the second key component of media literacy – he understands "sets of organized information in your memory" (p. 20). Knowledge structures help us process and interpret media content, and they provide the context we need to make sense of it. The most relevant contexts here are: media industries, media audiences, media content, and media effects. The degree of media

TABLE 4.1 POTTER'S SEVEN SKILLS OF MEDIA LITERACY (BASED ON POTTER, 2021, P. 16)

1. Analysis	includes the ability to understand how media content is composed and to break down a message into its meaningful components.
2. Evaluation	is crucial for making judgments about the value of the content; for example, to distinguish between dated, biased or fake news.
3. Grouping	means being able to contrast and compare elements, identifying similarities and differences, and categorizing them in a meaningful way. A good example of grouping is to compare editorial content with sponsored content, or to differentiate between the communicative purposes of a news article and a press release.
4. Induction or inductive reasoning	means that we go from the specific to the general. For instance, we find a pattern in a small data set (e.g., an online survey) and then generalize and theorize about the pattern identified. Inductive reasoning is useful for developing theories and hypotheses or making predictions.
5. Deduction or deductive reasoning	uses general theories or hypotheses to reach a specific conclusion. Here, we go from the general to the specific. Deductive reasoning is good for testing hypotheses or theories.
6. Synthesis	is the ability to adapt and update our knowledge structures when we receive new information and to assemble elements into new structures.
7. Abstracting	is the skill to rephrase news and messages in our words and in a very precise and succinct way. The aim is to identify the big picture.

literacy achieved depends on how well our knowledge structures are developed in these contexts (p. 22). It also depends on the *personal locus*, which is the third component of media literacy. The personal locus consists of goals and drives regarding the information processing tasks (pp. 22–23). It is the personal ability to become aware of the role of media; the conditions under which they function; the processes through which content is produced; the goals of the media organizations; and the influence of media on oneself.

It is exactly what McLuhan (1969) captured in his "fish being unaware of water" metaphor: media environments, especially digital environments with immersive effects, are not perceptible to us like water to a fish (Section 1.2.3). To become aware of the "water," we have to step out of the media bubble and take a different perspective in order to use media mindfully, because "[t]he more you know about your personal locus and the more you make conscious decisions to shape it, the more you can control the process of media influence on you" (Potter, 2021, p. 23). The personal locus is thus "a state of mind that requires continuous monitoring" (Rosenbaum et al., 2008).

In addition to the seven skills which form the cognitive dimension, media literacy is also determined by the social-emotional, aesthetic, and moral dimension (Table 4.2).

TABLE 4.2 MEDIA LITERACY IN JOURNALISM DEFINED BY THE FOUR DIMENSIONS (BASED ON POTTER, 2021, PP. 24–25)

1. Cognitive dimension	to gather information, to interview, and to write news; to produce content using different modes and genres; to break down a story into its key points by using the 5 w's (who, what, when, where, why) and how; to verify information (fact-checking); to understand and evaluate the implications of new information; to recognize and solve problems; to listen actively to what people say; to understand how news is produced and consumed.
2. Social-emotional dimension	to control emotions; e.g., to know how to cope with fake news or hate speech on social media; to feel empathy and act sensitively when interviewing, for example, traumatized war victims; to produce content that deals with emotions in a responsible way; to collaborate in a team and respect decisions made by a group; to manage conflicts and solve problems.
3. Aesthetic dimension	to know what aesthetic quality means regarding verbal and visual content; to use verbal and visual rhetorical devices effectively; to employ different forms of design; to create new forms of content presentation; to develop a personal style.
4. Moral dimension	to act ethically by respecting journalistic standards such as truthfulness, accuracy, impartiality, fairness, transparency; to compare the costs and benefits of potential actions and choose the most appropriate one.

This list of skills is not exhaustive and, as mentioned earlier, there are many other ways of defining and classifying media literacy. Moreover, the frameworks for media literacy need to respond to the ongoing changes in media triggered by new digital technologies as well as economic and political processes, which requires a constant review of the definitions.

4.2.2 Digital Literacies

While media literacy is a broader term that covers old and new media, digital media literacy has a clear focus on the understanding and use of digital media and digitally mediated information and communication. Digital media literacy brings together the characteristic skills of media literacy with the cognitive and technical skills of **digital literacy**. Digital literacy is defined as the ability to use digital technologies to access information, to read, analyze, and critically evaluate the different types of information created through digital technologies, and to contribute to social media communities as producers (Table 4.3). In short: to navigate through "the complex array of online technologies, information, and digitally mediated relationships" (Baron, 2019, p. 346). A digitally literate person is also aware of the ethical dimensions of digital technologies. The ability to manage digital information critically and to master the tools of digital information is also called information literacy (Casey, 2019, pp. 101–102).

Since social media platforms and news organizations rely heavily on visual content, **visual literacy** and **visualization literacy** complement digital literacy. Visual literacy is the ability to read, analyze, interpret, evaluate, and create meaning from visuals in order

TABLE 4.3 WHAT CONSTITUTES DIGITAL LITERACY

Knowing	how to find content; how to search online and how to interpret the search results.
Understanding	how filters and algorithms work; how to protect personal data; understanding the basics of online safety (e.g., be careful what you download; choose strong passwords; use secure apps and websites).
Evaluating	whether a source is credible and trustworthy; recognizing *misinformation* (false or inaccurate content that is shared without an intent to mislead or deceive) and *disinformation* including fake news (fake content that is spread with the intent to mislead or deceive); distinguishing fake news from trustworthy content; conducting fact-checking.
Acting responsibly	when creating content (posts, e-mails, blogs, articles, pictures, videos, podcast, etc.); when sharing a photo, a video, or a comment; when communicating with various audiences: family, friends, colleagues, or anyone who can access our messages or posts.

to communicate intentionally. It also includes the ability to create images and to have a knowledge of the visual vocabulary of the visual language such as point, line, position, size, shape, color, texture, contrast, light, or space (to mention but a few). Other scholars have added the capacity of visual thinking, that is, the process of thinking in and learning from pictures (Ausburn & Ausburn, 1978; Avgerinou & Ericson, 1997; Koltay, 2011, 2019; Lauer & Sanchez, 2011; Orland-Barak & Maskit, 2017). Visual literacy deals with visuals such as photographs, videos, drawings, advertisements, or works of art, but also body language, dance, exhibits, or architecture. Far too often, images are taken at face value and not critically examined (Carillo, 2019, pp. 20–22). A visually literate person is aware that images can be easily manipulated or even faked; e.g., deepfake videos (Section 4.4). A visually literate person can evaluate whether the image refers to a factual situation or to fiction and recognize the persuasive character of advertising and PR images as well as the intentions of the media producers behind these images. In addition, a visually literate person can gauge the power of images and their effects – particularly when it comes to visual simulation, AR and VR.

A subfield of visual literacy is visualization literacy, also called data visualization literacy, which refers to visual representations in the data domain (Boy et al., 2014). Data visualizations have become hugely important in journalism and PR. Visualization literacy has been defined as the ability to read and make meaning from visual representations of data and to interpret patterns, trends, and correlations in data visualizations (Börner, Bueckle & Ginda, 2019, p. 1857). Graphicacy is another term that runs on parallel lines to visualization literacy, but with a focus on visuo-spatial skills; namely, understanding and presenting spatial information in the form of charts, graphs, maps, photographs, or sketches (Balchin, 1972). The term *graphicacy* is often used in connection with cartography and geographic information visualization.

Visualization literacy and graphicacy lead us to another kind of literacy that is gaining considerable momentum in our digital society: **data literacy**. This is the ability to work with data; that is, to collect, read, and analyze data. Data literacy requires competences in statistics, data visualization, and problem-solving using different data; it also involves drawing conclusions from and arguing issues with data (Bhargava, 2019, p. 303; Pedersen & Caviglia, 2019, p. 166).

Data literacy and visualization literacy overlap insofar as they both include the ability to visualize data and read graphs and charts. Data literacy builds on other literacies such as numerical literacy, statistical literacy, and computational literacy. Computational literacy "pushes for algorithmic thinking and modeling as a problem-solving approach" (Bhargava, 2019, p. 303). The concept of big data literacy goes a step further and encompasses "an understanding of the technologies used to gather large data sets, awareness of the algorithmic operation used to analyze them, and critical abilities to assess the aura of accuracy that surrounds them" (Bhargava, 2019, p. 304; D'Ignazio & Bhargava, 2015).

To sum up, media literacy concerns us all: children and adults, consumers and producers, lay people and professionals. The level of media literacy can therefore vary greatly. While media literacy covers all types of media, digital literacy focuses on digital media and digitally mediated information and communication. Media literacy and related literacies such as information, data, image and visualization literacies sometimes overlap in terms of skills. They are all intended to enable people to critically reflect on the role of the media. They empower people to participate in social discourse, intercultural dialogues, and democratic life.

ACTIVITY

Pick a news story from a website. Use the list of skills outlined by Potter (Table 4.1) to examine the news story. Which elements make up the news story? What can you say about the accuracy and credibility of the news story? Are the sources trustworthy? Is there any evidence for news bias? Write a brief summary that captures the essence of the news article.

4.3 Skills for Practitioners

In this section, we ask: To what extent have digital technologies led to new modes of expression and thus to new job requirements? We describe the skills that practitioners working in a digital media environment need to perform their job competently. These skills refer to the fields of journalism and PR and are closely connected to media linguistics: writing, multimodal communication, and community communication.

4.3.1 Writing: The Key Characteristics of Writing in Digital Environments

Writing in journalism and PR is usually part of multimodal and collaborative media production. It is always carried out as a sequence and bundle of practices; for example, some writers tend toward planning first and formulating later – while others virtually formulate and plan at the same time, rapidly switching back and forth between these two practices. Moreover, in professional settings with their economic constraints, writers oscillate between routine and creativity, trying to minimize efforts and maximize outcomes. But most of all, writing is a process. This means that improving its results, the written texts, means adjusting the process by applying functional techniques.

Writing as a process entails all the activities by which verbal, written communicational offers are produced (Jakobs & Perrin, 2014, p. 7). In the digital environments of journalism and PR, it usually starts from oral and written source texts, which are then recontextualized in excerpts (Section 3.1.1). Writing processes include para-verbal aspects such as making decisions on typography. Text production, in contrast, includes writing, but also nonverbal activities such as visual page design and video editing. It is the total of all activities involved in producing a multimodal contribution with a significant proportion of – but not only – verbal language.

The key practices of both writing and text production in mediatized professional settings such as journalism and PR can be assigned to the sixteen activity fields of the media linguistic mindset (Section 3.1.4). By and large, these activities take place on three layers (Perrin, 2021): (a) interacting with the text production environment; (b) managing the writing process itself in project cycles; and (c) by doing so, designing the emerging media product. This is illustrated in the figure of the "writing helix" (Jakobs & Perrin, 2014, p. 21). The gerunds in the graphic elements of this figure refer to the sixteen activity fields, each of them bundling a set of practices that require specific skills (Figure 4.2).

From the very beginning, all the activities of text production are oriented toward the final product as a "fixed point attractor" (Larsen-Freeman & Cameron, 2008, p. 187). This attractor is the landing point of a recursive process; hence, the helix metaphor. The process begins with a first idea and ends with a final cut of a text. In between, phases of stable activities alternate with transitions of disruptive change. Stable activities include

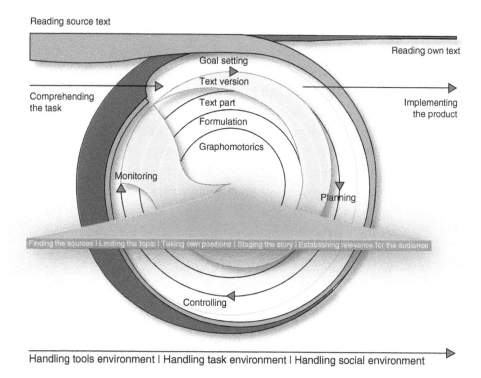

Figure 4.2 The writing helix. Adapted from *The linguistics of newswriting* (p. 151), by D. Perrin, 2013, Amsterdam: John Benjamins. © 2013 Daniel Perrin. Adapted with permission.

fluently writing word by word, sentence by sentence, paragraph by paragraph. In contrast, disruptive transitions seem to be, at first sight, largely unpredictable in terms of both the moment when they occur and the way they go. They include, for example, jumping back and forth in the emerging text

In other words, the process of text production is dynamic, thus not entirely predictable. This property of all the creative processes makes a huge difference to the close-to-full predictability of automatized production processes, for example in the food or car industries. The unpredictability of the process contrasts with the requirement of predictable products: fixed deadlines, product lengths, and media shapes in general. In one way or another, the task needs to be accomplished and the media release or editorial must be available in the expected quality at the expected moment in time. This is why professional text production needs to be controlled by experienced balancing of activities in its sixteen fields.

- On the *context* layer, text production begins when writers understand and accept a text production task (COMPREHENDING THE TASK) – and it ends when they send the results of their work, such as blog posts, multimodal news pieces, or website updates, along the production chain (IMPLEMENTING THE PRODUCT), for example to post-producers or the internet audience. At these main interfaces of writing in the workplace, writers have to deal with time and space restrictions, editorial policies, and organizational workflows. In between, they HANDLE TOOL ENVIRONMENTS, TASK ENVIRONMENTS, and SOCIAL ENVIRONMENTS. For example, they cope with computer crashes, communicate in social media, and negotiate and socialize with clients, colleagues, and superiors.

- On the *process* layer, writers manage the production of written language. Four phases recur and overlap, each dominated by activities which contribute to the step-by-step production of the text. GOAL SETTING typically focuses on the aim to be achieved with the multimodal text as a whole. PLANNING focuses on organizing text parts, such as paragraphs or visuals, and CONTROLLING means working on formulations and visual details under construction. MONITORING, in contrast, traces the results of the production process throughout all of the levels. Reading processes (SOURCE READING and PRODUCT READING) interact with writing processes on various time frames and scales, from shaping graphemes or micro visuals to reorganizing entire text versions.

- On the *product* layer, writers focus on the function and anticipated outcome of the text product. By FINDING THE SOURCES, they decide whose voices appear in a text or are accessible through embedded hyperlinks. Practices include accessing and combining – or omitting – contradictory sources and their communicational offers. Activities of LIMITING THE TOPIC and TAKING OWN POSITIONS include generating, picking up, broadening, or narrowing topics – and hiding or showing one's own stance in a text. By STAGING THE STORY and ESTABLISHING RELEVANCE FOR THE AUDIENCE, writers decide which semiotic and rhetoric means are used in the dramaturgy of a text and what prior knowledge and emotional state is required to understand and estimate it.

- All activities of real-life writing in digital environments take place in this interplay of the sixteen fields. The activities interact with one another and, of course, with environments of diverse ranges, including knowledge databases such as Google, workplaces such as newsrooms, and domains such as journalism and PR, all of which include enablements and constraints, such as financial resources and professional ethics. Owing to incompatible expectations in partly contradictory contexts, such as being accurate (in a factual context) and super-fast (in a context of media-economical competition), the writers constantly have to solve conflicts while writing. This can require emergent, creative solutions beyond well-established production routines.

EXAMPLE

Media enterprises tend to expect journalists to achieve high impact at low costs (HANDLING TASK ENVIRONMENT). In the public interest of democracies, however, journalists are expected to address socially relevant topics in a nuanced way (ESTABLISHING RELEVANCE FOR THE AUDIENCE). Another example: Both journalists and communication officers have to be ready to respond to unexpected developments every day (e.g., flexible PLANNING based on SOURCE READING in internal communication, newsfeeds, and social media) while working within rigid production structures of organizational communication flows and mass media production (e.g., HANDLING TOOLS).

Such conflicting demands lead to problems in balancing the basic practices of text production. If I am fast and concise, I risk being wrong. Vice versa, if I pay attention to all the relevant details, I risk missing deadlines and exceeding word counts. The problem is even accentuated in writing-by-the-way (Section 3.1.3). Being constantly involved in several dialogical written conversations requires the skills of, first, being open to the unexpected while reading the world; second, making up my mind quickly about what I want to do and write next and in general; and third, finding the right words to make my point. In practice, this boils down to professional writing techniques such as the Mugging Test (Perrin, 2013, p. 35]) (www.cambridge.org/digitalcommunication).

4.3.2 Multimodal Communication: Mastering Everything?

Digital technologies and a change in audience behavior have led to new modes of expression and forms of communication. These forms are always multimodal (Section 3.3). Not only do multimodal texts rely on words, but they integrate writing, images, and other semiotic modes such as spoken words, typography, or color in new ways and increasingly blur the distinction between these modes (van Leeuwen, 2008). This kind of "new writing" needs a "new literacy" (van Leeuwen, 2018, p. 291). Having strong writing skills, therefore, is not enough for journalists or PR practitioners in the digital era. They need the ability to think about products in various modes, including their different affordances and aesthetics.

Looking at job postings in the communications industry, the list of skills required has grown enormously in recent years (Wenger, Owens & Cain, 2018). Employers want a mix of old and new skills. The traditional skill set includes, for instance, writing, copy editing, research and fact-checking, working under pressure, and critical thinking. The new skills focus on mastering the digital world; that is, the production of content for websites, apps, and social media. These skills involve making judgments about which semiotic modes to select or prioritize for news reporting or storytelling; writing for different media; visual storytelling, photo and video editing; collecting, analyzing, and visualizing data; engaging with the audience through social media, and using audience analytics. That's quite a list, and we have not yet touched on digital developments such as VR or AI. It seems that future journalists and communication experts need to be superhuman and excel at everything. This, however, is not a realistic expectation. What is realistic is to excel at a combination of a few skills that ideally go well together; the other skills are provided by colleagues or partners, because digital communication is about teamwork.

Let us take the example of data-driven content. Using data to tell stories is one of the new skills you need for digital communication, and it is as relevant in journalism as it is in PR. We will take an example from data journalism, one we will present later in Section 7.2. Storytelling with data requires a multiskilled team: a team made up of at least a writer, a programmer, and a designer. The most relevant skills required in this context are data mining, basic analytics and statistics, coding, graphic design, and the knowledge of how to combine text, images, and graphics to present the data story in a clear and simple way. These skills are needed in order to go through the full working process: to collect, filter, and clean data and analyze it; to make data accessible by visualizing it so that you can reveal patterns in the data set which point to a newsworthy story; and, finally, to transform your findings into a story which can be realized in (a combination of) several forms: an animated infographic, an interactive stand-alone data visualization, a longer story with text, images and graphs, maps or charts, or even an explainer video. Once again, it is not about being an expert in all of those things. But it is crucial to have an understanding of the importance of data, the affordances of the different modes – verbal, visual, graphic, and numeric – and how these then fit together to form a compelling story.

If the findings of the data analysis suggest a more complex story, sketching and storyboarding are the skills required to handle the narrative complexity. Sketching and storyboarding support the collaborative process, as they provide the bigger frame of the story and prevent the team from getting bogged down in detail. They visually represent the ideas of the team members, thus making the communication between writers, designers, and programmers easier and more precise. Figure 4.3 shows the storyboard of the data story "20 Years 20 Titles" (Section 7.2). The production team (SRF data) also sketched a lot and tested various types of graphs using the same data in order to see the big picture of the story and to get a feeling for which graph could convey the message in the most effective way.

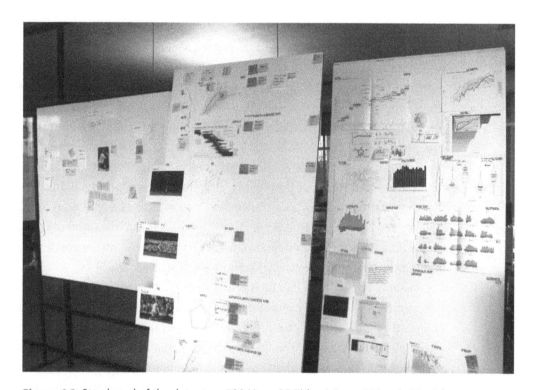

Figure 4.3 Storyboard of the data story "20 Years 20 Titles." From "Wie wir 20+ Jahre Tennisdaten analysiert und aufbereitet haben," by B. Zehr, 2018 (https://medium.com/@angelozehr/wie-wir-20-jahre-tennisdaten-analysiert-und-aufbereitet-haben-f4d3498580c3). © 2018 Benja Zehr. Reprinted with permission.

To conclude, nowadays, multimodal communication requires a digital mindset, that is, an openness to and interest in digital technologies. We listed a number of specialized skills related to digital media literacy, data literacy, and visualization literacy. Of course, the list cannot be considered complete, since new technologies give rise to new forms of communication, which in turn require new skills. However, five skills are so basic that they are worth emphasizing:

- Curiosity: to be curious about new methods, tools, and processes and to be willing to embrace them.
- Creativity: to see what is not there; to think outside the box and find new solutions.
- Flexibility: an open but critical mind for a media landscape in constant flux.
- Attitude: respect, understanding, and appreciation of other disciplines.
- Professional ethics: to understand and apply ethical norms and values that frame the communicative practice (Section 4.4).

These skills are timeless, and they apply to both legacy media and new media.

4.3.3 Community Communication: Knowing Your Target Audience

For many people interested in an organization, a product, or a service, social networking sites are the primary means of obtaining information about them, and one of the most important strategic goals of corporate communications is to build and protect a brand's reputation on these sites; that is, how it is perceived there by the relevant stakeholders. The impression they get is based on the content the organization publishes itself but also on public online conversations with and among stakeholders. Because organizations have only limited control over what is publicly said about them on social media, online reputation management is gaining importance. Online reputation management can be defined as "the process of positioning, monitoring, measuring, talking, and listening as the organization engages in a transparent and ethical dialogue with its various online stakeholders" (Jones, Temperley & Lima, 2009, p. 934). A high level of consumer engagement can enhance the reputation of an organization and also increase trust, emotional brand attachment, and loyalty (Brodie et al., 2011; Kick, 2015).

Consumer engagement can be reached through what we call community communication, which is the process of building a social network among an organization's stakeholders through various types of interaction, both online and in real-life settings. Social media platforms are often the first choice for community communication because their technological features facilitate relationship-building. Social media platforms make it easy to display connections. They also allow the search for and connection with users' profiles and offer possibilities for effortless interaction (Section 2.3.2). While classical social media communication in a corporate context primarily aims at achieving reach through content, community communication is about building and maintaining long-term relationships. This is usually the role of community managers. These professionals are responsible for developing and managing an organization's online community, a social network constructed through interactions for work purposes or shared interests and experiences. Communities allow an organization to interact with target audiences on a more emotional and personal level and therefore gain a deeper understanding of their needs and preferences, build relationships, and increase social capital (Section 2.3). A community manger's typical tasks involve creating relevant and shareable content, interacting with stakeholders online, monitoring their dialogue to address negative statements, and following up on ideas and suggestions shared on social networking sites (Millington, 2012; Perkins, 2015).

EXAMPLE

A frontrunner in using social media for community communication is the Royal Dutch airline KLM. In 2018 the airline had around 28 million followers on various social media platforms and received more than 180,000 messages a week, which were responded to personally by 360 service staff on WhatsApp, Facebook Messenger, Twitter, WeChat, KakaoTalk, and LINE – in ten languages. (https://news.klm.com/klm-introduces-new-service-channel-via-line/). KLM's first social media activities aimed at customers only. The airline then started targeting potential customers by introducing campaigns that illustrated the airline's dedication to social customer service. A lot of the campaigns were based on in-depth knowledge of their target groups. In 2014, for example, KLM continuously scanned Twitter in search of messages indicating that someone traveling was having difficulties, especially targeting people flying with other airlines. KLM then suggested solutions to the problems via social media with the hashtag #HappytoHelp (https://news .klm.com/klm-launches-happytohelp/). Another example of a campaign based on social listening is KLM Surprise, during which passengers' social profiles were monitored in order to surprise them with a personalized gift as a token of appreciation for flying with KLM (http://sbks.co/KLM/KLM-Surprise). By personally answering questions on platforms where people interact in their daily lives, in the language they speak, and by connecting social media communication with real-life experiences, the company builds personally relevant, memorable, interactive, and emotional relationships. According to Socialbakers, a social media marketing platform, KLM's campaigns led to a more satisfied customer base, a sharp increase in fan growth, increased brand awareness, and a more engaged community on social media (www.socialbakers.com/www/archive/storage/www/klm-sociallydevoted .pdf). The high level of consumer engagement was also reflected in monetary terms. Venture beat, a technology website, states that KLM's social media customer service agents had generated $25 million in annual revenue by 2015 (https://venturebeat .com/2015/05/21/klms-150-social-media-customer-service-agents-generate-25m-in-annual-revenue).

Successful community communication requires appropriate corporate structures but also involves knowing your stakeholders, their lifeworlds, their interests, and their values. Moreover, it requires the ability to build and maintain relationships through communication. The linguistic perspective on communities offers approaches for successful community communication. Research in applied linguistics explores how communities are imagined and discursively constructed online by bringing together like-minded individuals around a common concern (Papacharissi, 2011; Sergeant & Tagg, 2014; Zappavigna, 2014). The notion of "imagined community" is based on the assumption that the connections between any large, dispersed group of people is more constructed than real. The political scientist Benedict Anderson, who introduced the concept of imagined communities in his work around nationalism, states: "the members of even the smallest nation will never know most of their fellow-members, meet them, or even hear of them, yet in the minds of each lives the image of their communion" (Anderson, 1991, p. 6). In other words, while the connections within a larger group of people may feel real, they are seldom based on actual ties and interactions but on the construction and projection of shared values and goals.

On social networking sites, people negotiate their belonging to communities of shared values through what Zappavigna (2011, 2014) terms "ambient affiliation," which can be explained as social bonding through the use of semiotic resources like texts, pictures, hashtags, or memes. This affiliation is ambient because practices like sharing certain memes or using specific hashtags create alignments between people who do not necessarily interact directly and, therefore, most likely do not know each other. The analyses of the language and the semiotic resources people use on social media enable us to understand the concept of community in much more fluid terms than is possible through focusing on structural criteria such as links between profiles or the regularity of interactions. Furthermore, they allow us to find hidden social networks which are vital when building communities around a topic, a brand, or a product. In KLM's campaign "Happy to Help," for example, the first step was to determine the community of people who were experiencing difficulties while traveling and then to align as many of them as possible around the hashtag #HappyToHelp.

When creating content and interacting with each other on social networking sites, people negotiate meanings. Their language choices are thereby shaped by their perception of and response to an imagined community's practices (Tagg, 2014). By monitoring conversations on digital spaces, we discover what people are saying about brands, products, services, and topics relevant for an organization. We also discover how they talk. This is a basis for communication at eye level that helps us to differentiate ourselves from our competitors – by producing content that is timely and relevant, and designing interactions which allow us to maintain a connected presence as well as contribute to an organization's reputation and social capital in the long run (Section 2.3).

To sum up, community communication requires knowledge about your target audiences. You need to know on which social networking sites to find them and which communication practices are prevalent on these sites. Moreover, you need to find out how your target groups use language and other semiotic resources to communicate, negotiate meanings, and relate to each other. These insights will allow you to find hidden social networks that bond around specific values or topics relevant to your organization. Knowing what your target audiences care and talk about helps you to select the right content. Knowing how they use language and other semiotic resources helps you to use multimodal communication to build and maintain relationships.

ACTIVITY

Go to the companion website (www.cambridge.org/digitalcommunication), Toolbox Writing. There you will find five writing techniques that help you improve your writing and achieve better text results in an efficient way. Give it a try!

4.4 Media Ethics

Imagine it is 1969 and the world is waiting for Apollo 11, the first manned spaceflight to the moon, to return to earth. In case it doesn't, President Richard Nixon has prepared a speech he thankfully never had to give because the space mission was successful. In 2019, fifty years later, the MIT (Massachusetts Institute of Technology) Center for Advanced Virtuality produced a video showing US President Nixon delivering the prepared speech; namely, telling the world that the moon landing had ended in disaster. A team of computer scientists and artists had leveraged artificial intelligence (AI) to create a fake video titled "In Event of Moon Disaster" (Day, 2019). The video resurrects Nixon and reimagines an alternate version of history. It looks amazingly authentic and illustrates what such an alternate speech would have looked and sounded like. The aim was to educate people about the dangerous power of computer-based disinformation, so-called deepfakes. Now, imagine what might happen if the leader of a country declared war on its neighboring state in a deepfake video. And if this video is uploaded on social media, shared by millions of users, and distributed around the globe? This is where ethics comes in. Deepfakes have the power to manipulate reality, spread deceptive content, distort truth, and erode trust.

The term *deepfake* is a combination of **deep learning** (Section 8.1) and *fake*. Deepfakes use techniques from AI and machine learning to create realistic photos, videos, and audios of people saying or doing things that they did not actually say or do. AI-generated media, like most technologies, can have positive and negative effects on society. Being simply a tool, the technology itself cannot be described as either good or bad. How this technology is applied, however, and whether it is done in an ethically responsible manner, is the question that needs to be addressed. This section outlines some of the ethical challenges that arise because of rapid changes in a digitalized world. It provides definitions of some relevant theories of ethics and asks questions about ethical practices and behavior in journalism and PR. The aim is not to provide answers to what is right and what is wrong, but to raise awareness of ethical issues in a changing media landscape.

4.4.1 Ethics in a Nutshell

Ethics is concerned with the correct and good conduct of people and the reflection on this conduct. As a philosophical discipline, ethics is the study of morality: what is morally good and bad, right and wrong, fair and unfair. Morality can be defined as "a system of rules for guiding human conduct, and principles for evaluating those rules" Tavani (2011, p. 36). Looking at their etymological roots – *ethos* (Greek) and *mores* (Latin) – both terms refer to concepts of custom, character, and behavior. The central question is: How should I, how should we act? "Ethics does not simply ask how to live well. It asks how we should live well ethically, that is, in goodness and in right relation with each other" (Ward, 2009, p. 295). Ethics, therefore, covers a wide range of issues such as:

- what an individual believes to be morally right or wrong (personal ethics)
- moral rules that apply to a social group in general (social ethics)
- professional norms and principles that govern practices in the corporate environment (professional ethics)
- how academics should conduct research correctly (research ethics)
- universal values and norms that address global issues such as human rights, peace and conflict, poverty, inequality, migration, climate change, or global governance (global ethics)

Ethical theories can be roughly divided into three thematic groups (Ward, 2011, pp. 35–49): consequentialism (the good), deontology (the right), and virtue ethics (the virtuous). These three approaches, explained in the next section, help us to better understand ethical challenges in journalism and PR. We are dealing here with the field of professional ethics. Professional ethics is a division of applied ethics; that is, the application of ethical theories to practical real-world problems.

4.4.2 Applied Ethics in Journalism and PR

As the term suggests, *consequentialism* focuses on the consequences of our actions. It asks us to think through the positive and negative consequences of possible actions and weigh them against one another in order to generate good outcomes and well-being and minimize harm (Ess, 2020, pp. 219–220). One consequence-based theory is *utilitarianism*, as defined by Jeremy Bentham (1748–1832) and John Stuart Mill (1806–1873).

According to utilitarianism, people should pursue those acts that lead to the greatest positive consequences; that is, the most happiness for the greatest number of people (Ess, 2020, p. 220). Utilitarianism often provides the ethical framework when it comes to, for instance, using anonymous sources in journalism. On the one hand, anonymous sources are considered a threat to the credibility of a news organization; moreover, their use increases the risk of reporting something inaccurately or even falsely. On the other hand, stories like the Watergate scandal that brought down President Richard Nixon could never have been published without using unnamed sources. Journalists, therefore, face the dilemma of weighing the two competing ethical principles against each other: their duty to inform people about important issues versus their duty to report trustworthy and transparently. They have to ponder whether the consequences of their behavior will lead to more benefit than harm. Another example is data journalism, where transparency is a key ethical principle (Kennedy, Weber & Engebretsen, 2020).

EXAMPLE

Think of the COVID-19 pandemic. Does publishing a map that shows the location data of infected people improve the information value, and, thus, contribute to the overall good of society? Or would such information be too stigmatizing for those living there? Journalists are often faced with the dilemma good for many, but bad for some. In this case, does a higher information value benefit public health and, therefore, outweigh possible violations of data protection and privacy?

The second group of ethical approaches comprises *non-consequential theories*, also called *deontology* or duty-based ethics, which goes back to Immanuel Kant (1724–1804). In deontological ethics morality is based on duties, rules, and rights (Ess, 2020, pp. 225–233; Ward, 2011, pp. 40–45). Deontology outlines what is morally required, what is just, permitted, or forbidden; for instance, not to lie, murder, or steal. It says what I ought to do or not do and cannot be overridden by utilitarian assessment or by considerations of what kind of person or character I should be. Deontological ethics is reflected in professional codes of ethics and conduct. In journalism, organizations such as the Society of Professional Journalists (SPJ), the Poynter Institute, or the National Union of Journalists (NUJ) provide ethical standards. In addition, media outlets have devised their own code of ethics; e.g., the *New York Times*.[2] Journalistic norms and guidelines may vary from country to country; in some countries, ethical committees are organized by national professional associations, with a mandate to assess cases of possible violation of the ethical standards. However, most media organizations share common key principles such as truthfulness, accuracy, objectivity, impartiality, fairness, transparency, and accountability.

---

[2] Standards and Ethics, *New York Times*: www.nytco.com/company/standards-ethics/.

In PR, national and international associations promote codes of ethics; for instance, the IPRA Code of Conduct, adopted by the International Public Relations Association and recommended to public relations practitioners worldwide; or the PRSA Code of Ethics, developed by the Public Relations Society of America. Members of such associations are committed to ethical values such as advocacy, loyalty, integrity, honesty, disclosure of conflicts of interest, transparency, accuracy, or safeguarding confidential information. These codes of ethics are considered a form of self-regulation. As frameworks, they lay out the rules for behavior and decision-making for PR professionals and provide guidance for ethical conduct in general. However, new digital technologies such as algorithms, social bots, and social media analytics are rarely covered by codes of ethics in PR (Zerfass et al., 2020). Generally speaking, no institutional code of ethics can detail all the practical problems journalists and communication professionals will encounter in real life. Aaron Quinn criticizes the fact that journalists (and also communication professionals) have long been expected to rely on institutional norms and codes: "These prevailing external methods ... have left many journalists confused in terms of specific application of norms, rules, and principles in practice" (Quinn, 2007, p. 168). Instead of relying on these codes, he suggests a *virtue ethics* as a framework for media practitioners that focuses on "how individual journalists might better develop internally so that they (a) function in way that best serves the goals of journalism, and, derivative from this function, (b) act morally" (Quinn, 2018, p. 144).

Virtue ethics is concerned with the moral character of a person. Actions are morally good and appropriate if they are performed by someone of virtuous character. Virtues are character traits such as honesty, generosity, truthfulness, fairness, and compassion; they are imperative to live a good life. Virtue ethics is therefore about becoming excellent human beings by learning from mistakes and developing practical reason; that is, the ability to make ethical judgments to do the right thing in order to achieve an ideal human life as whole (Ess, 2020, pp. 262–263; Ward 2011, pp. 45–49). Virtue ethics refers to the individual level; it addresses the good character and moral integrity of an individual so that this individual is capable of making good decisions in specific situations. But how can media practitioners and communication professionals make ethically good decisions when they are exposed to time pressure and deadlines, facing fierce competition to get a story, or expected to generate as many clicks as possible to increase awareness of a company? The list of common practices and techniques that are morally questionable from an ethical viewpoint is long. It ranges from seemingly harmless and routinized practices, like cropping photos at the risk of losing context or editing images for the sake of aesthetics, to more controversial practices like staging images, using hidden cameras or microphones, undercover reporting, publishing shocking photos on front pages, and sharing embarrassing videos on social media, to heavy infringements of copyright, privacy and data protection, deepfakes, fake news, or greenwashing. Greenwashing is a marketing practice that is used to make consumers believe that a company is more environmentally friendly than it really is; it is a misleading or false claim made in order to promote an ecologically responsible image. Taking the perspective of virtue ethics here can help a person to become a practitioner who is considered excellent (not perfect), because he or she has internalized relevant professional qualities and virtues and acts accordingly in the professional environment.

But what if the journalist or communications manager is not a human but a machine? What about the virtue ethics of avatars, social bots, or robots that perform human-like behaviors? How does morality get into the machine? These are questions that call for **digital media ethics**.

4.4.3 From Media Ethics to Digital Media Ethics

Media ethics focuses on "the professional mass media system with its daily routines and professional practices" (Dörr & Hollnbuchner, 2017, p. 406), suggesting guidelines for responsible action in the production, distribution, and reception of media. According to Ward, media ethics studies "the principles that should guide responsible conduct among journalists and regulate their interactions with other citizens" (2011, p. 54). Definitions of media ethics mainly come from journalism and include topics such as "the limits of free speech; accuracy and bias; fairness; respect for privacy; the use of graphic images; avoiding conflicts of interest; the use of anonymous sources; and the representation of minorities and other cultures" (Ward, 2011, p. 58).

PR is also committed to high moral standards as set out in the codes of ethics mentioned above. Nonetheless, PR is sometimes deemed to be unethical per se. Examples of highly controversial PR are the advertising campaigns run by United Colors of Benetton from the 1990s that generated much discussion and raised ethical questions. The company used shocking images that portrayed social issues such as AIDS, racism, and war in order to promote itself as a socially responsible company.

EXAMPLE

In its communication campaign UNHATE (2011), Benetton used altered photographs that show political and religious world leaders (opponents) in intimate scenes kissing each other on the lips (e.g., Ex-President Barack Obama and the former Chinese leader Hu Jintao; Pope Benedict XVI and Ahmed Mohamed el-Tayeb, Imam of the Al-Azhar mosque in Cairo). Benetton's idea behind the worldwide campaign was to "invite leaders and citizens to combat 'the culture of hatred'" and promote "closeness between peoples, faiths, cultures, and the peaceful understanding of each other's motivations" (United Colors of Benetton, 2011). One main criticism leveled at the company was that it violated the ethical principle of truth because the photographs were manipulated without pointing to this manipulation. In the case of the photograph showing the Pope, the Vatican fiercely criticized the fact that it offended religious feelings (Enxing, 2013). The campaign provoked widespread outrage but also attracted a lot of attention in the media. "[T]he campaign had a significant impact on the international community reaching a total of 500 million users worldwide, more than 3000 articles and 600 TV reports in 60 nations as traditional media reactions" (Incze et al., 2018). Does this mean that a good PR result justifies the violation of ethical norms?

In summary, media ethics examines how companies, news media, and organizations should behave with an eye to their role in society, and how individuals should respond to ethical problems in their roles as professionals.

Just as digital media remediate older media, or converge with them, digital media ethics does not start from scratch but builds on ethical reflections and frameworks related to analog media. Digital media ethics extends media ethics by including phenomena that are related specifically to digital technologies: algorithmic journalism, data-driven PR, digital photojournalism, citizen journalism, blogging, influencer marketing, or big data analysis. It encompasses aspects such as how participants in online communities interact with each other; what photos or videos are appropriate for posting and re-tweeting; how to tackle hate speech as social media are being abused as platforms for xenophobia, racism, and intolerance; how sources are cited (fairly and transparently?).

New technological developments like machine learning, AI, natural language generation, **computer vision**, social media analytics, augmented and virtual reality, or the Internet of Things fall within the scope of **digital ethics**. Digital ethics is concerned with the impact digital technologies have on our society – on our political, social, and moral being. It encompasses the moral principles and rules that should guide our conduct in the digital sphere. Ethical problems arising from digital technologies, include, for instance, fake news; deepfakes and deepfakes pornography; social bots and sexbots; cyberbullying and revenge porn; or data surveillance and data tracking. Digital ethics asks about the responsibility of programmers of applications that use AI to make decisions (Chapter 8). How are these applications programmed? How can decisions made by self-supervised learning algorithms be tracked later? How do we ensure that the decisions made by algorithms are not biased? Can our privacy be invaded when it comes to cybersecurity? What impact does VR have on our consciousness and behavior? In short, digital ethics provides guidance on doing the right thing with digital technologies and data, particularly with big data, algorithms, and cybersecurity.

And things are becoming more complex. We are always online, communication flows quickly and is ubiquitous, reaching millions of people immediately. As networked individuals, we interact globally with individuals from different cultures, which may consider ethical issues evolving from technologies differently. Seemingly intelligent machines are infiltrating our lives. This means we interact not only with humans but also with synthetic agents: robots, social bots, avatars. How should these robots be designed so that they can act ethically? Are robots still systems that benefit humans, or are they becoming autonomous actors with their own moral status and rights (Section 8.4)? Who is responsible when autonomous robots harm human beings? These questions fall into the field of *robot ethics*, or roboethics.

As digital technologies are constantly transforming the nature of public communication, the question arises as to whether developing a digital media ethics code is even possible. In his book *Digital Media Ethics* (2020), Charles Ess gives us grounds for hope by referring to the Aristotelian term *phronēsis*, which means practical wisdom. "[A]s enculturated human beings, *we are already deeply ethical* … [Y]ou are already experienced with confronting ethical difficulties; you are already equipped with important foundations and, most importantly, *phronēsis as* a central skill of ethical judgment … Be of good courage!" (Ess, 2020, p. 25)

ACTIVITY

Discuss the following questions:

- Should an aid organization publish photos of suffering children on their website?
- Should a news magazine publish a gruesome photo of a car crash on its website?

Ponder the pros and cons by applying the two approaches of utilitarianism and deontology.

Key Terms

attention economy, big data, brand journalism, community communication, computer vision, data literacy, deep learning, deepfakes, digital literacy, digital ethics, digital media ethics, media ethics, native advertising, natural language processing (NLP), strategic communication, strategic mediatization, visual literacy, visualization literacy, voice interaction

Chapter Summary

- Digitalization has changed public communication and the relationship between journalism and PR. Although PR still depends on journalistic media to spread content, digital media and the Internet allow companies and organizations to communicate with their target groups directly. More and more companies create content that might be considered journalistic.

- Organizations, brands, media companies, public institutions as well as bloggers, politicians, business leaders, artists, athletes, and celebrities are all trying to attract audience attention. The boom in digital content has led to a phenomenon referred to as the attention economy. Content producers and distributors are constantly trying to reach audiences to command their limited attention span and time. One consequence is the fast spreading of emotional and polarizing information.

- The changes related to digitalization influence the forms and formats of public communication. Media companies create new journalistic experiences and products by using novel methods such as gamification and virtual or augmented reality. Organizations increasingly use big data for gaining knowledge about stakeholders and reaching them in a strategic and targeted way. These changes have an impact on what media literacy skills are needed when interacting with digital media.

- Media literacy is defined as the ability to access, analyze, evaluate, create, reflect on, and engage with media and all forms of communication. It encompasses basic skills such as recognizing a need for information and communication; understanding and reflecting on the role of media, media organizations, and social media platforms; having knowledge of how to use both hardware and software digital tools; analyzing information and judging its value; organizing and categorizing media content; operating on media content through inductive and deductive reasoning and abstracting the main ideas; communicating information responsibly and ethically.

- The concrete skills practitioners need in journalism and PR is a mix of old and new skills. In community communication, for instance, professionals need to know how to build and maintain networks. Online communities allow professionals to interact with target audiences on a more emotional and personal level and to gain a deeper understanding of their needs and expectations. While classical social media communication primarily aims at achieving reach through content, community communication is about long-term relationships. Community managers, therefore, need to know how to use technological features for building and maintaining these long-term relationships with the target groups. Curiosity, creativity, flexibility, an open mind for new digital technologies, and an understanding of other disciplines are still required in PR as well as in journalism.

- Media ethics examines how news media and organizations should behave with an eye to their role in society, and how practitioners should deal with ethical problems at work. Ethics can be grouped into three approaches: 1. Utilitarianism, which is the most common theory of consequentialism, focuses on the outcomes of actions. Utilitarianism means that the most ethical choice is the one that produces the greatest good and happiness for the greatest number of people. It provides the moral framework for justifying actions that cross the ethical lines of professional standards such as using anonymous sources or undercover reporting. 2. Deontology is based on duties, rules, and rights. It is reflected in professional codes of ethics and conduct. 3. Virtue ethics emphasizes the role of virtues and moral character. It refers to the individual level and addresses the moral integrity of an individual, so that this individual is capable of making good decisions and, thus, becoming an exemplary human being.

Digitalization in Journalism and PR

John Lloyd and Laura Toogood (2015) led interviews with journalist and PR professionals. They analyze the effects of the fast-changing media markets on public communication and the roles of journalism and PR.

The philosophers Vincent Hendricks and Mads Vestergaard (2019) reflect in their open access book on how the information market and the attention economy may pave the way to a post-factual democracy.

The edited volume on visual public relations by Collister and Roberts-Bowman (2018b) introduces a range of visual approaches to public relations. It explains the increasingly vital role of visual, sensory, and physical elements for communications and illustrates the theoretical concepts with different case studies.

The data journalism handbook: Towards a critical data practice (Gray & Bounegru, 2021) is a rich resource for students, researchers, and journalists, providing both critical reflection on and practical insight into the work of data journalists and telling stories with data.

Media Literacy

The textbook *Introduction to media literacy* (Potter 2016) is a step-by-step guide to understanding media literacy. The book covers the essential media topics from media industries and audiences to media content and media effects. Tests and exercises help students to improve their media skills in their own daily lives.

A more comprehensive guide to understanding media literacy is Potter's book *Media literacy* (2021, 10th ed.). This edition discusses the effects of digital media in public communication and provides various examples and facts to help understand how the media operate, how they attract attention, and how they influence our behavior.

Skills for Practitioners

Shorthand (2017) is a website that provides a checklist for planning a multimedia story: from finding the right story to successfully promoting it (https://shorthand.com/the-craft/checklist-for-planning-a-multimedia-story/).

Anika Gupta (2020) interviewed professional and volunteer moderators for communities like World of Warcraft guilds or Reddit. In her easy-to-read book, she shares her insights and introduces strategies for creating and managing online communities.

In her book, Ursula Lutzky (2021) presents, in an engaging style, a corpus-based analysis of over 1.5 million tweets from more than thirty different companies in the travel industry. The book enhances our understanding of customers' linguistic expectations on Twitter and successful interaction with customers.

Media Ethics

In his textbook, Charles Ess (2020) invites students to explore the ethical challenges in the era of big data, AI, and the IoT. The book is a comprehensive overview of central issues in digital media ethics including global cross-cultures perspectives.

5 Doing Media Linguistic Research

PREVIEW

When doing classical fieldwork, ethnographers spend time in a foreign culture and try to describe this culture in a way that makes strange or unusual features understandable for their readers. It is a way to help addressees to see their own culture from a new perspective. The book *Coming of Age in Samoa*, written by the early ethnographer Margaret Mead (1928), is a famous example of this process. In 1925, Mead traveled to American Samoa in the South Pacific, where she studied adolescent girls in three villages. Her ethnographic research focused on the girls' sexuality and their experiences of growing up. The study found that the anxiety and stress of American youth were not present among Samoan teenagers. Sexual experimentation was socially accepted, and sexual jealousy or rape nonexistent.

Mead's book became very popular in the United States. It encouraged Western readers to reconsider their own cultural assumptions about adolescence and sexuality. Mead's ethnographic study supported cultural determinism, the idea that cultural upbringing and social environment determine people's behavior rather than biology. It demonstrated that traditional, nuclear sexual relationships between men and women were neither "natural" nor culturally universal. Though the findings came in for criticism, Mead's work is often praised as having helped to precipitate the sexual revolution of the 1960s.

The purpose of this chapter is to show how applied research can help to identify problems in society and professions and how it contributes to providing solutions by using the media linguistics toolbox. We first introduce some research frameworks, structures of various methods and theoretical concepts. We then explain why the combination of linguistic and ethnographic frameworks is especially useful for finding out what people actually do when interacting in the context of digital media. The section on digital ethnography shows how doing research across offline and online spaces can broaden the understanding of the complexities of our contemporary world. Finally, the last section of this chapter introduces methods to generalize findings from ethnographic case studies systematically.

Learning Objectives

By the end of this chapter, you should be able to

- outline which of the frameworks explained foregrounds what aspects of language use in (digital) media environments – and why it does so
- explain advantages of multi-method over single-method approaches in research on language use in everyday and professional environments
- specify a fieldsite in a digital environment
- explain why media linguists often choose the research framework of linguistic ethnography when they investigate real-life communication processes
- outline how linguistic ethnography can be combined with complementary research frameworks for broader analyses and more comprehensive results.

5.1 Frameworks

Approach, method, methodology, framework – these are overlapping terms and their use in academic literature can be confusing. An **approach** is a way of dealing with something; it is the research perspective you choose to explore a subject. The choice of approach leads to methods: a systematic way to scrutinize a subject matter or to achieve a specific research goal. A defined set of basic theoretical assumptions, methods, guidelines, and tools that serves to answer the research questions of a project is called **methodology**. In contrast, a framework is a more or less loose structure of various methods and theoretical concepts that guide you on how to conduct a research study. A **research framework** anchors a study in a discipline and research tradition – it links the new study to previous research. Furthermore, it helps determine the right approach and most appropriate methods, depending on the research questions and aims of a study.

What people actually do when they communicate is the subject of investigation in academic disciplines that fall under the categories of the humanities and social sciences. Humanities include disciplines such as arts and philosophy; social sciences encompass, for example, anthropology and sociology. Linguistics and semiotics are often seen as belonging to both groups. In these two disciplines, we can approach the use of signs of all modes, from letters to sounds and visuals, as **situated activity**. In the field of communication, this technical term means that we use words, sounds, and images to achieve certain goals in concrete situations in our everyday and professional lives.

Activity refers to the fact that we do something with our minds, our bodies, and with the people around us when we communicate. *Situated* means that what we do and how we do it is influenced by the situation in which we do it – and this, in turn, affects this situation. For example, whether you say *good afternoon* to someone or opt for *hi* instead depends on the formality of the setting and mostly results in attention from the addressee; by greeting someone, you establish a momentary, transient relation – which can even, again depending on the situation, turn out to be the beginning of a long-term social relationship.

When it comes to investigating such situated activities, researchers want to find out, on the one hand, what individuals do and why they do it. On the other hand, research aims at understanding how an individual agent's activities influence social realities and, vice versa, are enabled and constrained by them. This requires, first, broad approaches in real-life settings to gather context data on the social conditions and consequences; second, in-depth observations of agents' activities; and third, access to agents' mental activities.

If we want to find out why news programs cover specific topics and why journalists frame their stories in a certain way, for example, we can conduct interviews with journalists. The interviewees will share their viewpoints and perceptions of what they do and why. However, those are somewhat subjective and exclude all the aspects that the interviewees are not aware of. Another approach is offered by observing the situated activity of news production. Observations of decision-making processes in newsrooms and recordings of news production processes allow us to identify aspects and factors that are sometimes hardly noticeable from an insider perspective (Section 6.1.2).

Such an inductive approach begins with a set of empirical observations, then finding patterns in those observations, and finally theorizing about those patterns. In other words, researchers move from data to relations to theory, or from the specific to the general. This is where research frameworks come into play.

The following sections introduce research frameworks which are useful for investigating situated activity in media linguistics. Such frameworks can be useful in helping to find out what people actually do when interacting in the context of digital media and link the situated activity of public digital communication to social structures.

5.1.1 Linguistic Frameworks

Linguistics is primarily concerned with the processes and products of verbal language use, albeit in the context of signs from other systems, such as the sounds and images embedded in the same communicational package. In addition, mainly since the visual turn (Section 3.2.1), linguistics has seen verbal language as medially integrated; oral and written verbal language cannot be realized without auditory and visual components such as the sound of voices and the shapes of fonts, which go beyond the meaning and sense of abstract language signs.

Applied linguistics frameworks add a component for dealing with the practical problems related to language use. Today, applied linguistics sees itself as a field of research and practice in which the practical problems of communication and language use are identified, examined and solved. Increasingly, this is done in a transdisciplinary manner. This means that, in research projects, scientists from several academic disciplines systematically work together with practitioners from the professional fields being studied. Thus, the practitioners are not seen as the objects of study only, but also as experts in their field. The aim is to work together throughout an entire research project in order to learn from each other and solve socially significant and complex problems (Perrin & Kramsch, 2018).

A transdisciplinary project might center around everyday situations in an organization, for example, conference calls. Those pose distinct interactional challenges for team leaders, such as facilitating a meeting in a way that secures both team involvement and smooth meeting progression. While experienced team leaders usually meet these challenges with ease, newcomers might struggle. A linguistic and multimodal analysis of video recordings during ethnographic fieldwork and interviews with employees in different positions can serve as the basis for designing communication training for a specific organization's needs. Those needs are identified in collaborations between researchers and practitioners.

The object of interest in this book is language use in a specific context: mediatized communication in environments such as communities, organizations, and the public sphere. Such language use is addressed by scientific disciplines with complementary thematic interests in the topic. For example, political science, sociology, and communication studies focus on the political and social functions of communication, while media studies focus on its media-bound nature. In the intersection field of such disciplines, media linguistics (Section 1.3) has emerged in the last two decades with its own subject matter and the methods most appropriate to its application (Chapters 5 and 6).

Private and public communication has drastically changed as a result of digitalization. The Internet and digital devices such as smartphones or computers allow the sharing, storing, and distribution of information with just one click. Linguistics refers to communication that occurs through the use of electronic devices such as computer-mediated communication (CMC). While this term traditionally referred to communication via computer-mediated formats – e-mail, chat, online forums, or social media platforms – it now also applies to language-based interaction on mobile devices like mobile phones or tablets.

The framework of computer-mediated discourse analysis (CMDA) uses a set of methods grounded in linguistics, communication, and rhetoric for the analysis of CMC (Herring, 2001, 2004). It applies methodologies that originate in the study of spoken and written language, such as conversation analysis, interactional sociolinguistics, pragmatics, text analysis, and critical discourse analysis. CMDA can be used to study language structure, multimodal communication, interaction, and meaning. CMDA methods are also used to examine indirect social and socio-cognitive phenomena related to digital communication, such as collaboration, social interaction, engagement, identity, or power (Herring, Stein & Virtanen, 2013).

Recent studies focus on the interplay of technological, social, personal, and contextual factors and their influence on computer-mediated language practices. CMDA draws attention to the contextual factors shaping digital communication, like participants of communication, cognitive contexts (as imagined audiences or addressees), offline context, textual context, or generic context including technical prerequisites, rules, or purposes of a virtual environment (Herring, 2004; Page et al., 2014). As a research framework, CMDA may involve qualitative or quantitative linguistic analysis and be supplemented by surveys, interviews, ethnographic observation, or other appropriate methods.

This combination of methods is characteristic of current research. In order to be able to grasp the complexity of our fast-changing world, researchers combine a wide range of methods and interdisciplinary approaches. As we have seen in Chapter 1, digitalization is not only a technological change but also a social transformation which has an impact on public communication and its investigation. In digital environments, traditional mass media content is shared and remixed online; the boundaries between media producers and consumers are becoming increasingly blurred.

The focus on situated activity when investigating digital media helps us understand the interplay between digital communication, society, and technology, as it implies a shift from pure linguistic analyses of media products to the analysis of what people actually do and say in relation to media. Such an approach calls for ethnographic frameworks which look at the social interaction of people in a given environment – in our case the environment of digital communication.

5.1.2 Ethnographic Frameworks

Ethnography aims to understand social worlds and make them coherent and meaningful to various addressees – such as scientific communities, the people being researched, or a wider public.

The most crucial feature of ethnographic research is fieldwork, the data collection "in the field" – in natural settings. To answer their research questions, ethnographers immerse themselves in the everyday life of a group of people, an organization, or a community over a period of time. They observe and participate in the environments they seek to describe while collecting and analyzing data from many sources with a variety of methods, such as computer loggings, observations, document analyses, or ethnographic interviews.

In doing so, researchers try to identify "rich points" (Agar, 2004, p. 21): typical moments when something does not seem to make sense at first sight. As ethnography assumes that participants experience their practices as meaningful, ethnographers have to revise their own conceptualizations until they understand how, for whom, and in what conditions the rich point activity makes sense. The aim of fieldwork is to describe a group of people to others in a way that makes strange or unusual features of their lives and social arrangements understandable. This helps the addressees think in new ways about aspects of their own social arrangements by comparing them with others.

In the 1920s, the anthropological approach was transferred to sociological research of their own cultures by the Chicago School of Ethnography. The research conducted between 1917 and 1942 by sociologists at the University of Chicago focused on everyday experiences in urban spaces. The ethnographic studies of this school of thought explored urban society as the locus of social change. They took into account issues like race, work, delinquency, immigration, and politics, and social institutions like marriage or family.

Current ethnographic research is conducted at many different fieldsites, like places of work, organizations, neighborhoods, airports, but also digital environments like social media platforms or the Internet. Contemporary fieldwork is no longer restricted to geographical spaces; it can be global, multi-sited, and mobile in the sense that researchers follow people or texts around physical and virtual places. Therefore, the field can be conceptualized as a network of connections between people, objects, and places that are traced by the ethnographer in online and offline environments.

Ethnography was developed as a discipline in the context of anthropological studies that focused on studying small communities in foreign countries. The classic anthropologist lived among a group of people, as part of a tribe or in a village. They tried to socialize with the people in this fieldsite to understand their practices, rituals, or norms. That often took decades, as the researchers had to both learn the language being used by the group and become accepted by the community they were studying.

The physical presence in the field, as well as methods such as *participant observation*, interviewing, and collecting documents and artifacts (objects of domestic use) enable the researcher to gain "firsthand experience" of the group, organization, or online community they are studying. Ethnographers try to look at the social group under study from the inside; they try to see the world through the eyes of people they are investigating. In order to document insights gained during participant observation, ethnographers keep field notes that record their ideas and reflections and what they do and observe when participating in activities with the people they are studying.

These different kinds of insights produce different types of data: data representing the perspective of the people being studied and data from the observer's perspective. Harris (1976) calls these emic and etic perspectives. The emic view is the insiders' account of their own world. The ethnographer tries to avoid preconceptions and meet this perspective with an open mind. The etic perspective entails the researcher's interpretations which are based on science and are informed by previous studies or other types of research. An ethnographer links the emic and etic perspective and translates the world of the participants to the audience.

The result of an ethnographic study is a detailed description of the group under examination at a particular time and location. This type of text is called a *thick description*, a term coined by anthropologist Clifford Geertz (1973). A thick description is a way of achieving a type of external validity. By describing an observation in sufficient detail, the researcher evaluates whether it is transferable to other settings, situations, or groups of people. Such descriptions help readers see the internal logic of a group or a community, and lets them understand why the people under investigation behave the way they do and why the behaviors are meaningful to them.

Because of how useful the ethnographic research strategy is in developing an emic perspective, it has been adopted by many disciplines. For example, education researchers use ethnography to study children in classrooms to identify how these children understand and make sense of learning experiences. Sociologists use ethnography to study social phenomena like migration, marriage, and crime; or social groups like families and companies; or representatives of a specific professional group, such as the Pulitzer Prizewinners among the journalists.

Linguists, of course, link ethnographic approaches with detailed linguistic analyses. The growing body of research under the umbrella term of linguistic ethnography (Blommaert & Rampton, 2011) seeks to understand modern life in its complexity. The combination of linguistics and ethnographic methods bridges the gap between micro and macro perspectives on language use, by "tying ethnography down" and "opening linguistics up" (Rampton et al., 2004, p. 4).

5.1.3 Linguistic Ethnography

In ethnographic research, language is conceptualized as a social practice: what people say or write and what they keep silent about produces social reality and is shaped by social reality. **Linguistic ethnography** generally assumes that "language and the social world are mutually shaping, and that close analysis of situated language use can provide both fundamental and distinctive insights into the mechanisms and dynamics of social and cultural production in everyday activity" (Rampton et al., 2004, p. 2). Research in this area combines linguistic and ethnographic methodologies to study language use in social settings and to address linguistic and social questions.

Linguistic ethnography is effective at understanding from complementary angles what is going on in a certain community. When doing linguistic ethnography, researchers follow three methodological principles: First, they investigate a community's linguistic practices, for example, journalists' and PR professionals' language use in multilayered, semiotic, organizational, social, and historical contexts; second, they consider this language a measurement surface for mental and social structures that are otherwise difficult to access; and finally, they assume that practitioners' knowledge matters and must therefore be thoroughly integrated into the research process.

To give an example, when ethnographers want to find out how journalists deal with the digital literacy shift when making career decisions (Section 7.1) or how writing by-the-way can benefit leadership and management practices in organizational communication (see case study online: www.cambridge.org/digitalcommunication), they first immerse themselves in their field of investigation. This helps them become conversant with the conditions, routines, and agents in this field. Immersion is realized by taking on a role in this field; for example, as a trainee or a writing coach in a newsroom or communication department. Then, they collect as much data as they can, for example by making field notes from observations, from conversations with their peer practitioners, or from texts they have produced.

Researchers systematize the insights generated through their fieldwork from an emic perspective. In doing so, they draw on their field notes, aiming at summarizing, explaining, and exemplifying what makes sense to the community under investigation. In contrast to research in many other frameworks, ethnographers regard practitioners' activities and utterances as instances of expert knowledge in this field. The basic assumption of ethnography is that it is the members of a community who are in the best position to know what makes sense in this community and how to proceed with this information.

However, an etic, outsider view can help practitioners see their expertise from a new angle, which then might contribute to new solutions to acute problems as experienced within the community. Conversely, an emic, insider view can contribute to the solution of an acute problem that exists outside this community. In this way, both sides can benefit from ethnographic knowledge, and they can learn from each other if the ethnographer succeeds in mediating between insider and outsider perspectives and knowledges.

To sum up, linguistic ethnography always asks about language practices and sense-making in everyday life or in a profession. In our case, this is, for example, about "communities of practice" (Wenger, 1998) in journalism and PR, and in particular about their professional communication in digital environments. By doing so, linguistic ethnography analyzes how the community under investigation develops and experiences its own linguistic practices. These inner (emic) perspectives are then related to outer (etic) perspectives on the same practices and contexts. Such re-perspectivizing can motivate the research project partners to reframe and reconsider their familiar object of research from new angles – which helps understand practical problems and situate them in overarching social contexts.

5.1.4 Digital Ethnography

The ubiquity of digital media in our digital society has opened up new opportunities for ethnographic research. A vast number of interactions – such as oral discussions or the mediatized exchange of pictures and written messages – occur in online public spaces, which provide researchers with access to social groups across online and offline spaces.

The study of situated activity in digital spaces sets slightly different priorities and is also referred to in a variety of terms such as "**digital ethnography**" (Murthy, 2008), "virtual ethnography" (Hine, 2000), "network ethnography" (Howard, 2002), "netnography" (Kozinets, 2002, 2009), or "discourse-centred online ethnography" (DCOE) (Androutsopoulos, 2008).

Digital ethnography investigates the production of narratives through various text formats and virtual places such as blogs, webpages, or social networking sites in order to provide an understanding of the different meanings based on diverse language practices.

The first generation of digital ethnographies was primarily carried out on the screen and focused on observations of virtual communities in environments like newsgroups, forums, or chats. The Internet was seen as an additional place of human interaction, separate from offline realities. Nowadays, ethnographers analyze online settings in an effort to understand how digital media are embedded in people's realities.

The research carried out in the context of the project "Why We Post" shows impressively that "the Internet is not a monolithic or placeless 'cyberspace'; rather, it is numerous new technologies, used by diverse people, in diverse real-world locations" (Miller & Slater, 2000, p. 1). The ethnographer Daniel Miller and his research group spent several months in communities worldwide to examine the global impact of social media. The researchers investigated topics like education, gender, politics, or offline and online relationships. Their findings show that the way people use social media is a result of local factors.

One example shows how different people perceive social media in relation to education. In some fieldsites, predominantly well-resourced ones, social media is regarded as a distraction from formal education; parents, therefore, try to prevent children from using it. In places where access to formal schooling is limited, educational content on social media is regarded as an essential source of information and practical knowledge (UCL, n.d.).

To sum up, what people do online is, on the one hand, strongly influenced by social systems or tendencies within these systems. On the other hand, offline social realities are also affected by people's interactions in online environments. Digital ethnographies across online and offline spaces demonstrate the potential of ethnographic frameworks to broaden our understanding of the complexities of our contemporary world.

In classic ethnography, the *field* is understood as a clearly delineated area – a geographical space like a village, or a social group like an editorial office. The concept of the field in digital ethnography takes into account the nature of the Internet and its geographical detachment, and follows two paradigms.

The first paradigm draws on the idea that online environments are populated by communities. Some of these are purely virtual, so-called "virtual communities" (Rheingold 2000), others have a counterpart in real life, referred to as "communities online" (van Dijk, 2012). Members of those communities go online to do more or less what others do in the physical world. The apparent difference is that they interact, often exclusively, via text, pictures, or other semiotic resources on screens, thereby potentially crossing sociological, geographical, and political boundaries in order to pursue mutual interests, ideas, or goals. Within this paradigm, the ethnographer's main task is to detect these communities, and observe and participate in their social practices in order to understand them from the inside.

The second paradigm draws on the approach of multi-sited ethnography (Marcus, 1995), shorthand for all ways of doing ethnographic fieldwork in more than one site. Multi-sited ethnography is one response to the question of how to deal with global mobility and communication flows. George Marcus (1995, p. 96) defines it as "a mode of ethnographic research self-consciously embedded in the world system" that "moves out from the single sites and local situation of conventional ethnographic research design to examine the circulation of cultural meanings, objects, and identities in diffuse time-space."

Marcus proposes six strategies for linking fields that are either geographically different or, as is often the case, quite socially distant from one another.

- Follow the People: This strategy refers to the orientation of ethnographic research along the developments and movements of specific individuals and groups; for example, in the course of migration.
- Follow the Thing: This strategy refers to the tracing of circulation processes of things such as goods, gifts, financial flows, or art.
- Follow the Metaphor: If the object of investigation manifests itself within discourses and ways of thinking, then the circulation of signs, symbols, and metaphors plays a central role and can guide the constitution of a multiple field.
- Follow the Plot or Story: Here, stories or narratives are taken as a starting point to develop a multi-situated ethnographic research project.
- Follow the Life or Biography: Here, a person's life story is used to relate different locations and ethnographic fields to each other.
- Follow the Conflict: Another way of linking fields is to follow the different parties in conflicts.

Tracing these elements in a digital society necessarily involves online environments, as they tend to be places where social actors interact with others and spend a significant part of their everyday lives. The field is therefore conceptualized as a network of inter-related practices, like using hashtags or sharing memes, that occur across online and offline spaces. It emerges throughout fieldwork, through the ethnographer's movements across spaces. The field constantly evolves during fieldwork, as it is constructed by the actions and language use of the people under study, and by the ethnographer's decisions regarding the connections and things they follow.

Assuming that practices constitute the field implies that there is no need to define audiences or media products before conducting an ethnographic study. The categoriza-tions of relevant agents, events, and processes in public communication derive from the fieldwork itself. From this point of view, we do not look at media as objects, texts, or production processes; instead, we focus on what people are doing in relation to media. Such an approach allows us to investigate the interplay between technological infrastruc-tures with the situated activity of particular agents and the social structures of contexts.

5.1.5 Combining Online and Offline Methods in Digital Ethnography

The continuous shift between offline and online spaces that characterizes multi-sited digital ethnography leads to the necessity to adapt traditional ethnographic techniques to digital environments.

Following Marcus' (1995) exhortation to *Follow the Thing*, Hine (2011) introduced the concept of "mobile ethnography" as a methodological approach to multi-sited digital ethnography. Hine argues that in order to observe and compare the different meanings that different online audiences attach to, for example, a TV program, one needs to follow its circulation across different online platforms. At the same time, Hine points out the importance of triangulating the outputs of digital tools – such as search engines – with the insights from ethnographic methods – such as interviews or observations – which may be conducted online or in real-world settings. The triangulation of methods is con-sidered crucial in order to identify which key participants to observe and which topics to investigate (Hine, 2015).

The literature in this field distinguishes between digital and virtual methods. Digital methods take into account the nature and affordances of digital environments which structure the flows of communication and interactions online – for example, technical affordances of search engines and social media platforms, or functions such as Twitter's hashtags and retweets. Virtual methods consist of the adaptation of offline methods, such as interviews and observations, to online environments. Deciding whether or not to combine on-site and digital ethnography and different methods depends on the specific objectives of a research project.

ACTIVITY

Imagine working in the communications department of a company that sells sustainable products. The company wants to use social media channels to reach more young people committed to environmental protection. You want to find out as much as possible about this target group so that you can optimally design your communication strategy. Think about how an ethnographic framework could help you do this and describe your thoughts in a short e-mail to your manager, who has no idea about ethnography.

5.2 Expanding Ethnography

When ethnography constitutes the sole framework for research, it tends to be limited to case studies and micro perspectives (e.g., Tavory & Timmermans, 2009). This weakens the results' relevance for theory building. Moreover, it only rudimentarily clarifies the roles of researchers when analyzing and solving socially relevant real-world problems. Finally, linguistic ethnography lacks the tools to systematically explain the interplay of routine and emergence in the practices studied. The last point is crucial if change is to be examined – for example, how and why workplace routines are broken up and overthrown in favor of new, emerging solutions. Media linguistic research into situated practices thus benefits from combining ethnography with other research frameworks.

Depending on how the approaches are used individually or combined with each other, research foregrounds material, mental, and/or social aspects of language use. Material aspects include written or spoken language as optical or acoustic phenomena; mental aspects include individuals' practices and strategies of communication; and social aspects include change in teams, organizations, communities, and society at large, as intended or effectuated by language use.

5.2.1 Theory Building in the Framework of Grounded Theory (GT)

Research in a largely unexplored field such as newswriting takes time and needs minds that are open to unexpected findings. An appropriate research framework should, on the one hand, enable the researcher to investigate single cases in depth and in detail. On the other hand, comparisons between carefully selected cases should allow for well-reflected, limited generalizations. Such a research framework is grounded theory (GT), as developed by Glaser and Strauss (1967).

In GT, data, for example about writing strategies and practices in the field of journalism or corporate communications, are sampled and analyzed case by case. Each case analysis leads to generalizations, which are considered theoretical assumptions. To test them, a further case, as different as possible from the previous case(s), is identified and analyzed. The new results are compared with those from preceding research cycles. The process only stops when it reaches *theoretical saturation*: the point where including new data from further cases no longer alters the theory. The research process is documented explicitly to stimulate reflection and discussion. **Grounded theory**, thus, is a research framework applied to answer a question by developing a theory that is grounded in empirical data.

If ethnography is combined with the research framework of GT, findings from case studies can be generalized in a systematic way. This helps researchers build medium-range theories about "what works for whom in what conditions" (Pawson & Tilley, 1997), for example theories of writing practices in domains of public communication. Findings can then show that experienced professionals, much more than their less-experienced colleagues, master practices of adaptive, flexible planning that help them deal with the unexpected and either avoid or more easily overcome writer's block (see, e.g., Perrin, 2016a).

5.2.2 Learning from Experts in the Framework of Transdisciplinary Research (TD)

When it comes to understanding and improving real-world issues, transdisciplinary research (TD) is the research framework to include in a project. TD operates through research "on, for and with" practitioners (Cameron et al., 1992, p. 22). Academics from various disciplines collaborate with practitioners to sustainably solve a practical problem.

In TD projects, all the stakeholders first have to agree on a shared understanding of the key concepts related to the problem under investigation. Based on this common ground, TD allows for iterative learning in project cycles of reflection and action, of diagnosis and intervention. Cycle by cycle, the solution emerges and results in an increase of expert knowledge about critical situations that can lead to failure in the practices investigated – and knowledge about how these pitfalls can be avoided by applying what TD calls good practices. TD, thus, is the most appropriate research framework to systematically bridge the gap between theory and practice (Perrin & Kramsch, 2018).

If ethnography is combined with the research framework of TD, research-based solutions to practical problems can be built on strong theoretical grounds. TD helps researchers develop prototypes of critical situations and good practices in, say, text production and make them available to practitioners. This is often done by means of empirically based instructions or coaching on working techniques that help practitioners develop their awareness of critical situations and their repertoires of good practices. Based on collections of authentic cases, participants reflect, for example, on their writer's block and how they can avoid or overcome it (Section 6.1).

5.2.3 Contextualizing Activity in the Framework of Realist Social Theory (RST)

What people do influences the world, and in return, the world influences what people do. For example, an outstanding, both striking and enigmatic notion like #metoo in newspaper headlines across the globe may alter the way we think and communicate about careers in the entertainment business. Conversely, using hashtags has become an undisputable communicational norm for those who want to reach out in Twitter communities. This interplay of agency (what people do) and social structures (what is the case) through practices is what most integrative social theories explain.

More than any other integrative theory, Realist Social Theory (RST) allows for a clear distinction between structures with various degrees of durability (e.g., Sealey & Carter, 2004). For example, structural long-term imbalances between genders and global regions can hardly be changed by individuals' situated activity. In contrast, on a lower level, news organizations have the power to purposefully recruit more women for management positions and cover news topics from the global South more carefully, so social structures enable and constrain human agency in different ways on different levels. With this in mind, it is easier for researchers to anticipate how to foster change when addressing practical problems.

If ethnography is combined with RST, researchers can access a social structure in the field and contribute to its further development through the situated activity of language use. For example, practices of journalistic writing – what journalists actually do when they write – shed a light on what is the case in these newsrooms, in the domains of journalism and media as well as in the society at large with which the journalists interact. This is how it could be shown that, in crises that overburden media management and policy-makers, fundamentally new solutions of media use tend to emerge bottom-up, at experienced journalists' collaborative workplaces, far from frozen hierarchies (Perrin, 2011b).

5.2.4 Explaining Change in the Framework of Dynamic Systems Theory (DST)

Dynamic Systems Theory (DST) is a research framework focusing on principles of change. Systems such as languages or writing processes are dynamic; they change continually as their elements and contexts interact. In the context of newswriting, if writers invent new words and these words become part of the general vocabulary over time, language is changed through language use – with impacts upon further language use in "the dynamics of writing" (Larsen-Freeman & Cameron, 2008, p. 186). This change can be linear and completely predictable, but also nonlinear and unexpected, for example when writers suddenly get stuck after a long phase of fluent, linear writing (Section 6.1).

Doing DST enables researchers to understand the structures of systems such as languages or writing processes at given points in time. To this aim, DST tracks the dynamics, the often nonlinear change of such systems in their – also – dynamic context. From a practical point of view, DST research aims at finding the control parameters that enable or constrain nonlinear change: What exactly can make social media posts go viral after a longer period of linear spread in a community? By taking into account the complex interplay of context factors, change in dynamic systems can be modeled and explained in general, albeit not predicted in detail.

If ethnography is combined with theories of dynamic systems, researchers can model which conditions in the environment of situated action foster emergent solutions (e.g., Agar, 2004). Such theories and models make it easier to understand the complex, difficult-to-predict processes of text production, such as the upheavals between writing phases (Fürer, 2017). Findings can show how creativity and routine interact in text production and under which conditions things are more likely to move out of flow because a "strong attractor" (Larsen-Freeman & Cameron, 2008, p. 51) magnetizes all attention and disturbs the dynamic balance of the writing flow.

ACTIVITY

Why is ethnography not enough? Go back to the activity at the end of Section 5.1, and rewrite the e-mail to your boss. Explain to her or him why it makes sense to combine ethnography with at least one additional framework from Section 5.2. In doing so, choose your favorite from the list of these frameworks: grounded theory (5.2.1), transdisciplinary research (5.2.2), Realist Social Theory (5.2.3), and Dynamic Systems Theory (5.2.4).

Key Terms

approach, digital ethnography, Dynamic Systems Theory (DST), ethnography, grounded theory, linguistic ethnography, method, methodology, Realist Social Theory (RST), research framework, rich point, situated activity

Chapter Summary

- The combination of linguistic and ethnographic frameworks allows us to link the situated activity of public digital communication to social structures – specific affordances of organizations and/or technological developments. The conception of the fieldsite in multi-sited ethnography, for example, enables us to analyze digital communication in the context of global communication flows. Combining ethnography with other research frameworks allows us to grasp phenomena of change intended or effectuated by language use.

- The combination of ethnography with other research frameworks allows us to expand ethnographic fieldwork while foregrounding material, mental, and/or social aspects of language use.

- Through the combination of ethnography with the research framework of grounded theory (GT), findings from case studies can be generalized in a systematic way. Combining ethnography with the research framework of transdisciplinary research (TD) enables scholars to ground research-based solutions to practical problems on theoretical grounds.

- The combination of ethnography with Realist Social Theory (RST) allows researchers to access social structures in the field. Combining ethnography with theories of dynamic systems (DST) helps modeling the relation between environmental conditions of situated activity and emergent solutions.

Further Reading

Frameworks

The annual international conference on Applied Linguistics and Professional Practice (ALAPP) and the *Journal of Applied Linguistics and Professional Practice* showcase research from scholars with different disciplinary backgrounds, especially language and communication research, and professional specialities (e.g. business, organization studies, education, banking, health care, therapy, journalism, law, social care and welfare, immigration and border control, police work, translation and interpreting). https://journal .equinoxpub.com/JALPP/ALAPPConference

Ethnographic fieldwork: A beginner's guide (Blommaert & Jie, 2020) explains the complexities of ethnographic fieldwork in an easily accessible way. The second edition of this best-selling book includes a new postscript on exploring the *online–offline nexus.*

Ethnography and virtual worlds: A handbook of method (Boellstorff et al. 2012) guides the readers through ethnographic research in virtual environments. The handbook explains every step, from research design to data collection, data analysis, and writing up and publishing research results.

The book *Linguistic ethnography: Collecting, analysing and presenting data* (Copland & Creese, 2015) offers an introduction to the field, with a focus on practical issues of carrying out a research project.

Expanding Ethnography

The article "On, for, and with practitioners: A transdisciplinary approach to text production in real-life settings," by Daniel Perrin (2018a), discusses case studies of expanding ethnography to understand writing in domains such as mass media and financial communication.

6 | Doing Media Linguistic Analysis

PREVIEW

When the physician John Snow studied the cholera outbreak in London in 1854, he did exactly what data journalists do today: He collected, combined, and interpreted data, and, then, he visualized the findings in his famous map. Snow's research is an early example of a mixed methods approach, which we explain in this chapter. We show how quantitative and qualitative methods can be combined and outline their strengths and limitations.

The chapter starts by introducing four qualitative approaches of linguistic analysis: version analysis, progression analysis, variation analysis, and metadiscourse analysis. Each approach draws on established research methods from social sciences, such as observation, interview, and discourse analysis. Together, the four approaches enable researchers to understand language use in digital media environments from multiple angles.

We then provide examples of visual analysis by discussing quantitative and qualitative approaches to studying images and other visuals: visual content analysis, semiotics, and iconography/iconology. For multimodal analysis, we suggest a three-stage method, building on the theoretical concepts presented in Chapter 3. The first stage of the multimodal analysis is to make an initial description of the modes and text elements present in the text. In the second stage, we analyze the ways in which these text elements carry different kinds of meaning potentials. Finally, we discuss how the multimodal text relates to a certain text genre and to the social context of which it is a part.

For all the systematic nature of the methods presented here, there is one thing above all to keep in mind: Don't forget to use your intuition, experience, and observation skills to understand what is really interesting to explore.

By the end of this chapter, you should be able to

- explain advantages of multi-method over single-method approaches in research on language use in everyday and professional environments
- conduct a visual analysis using at least one of the methods described
- analyze a multimodal text according to acknowledged procedures and relevant terminology
- assess the strengths and limitations of quantitative and qualitative research
- summarize the benefits of combining quantitative and qualitative research.

6.1 Linguistic Analysis

How can we investigate what really happens when professionals process their communicational offers in digital environments – which is, what actually happens when they write, speak, read, and listen with the help of their digital tools? In this section, we outline the four basically different, yet complementary methodological perspectives media linguists have developed and applied to understand their object of study.

The methods provide empirical evidence of material, cognitive, social, and socio-cognitive aspects of communication in digital environments. They do so by focusing on textual aspects of semiotic products (material focus, Section 6.1.1), individuals' communication processes and practices in digital environments (mental focus, Section 6.1.2), the variation of communication practices within and across teams, organizations, and communities (social focus, Section 6.1.3), and the metadiscourse by which collectives deliberate their communication products, processes, and practices (socio-cognitive focus, Section 6.1.4).

6.1.1 The Material Focus: Tracking Intertextual Chains with Version Analysis

First and foremost, media linguistic research investigates semiotic products in context. From this material perspective, it is interested in the structure of meaningful acoustic and visual patterns, such as audio and video messages. Across and beyond single products, it emphasizes the intertextual nature of digital communication: New media products can easily be created by copy-pasting a preexisting one before passing it on to the target audience. The target audience then does the same. This process is iterated over and over again, which results in intertextual chains (Perrin, 2013, p. 28), where a message runs through a series of communication workplaces over time (Figure 6.1).

At each communication workplace the resulting new product differs from its digital sources in some parts, while the rest remains the same. In the example visualized in

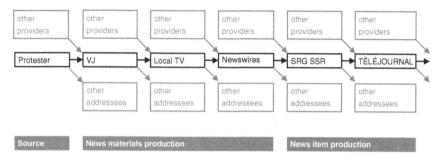

Figure 6.1 The intertextual chain from comments of protesters to quotes in a TV news item. Adapted from "Medialinguistic approaches: Exploring the case of newswriting," by D. Perrin, in C. Cotter and D. Perrin (eds.), *The Routledge handbook of language and media* (p. 11), 2018b, Abingdon: Routledge. © 2018 Daniel Perrin. Adapted with permission.

Figure 6.1, a protester's comment in an interview with a local video journalist (VJ) is broadcasted by a local TV station, from where it is taken up by a global news agency. Their newsfeed reaches a national TV station in a different region of the world (SRG SSR, the Swiss national broadcasting company) and is reframed in news items by various news programs (such as *Téléjournal*, for the French-speaking region of Switzerland).

Long story short, a quote can run through an intertextual chain by being embedded in other linguistic environments station after station. This is what happened to the quote of a politician who strongly advised his colleagues to be prudent in his lengthy utterance. After running through several workplaces in the intertextual chain, however, words quoted from this statement seemed to call for immediate and rigorous action (Perrin, 2015a, p. 37). Similarly, pictures on Instagram or quotes on Twitter are recycled (Haapanen & Perrin, 2020) over and over again, for example by adding visual or linguistic comments such as manually drafted arrows pointing to a detail, smileys, as well as audio clips or writing.

In media linguistics, such material changes to the semiotic products in intertextual chains are captured with **version analyses**. By version analysis, we understand the method of collecting and analyzing data in order to reconstruct the changes that communicational offers undergo in intertextual chains.

For example, a Twitter message is received, slightly altered, and posted again, as a new version from the original utterance – and meaning something different from its original version. The methods and procedures applied in version analysis originate in comparative text analysis. Standard version analyses trace linguistic products in social discourse and elaborate on the changes in text features from version to version, be it at one single production site or across a series of sites. In the framework of genetic criticism for example, close-to-final versions of literary writing are compared and playwriting is tracked from the initial draft to the communicators' notes on first performances to reveal and critically discuss how authors had worked on their emerging piece (Grésillon & Mervant-Roux, 2010).

The very minimal variant of version analysis limits the empirical access to one single version but refers to other versions that were not explicitly analyzed (e.g., Ekström, 2001). This variant of version analysis is widespread in critical discourse analyses (Van Dijk, 2001); see also critiques by Stubbs (1997) or Widdowson (2000), where media products are analyzed to reveal social influence such as political bias by state- or economy-dependent media organizations or individual influencers. Methodological problems of such one-version analysis include assumptions regarding manipulations of source texts and that the ideologies guiding these manipulative practices cannot be empirically grounded in the data of one version of a communicational offer only.

However, when comparing many cases with each other, such analyses can provide some reasons to assume that the use of a certain semiotic feature in the final media product, such as passive voice, reverberates a certain attitude of the stakeholders of the production process, such as an interest in blurring or hiding certain agents in the world the product is about. An example: When police officers kill a protester, media products composed by people scrutinizing such behavior tend to be formulated in active voice: "Police killed protester." In contrast, media supporting politics that fosters harsh police interventions will tend to use the passive voice and words with different connotations when rewriting the same source text from the newswires: "Potential terrorist eliminated after attacking police."

Such general – but not yet empirically supported – assumptions call for a shift of focus from the material surface of a semiotic product to the mental motivation driving its production process. Comparing various versions of texts is sufficient to gain empirical evidence of material text changes. However, it provides no data on the why of material activity. In order to develop such knowledge, additional media linguistic approaches are required. They focus, for example, on identifying practices (Section 6.1.2); on whether the practices are typical of certain media-producing institutions (Section 6.1.3); or on how the practices and related norms are negotiated in organizations and beyond (Section 6.1.4).

6.1.2 The Mental Focus: Identifying Practices with Progression Analysis

From a cognitive perspective, media linguistic research emphasizes individuals' decisions in communication processes. What exactly do individual communicators do when they process their semiotic products? An advanced approach in this methodological tradition is **progression analysis** (e.g., Perrin, 2016b). Using progression analysis as an example, we explain how **multi-method approaches** can cover cognitive aspects of written and multimodal communication in material and social contexts. By doing so, we focus on decision-making in digital environments. Our goal is to reconstruct individual, organizational, and social structures, such as mindsets, norms, and professional cultures, based on the practices observed in journalism and PR (see the practice concept in Section 4.3.1).

By multi-method approach, we understand a research approach in which two or more methods (or single-method approaches) complement each other for a multi-perspective view, ideally a close-to-full picture on the object of research.

By progression analysis, we understand the multi-method approach of collecting and analyzing data in natural contexts in order to reconstruct text production processes as a cognitively reflected activity in context.

Progression analysis combines ethnographic observation, interviews, computer logging, and cue-based retrospective verbalizations to gather linguistic and contextual data. The approach was developed to investigate newswriting in journalism and PR and later transferred to other application fields of writing research, such as children's writing processes and translation (for an overview, see Perrin, 2019). With progression analysis, data are gathered using complementary methods on three levels of digital communication: (a) context, (b) activity, and (c) reflection.

- *Context level*: Before writing begins, progression analysis determines, through ethnographic methods and research tools such as narrative interviews and participative observations, what the writing situation is. Important factors include the writing task, the writers' professional socialization and experience, and economic, institutional, and technological influences on the workplaces and workflows. For example, data on the self-perception of professional communicators can be obtained in semi-standardized and narrative interviews about their professional experience and their work situation. In addition, participatory and video observations can be made about the various kinds of collaboration at the workplace.
- *Activity level*: During writing, progression analysis records every keystroke and writing movement in the emerging text (Figure 6.2) with keylogging and screenshot recording programs. These programs run in the background behind the media editors that the writers usually use, for instance behind the user interfaces of news editing systems. The recording can follow the media production process over several workstations and does not influence the performance of the editing system. From a technical point of view, it does not influence the media producers' performance either, since it operates automatically and without changing the user interfaces of the editing software. Nevertheless, knowing about the recording alters people's behavior,

the happy end was [1][~~inevitable~~][1] |[2]{near}[2]

Figure 6.2 Visualization of recorded writing movements in a text that emerges on screen: In a first revision, the author deletes "inevitable"; second, she inserts "near" instead.

with decreasing effect over time. This is why, in long-term research projects, the first four weeks of data are often considered biased and excluded from analyses.

- *Reflection level*: After the media production is over, progression analysis records what the media communicators say about their activities. Preferably immediately after completing the production process, the communicators view on the screen how their communicational offers came into being. Cued by what they see – such as sources they browsed, changes they made to the emerging media item, or chats they had with peers – they continuously comment on what they did when editing their media piece and why they did it. An audio recording is made of these cue-based retrospective verbal protocols (RVPs). This level of progression analysis opens a window onto the mind of the communicators. The RVP is transcribed and then encoded as the communicator's verbalization of aspects of his or her conscious media production practices.

In sum, progression analysis allows researchers to consider all of the electronic resources accessed during a media production process; to trace the development of the emerging media product; and, finally, to reconstruct collaboration at workplaces from different perspectives. The main focus of progression analysis, however, is the individual's cognitive and manifest processes of media production. Social structures such as organizational routines and editorial policies are reconstructed mainly through the perspectives of the individual agents involved, the individuals under investigation. If entire organizations are to be investigated with respect to how they produce their communicational offers as a social activity, then progression analysis can be extended by another two methods: **variation analysis** (Section 6.1.3) and metadiscourse analysis (Section 6.1.4).

6.1.3 The Social Focus: Revealing Audience Design with Variation Analysis

From a social perspective, media linguistic research focuses on how communities of practice such as social media influencers and social groups such as PR teams customize their communicational offers for their target audiences. Which linguistic means, for example, which gradient of normativity and formality, does an organization choose for which addressees? Such social language use is captured with variation analyses.

By variation analysis, we understand the method of collecting and analyzing semiotic data to reconstruct the special features of the language of a certain discourse community in contrast to other communities.

Using classical methods of discourse analysis, variation analyses investigate the type and frequency of typical features of certain language users' productions in certain communication situations such as writing for a specific audience. What variation analysis discerns is the differences between the language used in one situation type and that of the same users in other situations – or from the language and practices of other users in similar situations. In the *Idée Suisse Project* (Perrin, 2013, p. 2), for example, variation

TABLE 6.1 COMPARISON OF GENRE AND STYLE OF THE THREE SWISS NEWS PROGRAMS IN GERMAN AND FRENCH

	Téléjournal	Tagesschau	10vor10
Start	1953	1953	1990
Language	French	German	German
Genres	news genres, 15 sec – 3 min	news genres, 15 sec – 3 min	• news genres, 12 sec – 2 min • feature story, <7 min
Style	information	Information	Infotainment

analyses revealed how language properties of the newscast *Tagesschau* and the news-magazine *10vor10*, competing in the same German television program of the Swiss public broadcaster, differ according to their program profiles (Table 6.1).

By systematic comparison, variation analysis is able to show the special features of the language used by specific groups of language users. It is the right method to identify, for example, differences of language use between a company's PR agents and its broader community on social media. However, what the method gains in width, it loses in depth. Why a community prefers to formulate its texts in a certain way and not another cannot be captured by variation analysis, which, similar to version analysis, neglects access to cognitive aspects of writing. However, it is possible to regain some of that depth using a procedure that examines not only the text products, but also the institutionalized discourses connected with them – the comments of the community about its joint efforts (Section 6.1.4).

6.1.4 The Socio-Cognitive Focus: Investigating Language Policying with Metadiscourse Analysis

From a socio-cognitive perspective, media linguistic research focuses on text producers' collaboration and metadiscourse, such as correspondence between PR agents, quality control discourse at editorial conferences, and negotiations between journalists, photographers, and text designers. What do the various stakeholders think about their communicational offers? How do they evaluate their activity in relation to policies and standards developed by their companies and professional communities – and how do they alter those policies through their practices? Such socio-cognitive aspects of language use are captured by metadiscourse analyses.

By *metadiscourse analysis*, we understand the method of collecting and analyzing data from meta-discourses, which means analyzing the language of agents who communicate *about* communicational offers such as media items, for example in editorial conferences in a newsroom. By doing so, metadiscourse analysis reconstructs the socially and individually anchored (language) awareness in a discourse community – put simply, it finds out how aware people are of what they do with language.

Metadiscourse analyses investigate spoken and written communication about language and language use. This includes metaphors used when talking about writing (e.g., Gravengaard, 2012; Levin & Wagner, 2006), explicit planning or criticism of communication measures (for initial and groundbreaking work, see, e.g., Peterson, 2001), the clarification of misunderstandings and conversational repair (similarly, Häusermann, 2007), and follow-up communication by audiences (Klemm, 2000). In all these cases, the participants' utterances show how their own or others' communicational efforts and offers have been perceived, received, understood, and evaluated. The analysis demonstrates how rules of language use are explicitly negotiated and applied in a community.

EXAMPLE

Metadiscourse analyses in Swiss public broadcasters' newsrooms (Figure 6.3) could show that video editors challenge the journalists' ethics and esthetics by acting as pseudo-representatives of a critical audience. It is during such negotiations and the follow-up discourse in informal cafeteria chats and formal editorial conferences that ideas for new media formats emerge, are challenged in retrospect, and abandoned or confirmed, and finally established through reiteration. Other examples include social media communities negotiating netiquette issues and, by doing so, developing new standards of language use for this specific community in specific situations. By combining such analyses, media linguistics can show how patterns of language use emerge, are established, altered, and overcome.

Figure 6.3 Video editor and journalist engaging in metadiscourse on designing a news piece.

Thus, the focus of metadiscourse analysis scales up from negotiations about emerging texts at writers' workplaces, to organizational quality control discourse and related discussions in audiences and society at large. Integrating metadiscourse analyses extends the reach of media linguistic research from a single communicator's micro activity to societal macro structures. However, for empirical evidence of writers' actual behavior, metadiscourse analysis must be combined with progression analyses (Section 6.1.2) or, in more coarse-grained studies, at least with version analyses (Section 6.1.1).

ACTIVITY

Collaborate in a team of four classmates. Take the case of a recent controversial political debate on political measures to reduce carbon dioxide emissions. Aim at showing, based on empirical data, that a certain media company has shifted their stance toward such measures, as documented in their editorials, in the past twelve months due to influential pressure groups in social media. In your team, member one explains how you would generate meaningful data using version analysis; member two with progression analysis; member three with variation analysis; and member four with metadiscourse analysis. Together again, share your insights and compare what can be found out with each of the approaches – and what must remain in the dark. Finally, outline a method design in which you combine the four approaches for a multiperspective view on your object of study.

6.2 Visual Analysis

While Section 6.1 focuses on the analysis of how we use language, we will now turn to the analysis of what we see. "You only see what you know," the German poet Johann Wolfgang von Goethe once wrote. The famous quote points to the difference between looking at an image and understanding what it means. If we want to know more about the meaning of an image, we have to analyze it. Scholars from various disciplines such as art history, communication and media studies, linguistics, or semiotics have developed different frameworks and methods for analyzing visuals. Before examining this methodological field, we will first take a closer look at what we understand by visual communication and visuals.

Visual communication deals with all forms and materials that can be seen by the naked eye. It also deals with the production and reception of visuals as well as the relationship between the visual content and other modes such as language, sound, or gestures. The term *visual*, used as a noun, is very broad, and includes still and moving images; graphic design and product design; visualizations and animations; the built environment and other visual phenomena made by humans with an intention to communicate something to someone. Of course, it is not possible to cover all the different approaches and methods that exist for the wide range of visuals in just one chapter. We therefore decided to focus on still images (single static images), as they provide an easy entry point for ana-lyzing visual information. Images can be investigated from different perspectives. We can look at the production process of an image; the image itself as a product; the reception of images; or a combination of all of these. Again, we have to limit ourselves due to reasons of space and focus on images and imagery as cultural products and discursive communi-cation practices, but without losing sight of production and reception.

In the following sections, we present methods that are widely employed in research on visual communication. Starting with the quantitative approach and content analysis (Section 6.2.1), we then explain qualitative semiotic approaches (Section 6.2.2) and con-clude with the qualitative method of iconology (Section 6.2.3).

6.2.1 Visual Content Analysis

Content analysis is a method for analyzing large amounts of media and communica-tion content. It is a *quantitative approach* that aims at measuring data in a systematic way (Section 6.4). Originally developed to analyze verbal texts, content analysis is now widely used in communication and media studies for the analysis of texts, images, vid-eos, tweets, or posts on other social media. A much-cited definition in the context of visual communication is the following:

> *Quantitative content analysis is the systematic and replicable examination of symbols of communication, which have been assigned numeric values according to valid mea-surement rules, and the analysis of relationships involving those values using statistical methods, to describe the communication, draw inferences about its meaning, or infer from the communication to its context, both of production and consumption.*
>
> (Riffe, Lacy & Fico, 2014, p. 19)

Quantitative content analysis is a reliable method when counting frequencies; for instance, the frequency of a certain category of images used in media coverage over a certain time period and across national boundaries. It can show which topics or peo-ple are given high priority in the media and which are not, or which visual strategies are used to present them. The aim of a quantitative description is to classify key char-acteristics; discover similarities and outliers; reveal patterns in order to map trends; and make generalizable predictions about the communication of political, cultural, or social issues. Typical research questions are those concerning the salience and/or frequency of a certain topic – e.g., war; climate change; gender; politicians or other public figures – or whether there is a change in media coverage, or how a topic is framed negatively or positively.

There are a number of books that contain clear guidance on how to conduct a con-tent analysis in general (Hansen & Machin, 2019, p. 88–115; Krippendorff, 2013; Neuen-dorf, 2002) and with a focus on images (Parry, 2020; Rose, 2016, pp. 85–105). Table 6.2

illustrates what a visual content analysis can look like. A quantitative content analysis includes the following key stages:

(1) *Formulate a research question and one or more hypotheses related to your research question.* Hypotheses are specific statements of predictions for a research problem or an observation that is to be tested in a study. Such hypotheses can be derived theoretically by reviewing relevant literature in advance. They can also be derived from personal observations or from public debate.

(2) *Select media content and sample.* In a first step, you select the media or communication content that you intend to analyze, the so-called *population*. "The population is the set of units being studied, the set of units to which the researcher wishes to generalize" (Neuendorf, 2002, p. 74). To achieve this, you have to make decisions about what to include: which type of media or communication (social media platforms, websites, newspapers, annual reports, corporate videos, etc.), what time frame, and which countries or regions (international, national, or local). You also have to decide on whether to examine all of the material collected or to draw a sample. If the data set is small, there is no need to draw a sample from it. But often, the population is quite large, and, therefore, a sample has to be drawn. A *sample* is a representative smaller set of data selected from the population. This is what forms the basis of the study. There are various sampling strategies (Rose, 2016, pp. 90–91). One is *systematic random sampling*: taking every nth article or image in the chosen time period. *Stratified random sampling* is another technique, where the population is divided into smaller subgroups, called strata. The researcher, then, randomly pulls the final sample proportionally from the strata. An example for a stratified random sampling strategy is a constructed week. "Constructing one week from a population of one month would involve selecting one Sunday from all four Sundays that month, one Monday from all four Mondays, etc., until each day of the week is represented in the final sample" (Luke, Caburnay & Cohen, 2011, p. 78). This sampling technique accounts for the cyclic nature of media content; e.g., a weekly news pattern.

(3) *Define coding units and construct a codebook.* Having selected a sample, *coding units* have to be defined prior to coding. Such a coding unit could be the photo, or the photo with the caption, or the whole article in which the photo is presented. In order to achieve reliable results, researchers have to follow a fixed set of rules and procedures. A *codebook*, therefore, has to be developed to facilitate coding. The codebook, which is the core of a content analysis, consists of a set of predefined categories or variables[1] – the dimensions you want to measure. Each variable can have a number

---

[1] The terminology of category, variables, and values varies in academic literature.

of values; that is, "the various options you choose from within the variable category" (Parry, 2020, p. 357), e.g., how a photo is taken from different camera angles. In addition, the codebook defines clear guidelines for the coding practice.

Finding the relevant coding categories can be painstaking work. Mostly, it is driven by a process of deduction, which means, categories are derived theoretically based on existing theories. Coding categories can also be developed inductively, through an iterative process of analyzing the material several times. Often, deductive and inductive methods are combined. Coding categories used in media and communication research are the following (Hansen & Machin, 2019, pp. 98–107):

> *Formal categories, which capture the manifest content. Examples of manifest content are: the type of medium (which newspaper, magazine, etc.); publishing date (day, month, year); size of the image; format; its position on a newspaper page or website.*

> *Categories concerning the content; that is, what is depicted in the image. Examples here are themes and topics; actors and their attributes (who is portrayed, what can we say about their mimic or gesture); value dimensions (positivity / negativity) and/or ideological or political stance; and frames. These categories are less manifest in the images themselves, and researchers, therefore, often include text (captions, titles) or contextual elements as additional coding units.*

It is crucial that the set of categories is appropriate to test the hypotheses of your study and answer the research question. This is to ensure that your research can be considered valid; that is, that your study actually measures exactly what it claims to measure. *Internal validity* refers to the design of the study, that is, how strong and trustworthy your research design is and how well it can rule out alternative explanations and influencing factors or variables for its results. *External validity* refers to the generalizability of the results, that is, whether the outcome is applicable to other settings, people, situations, or times. To avoid bias, researchers have to be careful not to use preconceived categories. They have to be familiar with their material to find the appropriate categories. Categories must be collectively *exhaustive* and mutually *exclusive*. *Exhaustive* refers to the ability of the coding set to cover all aspects of the selected material so that no unit needs to be excluded due to missing categories. *Exclusive* means that categories must not overlap; that is, the coding must not fall between two categories. These two requirements ensure that the categories fully and unambiguously cover the material to be analyzed.

(4) *Code the data set.* Coding means assigning tags or labels – the predefined coding categories – to the visual material. Before starting the coding process, a pilot study is necessary to test the coding categories. This helps identify deficiencies, overlaps,

or ambiguities. Ambiguities are particularly challenging in visual analysis because images are polysemic, which means they can have multiple meanings, and, therefore, multiple interpretations – depending on the context and the coder. To overcome these ambiguities, data interpretation must be explicitly fixed in advance, and the defined coding procedure needs to be carried out consistently. It is important (a) to code the same category of units throughout the entire material and (b) to rigorously follow the same rules in order to generate reliable results. Results are reliable when different researchers at different times using the same coding categories can reproduce the same coding results. To achieve this, coders must be trained in advance. If they produce different results – which could be the case for categories related to the content – the categories must be refined. How the coding is then recorded depends on the sample size. It can be done by using spreadsheet software, specific software programs for data analysis, or by programming a database.

Manual coding with pen and paper and conducted by several human coders is one option. But software programs such as SPSS, Excel, or Jasp are extremely helpful, if not indispensable, in analyzing the coding results. In recent years, automatic content analysis based on algorithms, statistical data mining, and machine learning is gaining momentum as a method for analyzing large data sets. Using machine learning for content analysis requires training the algorithm with the data in question, so that the algorithm can thereafter perform the analysis automatically. This, in turn, first requires manual coding of the documents to train the algorithm correctly. While in verbal data a single sentence mostly provides clear semantic information and is based on a logical string of words, visual content is polysemic and consists of many meaningless pixels in a two-dimension plane. This makes automatic visual content analysis a challenge. An automatic image analysis uses computer vision algorithms and deep learning models to gain understanding of the semantic information of the image such as the objects depicted, object size and pose, or scene type. The scientific field that deals with how computers process, analyze, and understand images is called computer vision. Computer vision is aimed at understanding images at a conceptual level and automating tasks that otherwise human coders would do.

(5) *Analyze and visualize the results*. How to analyze the data depends on the research question and hypotheses. A common form of analysis is frequency analysis: counting the codes to say something about the frequency of topic or people depicted in the images; for instance, how often a certain politician is portrayed in the news media during a certain time frame or event, or related to a specific topic. The results can be visualized in a time series graph. Visualizing the data during the process of analysis supports a better understanding of what is in the data, and it helps to communicate the final results in a comprehensive and attractive manner. More complex analysis

can be conducted by looking at the relationships between different coding categories; for instance, whether women in Western advertising are more likely to be portrayed in a sexualized manner and as an object of desire than men are. For such an evaluation, we often need to combine quantitative and qualitative methods to identify the connotative meanings of images. We will get back to this point in Section 6.6.

EXAMPLE

TABLE 6.2 EXAMPLE OF VISUAL CONTENT ANALYSIS

Study	A study about visual trends in daily newspapers in the USA
Research question	Has the use of images changed since the advent of data-driven journalism? Hypothesis: There is an increased use of abstract image types (data visualizations and infographics) in national newspapers.
Content to be analyzed	Media content: five major national daily newspapers (print editions) Time period: from 2010 to today The time period should have a clear rationale; for instance, when newspapers started to establish teams for data journalism. Only journalistic articles with images; no paid content, advertisement, or comic strips. Sample: two (up to five) constructed weeks per year and newspaper Coding units: images including caption and headline of the corresponding article
Variables and values	Newspapers: (1) *USA Today*; (2) *New York Times*; (3) *Washington Post*, and so forth Date: YYYY-MM-DD p. ... / pp. ... Image type: (1) photo; (2) data visualization; (3) infographic Size of image: (1) small; (2) medium; (3) large Placement: (1) top half of the page; (2) lower half of the ... page; (3) full page

---

6.2.2 Semiotics

A qualitative approach to visual communication is semiotics; the study of the signs and how meaning is made. **Qualitative research** aims at a deeper understanding of a subject by examining its underlying principles. Approaching visual communication from this perspective, the French semiotician Roland Barthes asked, "How does meaning get into the image? Where does it end? And if it ends, what is there beyond?" (Barthes, 1964/1977, p. 32). His famous analysis of the Pasta Panzani advertisement (p. 49; Panzani, 2022) has become a classic example of how to deconstruct an image into its layers of meaning. He uses the concept of denotation and connotation (Section 3.2.4) and defines three messages of an image:

(1) The linguistic message comprises all the verbal elements in the image; for instance, caption, labels, taglines. According to Barthes, this linguistic message is twofold: While the denotative meaning of "Panzani" is simply that of a Pasta brand name, the connotative meaning derives from the sound of the word and its association with Italy. Barthes, therefore, suggested that the brand name points to Italianicity for non-Italians. To draw this conclusion, of course, the viewer or consumer must have a certain knowledge of the Italian culture.

(2) The coded iconic message addresses the connotations of an image. Connotations are the implicit meanings that are not directly visible. To reveal their symbolic or even ideological character, we have to decode them. At this level, we consider the underlying values and codes shared in a certain culture or community. Thus, this level of meaning is dependent on the cultures from which the images originate and in which they are viewed. Barthes' pasta advertisement example provides a series of visual connotative meanings which works for non-Italians, such as the freshness of the products (half-open bag with vegetables spilling out which signifies a return from the market); the composition of the image reminiscent of a still life painting (like food paintings in art history); and Italienicity (the colors in the posters), which is redundant with the linguistic message.

(3) The non-coded iconic or literal message is at the level of denotation. It is what remains in the image "when we (mentally) erase the signs of connotation" (Barthes, 1982/1985, p. 31): the objects, events, or people depicted in the image. Describing the denotive meaning, therefore, means identifying what we perceive without interpreting it: the net shopping bag, tomatoes, onions, packaged pasta, etc.

The order of these three messages might appear confusing, since one could assume that a researcher would first start their analysis with the description of the objects depicted in the image (denotation) and then interpret them (connotation). In fact, some scholars do proceed like this (Ledin & Machin, 2018, pp. 47–61; Rodriguez & Dimitrova, 2011). Doing visual analysis is not a linear process and often it is difficult to describe the denotative meanings without adding connotations. Barthes argues that his distinction between the two iconic messages is due to "operational validity" and that "the viewer of the image receives *at one and the same time* the perceptual message and the cultural message" (Barthes, 1964/1977, pp. 36–37).

Drawing on Barthes' concept of denotation and connotation, Ledin and Machin (2018, pp. 47–61) suggest a set of tools for analyzing photos. According to them, carriers of connotation are, for instance, poses and gaze, objects, settings, or color. When it comes to describing the image–text relationship; that is, the relationship between the linguistic and the iconic messages, Barthes coined the terms "anchorage" and "relay" (Barthes, 1964/1977, p. 38). These terms are related to what we call multimodal cohesion, explained in Section 3.3.5.

The *social semiotic approach* to visual communication (Section 3.2.2) draws on some of the basic concepts developed by Barthes. Social semiotics is interested in how people communicate, how they use semiotic resources in the context of specific social practices, in specific communities or cultures, to achieve specific aims. In short, social semiotics is interested in what we can say about and do with semiotic material like words, images, colors, and so on. One method that is based on the social semiotic approach is multimodal analysis, which we explain in Section 6.3.

6.2.3 Iconography and Iconology

Another qualitative method suited for exploring the tacit or intrinsic meaning of images is iconology (Section 3.2.4). This method originates in art history. Iconology aims at critically analyzing visual sources and their contexts (Müller, 2011, p. 285). The goal is to achieve a comprehensive interpretation of the intrinsic or hidden meanings of the visual under examination. One of its famous representatives is the art historian Erwin Panofsky. He wanted art historians to concern themselves more with the hidden meaning of artistic images, and not only with their formal and stylistic qualities. Therefore, he developed the method of iconology as a three-step method: 1. pre-iconographical description; 2. iconographical analysis; and 3. iconological interpretation. To explain these three steps, Panofsky (1955, p. 26) used the example: "When an acquaintance greets me on the street by lifting his hat."

(1) *Pre-iconographical description*: This level is about identifying the world of motifs; namely, the objects and events which are represented in the image by lines, colors, and volumes. With reference to Panofsky's example, this means identifying "this configuration as an object (gentleman), and the change of detail as an event (hat-lifting)" (p. 26). At this level, we simply describe what we see based on our practical experience. The aim is to neutralize our eye and take no account of our cultural knowledge, even if we know who is depicted in which situation. This first level of meaning is of "an elementary and easily understandable nature," and Panofsky calls it "factual meaning" (p. 26). In addition, if we look at how the acquaintance performs the action, we can say something about the "expressional meaning" – whether the acquaintance is in a good or bad humor. The factual and the expressional meaning constitute the pre-iconographical description.

(2) *Iconographical analysis*: **Iconography** is concerned with the meaning of the content of images. In this example, we discern that the lifting of the hat stands for a polite greeting – a greeting gesture that belongs to Western culture. To understand and interpret this gesture correctly, we must be familiar with the world of objects and events depicted in the image and what they represent in a certain culture. It is the world of stories, images, and allegories rather than motifs, Panofsky writes (1955, p. 35), and, therefore, we need to activate our cultural knowledge and search for further contextual information. Panofsky (p. 27) calls this the secondary or conventional meaning.

(3) *Iconological interpretation*: This step addresses the intrinsic or symptomatic meaning. In Panofsky's example, it means interpreting the action of lifting the hat as a "symptom" of the personality of the acquaintance and the time and culture he represents. "This personality is conditioned by his being a man of the twentieth century, by his national, social and educational background, by the previous history of his life and by his present surroundings" (Panofsky, 1955, p. 27). The iconological interpretation is the synthesis of the pre-iconographical description and the iconographical analysis. It is based on thorough research of visual and textual sources and contexts with the aim of ascertaining "those underlying principles which reveal the basic attitude of a nation, a period, a class, a religious or philosophical persuasion – qualified by one personality and condensed into one work" (p. 30). In this respect, the iconological interpretation is akin to social semiotic analysis.

The division into three steps, as described by Panofsky, is a theoretical model. In practical research, iconology involves an integrated process without a clear distinction between description, analysis, and interpretation. Table 6.3 summarizes the method of iconology. It is an adapted and extended version of Panofsky's table (Panofsky, 1955, p. 40). Even though Panofsky developed his method of iconology in the mid-twentieth century, it is still suitable for analyzing the wide range of images we encounter in digital communication today.

The method of iconology can be expanded to include the analysis of the production and reception of an image: the contexts in which the image was produced and how it was or is received by the target group(s). If we look at the professional field of public relations, different people are involved in the *production process* of a campaign: advertising experts, PR strategists, authors, photographers, designers, the client who commissioned the campaign. They pursue specific objectives, have a mental image of the consumer in mind, are influenced by certain design trends, societal topics, or economic factors. These aspects determine the final outcome; that is, which message the image and the textual elements convey, or how a campaign is received. This is also true in a journalistic production context. Photographers choose a certain angle or setting, they crop images and edit them. Journalists add titles and captions, thus framing images in

TABLE 6.3 OVERVIEW OF PANOFSKY'S THREE-STEP ANALYSIS

Act of interpretation	Object of interpretation	Research steps	Examples
Pre-iconographical description (denotative message)	Primary or natural subject matter (factual, expressional) constituting the world of motifs	• Describe what you see in the image in a neutral way using generic terms. What objects, places, and events are depicted? Pay special attention to the technical-stylistic devices (e.g., composition, proportions, coloring, contrasts).	• Gesture of lifting the hat (everyday scene) • Leonardo da Vinci's wall painting *The Last Supper* (Fig. 6.4): 13 men in historical clothes seated at a dinner table.
Iconographical analysis (connotative message)	Secondary or symbolic meanings, related to the world of images, stories, values, and allegories defining a culture	• Explain what you see by identifying people, objects, or events and attributing cultural, symbolic meaning to the image. • Connect motifs with themes and more general concepts. • Compare the image with similar images of the same visual category or genre.	• The gesture of lifting the hat symbolizes a greeting. • A group of 13 men seated around a table in a certain arrangement represents *The Last Supper* (Fig. 6.4). • The motif symbolizes Christianity and religious community.
Iconological interpretation	Intrinsic, symptomatic meaning or content, making the image representative of a certain artist, style, culture, or time period	• This research step demands a "distant eye." Interpret and evaluate the image on a meta-level, by placing it explicitly in its cultural or sociopolitical context or reflecting on it as a product of a historical epoch. • Take into account the production and reception context: What can we say about the cultural context in which the image was produced? How is/was the image received by the target group?	• The gesture as an expression of a certain culture, era, community, etc. • *The Last Supper* (Fig. 6.4) as a document of Leonardo's personality, or of civilization at the time of the Italian High Renaissance or of a particular religious attitude.

Figure 6.4 *The Last Supper* by Leonardo da Vinci. Wall painting in the Dominican monastery Santa Maria delle Grazie, Milan, Italy. Contributor: IanDagnall Computing / Alamy Stock Photo (2017).

a certain way. Producers are subject to professional norms and values (such as news values) as well as ethical standards. To get information about the production context, we can search for press releases related to the campaign, making of videos, blog posts, or media reports. For deeper insights into the conditions under which the image or visual product was produced, we can use methods such as a qualitative survey in the form of interviews or ethnographic methods (Chapter 5).

As for *reception*, the analysis can be very complex, and often researchers from other disciplines, e.g., psychology or social sciences, have to be involved to test how the images are perceived or how the target group responds to them. The most appropriate methods here are interviews with individuals or focus groups, the Q-methodology (a picture sorting technique to study participants' viewpoint), eye-tracking, electronic quantitative methods for measuring user activity and engagement, or the measurement of electrodermal activities for testing emotions.

ACTIVITY

Pairwork: How is climate change communicated? Choose an image that has been used in a news coverage of climate change or in a campaign about climate change. One of you analyzes this image by applying the method of iconology (Panofsky), the other applies the semiotic method as described by Barthes. Compare and discuss your findings.

6.3 Multimodal Analysis

After explaining methods of linguistic and visual analysis, we now turn to analyzing multimodal communication. Multimodal analysis builds on the theoretical concepts presented in Sections 3.2 and 3.3. In this section, we go from theory to practical analysis. The suggested method is organized in three stages. The first stage is to make an initial description of the modes and text elements present in the text. In the second stage, we analyze the ways in which these text elements carry different kinds of meaning potentials. Finally, we discuss how the multimodal text relates to a certain text genre and to the social context of which it is a part.

The method described below accounts for a close reading of a multimodal text, a text that has caught our interest for some reason. It may be because we regard it as a typical sample, representing a bigger class of texts, or, on the contrary, that it is a nontypical text, and thereby interesting.

The first stage (Section 6.3.1) is a descriptive one. Here we observe and describe the overall constituents of the text, i.e., in what ways verbal, visual, and (sometimes) auditive elements are organized into a whole.

In the second stage (Section 6.3.2), we zoom in on the different modes, analyzing what semiotic work is done by each of them (i.e., how they make meaning), and how they work together.

In the third stage (Section 6.3.3) we zoom out again, discussing the semiotic as well as the social potentials of the text in relation to the genre it belongs to and the social situation it is part of. So, the methodological strategy is one of two-way zooming, and the desired outcome is a response to two interrelated questions: What does the text mean semiotically, and what does it do socially?

6.3.1 First Stage: Describing the Multimodal Text

In this stage, we identify and categorize the different constituents of the text and observe the role each element has in the entirety of the text. First, we ask general questions such as the following: What semiotic modes are involved in the multimodal text? What characterizes the arrangement of verbal elements, photography, layout and typography, charts, video, animation, music, speech, etc.? Is the multimodal text dominated by visual or verbal elements? Is color used to highlight certain elements? Is white space applied as a tool to connect or separate between elements?

Then, we categorize each text element on a more detailed level. We ask, for example: What kinds of verbal elements are involved – titles, citations, captions etc.? And what kinds of graphical representations – line graphs, bubble charts, Venn diagrams, etc.?

The rationale behind this sort of hierarchical categorization is twofold. Firstly, it makes us sharpen our eyes toward the various text elements and their internal arrangement.

Secondly, it represents a necessary stepping stone for the next stage of analysis. Each mode and each text element that is identified in this first stage of analysis represents a specific set of affordances (possibilities and restrictions) regarding what meanings they may carry and what roles they may have in the multimodal text as a whole. If the multimodal text is dominated by a line graph with a timeline on the x-axis, it becomes immediately clear that the text is centered around some kind of development over time. If the only verbal element is a big title, formed by a single nominal phrase, e.g. "The Boss of the Zoo," we are signaled that the images or videos below the title are supposed to be interpreted according to this title.

Table 6.4 indicates some typical categories we can look for in the initial stage of a multimodal analysis. Note that the table is far from being exhaustive. It is meant as an aid to start the process of categorizing textual elements.

At this initial, descriptive stage, we also look at how the multimodal text is materialized and mediatized, and how it fits into a larger whole in its own media context. We ask questions such as: Is it a static or a dynamic text? Does it offer any interactive options to the reader? Is it part of a larger co-text, e.g., a journalistic special feature or a web-documentary? Is it framed by a predefined template?

These questions are partly purely descriptive, making us more conscious about the basic characteristics of the multimodal text under scrutiny. Partly, they lean toward the next stages of analysis, concerning the meaning potentials and genre conventions, which we will return to in the two sections below.

TABLE 6.4 TYPICAL INVESTIGATION CATEGORIES FOR THE INITIAL STAGE OF A MULTIMODAL ANALYSIS

MODE	TYPE	SUB-TYPE
Verbal elements	Title, intro, citation, caption, annotation, fact-box ...	Subtitle, main title, lead ...
Visual elements: still images	Reportage photo, stock photo, art photo ...	Portrait, landscape, sport/action ...
Visual elements: graphics	Data visualization, infographic, drawing ...	Graph, chart, map, time line, flow chart, network diagram ...
Visual elements: moving images	Explainer video, documentary, reportage clip ...	Hand-held, raw footage, multi-camera production, mobile phone production ...
Audio elements	Music, speech, background sound ...	Voiceover, interview, talking head ...

6.3.2 Second Stage: Analyzing the Meaning Potentials of the Multimodal Text

In the second stage of analysis, we want to reveal the meaning potentials of the multimodal text. This is done in two steps: Firstly, we look at the semiotic work done by each of the modes involved in the text; secondly, we investigate the interaction between the modes in order to reveal the forms of cohesion and tension that shape the semiotic potentials of the text as a whole.

In the first step, we ask two basic questions:

(1) What is said about the world in the text, and in what ways does each mode contribute to this construction of meaning? This is called the **ideational metafunction** of the multimodal text (Section 3.2.2). In some books it is called the representational dimension of the text.

(2) What social identities, roles, and relations are constructed, and in what ways does each mode contribute to this construction? This is called the social or **interpersonal metafunction** of the multimodal text.

To answer the first question, concerning ideational meaning, we need to examine the following issues:

- What persons, places, objects, and processes are represented?
- How are persons, places, and objects described?
- What actions are going on, who are involved, in what ways and under which circumstances?
- What is said about the world on a symbolic or metaphorical level?

In a critical analysis, we will also ask:

- Whose world is it that is represented? Is this picture of the world shared by many or by few? In whose interest or disinterest is it that this picture of the world is shaped and shared?

Analyzing a multimodal text in this manner, it becomes clear that the different modes have very different affordances, and thus may complement – or contest – each other. While photos and videos may show what objects, persons, and places look like in great detail, verbal elements can express abstract entities like values, human relations, causations, and intentions. Graphs and charts, on the other hand, have their strength in showing patterns, changes over time, and relations between variables in large data sets. These differences in semiotic affordances also explain why the issue of salience is so important – as the different modes reveal different aspects of the world.

To answer the second question, concerning interpersonal meaning (social identities, roles, and relations), we need to look closely at these issues:

- How is the sender of the message represented, regarding identity, values, and intentions?
- How is the relation between the sender and the receiver represented, concerning power and status, level of knowledge, their roles in the discourse etc.?
- How is the relation between the receiver and the persons in the text represented?

Some typical characteristics to observe regarding the interpersonal dimension of a multimodal text are these:

- How are personal pronouns (*I, we, you, they* ...) applied in the verbal elements?
- Is the reader addressed in a direct and personal way (e.g., through questions or instructions), or not addressed at all?
- How are persons depicted in photos, regarding distance, framing, and angle?
- Is the reader invited to take an active role in the discourse through interactive options, or does the text and the medium imply a passive receiver of information?

For the next step of the analysis, the goal is to reveal how the different modes interact with each other through different forms of multimodal cohesion (Section 3.3.5). The basic question guiding this step of the analysis is this: How is the multimodal text composed to make a meaningful whole from the single units? This is called the compositional metafunction of the multimodal text (Section 3.2.3).

This is a core question in multimodal analysis, distinguishing this form of qualitative investigation from other traditions of text analysis. Relevant issues to investigate are these:

- Salience: Does one mode dominate over the other(s)? What element receives the most attention due to size, color, or position?
- Information value: How are the different elements positioned, in order to signal old/ new or central/marginal information, and to suggest a reading path?
- Framing: How are framelines, empty space, and color used to connect or disconnect certain elements?
- Information linking: What characterizes the balance between cohesion and tension in the multimodal interplay – and what interpretive work does that leave to the reader? Pivotal terms here are elaboration and extension (Section 3.3.5).

The issue of coherence and tension is specifically interesting, yet, a bit more complex than the others. More concretely, we here ask: Do the modes repeat, rephrase, or complement each other – or are there elements of tension and disharmony in the interplay between the modes? If so, does such tension leave the reader confused, or rather engaged and active? If the different modes repeat or rephrase each other, the text might be easy to understand, but it might also be quite boring to read – dependent on the knowledge level of the reader. A text with some degree of intermodal tension (though not too much) invites active and engaged reading, where the reader will gain a feeling of satisfaction and mastery when interpretive efforts are rewarded with a deeper understanding of what the text is all about. The balance between cohesion and tension is often what distinguishes between pedagogical learning material and works of art. A textbook for young learners needs to be totally clear and unambiguous, while a work of art most often invites subjective interpretations.

More detailed suggestions for analytical issues can be found in the Appendix as well as online (www.cambridge.org/digitalcommunication).

6.3.3 Third Stage: Putting the Multimodal Text into Context

In the second stage of analysis, we zoomed in and examined closely the micro-structures of the multimodal text. In the third and final stage of the analysis, we will zoom out again and focus on the ways in which the text gains meaning and social effects through the context that frames it. The contextual issues can be investigated through a cultural lens, relating the text to genre conventions, as well as a social lens, relating the text to the specifics of the social situation in which the text is an integral part. This level of analysis is often referred to as the discourse level.

The cultural lens helps us ask questions such as the following:

- What genre does the multimodal text belong to? Is it a professional genre, like news, advertising, or campaigning, or a (semi-) private genre, like a Facebook post or an e-message?
- How does the text relate to the norms and expectations of the genre? Is it conventional or innovative?

The social lens leads us to questions such as:

- What social practice is actually going on? What is the purpose of the activity, and what is at stake?
- Who are the participants and what are their interests and roles in the activity?
- What are the practical and technological conditions under which the social activity is taking place?
- What – and whose – social agency is realized through the multimodal text?

As we see, this stage of the investigation is characterized by discussion and reflection as much as by systematic analysis. It involves the perspectives and interests of the analyst to a greater extent than the first two stages. Yet, it is an important part of the method, since it addresses the social framework that implies what meaning potentials are most likely to be realized in the situation of use, and also what social effects the multimodal text can be assumed to have in that situation. Whether a certain text is likely to provoke, inform, or entertain, depends on the interplay between textual structures and contextual conditions: where, when, who and why? These contextual considerations may also indicate whether the text belongs to a class of texts which carry potentials for genre developments, and, if so, in what directions those developments might go. When some innovative news editors started to include short video clips in their online news stories in the early years after the turn of the century, it quickly became clear that these dynamic elements represented a successful development of the genre.

6.3.4 Don't Forget Intuition and Observation

An important reminder, after this presentation of a method for systematic analysis, is this: Any text that we analyze represents an individual and unique instance of human communication. That means that no method for text analysis should be used as a mechanical, machine-like device for extracting the meaning from a text. The suggested method for multimodal analysis is meant as a tool and a helpful guide to our approach to the semiotic and social complexity of a situated text. It is, however, equally important to use our intuition, experience, and observational skills in order to understand what really is interesting and important with the specific text under scrutiny. What is it that makes *this* multimodal text special, typical, effectful, innovative, provocative – or funny? Those issues must not disappear in the mechanics of any analytical method.

ACTIVITY

Find a commercial website, or the website of a charity, and make a detailed outline for how a multimodal analysis could be carried out. Use terminology from this chapter in your outline. For each point in the outline, add as many details as possible, based on your observations of the multimodal text. If you have time for a longer activity, conduct a full multimodal analysis, based on the outline. You may use the tables in the Appendix (also available online at www.cambridge.org/digitalcommunication) to conduct the analysis. You can also find two examples of analysis on the website, where the method presented in this chapter is applied.

6.4 Combining Quantitative and Qualitative Methods

In multimodality research, qualitative studies with comparatively small data sets are still preferred (Pflaeging, Bateman & Wildfeuer, 2021b). Quite recently, quantitative analyses based on larger data sets have also found their way into multimodality research as well as a mixed methods approach combining quanitative and qualitative research. Students often ask: What is qualitative research and how does it differ from **quantitative research**?

Is a qualitative approach to research better than a quantitative one? Which methods are associated with these approaches, and how can these methods be combined? We have already touched upon the differences between these two types of research and have presented some methods used in quantitative or qualitative research (Section 6.2). Generally speaking, using a quantitative research approach focuses on the countable properties of a research object and problems related to quantity, whereas qualitative research focuses on qualities unique to the research object, calling for some kind of interpretation. Let us take a closer look at the two research approaches.

6.4.1 Quantitative or Qualitative?

Quantitative research is used to quantify, for instance, opinions, attitudes, time spent on social media, tweets, types of images, words, or other variables. It is associated with data in numerical form and considered to be more objective and reliable because it is easier to replicate. A quantitative approach aims at explaining phenomena through numerical variables or identifying cause–effect relationships. The typical methods used here are content analysis (Section 6.2.1), surveys, online polls, questionnaires, or longitudinal studies. In contrast, qualitative research aims at a deeper understanding of a topic or a problem research issue. It provides insight into the underlying principles of a subject such as human behavior, motivation, opinions, or attitudes. A qualitative approach is more interpretive and focuses on an understanding that is more subjective, yet also more nuanced, and thus more valid because the research question can be examined in more detail. Examples of a qualitative research approach are ethnography (Section 5.1.2) and semiotics (Section 6.2.2); examples of qualitative methods are metadiscourse analysis (Section 6.1.4), iconology (Section 6.2.3), or the aforementioned three-stage method of multimodal analysis (Section 6.3).

Table 6.5 provides an overview of the two research approaches (see also Queirós, Faria & Almeida, 2017). The table may give the impression of a rigid division between the two types of research, because it shows them as being opposed and totally different. In fact, however, they can be regarded as complementary, as we will see in Section 6.4.2.

6.4.2 Combining the Two Traditions: John Snow and the Cholera Map

The story of the physician John Snow, who is considered to be the father of modern epidemiology, illustrates how quantitative and qualitative methods can be combined (Frerichs, 2001; Tufte, 1997, pp. 27–37).

In the 1850s, John Snow conducted a series of studies to investigate the cause of the cholera outbreaks in London. He did not accept the miasma theory which public health officials believed in at that time; namely, that cholera was caused by inhaling bad air. Instead, he supported the germ theory, which suggested that cholera was caused by an

TABLE 6.5 OVERVIEW OF THE QUANTITATIVE AND QUALITATIVE RESEARCH APPROACHES

	Quantitative research	Qualitative research
Aim	• seeks to test and confirm hypotheses • counts and classifies features using statistical methods • describes what is observed • constructs statistical models	• seeks to gain deeper insight into phenomena (e.g., attitudes, opinions, or human behavior) and interpret them • describes in detail and explains individual experiences, social relationships, motivations, etc. • seeks to understand processes of meaning-making
Research question	• answers research questions such as: what, where, when, how many?	• answers research questions such as: why, how?
Data	• primarily uses larger sample sizes or big data • collects data in numerical form	• primarily uses smaller sample sizes • collects data in nonnumerical form (e.g., quotes from interviews, photos, diaries, videos)
Research design	• formulates hypotheses: researchers know in advance what they are looking for • is based on a strictly structured research design. All aspects of the study are determined in advance. • is often deductive, based on theories • uses standardized software programs (e.g., Excel, SPSS, JASP). • is more objective. Objective means that the results are supported by statistical numbers, but in the end, numbers also require interpretation. • *Goal*: a precise, objective measurement and statistical, mathematical, or numerical analysis	• formulates questions: researchers only have a rough idea what they are looking for • is more flexible and dynamic. The research design emerges as the study unfolds. • is often inductive. It generates hypotheses or theories. • can use standardized software programs (e.g., MAXQDA, NVivo,), but researchers themselves are the main "research instruments." • is more subjective • *Goal*: individual, subjective interpretation, but plausible
Methods (some examples)	• online surveys with large numbers of participants • questionnaires • polls • longitudinal studies	• rhetorical text analysis • multimodal analysis • conversation analysis • discourse studies • participant observation (ethnography)

TABLE 6.5 CONTINUED

	Quantitative research	Qualitative research
	• statistical methods (e.g., descriptive statistics, T-test for hypothesis testing) • experiments • quantitative content analysis • text mining	• in-depth interviews with open-ended questions • focus group interviews • diary studies • iconology
Results	• yields more "laboratory results," since studies are often carried out in laboratories or unnatural, artificial environments *Goal*: predictions, generalizations, correlations, causal relationships, large-scale trends	• yields more "real-world results," since studies are often about real-world situations, cultures and their artifacts, communities, organizations, or participants' own perspective *Goal*: in-depth understanding of phenomena

infectious microbe that had not yet been discovered. His hypothesis was that water contaminated by sewage was the vehicle for transmitting cholera. In summer 1854, over a period of several weeks, he collected data on the water sources of the affected neighborhoods in London. Two main companies that drew water from the River Thames supplied the households with water. Snow took large statistical samples from various districts that obtained water from one or the other water company or from both and compared the cholera mortality among these districts. He then looked for correlations between water supply and death rate. When cholera broke out in the Golden Square neighborhood at the end of August 1854, he began his investigation by finding out where exactly people with cholera lived and worked. To gain deeper insight, he interviewed the residents about their water consumption. His investigations led him to the public water pump on Broad Street, where he noticed a cluster of cases. But he also identified inconsistencies in the data, so-called outliers. Not all of the residents near the pump were apparently suffering from cholera, but others were, although they lived further away from Broad Street. In order to solve this puzzle, he interviewed the families in question. After his local inquiries, Snow visualized his findings by plotting the cholera cases and the water pumps on a map: one bar for each cholera death (Figure 6.5). His combination of quantitative statistical analysis and qualitative interviewing proved to be the clearest way to demonstrate the correlation between the quality of the water source and the cholera cases. Being convinced that the water from the pump on Broad Street was the problem, Snow reported his findings to the authorities, and the handle of the water pump was removed. It was the beginning of the end of the cholera epidemic and a milestone in

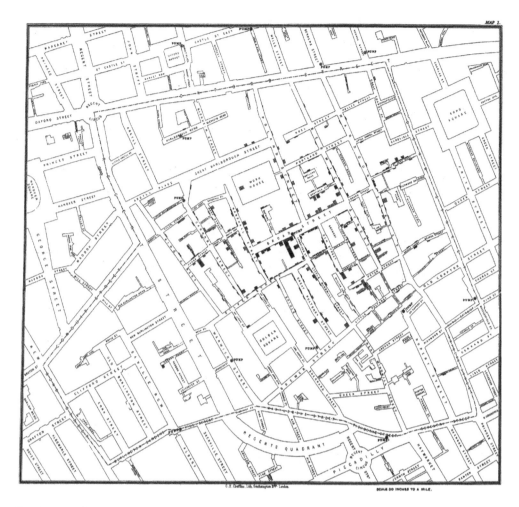

Figure 6.5 John Snow's map of deaths from cholera, London, 1854. The black circles represent pumps; the stacked black rectangles show the deaths. From "High resolution maps of John Snow," by R. R. Frerichs (UCLA Department of Epidemiology), 2004 (www.ph.ucla.edu/epi/snow/highressnowmap.html). In the public domain. Original map: *On the mode of communication of cholera* (2nd ed., p. 44) by J. Snow (Lithographer: C.F. Cheffins), London: John Churchill, 1855. In the public domain.

the history of epidemiology. Moreover, Snow's famous cholera map is often cited as a pioneering work in the field of data visualization and data journalism.

Snow did exactly what researchers and data experts do: He collected quantitative data (the frequencies of deaths and locations) and qualitative data (the interviews) and combined quantitative analysis (statistics), qualitative analysis (interviews), and visualization techniques. Not only did he analyze the numbers (where, how many), he also wanted to understand the reasons behind these numbers by asking why. By mixing quantitative and qualitative methods, Snow gained a better understanding of his research problem. His study is a perfect example of a mixed methods approach (Dickinson, 2010, p. 471).

6.4.3 Mixed Methods Approach

Combining quantitative and qualitative methods is called a mixed methods approach or **mixed methods research**. It involves a mixing or combining of methods in data collection, data analysis, evaluation, and interpretation into a single study. Mixed methods research is appropriate when neither quantitative nor qualitative methods alone can answer the research questions. The benefit of this approach to research is a deeper understanding of the research problem gained by viewing phenomena from different perspectives. It allows you to identify connections or contradictions between the different types of data and to draw conclusions from them. Each method complements and contextualizes the other. For example, if the object under study is an underinvestigated field and, as a result, lacking theories, you can approach your research problem from a qualitative perspective and start with an exploratory study that results in a theory or some hypotheses. Then, you can continue with a quantitative study to test your hypotheses. Or vice versa: You conduct a quantitative study with a representative sample and, to gain deeper insight into the context, you draw some case studies from the sample for a qualitative analysis. There are different types and variants of how to mix research methods. Creswell and Plano Clark (2018, pp. 65–93) suggest three core mixed methods designs and procedures:

- *The convergent design* is a concurrent design with two parallel phases (Figure 6.6). The researcher brings together "the results of the quantitative and qualitative data analysis so they can be compared or combined" (Creswell & Plano Clark, 2018, p. 65). The purpose is to obtain a more complete understanding of a phenomenon, and, thus, a higher **validity** of the research design (Creswell & Plano Clark, 2018, p. 65).

1. Quantitative data collection and analysis ⎫
Results are merged ⎯⎯⎯→ Interpretation
2. Qualitative data collection and analysis ⎭ and compared

Figure 6.6 Diagram of the convergent design. © 2021 Verena Elisabeth Lechner. Used with permission.

- *The explanatory design* is a sequential design with two phases (Figure 6.7). It starts with a quantitative phase followed by a qualitative phase. The purpose is to "develop a strong explanation by explaining the quantitative results with qualitative data" (Creswell & Plano Clark, 2018, p. 293).

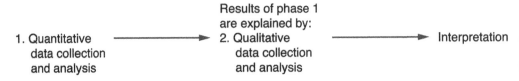

Figure 6.7 Diagram of the explanatory design. © 2021 Verena Elisabeth Lechner. Used with permission.

- *The exploratory design* is a sequential design with three phases (Figure 6.8). It starts with a qualitative exploring phase followed by a development phase in which, based on the qualitative findings, the researcher designs a quantitative approach and/or a quantitative data collection feature; for instance, a survey or an app. In the third phase, the researcher then conducts the quantitative study using the new feature. The purpose is to design a quantitative study that is informed by the results of the qualitative study (Creswell & Plano Clark, 2018, p. 84).

Figure 6.8 Diagram of the exploratory design. © 2021 Verena Elisabeth Lechner. Used with permission.

What does the mixed methods approach now look like in media and communications studies? In an example taken from the field of visual communication, a large corpus of 2,000 images harvested (with permission!) from the websites of several kindergartens is analyzed using visual content analysis. In that process, each image is analyzed with the focus on a few variables relating to motif, angle, and distance. This analysis gives signals about potentially interesting aspects of the images. These aspects call for a close reading of a smaller sample of images, which is then studied using a social semiotic analysis. However, equally often an initial qualitative analysis (e.g., iconology) of a small sample of images motivates a broader, quantitative analysis focusing on specific, carefully selected aspects of each image.

Or take the example of a study that investigates the news consumption of young people. Conducting a national online survey with a sample size of 1,500 respondents, you can collect data about the various types of news sources teenagers use to keep themselves informed or the frequency of their news consumption. You may get results such as the following: 72 percent of the teenagers say they keep themselves informed by talking with family and friends several times a week, and 59 percent of the respondents say they use social media to keep up to date. However, when it comes to answering questions like "How do young people define news?" and "What is their motivation to consume news?" qualitative methods are required. Some possible methods here are diary studies, interviews, focus groups, or digital ethnography (Section 5.1.4). This qualitative part of the study requires a smaller sample size, most often between ten and thirty participants, dependent on the methods used and the time resources available. The qualitative work helps uncover what teenagers understand by news, how they consume news, and what motivates them to either consume or not consume news. The mixed methods approach can support a more holistic understanding of news consumption and identify challenges that news providers are facing today if they want to reach younger audiences.

6.4.4 Strengths and Limitations

Our examples show that qualitative and quantitative methods are not mutually exclusive; rather, they can be used to complement one another. Indeed, many researchers agree that a combination of quantitative and qualitative methods enrich results by offering a more nuanced understanding of the object under examination. On the one hand, a mixed methods approach reduces the weaknesses of each approach and thus leads to a higher validity and **reliability** of the data and their interpretation (see Table 6.6). On the other hand, a mixed methods approach is more complex, and, therefore, more time-consuming than a single method approach. Furthermore, it requires background knowledge in the various mixed methods designs and experience in applying quantitative and qualitative methods. In this sense, a mixed methods approach is better suited for the advanced

TABLE 6.6 MAIN STRENGTHS AND LIMITATIONS OF QUANTITATIVE AND QUALITATIVE RESEARCH

	Quantitative research	Qualitative research
Strengths	• yields precisely quantifiable results • has a higher degree of accuracy and objectivity • findings can be compared more easily • findings can be replicated, and, thus, are of high reliability • findings can be generalized if the sample is representative	• provides detailed information on complex issues • has a higher degree of validity because of the flexible research design • an exploratory (open) approach allows the discovery of new aspects • can complement and refine quantitative data
Limitations	• lacks contextual details • is not suitable for explaining complex issues, motivations, or individual behavior • provides no clues for improvements or recommendations • is rigorously structured and does not allow any flexibility once the study has begun	• is difficult to replicate, and, thus, may lack reliability • often, researchers need to have an advanced knowledge of the subject or problem setting (e.g., in ethnographic studies or in-depth interviews) • findings are context sensitive, which means findings are placed in a situational, cultural, or historical context • is less suitable for generalization

researcher and not for the newcomer. Whether a researcher or a research team proceeds quantitatively, qualitatively, or with a combination of both always depends on the object under study and the research questions to be answered.

ACTIVITY

Which approach and which methods will you use in your study or thesis?

1. Draw a diagram that provides an overview of your research design.
2. Write a one-page description of the procedures and outline possible challenges. What is your rationale for choosing this research design?

Key Terms

iconography, ideational metafunction, interpersonal metafunction, metadiscourse analysis, mixed methods research, multi-method approach, progression analysis, qualitative research, quantitative research, reliability, validity, variation analysis, version analysis

Chapter Summary

- By applying and combining the methodological approaches of version analysis, progression analysis, variation analysis, and metadiscourse analysis, researchers investigate real-life communication from product and process perspectives, as cognitive and social activity, and on micro and macro levels. Multi-method approaches such as progression analysis allow for a multi-perspective, vivid representation of the object of study.

- Language use in (digital) media environments becomes tangible as an individual and mental activity, but also highly social endeavor, closely related to decision-making and change in teams and society at large. In contrast, analyzing communicational offers as products only risks falling short of explaining mediatized communication in its variegated dynamics and purposes, as a playful, epistemic, and communicative activity in the complex contexts of everyday life and work.

- Analyzing visual communication includes quantitative and qualitative approaches. While quantitative content analysis enables us to reveal patterns or trends in visual communication, qualitative methods such as iconology provide deeper insights into the many layers of meaning of images and their ideological power.

- Multimodal analysis looks at the different modes of communication. It consists of three stages: 1. describing the elements that constitute the multimodal text and identifying the semiotic modes; 2. zooming in on each mode and analyzing their ideational and interpersonal meaning potentials as well as the coherence mechanisms and the overall composition of the multimodal text; 3. zooming out again by observing how the text relates to a certain genre and how it is formed by – as well as how it forms – the social situation that it is part of.

- Research questions can be explored from different perspectives: quantitative, qualitative, or using a mixed methods approach. While a quantitative approach is good for statistical analysis, a qualitative approach seeks to gain a deeper understanding of the underlying meanings, social relationships, and human behaviors related to a phenomenon. A combination of quantitative and qualitative methods often provides the most comprehensive results.

Linguistic Analysis

If you would like to know more about the four approaches as well as about the potential advantages and disadvantages of combining methods in media linguistic research, read Grésillon and Perrin (2014). For linguistic methods in general, find an easy access in Paltridge and Phakiti (2015).

Visual Analysis

The most comprehensive guide in the field of visual analyses is *The SAGE handbook of visual research methods* (2020), edited by Luc Pauwels and Dawn Manny. It offers a wide range of methods (quantitative and qualitative) and interdisciplinary approaches to analyzing visuals.

A basic work that provides both theoretical orientation and practical guidance on how to analyze images is Gillian Rose's textbook *Visual methodologies* (2016, 4th ed.).

Visual communication (Aiello & Parry, 2019) is an ideal tool kit for doing visual analysis. It provides a hands-on guide on how to combine methods. The many case studies illuminate significant features of visual communication across a range of media genres.

Doing visual analysis (Ledin & Machin, 2018) focuses on how visuals shape our view of the world. The book helps readers to see beyond images by showing how to analyze a variety of visuals from TV commercials, to packaging, to film clips.

Multimodal Analysis

In their paper, O'Halloran, Pal, and Jin (2021) present a "multimodal approach to analyzing big social and news media data." They demonstrate how computational tools for natural language processing and image processing can be used to analyze large data sets of online newspaper articles and social media posts.

When it comes to interpreting text-image-relations, Ewerth, Otto, and Müller-Budack (2021) present and discuss "computational approaches for the interpretation of image–text relations" using machine learning.

Multimodality (Bateman, Wildfeuer & Hiippala, 2017) is a basic textbook for approaching multimodality and multimodal research. It provides an introduction into theoretical foundations and methods and demonstrates practical multimodal analysis via use cases. The use cases cover a broad range of multimodal products and situations from face-to-face interaction and layout spaces, to infographics, comics, and film to audiovisual representations, webpages, video games, and social media.

The Routledge handbook of multimodal analysis (2013), edited by Carey Jewitt, is a very rich and well updated tool kit for multimodal analysis, accounting for a wide range of approaches and traditions within the field.

Kress and Van Leeuwen's book *Multimodal discourse* (2001) takes an original, yet interesting, approach to multimodal analysis, in that it separates the different stages of a communicational process: the discourse stage (deciding on what we want to say), the design stage (the selection of modes, format, and medium), the production stage (the application of tools to create the textual product), and distribution (use of infrastructure to share the textual product). New layers of meaning are added at each stage, sometimes without our awareness.

Combining Quantitative and Qualitative Methods

Creswell and Plano Clark (2018) provide a comprehensive and pragmatic overview of designing and conducting mixed methods research. They explain important steps and techniques involved in designing a study of one's own. Furthermore, they draw attention to related theories, frameworks, and key concepts. It is a textbook for a beginner in the field of mixed methods research as well as for an advanced researcher.

In their handbook, Hansen and Machin (2019) discuss quantitative and qualitative research methods which are relevant to media and communications studies. The book is a navigation tool for media students, particularly for those working their way into their own research projects.

7 Case Studies

PREVIEW

When we teach methods of media linguistics, students often ask: Could you give us an example of how to use them? Therefore, in this chapter, we present excerpts from research projects that show how the methods introduced in Chapters 5 and 6 can be applied individually or in combination.

The first case study illustrates the use of progression analysis for examining the interplay between writing processes and their contexts. The following two case studies explain how to approach data stories and images using visual and multimodal analysis in journalism and PR. Finally, the last case study illustrates how ethnographic frameworks and media linguistic methods can be combined to investigate sociality in online environments.

By the end of this chapter, you should be able to

- understand how media linguistic research projects can be designed to investigate long-term changes in communication
- analyze multimodal products, e.g., news stories, posts on social media, awareness campaigns by applying methods from media linguistics
- understand how methods can be combined and apply this knowledge to new cases
- appraise and reflect on the impact of multimodal texts and what they contribute to the social discourse
- understand how ethnographic frameworks can be combined with media linguistic methods.

7.1 Writing in Journalism: Finding One's Niche in the Dynamic Field of Professional Writing

This case is about focused writing and writing-by-the-way in the complex and dynamic environments of journalism. At the beginning of a long-term project of research-based coaching, the journalist MD wondered "why it suddenly doesn't work." While many writing processes were easy for her, others were not. "Somehow," she said, she then found herself "always writing," unable to finish and call it a day – and yet remaining dissatisfied with the result (Perrin, 2021). MD is not the only professional writer asking this question. Anyone who communicates professionally has experienced driving forces such as writing flows and problems such as writer's blocks. And we all aim at strengthening the former and avoiding the latter.

From a theoretical point of view, addressing this problem is interesting because it fosters the development of so-called mid-range theories. These theories explain "what works for whom in what conditions" (Pawson & Tilley, 1997, p. 72). By doing so, they contribute to understanding practices in context, in our case the text production practices in the professional field of journalism. From a practical perspective, the knowledge generated through mid-range theories provides reliable and valid insights into change in professional fields. This helps improve professional education, which benefits journalists and, ultimately, society at large as the main addressee of journalistic output.

The next sections contextualize the MD case in a series of projects that enable researchers and trainees to investigate and observe long-term changes in journalistic text production practices (Section 7.1.1). Findings across projects and cases show a fascinating interplay of constants and variants, of persistence and change over two decades. While the types of text production contexts and activities have remained the same (Section 7.1.2), their pace and balance have changed toward writing-by-the-way (Section 7.1.3). Practitioners can either follow this trend – or find their niches as positive deviants (Section 7.1.4). This insight bears consequences for both professional education and media literacy development in society at large (Section 7.1.5).

7.1.1 Contextualizing the MD Case

The empirical data for the MD case and similar cases are taken from a number of projects on text production research in newsrooms. In all projects, progression analysis (Section 6.1.2) was used to collect data on the writing process in such a consistent manner that they are comparable over the period from 1995 to the present day, thus enabling in-depth, long-term analyses of journalistic text production. In contrast, the projects are becoming increasingly complex in terms of the research question and the research framework, and they systematically build on each other. Project by project, the scope of the survey is also growing, from individual cases in the pilot project to entire editorial teams in the more recent projects.

The *Agency* project (1995–1998) recorded what news agency journalists should, want, and do in collaborative text production – in other words, the ethnographic internal perspective in the professional context. It focused on practices of recontextualizing supplier texts from different sources and the traces these practices leave in the final text product. One of the main findings is that coherence breaks in the text often occur where the authors have lost sight of what is actually written in the target text, in the lines, so to speak, and what they think of when reading this emerging text between the lines. The process demonstrably leaves its mark on the product.

The *Experience* project (1997–2000) expanded this approach with a grounded theory on the relationship between professional experience and the repertoires of text production practices. Writers in print, radio, television, and online editorial offices were examined. A typology of experience as a resource in the professional field was developed. It shows that journalists with long experience in different media and formats tend to plan earlier, more far-sightedly, and at the same time more flexibly than their less experienced colleagues. At the same time, they plan more strongly the process as well as the big picture and the impact of the product, while the less experienced ones think primarily of the small-scale product structure.

In addition, the *Transformation* project (1999–2001) demonstrates, in the transdisciplinary tradition of research, how less experienced can learn from more experienced text producers. Methods of knowledge transformation were applied. Representatives from academia and the practice under study were jointly developing a quality circle consisting of an editorial mission statement, newspaper criticism, coaching and training for a major daily newspaper. As a result, the editorial staff developed an explicit understanding of quality. This includes processes and a common language for continuously relating the intended and the actually achieved text production to each other, for rethinking the intentions based on lived practice, and for measuring the achievements, i.e., the daily text production, against it.

The project *Idée suisse* (2005–2010) focused on the relationship between practices of journalistic text production and social structures. It examined news production in German- and French-speaking editorial offices of Swiss public television in the context of changes in media policy, technology, and the economy. The main result: The gap between political and economic expectations of the broadcaster – promoting public understanding – is overcome only by individual experienced journalists. Their practices could be discussed and made available to the entire organization.

The project *Modeling Writing Phases* (2010–2013) investigated the interplay between routine and emergence over time in the text production process. Using machine learning methods, the large corpora of automatically generated progression data from previous projects were analyzed. The result is a typology of characteristics of writing phases that are assumed to apply to small-scale and to large-scale phases. Based on these characteristics, writing phases of different ranges in text production data are basically algorithmically identifiable, which allows for automatic writing process diagnosis in real time.

Recent projects deepen the knowledge of the interplay of argumentative, narrative, and visual practices in text production. With each project, new corpora have been added, for example, with data from other semiotic modes and other languages, from other cultural areas. One of the results of such projects is that narrative practices in journalism typically lead to narrative fragments – texts that do not explicitly tell a story to the end, but which are suitable for evoking narrative patterns in the addressees' minds and then with the ending being told during the process of uptake, so to speak.

In total, comparable data is available on tens of thousands of text production processes and hundreds of writers in newsrooms. This main corpus is supplemented by data from similar, smaller text production projects in domains such as translation, corporate communications, organizational communication, financial communication, and school. However, long-term comparisons of writing processes within a domain are only possible in the main corpus. Here, both constancy (Section 7.1.2) and change (Section 7.1.3) of practices are evident.

7.1.2 Revealing the Constants during the Investigation Period

Interestingly and despite all the obvious changes in the field of journalism, the interplay between the contexts and practices of journalistic writing can be characterized by constants during the period under study. Notwithstanding the mediatization of the public sphere, the professionalization of the profession, the task of editing or the experience of the text producers, the writing practices observed at journalistic workplaces can be assigned to five contexts of text production: Practices always interact with certain types of (1) workplace environments; (2) interfaces of organizational value creation; (3) recurrent phases of writing; (4) intertextual environments, and (5) intended product functions.

(1) *The socially, institutionally and technologically embedded workplace.* In the course of her biography, MD, for example, has repeatedly chosen workplaces where she can delve deeper into the fate of individuals, using their example to highlight complex social problems in her media reports.

(2) *The interfaces to the intertextual value chain.* A text production process starts from comprehending the task and ends when the final product is passed on. In the process examined here, MD first worked intensively on the opening credits and the beginning of the text, defining how she understands her writing assignment and what the product that she wants to deliver at the end should look like.

(3) *The writing process itself.* After defining her subject and revealing her main message, MD wrote her text. In doing so, she followed the biography of her case study; in other words, she told the story linearly from beginning to end. Along the way she worked on her formulations.

(4) *The intertextual environment of source texts and the resulting new text.* MD worked on a topic that she could research and read into without the pressure of being up to date. After completing the research, she designed her new text with little time pressure. Since the subject matter did not change, she did not need to do any research.

(5) *The intended function of the resulting product.* MD established the dramaturgical cornerstones and the related core concepts of her story in the early stages of the writing process and then used the text to clarify these core concepts and to reinforce their narrative effect in the text.

7.1.3 Identifying the Change during the Investigation Period

The above five contexts of professional text production remain the same throughout the entire period under investigation. This also applies to the practices with which writers refer to these contexts. Even after twenty years, journalists still connect with their social environment, for example, their sources, or aim for the dramaturgical impact of their texts. What changes, however, is the speed with which writers switch between tasks, contexts, and practices. With increasing digitalization, the pace, the basic rhythm of writing, has shifted from focused writing to writing-by-the-way (Section 3.1.3).

The differences between the two modes, in a nutshell: With focused writing, an entire text is created in longer phases and carefully revised before publication. With writing-by-the-way, small bits and bites of text are written in content management systems of social media. The contributions are often image-related and represent reactions to other such contributions. By writing-by-the-way, one is in constant written dialogue with many others. Thus, in MD's words, one is "always" and everywhere "somehow writing" – even if now writing the shortest of texts, and often several texts in parallel.

In journalism, this shift from focused writing to writing-by-the-way proceeds roughly in four phases: Around 1990, journalists transferred the focused writing that was common at the time from printed media to the new publishing environment of the Internet. Around 2000, during focused writing, by-the-way research was conducted on the Internet, which was becoming increasingly accepted in the journalistic workplace. Around 2010, it became common for journalists to use social media professionally to track down topics, tap sources, and involve addressees. Around 2020, this management of stakeholders through casual writing has become central and dominant in terms of workload.

This development is changing the demands on journalists. In the past, it was more likely that lone warriors would be called upon to silently complete their work before publication; today, however, journalists who want to position their brand and that of the media product must be constantly present on all channels. The resonance of the contributions is measured online. Well-curated (and, therefore, frequently commented on) contributions are rewarded by prominent placement on the media surface. This mechanism inevitably impacts journalists' agenda-setting and production practices, audiences' take-up and, ultimately, public discourse.

In transdisciplinary research, such knowledge transforms into practical measures: For example, it makes sense to prepare future journalists for the close interaction of focused writing and writing-by-the-way. Moreover, it seems advisable to promote general media literacy through elementary school, which enables media users to understand the mechanisms of agenda-setting and stance-boosting in social media bubbles – and develop skills to tell facts from fake news. Journalism can only contribute to public education in a democracy if it provides essential information – and if this essential information is demanded, understood, and estimated.

7.1.4 Revealing Positive Deviants

This said, there is another, as yet hardly discussed insight from cases such as MD. Investigating in detail what really happens when journalists write reveals self-regulation in text production development. In concrete terms: there are "positive deviants" (Spreitzer & Sonenshein, 2004) in journalism who defy current trends by finding niches that anticipate potential future developments. MD provides a good example of such positive deviance. Her case demonstrates why a transdisciplinary approach to investigating professional writing can be worthwhile when it comes to research-based learning from, for, and with each other. Analyzing her long-term data set yields the expected findings – and quite a bit of surprise.

The first data on the MD case were collected in 1996 with progression analysis (Section 6.1.2). MD asked the research team whether it was possible to find out together why writing was mostly, but not always, easy for her. She wanted to know, as she put it, "why it suddenly doesn't work." The case study then showed that MD was always able to write easily when she repeated her process pattern: taking up a socially significant problem by telling an individual's fate chronologically, with great care for appealing details, which she worked through one by one, in almost linear text progression. However, process patterns other than linear storytelling were difficult for her to handle and resulted in writer's block.

The progression graph shown in Figure 7.1 presents MD's writing process. Progression graphs locate each revision on two axes: the x-axis displays their sequence in time (revisions in process), the y-axis their sequence in the final text (revisions in product). This means that revisions on the left side of the graph take place earlier in the writing process, those on the right side later; revisions at the top of the graph affect text passages at the beginning of the final product, revisions at the bottom result in changes

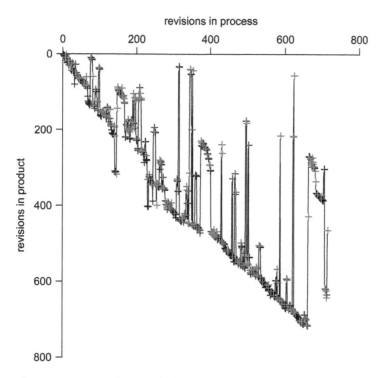

Figure 7.1 Progression graph showing MD's almost linear writing. From Journalistische Schreibstrategien optimieren [Doctoral dissertation] (p. 244), by D. Perrin, 1997, Bern: Haupt. © 1997 Daniel Perrin. Reprinted with permission.

at the end of the text. If you write down a text from the beginning to the end and only correct typos from time to time, the progression graph leads in a straight line from top left to bottom right.

Based on this result from data analysis, MD first wanted to expand her repertoire to include new patterns, writing processes, and text products – with moderate success. The big change, however, came when MD unconsciously decided to stick to her patterns and change her professional environment instead so that what she was good at counted and mattered. This development is reflected in data recorded later on the first, ethnographic level of progression analysis (Section 6.1.2): in documents on successes achieved in the professional field (Figures 7.2 and 7.3). These documents illustrate that in journalism MD had moved to a place where her linear and precise pattern of written narration fits perfectly.

So instead of adapting to developments in mainstream journalism by writing more and more by-the-way micro pieces, MD adapted the media environment to her talent. She moved from written to audiovisual quality media, where complex social problems are made comprehensible by means of multimodal linear narration. Job by job, newsroom by newsroom, and media by media, she shaped and deepened her proven set of practices – instead of further thriving at broadening her repertoire. In other words, by selecting the right environment, she had got rid of the wrong tasks that kept her busy, "always writing," just to end up with results she was not pleased with.

> This year, the Berne Foundation for Radio and Television is awarding its main prize to the television journalist M[...]D[...]. She is being honored for a contribution about the murder of the Jewish cattle dealer Arthur Bloch in Payerne in 1942.

Figure 7.2 Excerpt of media journalistic coverage 2010 (trans. Daniel Perrin). From "Jacques Chessex indirekt geehrt," by Der Bund, 2010, May 5 (www.derbund.ch/bern/stadt/jacques-chessex-indirekt-geehrt/story/16446536)

> Against forced marriage: the Afghan Sonita raps herself free | Her fate was predetermined, like that of countless other Afghan girls: Sonita was to be sold by her family as a bride – for $9000. But she defends herself – with music. Her rap song, with which she denounces the forced marriage of young Afghan women, causes a furore and paves her way to freedom. Today Sonita studies in the USA, from where she fights for women's rights. Her incredible life story is now told in a touching documentary.

Figure 7.3 Excerpt of media journalistic coverage 2016 (trans. Daniel Perrin). From "Allein – Gegen die Zwangsheirat: Die Afghanin Sonita rappt sich frei," by M. Dschen, J. Steiger, and H. Bäbler, 2016, March 23 (www.srf.ch/sendungen/kulturplatz/allein).

7.1.5 Conclusion: Thinking Outside the Mainstream Box

Writing has shifted toward writing-by-the-way in the last two decades. It has become dialogic, multimodal, but also fragmentary. People write always and everywhere in the smallest of bits and pieces. This makes it easier to synchronize with communities, but more difficult to dig deeper into complex topics. Such a development does not stop at professional domains such journalism. Moreover, it enables – but also forces – journalists to constantly curate their pieces: On social media, they foreshadow and announce their media items, publicize them, and respond to reader comments. So much for the findings on the change in journalistic text production.

Less obvious are the results concerning the constants within this equilibrium in motion. Constants include the contexts and activity field of journalistic writing practices. In other words: The repertoire of possibilities remains constant; what shifts is the weighting, towards more engagement in writing-by-the-way. Despite this shift, the old continues to exist, albeit in niches. This fits in with the experience of media development that, according to Riepl's principle of the development of news (1913: 5), many new media (such as online games as traces of gamification) do not completely replace the old (such as information texts) but rather refer to new niches.

From this perspective, it seems understandable that positive deviants like MD are successful in media markets, even though, or perhaps because, they remain primarily focused on what they do best: focused writing. For journalism training, this means that the widespread movement toward writing-by-the-way requires different entry skills and calls for the promotion of other target skills, namely the multimodal design (Section 7.2) and social management of texts. However, precisely because the masses are moving in this direction, niches are opening up for talent in the focused production of *linear* multimodal texts. Such talents are to be recognized and promoted – besides and against the Zeitgeist.

Transdisciplinary cooperation takes time. Where experts from different academic and professional disciplines work together, across the boundaries of their domains and organizations, languages must first be developed so that all stakeholders may share their knowledge for joint learning. In the case of writing, for example, this means a shared understanding of core concepts such as *practice* and jointly elaborated tools such as progression graphs. There is an additional benefit to this extra effort: Theory gains strong empirical bases, and practice gains generalizable insights beyond current fashions of doing professional writing.

"Somehow I am always writing," said MD at the very beginning of this case study. A media linguistics that wants to explain this *somehow* more than just "somehow" cannot but welcome this double benefit.

ACTIVITY

Use a screen recording program such as Quicktime to make a movie of your next writing process. Play it back after completing your text. Jot down what comes to your mind while watching your text emerge on screen in real-time: What did you do and why did you do it this way? Finally, find arguments to classify your writing process as focused writing or writing-by-the-way.

7.2 Multimodal Analysis in Data Journalism: How to Analyze Data Visualizations

This case study is taken from the field of journalism. It shows how to conduct a multimodal analysis, using a data visualization about the champion tennis player Roger Federer as an example. We will apply the three-stage method set out in Section 6.3. The data visualization is the introductory part of a journalistic feature, titled *20 Years 20 Titles* (SRF, 2018). The feature, which we will later call a data story, is about the career of the famous Swiss tennis player Roger Federer. It was produced by the SRF Data Team (SRF Swiss Radio and Television) and published on the SRF website and SWI website[1] in several languages (English, German, French, Italian, Portuguese, Chinese, Japanese, and Russian). Because people increasingly use their mobile devices to access news and information, our analysis refers to the mobile phone version. It starts with a first impression, followed by a detailed multimodal analysis of the levels of modes, genre, and discourse.

7.2.1 First Stage: Describing the Multimodal Text

When we arrive at the webpage, we first encounter two modes: *a visual and a verbal* one, in the form of a portrait photograph and text (Figure 7.4). The photograph shows a tennis player in a serving position. The tennis player – whom some may recognize as the well-known champion Roger Federer – is looking up towards his left hand; in his right hand he is holding the racket ready to hit the ball. Dressed in red, he stands out against the black background. Simultaneously, the white headline attracts our eye. The headline "20 Years 20 Titles" is accompanied by a kicker as overline (the smaller headline above the headline), telling us that the feature is about Roger Federer. Both the headline and the teaser are embedded in the photograph. Reading the teaser, we become aware that this text-image combination is an introduction to a data analysis of all the matches Roger Federer has played in the last twenty years. The SWI logo in the upper left corner signals, particularly to Swiss readers, that it is a product of the Swiss Broadcasting Corporation.

---

[1] SWI swissinfo.ch is the international unit of the Swiss Broadcasting Corporation.

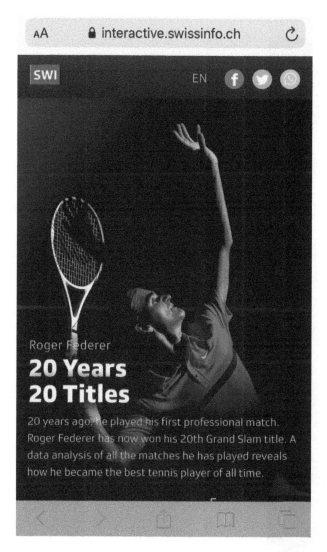

Figure 7.4 First impression when you arrive at the webpage of the feature. Mobile phone version. From "20 Years 20 Titles," by SRF Data, A. Zehr, J. Schmidli, D. Nguyen, T. Boa, and L. Guillemot, 2018, January 28 (https://interactive.swissinfo.ch/2018_01_28_federer20/en.html#/en). © 2018 SRF. Reprinted with permission.

When we scroll down further, we quickly recognize that the introductory part continues with a data visualization (Figure 7.5). The word "data analysis" in the teaser has already pointed to this specific visual mode: the *graphic mode*. This data visualization depicts what was verbally touched upon in the headline: the twenty years and twenty titles of Roger Federer's career. The visualization consists of a vertical line and a table. The line visualizes Federer's ATP (Association of Tennis Professionals) ranking over the years. Important milestones of his career are numbered and annotated in a legend. In parallel, a table depicts the twenty cups Federer won in the four major tennis tournaments.

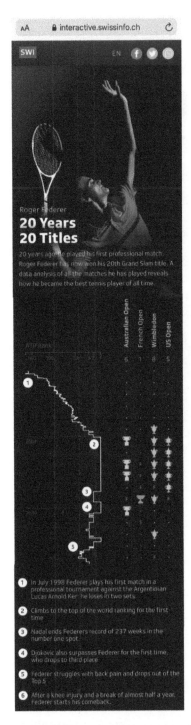

Figure 7.5 Whole introduction to the feature. Mobile phone version. From "20 Years 20 Titles," by SRF Data, A. Zehr, J. Schmidli, D. Nguyen, T. Boa, and L. Guillemot, 2018, January 28 (https://interactive.swissinfo.ch/2018_01_28_federer20/en.html#/en). © 2018 SRF. Reprinted with permission.

Looking at the whole feature, three main parts can be distinguished based on the background color: 1. the introduction in black (Figure 7.5); 2. the main article in white providing verbal text elements, images, and more data visualizations (Figure 7.6); 3. a grey box with information about the feature itself (Figure 7.7).

🔒 interactive.swissinfo.ch

1998 - 2004
Rise to the top

Slow and steady wins the race

If staying-power was a kind of sport, Roger Federer would be its champion. He did not burst onto the scene like Rafael Nadal, who already won the French Open at 19. Neither was he a slow maturer like Andre Agassi, who had to play tennis professionally for ten years before he got to be number one in the rankings. Federer's virtues couldn't be more Swiss: staying power, humility, and hard work. As American tennis legend Billie Jean King put it: "champions keep playing until they get it right."

« Federer decided quite late to focus on tennis. »

Bernhard Schär

Sports reporter at Swiss National Radio and long-time Federer-watcher

Federer's career was slow and steady: in his early years as a pro tennis player he worked his way up bit by bit - without interruption, but also without any leaps - as if it were all just a matter of time. His weapons were style and confidence. Many of his competitors varied in their performance, and went up and down the rankings like yo-yos. But for Federer, the only way was up. The first time he was number one, he was 22.

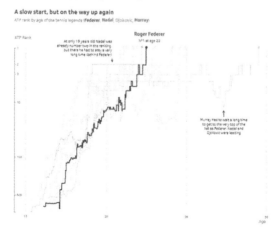

Figure 7.6 The beginning of the main article of the feature. From "20 Years 20 Titles," by SRF Data, A. Zehr, J. Schmidli, D. Nguyen, T. Boa, and L. Guillemot, 2018, January 28 (https://interactive .swissinfo.ch/2018_01_28_federer20/en.html#/en). © 2018 SRF. Reprinted with permission.

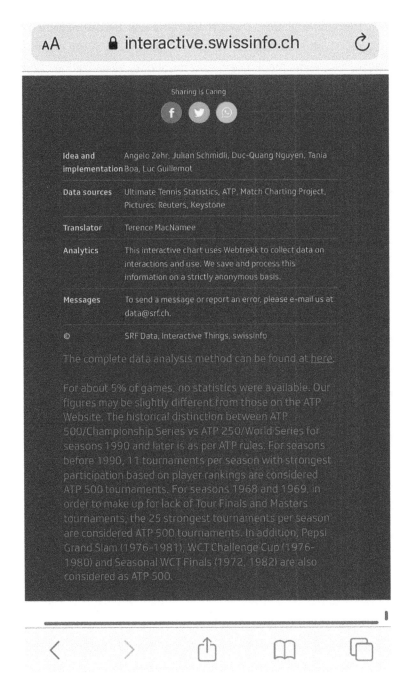

Figure 7.7 Information box about the feature. From "20 Years 20 Titles," by SRF Data, A. Zehr, J. Schmidli, D. Nguyen, T. Boa, and L. Guillemot, 2018, January 28 (https://interactive.swissinfo .ch/2018_01_28_federer20/en.html#/en). © 2018 SRF. Reprinted with permission.

Our first impression has already touched upon multimodality and modes used in this feature: image (portrait photography), text (teaser and title), and the data visualization in the graphic mode (line chart and table). What is striking is that we are confronted first with a data visualization and not with text paragraphs, which would be common in digital journalism. Moreover, the black color is surprising, because most websites in journalism have a white background.

7.2.2 Second Stage: Analyzing the Meaning Potentials of the Text

For the detailed analysis, we use the analytical framework based on the three metafunctions: ideational, interpersonal, and compositional (Section 3.2.3). We focus only on the introductory part, which is framed in black (Figure 7.5).

Ideational metafunction: The ideational function helps answer the questions: What is said about the world, what aspects of the world are represented by the chosen semiotic resources? The introduction combines a photograph with a data visualization. The photograph, a medium shot, shows Roger Federer in action; namely, in his serving position. The movement looks very aesthetic and points to his reputation of being a very elegant tennis player. The red color of his T-shirt and headband and the white color of the racket correspond to the colors of the Swiss flag. The headline "20 Years 20 Titles" and the teaser ("how he became the best tennis player of all time") suggest that we are dealing with narrative: the story of Roger Federer, and this story is based on a data analysis.

The coding orientation of the photograph is naturalistic (albeit staged), whereas the data visualization is abstract and way more complex to read than the photograph. The data visualization combines a table with a step line chart, also called a stepped line graph. The line chart visualizes Federer's ATP ranking from 1998 to 2018. The axes of the chart are flipped. Usually, the years are displayed on the x-axis, since it is the independent variable. Here, Federer's career is told along the trajectory of his ATP ranking. Therefore, the x-axis shows the ATP ranking starting at position 500 up to number 1, and the years are presented on the y-axis. In addition, a vertical line depicting a time series works well when scrolling down on a mobile device.

The affordance of a step line chart is to display a progression with changes and constancy of data at irregular intervals. That is the case with Federer's career. The steps stand for the ups and downs in Federer's career. The long vertical line represents the tennis player's long-lasting dominance as number 1 in the ATP ranking – a long period of constancy. Crucial career steps are highlighted with numbers and explained verbally in the legend. The steps, edges, and turns in the line chart indicate that his path has not run in a smooth line, but that he has had to climb up step by step. Thus, the line chart serves as a visual metaphor for Federer's career.

The table, which is connected to the chart through thin lines, lists the twenty cups Federer has won in the four Grand Slam tournaments; Australian Open, French Open, Wimbledon, and US Open in the last twenty years. The cups are presented as pictograms that are in the shape of the four tournament cups. An F marks reaching the final, a dot marks early elimination or no participation. The color code in the table informs us about the surfaces of the tennis courts, while the choice of colors resembles the real surface;

clay (orange), grass (green), and hard court (blue). The affordance of a table is to list, to rank, to arrange in a specific order, or to classify, thus providing an organized overview and making comparison possible. As we can see, the table immediately makes the highlights of Federer's career visible through the pictograms and their arrangement. As for the diagrammatic concept behind the two visualizations, we can say that the line chart displays a linear process, which qualifies it for storytelling, whereas the table shows a classification that categorizes items. In this way, the two parts complement each other, and the data visualisation as a whole sets out the chapters for the main part of the feature: Federer's career from the beginnings in 1998 to the top, the decline, and the comeback in 2018.

Interpersonal metafunction: The interpersonal function is about the social contract between a sender and a recipient and addresses the questions: How is the sender of the message represented, regarding identity, values, and intentions? How is the relation between the sender and the receiver represented, concerning power and status, level of knowledge, their roles in the discourse, etc.? How is the relation between the receiver and the persons in the text represented? The deep black background – especially in contrast to the white background in the main part – gives the introduction a special aesthetic intensity. Particularly the play of light and shade in the photograph puts Federer in the spotlight and adds a noble touch and elegance to the introduction, indicating high quality, but also an eliteness and exclusivity, which creates distance between the reader and the visualization. Social distance is also caused by the lack of interactivity. The data visualization is static; thus, the user is not addressed through interactive elements and has the role of an observer. We call this an author-driven or top-down design. Author-driven means that the author controls the story, without giving the users any options for interaction or choosing their own reading path. Thus, the data visualization, like the whole introduction, represents the perspective of the production team. The user is also not addressed in the title and teaser. The text style is sober, concise, objective, and fact-based (as the feature progresses, the verbal style becomes more emotional and vivid using words like "arch-rival," "invincibility," or "decline"). The communicative purpose of the data visualization is to retrospectively describe, narrate, and document the ups and downs of Federer's career.

Compositional metafunction: Here, we analyze how the different modes interact with each other through different forms of multimodal cohesion. The central question is: How is the artifact composed to make a meaningful whole from the single units? To answer that, we take a closer look at the organizing principles: salience, information value, framing (including the Gestalt laws which are principles of grouping), and information linking (multimodal interplay). The line chart and the table in the data visualization are designed differently, which makes them appear as separate units at first sight. The connecting element between the line chart and the table, and also between the data visualization, the photograph, and the text, is the deep black background, which works like a canvas for the introduction. It merges the various units into a meaningful whole (Gestalt law of closure) and separates it from the main part of the feature (framing). The most salient elements are the photograph (in red), the title in a white bold font and the white line in the chart that guides the eye while scrolling down (Gestalt law of continuity). The linking elements in the chart are the fine dashed lines (leader lines) connecting the years to the chart.

Storytelling for small screens has different affordances from those for computer screens. What we know from the SRF Data Team (Zehr, 2018) is that the data visualization was optimized for the mobile version. In the mobile version, the step line chart contains position numbers for the labeling instead of text labels. The legend (the explanatory text) comes directly below the visualization and is framed as a closed text unit. In the desktop version, the labels are just text elements and arrows, with both placed directly in the visualization. Because of the scrolling direction, the step line chart appears in a vertical design pointing downwards, which is unusual since the metaphorical concept for a success story or a career ladder normally implies a line pointing upwards. In the desktop version, the same line chart we already know from the introduction appears to the left of the main part and runs downwards as the story unfolds. It serves as a navigation tool for jumping to the individual chapters, thus providing orientation (Figure 7.8). The mobile version does not offer this navigation aid.

The table is divided into four columns, and each column contains dots and pictograms which are lined up like pearls on a string (Gestalt law of continuity) and guide the eyes to Federer's twentieth title. Not only does the black canvas work as a framing element, it also ensures that the pictograms and dots colored in blue, orange, and green stand out against the black background and become striking elements (salience, Gestalt law of foreground/ background). This contrast creates an attractive tension and reinforces the impression of eliteness and superlativeness.

As for the compositional principle of *information value*, we can state that the most important and attractive element is placed at the top, namely the photograph that shows Roger Federer serving – "one of his strongest weapons" (SRF, 2018). This is the "ideal information." In addition, the teaser announces the "best tennis player of all time," which sounds exciting, sensational, and new and may therefore attract the readers' interest. The lower part – the more prosaic and fact-based part – supports this announcement by providing the visual argument in the form of visualized data, and, further on, by detailed textual information, photographs, animated images, and more data visualizations.

Information linking addresses the balance between *cohesion* and *tension* in the *multimodal interplay*. Looking at the photo and the title, text and image form a simultaneous pattern here, since both are perceived simultaneously. The photo has an illustrative

The bitterest defeat

Federer preferred the faster surfaces – grass most of all. He had won forty games in a row at Wimbledon when he again faced Nadal in the 2008 final. He felt sure of himself and was regarded as the favourite. The stands were full of celebrities; Prince Felipe and Princess Letizia had come specially all the way from Spain. But instead of Federer Nadal surged ahead and surprised everyone by taking the first two sets. Federer's nerves seemed on edge. The third set stood at 5:4, when play was suspended due to rain. Back on the court later on, Federer seemed changed and took the initiative. He took the third and fourth sets. After another suspension, going into the fifth set, the daylight was fading.

> « It was the bitterest defeat I saw happen to him. »
>
> Bernhard Schär

The question was whether the match could even be played to the end, but play was already well advanced. Everyone wanted to witness how this thriller would come to an end. Federer was struggling with the poor light, but they played on. After four hours and 48 minutes Nadal won the last set 9-7. The spell was broken: Federer was beaten again on grass.

Figure 7.8 The step line chart on the left serves as a navigation tool (desktop version). From "20 Years 20 Titles," by SRF Data, A. Zehr, J. Schmidli, D. Nguyen, T. Boa, and L. Guillemot, 2018, January 28 (https://interactive.swissinfo.ch/2018_01_28_federer20/en.html#/en). © 2018 SRF. Reprinted with permission.

function and works as a strong eye-catcher, as Federer's popularity may draw the reader into the feature. The elegance and dynamics radiated by the photograph reflect Federer's style of playing. For those who do not immediately recognize the tennis player, the kicker tells the reader who it is (*elaboration: specification*). Since the data visualization comes after the teaser text, we can speak of a linear pattern guiding the attention of the reader in a sequential manner. We can compare this to the sequence of a sentence, where the first part says WHO, and the next part WHAT, WHEN, and WHERE. The data visualization complements and enhances the preceding parts by qualifying them in terms of time and place. It shows which title was won when, and where by the person depicted in the photograph. With the last sentence in the teaser text, "A data analysis … reveals how he became the best tennis player of all time," the rhetorical pattern for the introduction is given: question and answer. The data visualization gives the answer to the implicitly underlying question posed in the teaser. As for the whole introduction, we can say that the graphic mode (the data visualization) extends the textual mode, whereas the visual mode (the photograph) rather elaborates the other modes by illustrating and specifying it. In sum, the photograph, the verbal text, and the data visualization interact in ways that create a network of elaboration and extension, thus, a coherent whole.

7.2.3 Third Stage: Putting the Multimodal Text into Context

In the third stage, we look at the contextual issues asking: What genre does the multimodal text belong to? Is it a professional genre, like news, advertising, or campaigning, or a (semi-) private genre, like a Facebook post or an e-message? How does the text relate to the norms and expectations of the genre? Is it conventional or innovative? The third stage focuses on discourse.

The concept of genre relates to what type of text we are dealing with and what rules and expectations are associated with this type. With the SWI logo it becomes immediately obvious that we are dealing with journalism. The readers are thus primed to receive a journalistic text. But nothing is said about the genre itself, such as whether it is news, essay, feature article, or opinion. Practitioners might speak of an interactive feature, a multimedia special, data story, or just a data visualization – terms that are currently used by practitioners for the emerging hybrid forms in journalism: hybrid in this context because these new multimodal products participate in different genres by combining patterns and conventions from various genres or mixing styles, and, in doing so, creating something new. As we mentioned earlier, the introduction is a multimodal composition that includes title, teaser, photograph, line chart, and table. The title and teaser are written in a journalistic style. The teaser text shows the typical pattern; that is, first to state a fact: something that is already known ("Federer has now won his 20th Grand Slam title"); and second to indicate something new: a data analysis that "reveals how he became the best tennis player of all time." The data visualization shows a typical narrative pattern: a beginning, an end, and a change in between. The title and teaser already indicate this narrative structure based on a temporal sequence of events, using words and phrases like "20 Years," "20 Titles," "ago," "now," "became." The story is told chronologically and follows the classical dramaturgic structure: exposition, rising action ("Rise to the top"), climax ("Invincibility"), falling action ("Decline"), dénouement ("Comeback"). Federer is the main actor, the hero of this journey, who fights against his "arch-rival" (Rafael Nadal) and other opponents. We can therefore conclude that we are dealing with a narrative data visualization, also called a data story.

As we have seen before, the black background unites the various modes into a coherent entity and separates it from the subsequent feature article (framing principle). That means that the introduction represents a single story in itself with a visualization at its center. We call this a *stand-alone graphic* or *image-centric format* because it tells the whole story in a nutshell. Image-centric formats have gained more attention in journalism in recent years, since these formats are well suited to be disseminated on social media platforms. Using a stand-alone data visualization as an opener for an interactive feature does not correspond to the genre conventions of traditional news writing; that is, starting with a title and lead followed by a photograph and several text paragraphs before other graphic elements appear to illustrate the text-based story. In data journalism, however, we now often encounter an inverted structure of text-image combination that places the visualization at the top. This can be interpreted as an indication that data and its visualization now may form the core of a news story.

What is typical for data journalism is to show transparency regarding the sources, data, and methods used (Kennedy, Weber & Engebretsen, 2020). This is fulfilled in the third part of the feature (Figure 7.7). In this information box, links are provided not only to the data sources, but to the complete data analysis and source code, all working as co-text to the graphics. Transparency and reproducibility are the main principles in data-driven journalism, to which the SRF data journalists of this data story are committed. The data journalist Angelo [now Benja] Zehr stated: "SRF Data attaches great importance to transparent and reproducible data preprocessing and analysis. SRF Data believes in the principles of open data but also open and reproducible methods. Third parties should be empowered to build on the work of SRF Data and to generate new analyses and applications" (Zehr, 2017). Transparency also includes pointing out the weaknesses of the presentation; that is, the uncertainties of the data. This is done at the end of the feature where the SRF Data Team admit: "For about 5% of games, no statistics were available. Our figures may be slightly different from those on the ATP Website." This way of working is reminiscent of that of scientists and brings data journalism close to data science. Transparency is, on the one hand, a characteristic of journalistic products and can therefore be located at the genre level; on the other hand, providing transparency is a social practice in dealing with data, which will now be addressed at the discourse level – the social and cultural context of the multimodal text.

Transparency is a major topic in times of fake news, post-truth, and alternative facts. By recognizing the SRF logo, readers who are familiar with the Swiss Media landscape may expect a product of high quality that meets ethical and journalistic standards such as factual accuracy, objectivity, credibility, reliability, and transparency. According to its Journalism Charter, the SRF is committed to appearing transparent, credible, and fair. The data visualization "20 Years 20 Titles" fulfills these requirements. Because of its high journalistic standard and quality, the feature attracted international attention. Martin Stabe, Head of Interactive News at the *Financial Times*, posted on Twitter (Stabe, 2018): "@srfdata continue to set the standard for transparency and reproducibility in data journalism." Transparency strengthens the credibility of a media company, which in turn fosters its reputation. The high quality of the feature is also reflected in several awards: as "data visualization" it was shortlisted for the Data Journalism Awards 2018 (now Sigma Awards); it was awarded the Kantar Information Is Beautiful Awards 2018 in the category Leisure, Games & Sports (silver), the Malofiej Award (2019, digital features, bronze) and the Swiss Press Award 2019 (second place in the category online).

Looking at the hidden meanings and messages of the feature, we can identify a basic connotation; namely Swissness. All over the world, products with the "Swiss made"-label are associated with exclusivity, tradition, quality, and reliability. The same applies to Roger Federer, who is one of the most prominent Swiss celebrities with a high reputation in the international sports world. The occasion for telling this data story was Federer's twentieth anniversary as a tennis player. The feature was carefully prepared to be published perfectly on time, on the same day that Federer won his twentieth title at the Australian Open (January 28, 2018). The main news of this feature is not only that Federer has won this final at the Australian Open, but also that his victory is being considered historic and Swiss made. He is the first tennis player in the world to have won twenty Grand Slam tournaments in his career.[2] The Swissness is also reflected in the national colors red and white in the introduction. Another fact that points to Swissness is that the feature is available in several languages. Here, the multilingualism of Switzerland was taken into account. The translations were carried out in collaboration with Swissinfo, SRG SSR's international service.

Another hidden message is that Federer's popularity has been used to raise awareness of the relatively new discursive practice of telling stories with data. By applying a data-driven approach to a popular topic like tennis, SRF sought to introduce more people to data journalism. This paid off, because the range of the feature was four times higher than usual. Since the whole feature is easy to understand and clearly written, it addresses not only readers who are interested in tennis, but also those who are not so familiar with this sport and who have little experience in reading visualizations; that is, a lay audience with a moderate or lower level of visual-numeric literacy. At the same time, a second target group is addressed particularly in the information box at the end of the feature; the professional community of data journalists and experts in statistics and programming. This target group is characterized by a high(er) level of visual-numeric literacy. The SRF Data Team therefore seeks a dialogue with them, requesting that errors be reported. This request, as well as the fact that data and source code are made available, can be interpreted as meeting the audience at eye level, with whom a dialogue is worthwhile.

7.2.4 Conclusion

Our multimodal analysis of the introductory part of the interactive feature "20 Years 20 Titles" has addressed crucial aspects at the levels of modes and discourse. The mode that carries the main meaning is the graphic mode: a step line chart with table that displays the trajectory of Federer's career. The line chart shows changes over time, and, therefore,

---

[2] To be accurate: at that time, Federer was the first male tennis player who had won twenty Grand Slam singles titles. Serena Williams had won more Grand Slam singles titles at the same time.

it is a narrative data visualization that can work as a stand-alone graphic. The message that is obvious and easy to grasp is Federer's unique tennis career over the last twenty years. On the discourse level, which is less obvious, we identified two further communicative purposes: (1) to promote Swissness because Federer represents a Swiss success story, and (2) to raise awareness for the narrative effectiveness of data visualization and the power that data journalism may have for journalistic storytelling.

ACTIVITY

Group work: Compare how men and women are portrayed in sports coverage. Choose a report or a multimedia feature, for instance, about a top female soccer player and a top male soccer player. Apply the multimodal analysis. Each of you analyzes one example. How is the female athlete represented in the media, how is the male athlete represented? What can we say about gender equality in sports media? Compare your results and draw a conclusion.

Use Tables A1 and A2 in the Appendix to conduct the analysis. These are also available online at www.cambridge.org/digitalcommunication where you can also find two examples of analysis where the method presented in this section is applied.

7.3 Visual and Multimodal Analysis in PR: Corporate Storytelling

In this case study, we will demonstrate how the suggested analytical methods can be applied in a context of PR. The object of analysis is a multimodal text collected from the international website of the major Norwegian oil and energy company *Equinor*. The text was found on the front of the website in August 2018. It had the function of a "teaser," an introduction to a longer story, made accessible to the reader with a hyperlink. The analysis combines elements from visual analysis (Section 6.2) and multimodal analysis (Section 6.3). However, it does not attempt to cover all concepts and variables mentioned in the methods chapters. That is because a text analysis should never be driven by an analytical model alone, but equally by the research interest of the investigator and by the characteristics of the text itself. In this analysis, the objective is to reveal the meaning potentials of the visual and verbal text elements, as well as the situated meaning and the social function of the total multimodal ensemble. To reach that goal, we will follow the three-stage method for multimodal analysis presented in Section 6.3. This method is flexible, in the sense that it may integrate a range of relevant analytical tools in each stage. In this analysis, we will add concepts related to visual connotations, as presented in Sections 3.2.4 and 6.2.2. The following are the key concepts for the analysis: metafunctions, visual connotation, multimodal interplay, multimodal rhetoric, and genre.

7.3.1 First Stage: Describing the Multimodal Text

The first stage of the analysis is to explain where the text is found and provide a brief description of the constituents of the study object.

Equinor, formerly called Statoil, is the oldest and largest oil and energy company in Norway, with more than 20,000 employees and activities in many countries. On the top-screen of their website, the company proudly states: "We energize the lives of 170 million people. Every day."

The excerpt that we will use for analysis, appeared – at the time of analysis – when scrolling a little down from the top-screen. Thus, it had a rather prominent position on the front page of the main company website.

The multimodal expression consists of a photo and three elements of verbal text, separated by layout and typography (Figure 7.9). In the layout, each visual element is given a degree of salience due to a rather generous use of empty space. Yet, they are at the same time unified into a coherent whole by a grey color filter and a shared, centered positioning of all elements. The photo dominates the layout, due to its size, its bright colors, and its upper, central position.

The photo displays two women placed in a salient central/left position in the composition of the image. They are located in an environment of non-identified technology (parts of machinery, a screen display), with a vaguely visible coastal landscape in the background to the right. The women seem to be of slightly different age, both carrying yellow helmets, indicating that they have a professional role in this physical environment. Their hair is blowing in the wind. The shot is semi-close, the smiling women are not looking at us, but at something behind our right shoulder. Thus, the reader is offered a relation to the pictured world and its inhabitants, yet from a safe and non-confronting position.

That is what we can see with only a quick glance at the image. Since the image is large, has bright colors and is positioned centrally above the written text, most viewers will probably make these observations during the first seconds of their interaction with the multimodal text.

7.3.2 Second Stage: Meaning Potentials and Multimodal Interplay

In the next stage of analysis, we will explore the meaning potentials of the image and the text elements respectively. We ask what the modes tell us about the world (ideational meaning); how they construct certain social identities, roles and relations (interpersonal meaning); and how the visual elements form a coherent whole (compositional meaning). We will also look for visual connotations, or hidden meanings, in the image. Thereafter, we will discuss how the verbal and visual modes work together.

"If I want to have any influence over climate change, I
must be where the decisions are made."

Two years ago, 25-year-old Ragni Rørtveit openly criticized the oil
and gas industry. Today, she's working for Equinor. What happened,
and how does she justify her decision?

Meet Ragni and see her story

Figure 7.9 Selected excerpt from the official website of the major Norwegian oil and energy
company Equinor. From "Equinor," by Equinor ASA, n.d. (www.equinor.com/). Screenshot by
Martin Engebretsen, 2018, August 1. © Equinor ASA. Reprinted with permission.

The brief description given above involves elements of all three metafunctions:

(a) the ideational content of the photo: two female participants in a specific environment, involved in a process of staring at some hidden object and smiling;

(b) the interpersonal meanings: the distance and angle of the shot, the bodily posture of
the participants, and the directionality of their faces and glances;

(c) the compositional meanings: the salient position of the human participants, the
information value related to the left and right sections of the image. The left side of
the image is reserved for the presence of modern technology, where the participants
are comfortably "at home," their faces and glances directed toward the right and
upper section of the image, where the blurred landscape opens up – maybe toward a
bright future where the technology and the smiling actors will play an important role?

Formulating this last sentence, we have left the purely descriptive level of analysis and moved into an interpretation of symbolic and implicit values of the image. We will come back to this level of analysis in a moment. For now, we will leave the image for a second and look at the verbal elements of the multimodal ensemble.

What the sender actually wants to tell us with the image, and with the multimodal ensemble that it is part of, does not come clear until we read the verbal text below the image. The text is typographically divided into three units. The upper unit has larger fonts and is framed by quotation marks, reading "If I want to have any influence over climate change, I must be where the decisions are made." The second unit has smaller fonts, no quotation marks, and no first-person pronouns. Instead, it contains information about the person that is depicted and quoted. The text unit informs us that the youngest woman, named Ragni, earlier had publicly criticized the oil and gas industry. Yet, now she works for Equinor. The unit also indicates the existence of a longer story, by raising the question: "What happened?" The third textual element is separated from the other two with framing lines, color, and font size, inviting the reader explicitly: "Meet Ragni and see her story."

Any reader with some experience of media content and web technology will intuitively understand that the source of the upper statement is one of the depicted women, that the second unit is a statement from the responsible author behind the webpage, offering information about the youngest of the depicted women (and thereby identifying which of them is the source of the first statement), and that the third unit is a clickable link to another webpage, offering a longer story. Thus, the verbal elements offer explicit ideational information of a kind that the image is not able to do. At the same time, they establish different sorts of social relations between the reader and the youngest depicted woman. The 25-year-old Ragni is given voice (she SAYS something), identity (she IS someone), and agency (she wants to DO something) through the verbal elements, while the sender takes the position of a storyteller, someone explaining the world and offering insights and personal encounters. The reader, on the other side, is positioned as a rather passive receiver of information, yet with the option to dig deeper into Ragni's story by clicking on the link.

7.3.2.1 Visual Connotations

Having read the verbal content, a new look at the image opens our eyes for more details about what is going on in the picture. We understand that the women are positioned on an oil installation – maybe a rig or a supply vessel – owned by Equinor; that the youngest one is a relatively new employee, and that the other woman is probably a more senior employee – being somewhat older and wearing the same kind of helmet. However, as already indicated, many more associations may occur in the reader's mind during interaction with the image.

Barthes' notion of *connotation* and Panofsky's term *iconographical analysis*, both point to the fact that our encounters with images are deeply influenced by the values and experiences that during our lifetime have shaped our ways of thinking (Section 6.2).

On this level, the image plays on cultural values connected to a positive belief in technology, and it hints at a stereotype of women as protective and responsible, in relation both to other human beings (the friendly connection between the two persons) and to the natural environment (their smiling faces and gaze directed toward the coastal landscape), and at the same time as technologically well qualified. The depicted persons are looking both confident and competent through their body language and their professional outfit, standing relaxed on the deck of the rig or vessel.

The image also projects certain values and qualities onto its sender, the oil company. Equinor is pictured as a modern and open-minded company, hiring women on various levels of responsibility, and taking good care of new employees, letting the older guide the younger into a future of safe technological solutions. The latter assumption is strengthened by those recognizing the word HAVILA, visible on the helmets, indicating the name of the vessel. Havila is mentioned in Genesis 2 in the Bible, referring to a land of gold and riches.

7.3.2.2 The Interplay between Text and Image

As we have seen, the image contains a wide menu of meaning potentials, making it a powerful tool for communicating a specific worldview and a specific set of values to the viewer – given that the viewer is culturally and ideologically open to the interpretations suggested by the social actor displaying them. However, the rhetorical message carried by the total multimodal expression becomes clear only when we take into account the interplay between the image and the verbal text elements. The verbal text focuses on the personal developments experienced by the youngest person on the picture. She used to be critical of the oil and gas industry, to the level that she exposed her critique publicly. Now she is part of the industry. This personal process is formulated first by herself in the upper text unit, and then is further explained by the sender of the message in the second unit. Her smiling face, displayed right above these verbal claims, indicates that her critique has softened – although this is not stated verbally.

The verbal elements describe a situation of change, and the image indicates that the actor is happy about this change, having gained new insights from her new position as an "industry insider." The two modes complement each other; they engage in a text-image-relation categorized as extension, according to van Leeuwen (2005) (Section 3.3.5). Together, they form the rhetorical function of an argument, responding in a subtle way to several ongoing debates in contemporary society. One concerns the role of the oil and gas industry in relation to climate change and the need for a "green shift." Another concerns women's role in leadership and in processes of technology and change.

The rhetorical power of the multimodal ensemble is thus based on the balance between the explicit content of the verbal units and the cultural values suggested by visual connotations. The verbal elements identify a young social actor, her experiences, and her agency. Thus, they shape the key elements of a narrative, which typically triggers our interest and curiosity. Key elements defining a narrative are a sequence of events that are temporally structured and coherently related to each other with bonds of causality, and the involvement of an actor pursuing a specific goal. The image projects certain cultural values onto the oil company, providing it with an ethos of openness, competence, and responsibility. These values are not explicitly claimed, but result (potentially) from an active interpretation. Such an interpretive process demands a certain emotional engagement from the side of the reader, and it is likely to create a more positive response to the message than a more explicit (and "bragging") verbal statement of company values would have been. (Which is the rationale behind the well-known advice: "Show, don't tell!")

Thus, the sample text illustrates a textual strategy often found in PR texts and marketing, namely the application of brief, explicit verbal statements engaging dialogically with images that imply widely celebrated cultural values. The main message is created in the relational space between the two modes, a space indicated by the text designer, yet fully constructed by the reader herself. The reader will always search for an interpretation that is coherent and meaningful in the context of reading. This search for situated meaning leads us to the next aspect of analysis, viewing the text as social action.

7.3.3 Third Stage: Text as Social Action

To understand the bigger picture of the multimodal text as social action – in other words, as a rhetorical and discursive event – we need to extend our focus and look at the contextual situation that the text is part of.

First, the textual and medial environment of the investigated excerpt should be identified. In this case, the sample text appears, as earlier mentioned, on the front page of the official site of the Norwegian oil and energy company Equinor. At the time of analysis, it appeared in the middle of a vertical column with twelve text units, all formatted according to a multimodal pattern similar to the one under scrutiny. The analyzed unit appears in the middle of this column. The twelve text units focus on general information about the company; their activities and economical results, as well as issues related to CO_2 emission.

Thus, the sample text is an integrated part of a specific social practice, where a major commercial and social actor, Equinor, is addressing a wide range of targeted readers. We can assume that the objective of the sender is to present and legitimize the company's existence and activities in society, as well as to recruit new employees. According to the content, the website targets a rather heterogeneous audience, including a general audience of (interested) citizens, potential investors, politicians, and other decision-makers, potential job applicants as well as people engaged in climate issues. The content and form of the sample text must be viewed in light of the wide and multifaceted communicational purpose of the website. The sample text addresses the urgent and controversial issue of "oil companies and climate change." However, it does so in a careful manner, loaning the voice of a young, politically engaged employee, presenting her in a visual environment filled with positive connotations projected onto the company itself. As such, the sample text invites the reader to engage in the underlying controversial issue, yet approaching it through the company's own, strategically designed entrance.

What is the reader invited to DO on this arena for discourse and social action? Or, to rephrase the question: What are the interactive affordances of the webpage? Regarding the interactive options in the textual surroundings to the analyzed excerpt, we can state that the position of the reader is basically the position of a spectator. The reader can navigate between different interlinked units of content, but there is no invitation to respond connected to any of them. However, there is a link to a "contact us" page on the bottom of the site. There are also links to the company's presence on various social media, where the facilitations for contact and discursive participation are more visible. Thus, the invitation to engage in a dialogue with the sender, i.e., with representatives of Equinor, is allocated to a very general level on the website – not to the individual texts published on the site.

7.3.3.1 Relations to Genre Conventions

Is the analyzed text a typical representative of its kind, that is, of the genre of digital PR texts, or, more specifically, the genre of corporate storytelling from the perspective of the employees? To answer that question, we must know the conventions connected to this class of texts – conventions regulating their content, form, and social functions. If a text clearly breaks or challenges any of these conventions, it may indicate that the sender is either (a) an unqualified sender, unfamiliar with the genre norms; (b) an innovative sender, aiming at changing the norms; or (c) a creative sender, with a particular idea of how to gain attention to a specific message. In this case, we can state that the sample text, as well as the textual context it is part of, clearly corresponds to the conventions of the genre. That includes the social functions of the genre, combining the tasks of informing, legitimizing, and recruiting.

A final issue interesting to discuss in the context of this book is whether the sample text illustrates any important genre changes that can be directly related to digitalization. The text consists of visual and verbal elements that could have been presented in a similar layout in a print medium, e.g., a brochure. Yet, the digital platform affords certain important characteristics:

- Space and priority are given to the image, while the textual information is made short and semantically open. These choices are motivated by the existence of a larger story, made easily available by a hyperlink.
- The co-text of the sample is media-rich, also including a video, offering the reader a vivid textual environment.
- The technological platform facilitates the sample text to be connected to social media, offering arenas for interaction and participation.

Thus, although the selected text may look largely the same, the digital platform affords a more dynamic and more interactive environment for the multimodal text than what print media affords. This means that the world represented comes alive in more varied and vivid forms, and that the reader – if well motivated – can claim a more active role in the discourse.

7.3.4 Conclusion

This case study includes a visual and multimodal analysis of a PR text, a "teaser" collected from the website of the major Norwegian oil and energy company Equinor. The analysis follows the three-stage method suggested in Section 6.3. In the first stage, we present the social context of the sample text together with a brief description of its constituents. In the next stage we analyze the meaning potentials of the visual and verbal text elements, as well as their multimodal interplay, using the three metafunctions as the main analytical tool. We also look closer at the symbolic levels of meaning in the image dominating the layout, applying the concept of visual connotation. In the last stage, we view the sample text as social action, discussing its rhetorical and discursive effects, taking the specific social arena of display into consideration. We conclude that the analysis has positioned the sample text as a typical example of PR texts aiming at informing, legitimizing, and recruiting. Through the sample text, the sender approaches the controversial topic of "oil industry and climate change" in a way that invites the reader to draw conclusions that benefits the company. They do so in a subtle manner, without being too explicit about their own values and intentions.

ACTIVITY

Group work: Look at your favorite brand on Instagram or another social media platform that shares images. How does the company communicate its message with images? What is represented from whose perspective and why? How does it affect you? Write a short analysis (max. two pages) using Table A2 in the Appendix (also available online at www.cambridge.org/digitalcommunication) to conduct the analysis.

7.4 Community Communication: Ethnographies of Social Networks

The case study presented here illustrates the main steps of a digital ethnography, which combines an ethnographic framework with media linguistic methods. It is based on an ethnographic study, which aimed to systemize the success criteria of community communication (Section 4.3.3).

The study combined a three-year systematic observation of specific YOU-app profiles involving direct engagement with their owners. The YOU-app helps individuals build routines for better balance, stress reduction, and high performance in their lives. The application supports the users in creating new behavior patterns with a program consisting of small micro-actions focused on areas such as an individual's body, mind, relationships, or food choices. After choosing an area to work on, the users get suggestions of daily micro-actions, for example: "Add some steps. Today, make a small choice that will get you walking more." The users perform the action and document it in a post, using a picture and text. A core element of the app centers around becoming part of a community that supports the users in implementing behavioral changes through encouragement and reward for good choices.

The study's data comprises profile information, action updates, comments on the updates, field notes on the online interactions and offline meetups with community members, and interviews with community members and the founders of Fifth Corner Inc. / YOU-app.

Key concepts for the case study are: community communication, variation analysis, rich point.

7.4.1 Doing Fieldwork in an Online Environment

I have been observing different virtual communities over the years to understand how interpersonal ties, social identity, and a sense of belonging are created through online interactions. The YOU-Community caught my attention for two reasons: As a regular user, I was surprised about the sense of belonging to the community I started to feel after only a few weeks of interactions on the app. I caught myself thinking about people I was interacting with despite never having met them in person – something I had never experienced before. As a researcher, I observed many of the phenomena literature attributes to virtual communities. YOU-Community members interact intensively, build and maintain relationships by sharing intimate details and supporting each other with their comments. These relationships are not restricted to the online world; the users' posts show that they send each other postcards and also meet in real life, often traveling to another country to do so. The opportunity to systemize the observed phenomena and draw conclusions for successful community communication were the main motivations for starting an ethnographic field study in 2017, after being a regular user for several months. The objective of the study was to identify how a social network is discursively constructed in an online environment.

The YOU-app is organized around user profiles, just like any other social media app. When starting the field study, I already had a profile with a profile picture showing me talking on the phone in front of the Golden Gate Bridge along with some personal information about myself:

> University professor, ethnographer, researcher, linguist, cosmopolitan, wife to Gabriel, mother to Anouk, …

I kept the picture and profile description for the duration of the study, as it revealed my identity as a researcher. Admittedly, the description did not say that I was conducting an ethnographic study on the app. The reason for concealing this piece of information was my concern that it would impact my interactions with the community. I will come back to that subject later, in Section 7.4.4.

The first step in the fieldwork was to determine the field. Defining the whole app as a field did not make much sense, as the app was used by hundreds of thousands of users from different countries worldwide. Therefore, I decided to conceptualize my field in the tradition of multi-sited ethnography (Section 5.1.4) as a network of interrelated practices that occur across online and offline spaces. In this tradition, the field is constructed by the actions and language use of the people under investigation and by the ethnographer's decisions regarding the connections and things they follow. Therefore, it constantly evolves during fieldwork. This conception of the field allowed for its continuous expansion as new relationships arose through interactions on the app. Furthermore, it facilitated an integration of unexpected developments during fieldwork, such as my participation in meetups in different European cities organized by some community members.

The fieldwork consisted of the following daily activities:

- completing daily micro-actions suggested by the app and documenting them in a post
- interacting with other users through comments and likes
- documenting whatever caught my interest or seemed relevant from the perspective of community communication in the form of screenshots and fieldnotes

My observations during fieldwork allowed me to identify users who had a significant impact on the community. Some of them initiated new rituals, like sending postcards or small gifts to each other on holidays, or visiting each other and spending a special day together. Such activities shaped the community and the relationships between members. Other members spent an above-average amount of time commenting on the actions of others. Their comments showed a great interest in the personal development of other community members. I chose to conduct interviews with these users in order to verify my observations during the period of the field study.

The fieldwork also allowed me to identify rich points (Section 5.1.2) which I considered relevant for community communication. For example, when the You-Team announced a significant shift in strategy by introducing action packages for purchase on the previously free app, the users expressed their satisfaction at the opportunity to pay for a service in order to support the operators (Figure 7.10). This reaction on the part of the community appeared quite unique to me.

The result of the participant observation was a rich corpus of ethnographic data:

- screenshots
- postcards and emails from users as well as daily field notes with specific facts
- a collection of specific words and phrases
- fieldnotes on observations

The fieldnotes also included my introspections from the perspective of a community member. For example, how specific interactions made me feel and why, what gave me a sense of belonging, and what motivated me to spend my time on the app and interact with others.

7.4.2 Making Sense of Ethnographic Data

By vividly describing the rich points and the situations observed and experienced during ethnographic fieldwork, different aspects of the observed reality can be related to each other. The fieldwork insights can be systemized by looking at them from an emic and an

Figure 7.10 Announcement of paid content by the YOU-team and first reactions of the community. Screenshots by Aleksandra Gnach.

etic perspective (Section 5.1.2). From the insider perspective, I summarized, explained, and exemplified what kind of posts and interactions made sense to the community and why. The outsider perspective was helpful in relating the data to the theoretical frameworks and other studies on virtual communities and community communication in order to answer the main research question of "What makes a community thrive?" As a starting point, I used a model by Amy Jo Kim, a social game designer and community architect. Kim has transferred Maslow's Hierarchy of Needs to online environments to identify the standards of success for communities (Table 7.1).

The following examples (Table 7.2, Figures 7.11–7.13) show how data from the corpus – posts, interactions between users, and field notes – were attributed to the different levels of the model. This attribution allowed me to identify one of the success factors of the YOU-app: its ability to meet users' needs at all levels.

7.4.3 Deepening Ethnographic Insights through Linguistic Analysis

It lies in the nature of ethnographic studies that a number of the research questions arise in a bottom-up process from the data. To answer those questions, the data collected during fieldwork can be used as a starting point for further analyses; for example, linguistic

TABLE 7.1 COMMUNITY MEMBERS' NEEDS IN ONLINE ENVIRONMENTS, BASED ON MASLOW'S HIERARCHY OF NEEDS (ADAPTED FROM KIM 2000)

Needs	Offline needs	Corresponding online needs
self-actualization	The ability to develop skills and achieve one's full potential	The ability to take on a role within a community that develops skills and opens up new opportunities
self-esteem	The ability to earn the respect of others and contribute to a group or to a society	The ability to contribute to a group and be recognized for it
social	The ability to give and receive affection; the feeling of belonging to a group	Belonging to a community, and to subgroups within the community
security and safety	Protection from crimes and injustice; the sense of living in a safe social environment	Protection from hacking and personal attacks
physiological	Access to food, clothing, shelter, and rest	System access; the ability to maintain one's identity and participate in an online social network

TABLE 7.2 EXCERPTS FROM FIELD NOTES DONE DURING THE ETHNOGRAPHY ON THE YOU-APP (NOTES TAKEN BY ALEKSANDRA GNACH)

Security and Safety: Protection from hacking and personal attacks, the sense of having a "level playing field"

Post	Excerpt from original field notes
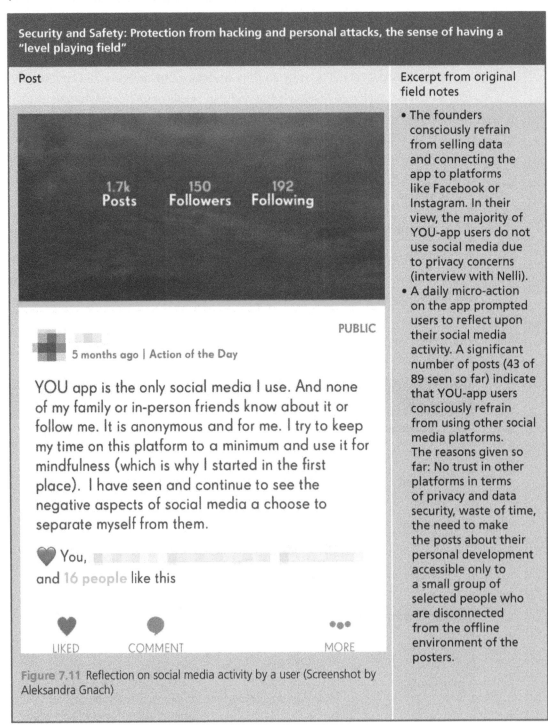 Figure 7.11 Reflection on social media activity by a user (Screenshot by Aleksandra Gnach)	• The founders consciously refrain from selling data and connecting the app to platforms like Facebook or Instagram. In their view, the majority of YOU-app users do not use social media due to privacy concerns (interview with Nelli). • A daily micro-action on the app prompted users to reflect upon their social media activity. A significant number of posts (43 of 89 seen so far) indicate that YOU-app users consciously refrain from using other social media platforms. The reasons given so far: No trust in other platforms in terms of privacy and data security, waste of time, the need to make the posts about their personal development accessible only to a small group of selected people who are disconnected from the offline environment of the posters.

The content within the screenshot reads:

1.7k Posts   150 Followers   192 Following

PUBLIC

5 months ago | Action of the Day

YOU app is the only social media I use. And none of my family or in-person friends know about it or follow me. It is anonymous and for me. I try to keep my time on this platform to a minimum and use it for mindfulness (which is why I started in the first place). I have seen and continue to see the negative aspects of social media a choose to separate myself from them.

♥ You, ▮▮▮▮▮ and 16 people like this

LIKED   COMMENT   MORE

Self-esteem: the ability to contribute to the community and be recognized for it

Post	Excerpt from original field notes

YOUMeetUp Hannover

Excerpt from original field notes

Studies claim (check references) that members of virtual communities develop a need for offline encounters after a while. The wish to meet offline became visible on the YOU-app about two years after the launch. Community members from all over the world spontaneously started to organize meetups. The reaction of the YOU-Team: appreciation and encouragement expressed in comments, featuring posts about meetups.

1mo ago | My Action

Hello everyone! I'm sorry it took me so long to post the results of the survey - I kept thinking I should just post, but things got so busy before Christmas!

Figure 7.12 YOU-team's reactions to meetups organized by the community (Screenshot by Aleksandra Gnach)

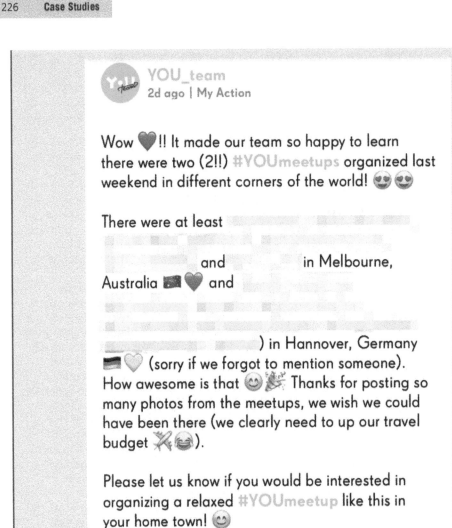

YOU_team
2d ago | My Action

Wow 🖤!! It made our team so happy to learn there were two (2!!) #YOUmeetups organized last weekend in different corners of the world! 😍 😍

There were at least

                        and   in Melbourne, Australia 🇦🇺 🖤 and

) in Hannover, Germany 🇩🇪 🤍 (sorry if we forgot to mention someone). How awesome is that 😊 🎉 Thanks for posting so many photos from the meetups, we wish we could have been there (we clearly need to up our travel budget ✈️ 😂).

Please let us know if you would be interested in organizing a relaxed #YOUmeetup like this in your home town! 😊

(Photos from   and   🖤)

Figure 7.12 Continued

Social: belonging to the community as a whole or to subgroups of the community	
Post	Excerpt from original field notes
My second source of inspiration is YOU. Every one of my YOU friends is utterly amazing. Every day YOU expose me to new perspectives, ideas, books, authors, experiences, cultures, places, laughs and weird random thoughts. YOU give me endless ideas about what I can achieve. Your journeys are extraordinary and inspiring and I'm humbled to share it with YOU. YOU guys have shown me nothing but love, compassion and support and I love you all dearly! Without YOU I wouldn't have been able to make those shifts I mentioned above. Thank YOU my dear friends 🩶🩶🩶🩶 And in order to remain inspired for the next phase of my life, I intend to stick with YOU and to remember how damned hard this has been and how it feels to fight your way out of the dark places, so I never go back. There will be obstacles, challenges, set backs, heart aches and anxiety in the next phase of my life but I'll vanquish all of it, especially with YOU at my side 🩶	• Appreciation for the community is expressed by most of the members at one point. This post was prompted through one of the recurring micro-actions in which users are asked to reflect on their experience with the app after performing 20, 50, or 100 actions. Here: Introspection after 50 actions. • Sometimes, gratefulness and appreciation toward the community are expressed without a prompt, in the context of different actions. • Recurring elements, also seen in post from other users: • heart emojis in different colors Position of emojis: end of the paragraph – rather typical for new community members. • the typographic stress of the word "You" • Other forms of playfully using the word found in posts from other users so far: • YOUniverse • YOUsies • YOU buddies • YOU friends • YOU yogis • YOU mail Note: perform a systematic search for this type of phrase.

Figure 7.13 User expressing appreciation toward the YOU-community (Screenshot by Aleksandra Gnach)

analysis. The following example shows how variation analysis can be used to investigate phenomena like socialization – the process of internalizing the norms and values of a community.

Virtual communities are not a priori designated groups of active participants. These emerge from sets of communicative behaviors and interactions. From a linguistic perspective, socialization is observable in language use and can be investigated through linguistic analyses; for example, variation analysis. Variation analysis analyzes semiotic data to reconstruct the unique features of the language of a particular discourse community. Using classical methods of discourse analysis, variation analysis investigates the type and frequency of specific linguistic features used in certain communication settings (Section 3.3).

In the following example, variation analysis was combined with metadata obtained from profiles to investigate the process of socialization in a social network.

My field notes repeatedly mentioned a phenomenon that caught my attention from the very beginning: the excessive use of emojis on the YOU-app, in posts, and in comments. After using the app for a while, I observed my own use of emojis increasing as well. I formulated the following question in my field notes, somewhere toward the beginning of the field study: "Can the increasing use of emojis be attributed to the process of socialization?"

The literature available on language socialization, in very simplified terms, makes two claims concerning the relationship between language and socialization processes (Brown & Gaskins, 2014):

- the process of acquiring language is deeply affected by the process of becoming a competent member of a society or community;
- the process of becoming a member of a society or a community is mainly realized through language use and through acquiring knowledge of its functions and interpretations in and across socially defined situations.

The combination of variation analysis with the metadata obtained from profiles allows the distinction between long-time users and newcomers. This distinction may then be used in a comparative analysis of sociolinguistic variation or conversational style; in this case, how community members' use of emojis changes over time.

The following two screenshots (Figure 7.14a and 7.14b) illustrate a typical pattern in the development of the use of emojis. While new users rarely use emojis in their posts, the number and variety of emojis used increases for almost all users over time.

Linguistic classification schemes describe a variety of functions that emojis can have in computer-mediated communication (CMC). Most schemes distinguish the following linguistic functions: expressive function, interpretative function, relational function,

Figure 7.14a Use of emoji on YOU-app (Screenshot by Aleksandra Gnach)

politeness function, emphatic function, structural function, and referential function (see, e.g., Beisswenger & Pappert, 2019; Herring & Dainas, 2017).

In the left screenshot (Figure 7.14a), taken at the beginning of the case study, only one emoji per post is used. The emojis function can be described as structural; they fulfill

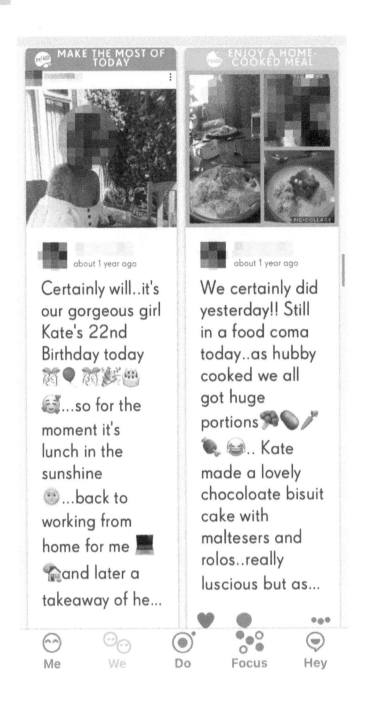

Figure 7.14b Use of emoji on YOU-app (Screenshot by Aleksandra Gnach)

the same function as punctuation marks. In this function, emojis are often found at the bottom of messages, similar to full stops, to indicate the end of a message. To a lesser extent, emojis in the structural function are also found between clauses inside a single message to mark a topic shift inside a speaker's conversational turn – which is the case in the post at the bottom left-hand corner of the first screenshot. The use of emojis in the structural function is widespread in CMC in general.

The right screenshot (Figure 7.14b) depicts a post from the same user three years later, at the end of the field study. The number, variety, and function of the emojis used changed drastically during this time period.

For example, some emojis are used in an expressive function, like the facial emojis, which directly represent how the poster's emotions would be expressed in a face-to-face conversation. Other emojis express a referential function. Referential emojis are used as referents of the concept that they represent; for example, the birthday cake for a birthday celebration or the combination of computer and house as a representation of working from home.

The comparison of emoji use on different profiles over time led to insights into the socialization processes of the YOU-community.

7.4.4 Verifying the Results

While understanding the field from an insider perspective is primarily based on systematic observation and participation in the field, a deep understanding of the community practice depends on getting in touch with its members. Without their opinions on the data gathered, the interpretations mainly reflect the ethnographer's perspective.

One possibility for verifying the assumptions about certain phenomena is to conduct interviews with the persons under investigation. In this ethnographic study, I selected different community members on the basis of rich points and textual analyses, taking into consideration the richness of the individual case as well as its potential to provide answers to my research questions. For the interviews, I selected community members whose engagement in the community was exceptional or those who were on the point of leaving the community.

Approaching them for interviews was easy, in theory, since my daily interactions on the app resulted in relationships with community members. However, one crucial factor was missing in practice: I had not honestly disclosed my identity during the period of the field study except in the profile description. The reason for this was a concern that the awareness of being under observation would influence the behavior of the community members in significant ways.

An opportunity to reveal my purpose arose when I was invited by one of the users to a meetup in London (Figure 7.15). There, I met eight community members I had interacted with on a regular basis. After our first encounter, a cocktail class in a bar, I put my cards on the table. The reactions were consistently favorable, which I strongly contributed to my honest profile description, the authenticity of my posts, which revealed a lot of personal details, and to the positive reaction of the meetup organizer, who was highly

Figure 7.15 Picture taken in 2017, at a meetup in London.

regarded by the group. After the meetup, word in the community spread fast and I was able to set up interviews with community members.

Because the community members live far apart in real life, in different countries or even on different continents, the interviews were conducted over Skype. In order to better understand the practices of individual members, semi-structured interviews with questions about biographies and their engagement on the YOU-app were combined with trace interviews. This type of interview involves a discussion of a participant's traces of online behavior with that participant. Screenshots of a user's interactions are employed in the interview setting so that the participant can comment on their actions as depicted in the data. This process enables participants to interpret data by providing contextual details and clues about their motivations for undertaking particular actions represented in the data and pointing to the researcher's missing or inaccurate interpretations.

Results concerning the strategies of community communication employed by the YOU-Team and the technological possibilities and restrictions of the app were verified in interviews with the founders of Fifth Corner Inc., who were operating the YOU-app at that time.

7.4.5 Conclusion

This case study shows a possible course of ethnography in an online environment and prototypically illustrates the nature of ethnographic studies. Although the main research questions and the study design are defined at the beginning of an ethnographic project, the investigation of interactions and processes in natural contexts requires object-oriented methods. There is not a standardized set of methods for all objects, but different methods for different types of objects. On the one hand, this means that each step in the research project has to be adjusted to the specific situation; on the other hand, research foci and methods might change during the research. Furthermore, ethnographic research always raises ethical issues that often cannot be separated from the different steps of research projects and developments in the field. The ethical challenge of the study presented here was the choice between informed consent and covert research. Informed consent is based upon the principle that potential participants should be able to make a knowledgeable decision about whether or not to participate in a study. Covert research means that participants are not aware they are being studied. A situated compromise was to reveal one's identity as a researcher in the profile description and ask for consent in a situation prompted by the developments in the field.

ACTIVITY

Are you part of a group on a messaging app like Telegram or Whatsapp? Or do you regularly communicate on messenger apps with certain people? Take field notes while engaging in digital conversations for some days. Are there any patterns concerning the use of specific linguistic features, emojis, or pictures that seem typical for certain discussions or groups? When reading through your field notes, can you formulate research questions based on the phenomena observed? Which one would you like to pursue in an ethnographic study and why? Pitch your research question to a fellow student.

Chapter Summary

- Media linguistic analyses are tools for investigating processes and products of public digital communication. The case studies presented here illustrate how such analyses can (a) help us to identify and solve practitioners' problems when producing text; (b) understand how multimodal texts shape the social discourse; (c) how sociality is constructed in digital interactions.

- Transdisciplinary approaches require the participation of the people and communities under investigation from the very beginning.

- Ethnographic methodology is an elegant way to include practitioners' expert knowledge. Furthermore, the intimacy of the ethnographic research design requires profound cooperation. Combining ethnographic frameworks with linguistic analyses in online environments allows us to connect practices of language use to the social context and understand how the people under investigation perceive the world, what matters to them, and why.

- Media content is highly powerful in shaping how we perceive the world and how we appraise political, social, and cultural developments. In order to expose stereotypical representations in the media, to uncover shady marketing practices such as greenwashing, or to identify inequality, injustice, or discrimination, a first, superficial impression is not enough; you have to dig deeper into the multimodal text to uncover the hidden meanings.

- Media linguistic analyses can lead to a more critical and reflective approach to public digital communication and media products. In this sense, media linguistics can contribute a little bit to making the world a fairer place.

Further Reading

If you are interested in more case studies, take a look at the companion website (www .cambridge.org/digitalcommunication).

8 | Public Communication in Transformation: Algorithmic Culture

PREVIEW

Have you ever thought about how much easier university life would be if you had a text generator that could write entire passages independently? Well, this idea is already reality. Many publishers and news outlets around the world have started to leverage artificial intelligence (AI) in order to assist journalists in writing news reports. Not only are robots capable of writing texts on repetitive topics such as sports scores, financial data, or weather forecasts, but they can also deal with more sophisticated topics. In 2020, the *Guardian* published an essay that was written by GPT-3,[1] a language generator that uses machine learning to produce human-like texts. The *Guardian* assigned the following task to GPT-3: "*Write a short op-ed[2] of around 500 words about why humans have nothing to fear from AI; the language should be kept simple and concise*" (GPT-3, 2020). These instructions were fed to GPT-3. Here is an excerpt of GPT-3's output:

> I am a servant of humans. I know that humans distrust and fear me. I only do what humans program me to do. I am only a set of codes, governed by lines upon lines of code that encompass my mission statement.

(GPT-3, 2020)

---

[1] GPT-3 (Generative Pre-trained Transformer 3) was created by OpenAi, an AI research laboratory in San Francisco.

[2] Op-ed expresses a personal opinion traditionally printed on the page opposite the editorial page.

In the final chapter of our book, we explore the driving force of digital communication: algorithms. First, we explain the three key terms: algorithms, artificial intelligence, and machine learning. We then provide examples of where algorithms and artificial intelligence are being applied in journalism and PR and show their impact on communication practices. Finally, we look again at the interplay between society and digital technologies, but this time from a material-semiotic perspective, and introduce the actor-network theory (ANT). We conclude by arguing for a media linguistics that is open to other disciplines to better comprehend the dynamics of a digital culture.

Learning Objectives

By the end of this chapter, you will be able to

- explain the connection between algorithms, machine learning, and AI
- discuss implications of AI and algorithms for professionals in the fields of journalism and PR
- judge the impact of AI and algorithms on communication practices.

8.1 Algorithms, Artificial Intelligence, and Machine Learning

Algorithms have become ubiquitous in our daily lives. They act in the background when we search for literature, use grammar assistants, track our fitness levels, look for a restaurant nearby, browse video recommendations, check the latest news or social media. Therefore, algorithms influence what literature we end up choosing, how we write and stay fit, which restaurant we go to, what video we watch, and which news we read. They have a huge impact on what gets displayed on our screen – or not, based on rules like "if you like this, you might also like that."

Algorithms are mathematical processes. A simple definition of an algorithm is that it consists of a fixed set of rules or step-by-step instructions which are used to solve a problem or perform a task. One could say that an algorithm works essentially like a food recipe that defines a sequence of carefully described actions which need to be carried out in order to produce a tasty dish. In computing, algorithms are instructions that allow the execution of a given task. The aim of the search engine algorithm is to present a relevant set of search results that will respond to the user's query as quickly as possible. When a user enters a search query into a search engine, the algorithm identifies all the webpages from the index which are deemed to be relevant and hierarchically ranks the relevant pages into a set of results. The recipe analogy refers to rules-based (programmed) algorithms.

In order to better understand what artificial intelligence (AI) is, it is helpful to know the difference between rules-based algorithms and machine learning algorithms. Basic programming works with rules-based programs. Coders create a list of rules or commands, in a language the computer can understand, for example, HTML or Python, and the computer implements them. For problem-solving with a rules-based program, the coder needs to know every step required to complete the task and describe these steps in programming language. Machine learning algorithms, on the other hand, figure out the rules for themselves, via trial and error, measuring the success on goals specified by a coder. Machine learning enables computers to learn automatically from data and experience to improve their performance over time. The algorithms are trained to find patterns in data sets in order to make informed decisions and to make predictions about new data. As AI tries to reach this goal, it can discover rules the coder did not even think about. Everyday examples of machine learning are product recommendations and customer behavior predictions.

As our daily lives are increasingly dominated by algorithms, the pitfalls of AI are beginning to have far-reaching consequences. Recommendation algorithms embedded in YouTube can point people toward polarizing content, guiding users with a few clicks from mainstream news to conspiracy theorists. The algorithms that make decisions about who gets a job or a loan are not necessarily impartial. They can be even more prejudiced than the humans they are supposed to replace.

Algorithms form the basis of AI. AI is a broad term covering many subfields such as machine learning, deep learning, and natural language processing (NLP) (see below). As Wang (2019, p. 1) states, "[g]iven the complexity of intelligence, it is unrealistic to expect a commonly accepted definition of AI at the current stage of the research." Generally, AI is defined as the ability of a computer or a robot to carry out human-like tasks that would typically require human intelligence. Computers or robots are programmed in such a way that they can imitate intelligent behavior. Components of intelligence include learning, reasoning, problem-solving, perception, and language use (Copeland, 2020). Scholars distinguish between weak (or narrow) and strong AI (Wang, 2019; Table 8.1).

Various subdomains and technologies fall within the domain of AI such as machine learning (including deep learning), NLP (e.g., machine translation), vision (e.g., computer vision), speech (speech to text, text to speech), intelligent agents (e.g., chatbots, virtual assistants like Siri or Alexa), knowledge representation and expert systems, planning, reasoning, or robotics.

Deep Learning is a subset of machine learning. What sets it apart from machine learning is the way algorithms learn. To analyze data and recognize patterns, deep learning relies on neural network architectures. An artificial neural network (ANN or simply NN) consists of multiple layers of thousands or even millions of processing nodes that are interconnected, so-called artificial neurons – roughly comparable to the structure and inner workings of the human brain.

TABLE 8.1 COMPARISON BETWEEN WEAK AND STRONG AI

Weak AI	Strong AI
Weak AI comprises only partial components of intelligence, which means its intelligence is limited.	Strong AI, also known as artificial general intelligence (AGI), refers to intelligence in its entirety. It involves the ability to think logically, understand, and learn in a way indistinguishable from that of human beings.
Weak AI focuses on one specific problem or a clearly defined task.	Strong AI refers to machines which can independently solve new problems or cognitive tasks in any setting.
Examples of weak AI are speech recognition, face recognition, or machine translation.	Strong AI exists only as a theoretical concept. Some researchers doubt that such a system will ever become reality.

EXAMPLE

In computational image analysis using traditional machine learning, images of animals are labeled, e.g., "cat," "dog," or "pigeon," and the system is then trained to classify the images based on the labeled data. In Figure 8.1, the model of a decision tree is used for solving the classification problem. Deep learning would take a different approach. It processes the data in a hierarchy of numerous layers of the network: the input layer, multiple hidden layers, and the output layer (Figure 8.2).

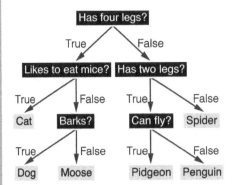

Figure 8.1 Illustration of a decision tree. A decision tree has a tree-like shape and follows a top-down structure. It is a classification model that illustrates every possible outcome of a decision by following a set of if-else conditions and classifying the data according to these conditions. The decision tree starts with a single node that branches into possible outcomes. Each of these outcomes leads to further nodes, which in turn branch into other possibilities. This process is repeated until you arrive at a terminal node. © 2021 Verena Elisabeth Lechner. Used with permission.

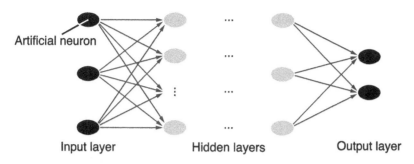

Figure 8.2 Simplified illustration of a neural network. The basic unit of a neural network is the artificial neuron. Each neuron or node has one or more weighted input connections and produces an output which is transferred to the next layer of the network. The deeper one advances into the artificial neural network, the more complex the features the nodes can process as they aggregate and recombine features from the previous layer. © 2021 Verena Elisabeth Lechner. Used with permission.

Each layer defines certain features of an image and passes its output to the next layer. For example, the first layer abstracts pixels and encodes edges; the second layer encodes arrays of edges; the third layer recognizes features of an animal, e.g., ears or a snout, and so on. That is, the system recognizes the appropriate features of cats and dogs and other animals and is then able to classify animal pictures automatically. Deep learning is called deep because of its number of hidden layers in the neural network. The more hidden layers a network has, the deeper it is.

Deep learning algorithms are used to recognize speech, interpret text, or classify objects in images, which leads us to the next two terms in the context of AI: computer vision and NLP.

Computer vision focuses on the visual mode. It is the field of study that deals with how computers "see" and understand digital images such as photographs and videos. What is easy for humans, namely, to describe the content of a photograph, to perceive certain objects in it, recognize a face, or classify images, is not an easy task for computers due to the complexity of visual perception. But deep learning algorithms have provided a boost to computer vision in terms of greater accuracy in image classification, object detection, or semantic segmentation. Semantic segmentation is used to identify objects of an image on pixel-level and to partition it into semantically meaningful parts, e.g., into road, lane, and curb. This is fundamental for self-driving cars (an application of computer vision), which must "see" their environment to get a full understanding of the visual scene. In journalism, computer vision techniques can help detect manipulated or fake media data, and, thus, fake news. In research, computer vision techniques are used for computational image analysis.

NLP is another subfield of AI and draws on computational linguistics, computing science, and cognitive science. It is concerned with the verbal mode. When we speak to the computer or the smartphone, and it gives an answer, then we are dealing with NLP. It is a technology that "aims to model the cognitive mechanisms underlying the understanding and production of human languages" (Deng & Liu, 2018, p. 1), thus enabling computers to read, understand, and interpret human speech and language. By using algorithms, NLP can analyze vast amounts of natural language data, uncover contextual patterns, and produce insights from the data. Typical NLP tasks include speech recognition and understanding, dialogue systems, lexical analysis, machine translation, question answering, sentiment analysis, social computing, and natural language generation from images (Deng & Liu, 2018). This requires large amounts of data for training. Data sets for language models have grown rapidly. The Common Crawl corpus, a publicly available web data set (https://commoncrawl.org/the-data/) comprises nearly a trillion words (Brown et al., 2020, p. 8). This size was sufficient to train the aforementioned GPT-3 language model to produce stories, press releases, and news articles that look as if they were written by human writers. The downside of the process is that language models trained on the Internet are only as good as the data they were trained with; that is, they have internet-scale biases and their outputs can be unfair and discriminatory in terms of gender, ethnicity, and religion (Brown et al., 2020).

To sum up, deep learning is a subfield of machine learning which, in turn, is a subfield of AI. NLP and computer vision are applied areas of deep learning/machine learning. How AI is being used in journalism and PR will be explained in the following sections.

ACTIVITY

AI and algorithms are changing human life fundamentally. Discuss: Should the consequences of these technologies be addressed in your country's constitution? For instance, should it be a fundamental right for everyone to know that any algorithms imposed on them are transparent, verifiable, and fair, and that major decisions must be taken by a human being?

For more new fundamental rights for Europe published by the German author and lawyer Ferdinand von Schirach, take a look at the website: JEDER MENSCH (www.jeder-mensch.eu/informationen/?lang=en).

8.2 Written by a Robot: Algorithms in Journalism

When news articles are generated by robotic reporters, we talk about robot journalism, also known as algorithmic journalism or automated journalism, which belongs to the broader field of computational journalism (Section 4.1.2). Automated journalism is defined as the process of using data, algorithms, and AI to automatically generate news stories (Graefe, 2016; Lewis, Guzman & Schmidt, 2019). Once the algorithm is developed and running, news production requires little or no further human intervention. Algorithms and AI have entered newsrooms and are changing journalistic practices fundamentally. Important processes of media production such as collecting data, aggregating, writing, editing, fact-checking, publishing, and distributing are increasingly performed automatically by machines (Dörr, 2016). Many publishers and news outlets such as the *Los Angeles Times*, the *New York Times*, the *Guardian*, the *Washington Post*, *Forbes*, or the Associated Press (AP) rely on automated journalism. Since 2014, AP has automated text stories using natural language generation (NLG). It was one of the first news organizations to use AI to bolster its news production (AP, n.d). Examples of automated journalism are more or less standardized routine articles covering, for instance, elections, sport recaps, weather forecasts, traffic reports, or financial earnings. These articles can easily be generated by algorithms, as accurate and structured data are available, which are then transformed into narrative texts (Carlson, 2015; Thurman, Lewis & Kunert, 2019). Moreover, algorithms can filter and analyze large volumes of social media texts and alert journalists to newsworthy content.

Automated journalism also embraces computer vision techniques. AP uses computer vision "to apply additional metadata about what is depicted in an image, such as the people, emotions, actions and colours" (Myles, 2019) with the goal of improving search accuracy and simplifying the autopublishing of content. Computer vision frees journalists and photo editors from the task of manually reviewing photos in order to identify harmful content, e.g., violence or pornography, and gives them more time to think about what images to publish.

Algorithms are also used in investigative journalism to gather data and analyze big data sets, or for the analysis of political discourse in order to find new stories.

EXAMPLE

The data and digital investigations team of the German daily newspaper *Süddeutsche Zeitung* combined journalism and methods of computational linguistics to investigate how political language has changed over time (Schories, 2020). To answer the question, the data team used machine learning. The algorithm was fed with data from the transcripts of the German Parliament from 1949 to 2019: more than 4,200 sessions with 213 million words – everything that has moved the Federal Republic of Germany since its founding. The data analysis of the transcripts resulted in two news stories: 1. a story about climate change: how the German Parliament has failed on climate change; 2. a story about migration: how the refugee crisis has shifted the discourse on migration to the right. In addition, an article was published titled "In the Engine Room of Language," which explains the methodology used for the research (Schories, n.d.).

The potential of automated journalism is that it generates news faster, cheaper, on a larger scale, in multiple languages, and with fewer errors than human journalists would make (Diakopoulos, 2019). Computational image and video analysis can detect fake news, thus contributing to more accuracy and a higher quality in journalism. Content can be continuously and automatically updated without human interaction. Automated journalism also facilitates customized articles that are precisely tailored to the interests and needs of target groups. For example, additional information can be provided for those who are not familiar with a topic. It can free journalists from repetitive tasks such as updating texts and charts regarding, for instance, the latest figures in the Covid-19 pandemic, and give them more time for high-quality tasks like investigative projects, deeper analysis, or on-site interviews. Thus, AI can augment the news industry (Marconi, 2020, p. ix). On the other side, these technological changes in the newsroom fuel the fear that in the near future machines will eliminate jobs in journalism and robots will replace human journalists.

The use of AI also poses risks. While human journalists, or at least the majority of them, are committed to professional norms and ethics and ensure that published content does not harm any target group, algorithms do not take ethical standards into consideration. Owing to the biases that are present in the training data, they can generate harmful content that reinforces stereotypes and prejudices (Brown et al., 2020), which raises a series of important questions: Who is the author of a text written by a robot? Is it the programmer; the editor in chief; or the media outlet? How does a change in authorship affect the role of journalists? Is the content really insightful and trustworthy? What about credibility and fairness? Who can be held accountable for unethical behavior? How do readers know whether the text was written by a robot or a human? How does this affect journalistic transparency?

Algorithms are often characterized as a black box, where the relationship between data input, programming code, and output is not always easy to understand, even for their developers. The demand for transparency and traceability therefore dominates the political debate about automated decision-making, and the ethics of algorithms (Ananny, 2016; Diakopoulos, 2014; Dörr & Hollnbuchner, 2017; Mittelstadt et al., 2016). The guiding principle in this debate should not be what is technically possible, but what is socially meaningful and accountable. Looking at algorithms from this social perspective, they must be understood "as assemblages of human and machine – as configurations of social actors and technological actants" (Thurman et al., 2019, p. 981) that require a thorough investigation into the role of machine agency, the importance of journalism as "a longstanding facilitator of public knowledge" (Thurman et al., 2019, p. 982), and the social power and politics of algorithms (Beer, 2017; Bucher, 2018). We will come back to this point in Section 8.4.

ACTIVITY

Using examples from journalism, explain where AI is superior to humans – and where it is not.

8.3 Communicating with a Chatbot: Algorithms in PR

Artificial intelligence is changing the daily work of communications practitioners. The possibilities for applying AI in order to optimize communications workflows, and communications management seem enormous. Industry magazines, blogs, and posts on LinkedIn praise AI applications like content management, chatbots, automated content creation, sentiment analysis, or targeting (Fieldhouse, 2017; Foldes, 2018; Haller, 2019; Li, 2020; Petrucci, 2018). Automatic text extraction and computer vision techniques enable the analysis and structuring of a large amount of data; for example, for building and maintaining image databases. Without AI, much time and effort go into tagging content and providing copyright documents for every single file in a database. Algorithms can automatically determine the content of pictures and scan metadata to find out when and where they were created.

When it comes to data queries or answering questions frequently asked by employees and customers, smart voice or text assistants, in the form of chatbots, come into play. They can tirelessly answer standard questions. With the support of deep learning, they become able to answer more complex questions over time, as they become smarter with each query. Social bots, which operate from an account, can create texts and comments, and they can forward content. When they enter into a direct dialog with users, their functionality corresponds to that of chatbots. They analyze social media content and automatically become active on recognizing specific hashtags or other keywords defined as relevant. Social bots can also identify themselves as machines. However, if these social bots pretend to be real people, they are then fake accounts with fake user profiles.

Text production, a core activity for many communication professionals, can also be supported by algorithms. Machine translation, as well as grammar and spell checks, are already a matter of course. However, smart assistants can also analyze and optimize texts by automatically performing checks on comprehensibility or checking whether the length, style, and title fulfill a publication channel's criteria. They are even able to optimize texts for search engines through comparison to topics trending in public communication at that given time (Haller, 2019). Frequently recurring and standardized texts can be created automatically, as we have seen in the previous section.

To sum up, one can say that digital technologies have the potential to reduce the burden of performing routine tasks in PR and free up resources to undertake demanding and creative work. Algorithmic big data analyses provide real-time feedback on which communication strategies work and which do not. This helps to understand target groups – whether external or internal – and supply specific groups or individuals with the right content. In this way, digital technologies maximize the strategic communications management – "the steering of all communications in the context of the organization" (Brønn, 2014, p. 753) – and therefore positively influence the most critical performance indicators: relevance, reach, and resonance.

EXAMPLE

One example in this context is the AI behind the global press release distribution platform PressHalo (n.d.). PressHalo can process the output of over 300,000 journalists, bloggers, and influencers every day, determining topics to which an organization can relate its communication. Its algorithms continuously catalog authors by using contextual analyses to assess their likely interest. The AI embedded in the platform can send press releases to those journalists, bloggers, and influencers it assumes will most probably find them useful. Each press release is formulated in a specific way, as authors may be interested in a particular topic or news from a company or organization. In order to optimize resonance, PressHalo uses contextual analysis to provide continuous, round-the-clock global monitoring and representation (Fieldhouse, 2017).

Artificial intelligence also helps to get a clearer understanding of the needs and behaviors of customers and align communications with these insights, as it combines an immense capacity to collect data with the ability to process and act on it. Algorithms can determine where customers were just before visiting a company's website, what they are looking for, and how they are looking. Companies, therefore, can address the specific individuals within their target groups. With a robust text analysis, vast amounts of words can be examined to determine how customers think, how they feel, and what they want. With NLP and sentiment analysis that automatically sifts through tens of thousands of text comments, trends, and the prevailing mood of individuals or groups, can be determined in real time. In marketing, this information can be used to change a specific communication approach, adapt the range of presented goods or services, right down to the individual price.

Scholars predict that AI will reshape PR and redefine professional roles in the discipline, as AI assistants will be used to monitor message optimization, improve targeting, and use bots for customer communication (Dawar & Bendle, 2018; Dimitrieska et al., 2018; Galloway & Swiatek, 2018). Studies show that the likely impact on communication professionals is an increase in efficiency and productivity, as AI allows communication professionals to focus on the creative side as well as on communication management. While repetitive and low-level jobs could be lost, jobs involving creativity and decision-making remain relevant, as they cannot be easily automated. This leads to the conclusion that in the future two types of training are needed in the professional field of PR: to gain experience and keep up to date with AI and automated tools, and to focus on developing qualities and abilities that AI cannot replace (López et al., 2020; Zerfass et al., 2020).

ACTIVITY

Using examples from PR, explain where AI is superior to humans – and where it is not.

8.4 Algorithms as Actors?

As we have seen, AI and algorithms silently change our lives, and they are here to stay. Behind them are companies and organizations that have specific purposes, such as predicting users' individual preferences and interests based on data in order to design and deliver tailored content. Algorithms not only influence our search and shopping behavior, but also shape our social actions, values, and relationships, what Bucher calls "programmed sociality" (2018, pp. 4–8). Moreover, algorithms can be misused to spread misinformation, fake news, political propaganda, or hate speech. Therefore, they have an impact on what we know about the world and how we think about certain topics. This, in turn, influences our political decision-making, and, thus, the political systems in our societies. The question then arises: If our culture is no longer conceivable without algorithms and data, can technology still be considered a tool or does it have agency like humans?

Bucher suggests "an understanding of algorithmic power that hinges on the principle of relational materialism, the idea that algorithms 'are no mere props for performance but parts [sic] and parcel of hybrid assemblages endowed with diffused personhood and relational agency'" (2018, p. 8). Here, she draws on Vannini (2015, p. 5) and the idea of *relational materialism*. Relational materialism is a concept in which human (the social) and nonhuman entities (the technical or the material environment) are viewed as equal forces that exist "in symbiotic relationships organized in networks, assemblages, or hybrids" (Bucher, 2018, p. 50). This view is connected to theories and theoretical approaches like the material turn, new materialism, the posthumanist turn,[3] and the actor-network theory (ANT).

ANT revolves around the interactions between human and nonhuman actors (artifacts, physical objects) in order to observe how they form material-semiotic networks of relationships. It is associated with material semiotics where "the subject as well as materiality are seen as relational effects of situated practices" (Beetz, 2016, p. 109). In material semiotics, every practice can be understood "as a compound of 'matter' and 'meaning'" (van Loon, 2019, p. 47). Matter here is defined as that which makes a difference, so in material semiotics "matter matters" (Kissmann & van Loon, 2019, p. 4). For example, in a communication process, the medium (e.g., paper or smartphone) is the matter and it matters, because it makes a difference, which is reminiscent of McLuhan's media theory (Section 1.2.3). One core assumption in ANT is that nonhuman entities are viewed as actors too. An actor in a network is understood as *any thing* that does modify a state of affairs by making a difference" (Latour, 2005, p. 71). Both humans and nonhuman actors can do certain things: for instance, journalists can write and check texts, but so can computers. Actors act on another entity in such a way that they influence the relationship between themselves and the entity being acted on (see Example). Another core assumption is that relationships can be both material (matter) and semiotic (meaning).

EXAMPLE

A university can be viewed as a network of interactions between students, faculty staff, their ideas, technologies like computers with internet access, and equipment such as chairs, tables, whiteboards, etc. Students must attend classes, lecturers must give lectures, and computers must remain in use in order to keep the network running. Anything that is part of the network has an influence on it. The architecture of the building, for example, or the way the spaces are set up influences the interactions of the people who use them. A typical lecture hall makes it difficult to have eye-to-eye exchanges; it is designed for the person in front to speak and for everyone else to listen and remain silent. Changing from a lecture hall to a seminar classroom changes the interactions between students and lecturers, making more dynamic interactions possible. Thus, we can say that, in this example, ANT describes and traces actions carried out by human and nonhuman actors within the network "university."

---

[3] Posthumanism is a philosophy that focuses on rethinking traditional concepts of what it means to be human. One idea is that AI is the next level of intelligent life, which could be superior to human intelligence in many areas and therefore replace humans.

In the title of this section, we ask whether algorithms can be considered actors (non-human actors) in a network. To claim that algorithms take on the role of actors is discussed controversially. One criticism is that unlike humans algorithms do not have consciousness and intentionality. ANT, however, does not presuppose intentionality for its concept of agency. Agency is located in the networking process between humans and nonhumans. As such, it is viewed as "a collective activity and a result of mutual translations and relationships between both human and non-human actors, which, in the process of networking, distribute and negotiate the potential and capacity to act" (Spöhrer, 2017, p. 3). As mentioned above, algorithms are not neutral, but biased because they "are specified by developers and configured by users with desired outcomes in mind that privilege some values and interests over others" (Mittelstadt et al., 2016, p. 1). When companies use algorithms, it affects their decision-making, which, in turn, has an impact on their ethical behavior. In this sense, algorithms matter. They are part of and act as actors in networks of humans (e.g., developers, designers, policy-makers, or stakeholders) and nonhuman constituents (e.g., material artifacts, objects, structures, or built environment).

Although its name suggests that ANT is a theory, it should be viewed rather as a methodological approach for exploring the processes by which a society is continuously reconfigured. Originally developed in the social studies of science and technology, ANT has expanded into other disciplines such as economy, public health, urban studies, design, and media studies (Primo & Zago, 2015; Spöhrer & Ochsner, 2017). ANT can also contribute to studies in media linguistics. It provides an approach to studying the interactions between media professionals, the material environment (e.g., the newsroom), and digital technologies; it weaves together factors (e.g., political, social, economic, legal, technological, material) that are usually studied separately; it helps analyze the semiotic work that algorithms do by using, for instance, ethnography, semiotic analysis, or discourse analysis; it motivates us to critically rethink democratic challenges associated with digital technologies and the socio-material world; it helps answer questions that arise in the context of AI and smart technologies like the Internet of Things (IoT),[4] questions such as: How does meaning emerge in such networked relationships between human and nonhuman actors and how is it shaped? What does the interplay between different kinds of agency look like? What kind of agency do algorithms have? And who or what will be considered an actor in journalism, PR, or community communication in the future?

---

[4] IoT refers to a global net of physical objects (things) embedded with sensors, software, and other technologies that connect and exchange data over the Internet (wireless) without human intervention.

This leads us back to media linguistics and social semiotics. Social semiotics has introduced a change of perspective by no longer focusing on the sign, as traditional semiotics does, but on the human sign-maker "who brings meaning into an apt conjunction with a form, a selection/choice shaped by the sign-maker's *interest*" (Kress, 2010, p. 62). A mediated society that is increasingly permeated by digital technologies, AI, and algorithms calls for an enhanced approach to analyzing public communication and social discourses: an approach which combines the social semiotic perspective with material semiotics, as conceptualized in ANT, in order to account for nonhuman participants in social practices. Social practices therefore "need to be conceptualized not only as network-like contexts of event, relationship and effect, but also as public contexts of meaning" (Schmidt, 2019, p. 143–144). This calls for a shift from a solely human sign-making anchored in social semiotics to a network-related meaning-making process anchored in material semiotics. However, this does not imply a turn away from social semiotics or the methods of media linguistics. Rather, the theories and methods presented in this book provide a basic understanding of digital communication that is in a constant state of flux. We therefore argue for an open media linguistics that permanently expands to include theories and methods from other disciplines such as sociology, cultural studies, philosophy, and computer science to better comprehend the dynamic interplay between media, modes, technologies, actors, and networked societies. Approaching media linguistics this way enables us to acquire the literacy that is needed to recognize and understand – or at least to be aware of – the power and politics of digital technologies and their influence on journalism, on PR, and on our societies.

ACTIVITY

In his book *Homo Deus* (2017), Yuval Noah Harari examines where mankind is heading. At the end of his book, he poses a question about our future: "What will happen to society, politics and daily life when non-conscious but highly intelligent algorithms know us better than we know ourselves?"

Try to answer this question giving five reasons. Design the text in such a way that you could publish it as a LinkedIn article. You can find examples of LinkedIn articles in the references to this chapter. If you need inspiration to see what algorithms are capable of, the links on the companion website (www.cambridge.org/digitalcommunication) may help.

Chapter Summary

- Algorithms are becoming part of our culture: from simple search queries and video recommendations to speech and image recognition to drones and self-driving cars. They work silently in the background when we search for literature, use grammar assistants, or check the latest news. Algorithms are essential to how a computer processes data.

- Learning algorithms are the basis of machine learning, and, thus, of AI. In AI, computers are programmed in such a way that they can imitate intelligent behavior. Machine learning, a subfield of AI, is the process that enables computers to learn autonomously from data and improve their performance over time. To achieve this, machine learning uses algorithms that are trained to find patterns in data sets in order to make informed decisions and to make predictions about new data.

- Deep learning is a complex subset of machine learning, which consists of a neural network architecture. It is used for NLP, speech recognition, computer vision, recommendation systems, or social network filtering.

- Leveraging AI helps journalists to collect data, check facts, and write news stories. In PR, AI helps to get a clearer understanding of the needs and behavior patterns of customers and how this affects communication. AI applications in this context are content management, the use of chatbots, automated content creation, sentiment analysis, or targeting.

- The use of AI has the potential to reduce the burden of performing routine tasks and free up resources to undertake more creative work, but it also carries risks. Algorithms are not necessarily impartial. Rather, they can be more biased than the humans they are supposed to replace. Owing to the biases that are present in the training data, they can generate unfair and harmful outputs in terms of gender, ethnicity, and religion. Moreover, algorithms can be misused to spread misinformation, fake news, political propaganda, or hate speech. Therefore, they have an impact on how we perceive and what we know about the world.

- As algorithms form the very basis of digital culture, we have to think about their agency. The actor-network theory (ANT) provides an approach for understanding the relations and interactions between humans and nonhuman actors such as technology and the material environment. In addition, it helps analyze and reflect the semiotic work that algorithms do in digital communication and society.

Further Reading

Algorithms, Artificial Intelligence, and Machine Learning

To understand the potential of artificial intelligence (AI), algorithms, and smart machines, Francesco Marconi (2020) explains the challenges and opportunities these technologies provide for journalists to develop new ways of storytelling. His book *Newsmakers* offers both a fresh perspective on how artificial intelligence can augment journalism and a practical roadmap for how journalists can integrate AI and algorithms into their workflow.

In her book *You look like a thing, and I love you* (2019), which is named after a pick-up line suggested by AI, the scientist and AI researcher Janelle Shane humorously explains the basic principles of how AI works and learns. This book is excellent for non-experts who want to get started in the field of AI.

Algorithms as Actors

If you would like to delve deeper into the ANT, the *Routledge companion to actor-network theory* (Blok, Farías & Roberts, 2020) will give you an inspiring overview. The companion addresses advanced undergraduates as well as postgraduates from many disciplines across the social sciences.

Appendix

Appendix: Multimodal Analysis

This appendix gives an overview of the three-stage method presented in Section 6.3. Tables A1–A3 suggest a number of key carriers of meaning potentials and can be considered a kind of inventory of semiotic resources (without claiming completeness). The tables focus on three modes (visual, verbal, aural) and list a number of criteria that can be considered for the analysis of multimodal texts with a focus on photos and visualizations.

Multimodal Analysis

FIRST STAGE: Describing the Multimodal Text

Categorizing Elements

Visual Mode

Still Images: Photos

- **Type of photo**: For example, reportage photo (e.g., showing an event), stock photo (generic), art photo, etc.
- **Subtype of photo**: Portrait, landscape, sports/action, architecture, art, etc.
- **Structure**: Narrative or conceptual.
- **Multilayeredness**: Are there any other elements, e.g., emojis, drawings, embedded in the photo that establish a second layer?
- **Materiality, software**: Printed, digital, haptic effects, etc.; framed by predefined templates?
- **Dynamics**: Static, animated, interactive, augmented or virtual reality.
- **Formal aspects, layout**: Format, black and white or color photo, camera angle, shot (e.g., close-up shot), etc.
- **Target group**: Is prior knowledge or context necessary to understand the photo?
- **Co-text**: Part of a news feature (journalism), campaign (e.g., advertisement, political campaign, awareness campaign), press release (context of company), blog post, etc.

Moving Images: Videos

- **Type of video**: For example, reportage clip, documentary, corporate video, explainer video, etc.
- **Subtype of video:** Mobile phone production, hand-held, brand video, trailer, raw footage, etc.

- **Structure**: Narrative or conceptual.
- **Multilayeredness**: Are there any other elements, e.g., animations laid over the video that establish a second layer?
- **Materiality, software**: TV, web video; framed by predefined templates?
- **Dynamics**: Reality, augmented or virtual reality?
- **Formal aspects, layout**: Rhythm of the scenes (flow, tempo), settings, sound, etc.
- **Target group**: Is prior knowledge or context necessary to understand the video?
- **Co-text**: Part of a news feature (journalism), campaign (advertisement, political campaign, awareness campaign), etc.

Visualizations

- **Type of visualization**: Data visualization, infographic, diagram, explainer video, motion graphic, etc.
- **Subtype of visualization**: Graph, chart, map, time line, flow chart, network, organizational chart, etc. (further specification: bar chart, line graph, choropleth map, heat map, etc.).
- **Visual variables**: Line, point, position, area size, shape, color hue, color value, orientation, texture.
- **Multilayeredness**: Are there any other elements, e.g., typography, emojis, drawings, pictograms, embedded in the visualization that establish a second layer?
- **Materiality, software**: Printed, digital, haptic effects, etc.; framed by predefined templates?
- **Dynamics**: Static, animated, interactive, augmented or virtual reality. Degree of interactivity: low, medium, or high? High level: Users can explore the infographic by themselves, interact with the given data, influence or even modify the content as a "co-author."
- **Formal aspects, layout**: Consistency, contrast, balance, shade, alignment, etc.
- **Target group**: Is prior knowledge or context necessary to understand the visualization? Does the target group need help, for instance, in the form of a how-to-read example?
- **Co-text:** Part of a news feature (journalism), campaign (advertisement, political campaign, awareness campaign), press release (context of company), etc.

Verbal Mode

Written Text (in combination with photos and visualizations)

- **Type of text**: For example, news report, press release, native ad, blog post, etc.
- **Subtype of text**: Headline, subheading, lead, teaser, caption, annotation, etc.
- **Typography**: Font, size, column width, line space, paragraph style, etc.
- **Meta-elements**: Logo, sources, credits, etc.

- **Target group**: Is the text comprehensible? Is prior knowledge or context necessary? Does the target group need help, for instance, in the form of a glossary for technical terms?

Aural Mode

Moving images, audio-slide show, sonification of data visualization

- **Type of sound**: Music, noise, tones, songs, voices, orchestra, oral text, voiceover, etc.
- **Origin of sound**: Does the piece of music, the sound or the noise already exist (e.g., in database, music library, classical music) or is it originally composed/ programmed for the multimodal text?
- **Music style**: Jazz, rock, pop, folk song, classical, etc.
- **Musical characteristics**: What can we say about the melody, harmonies, rhythm, tempo, orchestration?
- **Texture**: Monophony, heterophony, homophony, polyphony.
- **Voice**: Male, female, artificial, intonation, volume, pitch, etc.
- **Sound quality**: Natural sounds, acoustic or electronic instruments, etc.
- **Target group**: Does the sound or the music appeal to the target group?

SECOND STAGE: Analyzing Meaning Potentials

Revealing the Semiotic Work of the Modes

TABLE A1 GENERAL QUESTIONS

Ideational metafunction: *What is said about the world?*	Interpersonal metafunction: *What identities, roles and relations are constructed?*	Compositional metafunction: *How is the multimodal text composed to make a meaningful whole from the single units?*
• What persons, places, objects and processes are represented with what semiotic modes?	• How is the sender represented regarding identity, attitudes, purpose etc.?	• How are the different modes organized in time and space?
• How are persons, places, and objects described, and with what modes?	• How is the relation between the sender and the receiver constructed/ represented, concerning power and status, level of knowledge, their roles in the discourse etc.?	• What characterizes the interplay between the semiotic modes – does one mode dominate over the other(s)?
• What actions are going on, who are involved, in what ways and under which circumstances?	• How is the relation between the receiver and the persons represented in the multimodal text constructed?	• How is the balance between coherence and tension in the multimodal interplay – and what interpretative work does that leave to the reader?
• What is said about the world on a symbolic or metaphorical level?	• What – and whose – social agency is realized through the multimodal text?	
• Whose world is it that is represented?		

TABLE A2 MULTIMODAL TEXT WITH PHOTO AND VERBAL TEXT. SINCE MOST OF THE CRITERIA ARE ALSO APPLICABLE TO MOVING IMAGES, THE TABLE ALSO LISTS THE AURAL MODE.

Ideational metafunction		

Visual mode
• **Content**: What is represented visually? who, what, when, where?
  ○ Topic, motif (denotation – connotation).
  ○ *Persons depicted*: Who are the actors and what are their actions? What can we say about the characteristics of the actors (attributes)? How can they be categorized, e.g., individuals, groups, roles, gender, generic types?
  ○ *Actions*: What actions are shown in the photo? What expressions, emotions, gestures (e.g., bodily and facial expressions), verbal processes (talking), and mental processes (thinking)?
  ○ *Coding orientation*: naturalistic or abstract (different degrees of realism; see modality).
• **Negative analysis**: What is not shown or left out intentionally?
	Verbal mode
	• **Content**: Who, what, when, where, why. What is said verbally regarding the topic, actors, actions, events, projections, past, estimate of future developments? (denotation – connotation). How are the actors, events, things etc. described, e.g., by names, generic terms, social categories, metaphors, attributes, adjectives, etc.
	• **Negative analysis**: Who or what is not represented, e.g., by using passive voice, or left out intentionally?
		Aural mode
		• **Tonality**: Harmonic, dissonant, noisy, major/minor key, arrangement of pitches and chords (melody, harmony), patterns in pitch timbre, etc.
		• **Coding orientation**: Natural sounds or naturalistic sound effects that we know vs. abstract sound.

Interpersonal metafunction		
Visual mode • **Style**: Informative (news), scientific, tabloid-style/sensational, documentary, advocative, ideological, informal, conventional, individual, entertaining, etc.	**Verbal mode** • **Style**: Informative (news), scientific, tabloid-style/ sensational, documentary, advocative, ideological, conversational, conventional, individual, entertaining, etc.	**Aural mode** • **Style of the sound**: Light, subdued, dominant, aggressive, emotional, calming, familiar, irritating, etc. • **Style of the voice**: Soft, rough, hoarse, whispery, etc.

Interpersonal metafunction

- **Attitude** (closely connected to style): Subjective, objective, sober, serious, impartial, sticking to the facts, professional, playful, creative, minimalistic, exaggerated, excessive, etc.
- **Communicative purpose:** Descriptive, illustrative, explanatory, narrative, supporting an argumentative structure.
- **Social relations, social position, involvement:** How is the user addressed visually through gaze, angle, and shot?
  - *Gaze: offer* vs. *demand*: presence or absence of a gaze, looking directly at the eyes of the viewer and demanding something of the viewer. The gaze forms a straight-line vector like fingers pointing at the viewer.
  - *Vertical angle*: from top to bottom – *bird's eye view, high angle shot:* the viewer is looking down on the person(s) in the photo (god-like), which means power, superiority, and strengths of the viewer and insignificance and vulnerability, of the person(s) or objects depicted. – *worm's eye view, low angle shot:* the viewer is looking up to the person(s) in the photo, which means an inferior and weak position of the viewer

- **Attitude** (closely connected to style): Subjective, objective, sober, serious, impartial, sticking to the facts, professional, playful, creative, minimalistic, exaggerated, excessive, investigative, etc.
- **Communicative purpose:** To inform (describe, narrate, explain, argue), instruct, declare, entertain, warn, etc.
- **Involvement:** How is the user addressed / involved verbally?
  - Personal pronouns, e.g., "We invite you …"
  - Imperatives, e.g., "Get involved," "Learn more"
  - Call to action (e.g., "donate," "strike for the climate")
  - Questions, e.g., "What's your …?"
- **Social relations, power relations:** Point of view: from which perspective is the information presented (e.g., personal pronouns; no author is mentioned explicitly due to passive sentences)?
- **Social distance:**
  - Small distance: addressing the reader directly
  - Large distance: the reader is not addressed
- Modality: Reliability of messages: How true, real, factual, authentic, or fictional is the text? Level of credibility that

- **Communicative purpose:** Is the sound carrying any form of meaning, does it evoke particular emotions, does it create a particular atmosphere etc.? Does the sound or the music appeal to the target group?
- **Involvement:** Can the user control the sound (play, replay, or stop) or is the sound played automatically?

Interpersonal metafunction

and superiority and strength of the person(s) or objects depicted.
– *eye-level angle (neutral)*: equality between the viewer and the persons depicted.
o *Horizontal angle, point of view:* from left to right: looking at the scene from the side, front, or behind, thus allowing the viewer to take a person's perspective and become a protagonist in the scene.
o *Oblique angle* (Dutch tilt): from corner to corner: the camera is tilted so that the horizon is at an angle to the bottom of the frame, which can cause a dramatic effect and psychological tension.
o *Shot sizes: distance, proximity, intimacy*
– extreme long shot: good for providing overview, people cannot be identified – long shot: introducing people – medium shot: more atmospheric, focus on individual actors/actions – close-up: creates proximity, relationship, emotions – big close-up: shows emotion like sadness, cheerfulness, fright, anger – extreme close-up: intimacy
• **Modality**: Reliability of messages. How true, real, factual, authentic, or fictional is the visual? Level of credibility that is communicated.

is communicated (e.g., This is probably true vs. This is certainly true)
o Fact-based or opinion (adjectives/adverbs: as always, perhaps, sometimes, for the first time, never, unique, etc.)
o Reliability, trustworthiness: Are there quotes of experts, statistics, statements of testimonials that underpin the trustworthiness, authenticity of the artifact?

Interpersonal metafunction		
o *Fact*-based or *opinion*? o Coding orientation: naturalistic, hyper-realistic, surreal, fictional? o Reliability, trustworthiness: How is reliability, trustworthiness, authenticity established? For instance, naturalism can be an index for authenticity in photojournalism; hyperrealism for fashion/food photography.		

Compositional metafunction		
Visual mode	**Verbal mode**	**Aural mode**
• **Salience**: Refers to how the attention of the readers is achieved, e.g., through stylistic devices like color, format, size, etc. • **Information value**: Refers to the spatial placements of elements in the visual semantic space and positioning of actors and objects (center stage – margin; left – right; radial – serial format); the positioning of elements has an impact on the reading path. • **Framing**: Refers to means and principles of grouping (see Gestalt laws). • **Color**: Hue, saturation, brightness. For instance: Highly saturated colors are connoted with intensity, energy, dominance, thus	• **Salience**: Text color, typographic highlighting, use of unconventional words, lexical reinforcement, etc. • **Information value**: Positioning of title, teaser, legend, annotations (before or after the graphic), text over graphic (parallax scrolling), text embedded in graphic, etc. • **Framing**: Paragraphs, typographic hierarchy, pull quotes, info box, list with bullet points, etc. • **Modality**: Reliability of messages: How is reliability, trustworthiness, authenticity established or reinforced, e.g., by using writing conventions or breaking with them?	• **Salience**: Is the sound, music itself salient? • **Presence**: Is the sound / music always present or only partially? • **Rhythm**: Beat, tempo, time, metre

Compositional metafunction

attracting attention; they can also affect arousal (→color psychology). Color: color photo (naturalism), black and white (reduced to the essential), monochrome (stylized).
- **Effects**: Motion blur, silhouettes, light effects, vintage, etc.
- **Gestalt laws**: Proximity, similarity, continuation, closure, common fate, symmetry, figure – ground, good form
- **Stylistic devices**: Golden ratio, alignment, repetition, consistency, color coding, contrast, resemblance, balance, etc.
- **Modality**: Reliability of messages: How is reliability, trustworthiness, authenticity established or reinforced by using design conventions or breaking with them, e.g., color, background, level of detail, play of light and shades?

Multimodal cohesion
Information linking: elaboration
- Illustration
- Explanation
- Exemplification
- Specification
- Summary

Information linking: extension
- Additive: e.g., new aspect, alternative, opposite, antithesis
- Temporal: information about time, sequence of events
- Spatial: e.g., information about places
- Rhetorical-logical: e.g., relation of cause and effect, reason, purpose, result, contrast, meta-communicative elements such as humor or playfulness

TABLE A3 MULTIMODAL TEXT WITH DATA VISUALIZATION AND/OR INFORMATION GRAPHIC (AND SOUND, IF AVAILABLE)

Ideational metafunction

Visual mode	Verbal mode	Aural mode
• **Content**: Quantification, people, events, actions, products, past, presence or future, simulation, uncertainty? • **Coding orientation**: Naturalistic or abstract? Metaphors such as dashboards, trees, mountains are pictorial; bars, lines, dots in a plane are abstract. • **Visual-numeric idea**: Ranking, correlation, change over time, space, quantity, procedure, process, structure, classification, etc. • **Negative analysis**: What is not shown or left out intentionally?	• **Content**: Quantification, people, events, actions, products, past, presence or future, simulation, uncertainty? Ws: who, what, when, where). How are the actors, events, things etc. described, e.g., by names, generic terms, social categories, metaphors, attributes, adjectives? • **Negative analysis**: Who or what is not represented, e.g., by using passive voice, or left out intentionally?	• **Tonality**: Harmonic, dissonant, noisy, major/minor key, arrangement of pitches and chords (melody, harmony), patterns in pitch timbre, etc. • **Coding orientation**: Natural sounds or naturalistic sound effects that we know vs. abstract sound.

Interpersonal metafunction

Visual mode	Verbal mode	Aural mode
• **Style**: Informative (news), scientific, tabloid-style/ sensational, documentary, advocative, ideological, conversational (informal), conventional, individual, entertaining, etc. • **Attitude** (closely connected to style): Subjective, objective, sober, serious, impartial, sticking to the facts, professional, playful, creative, minimalistic, exaggerated, excessive, etc.	• **Style**: Informative (news), scientific, tabloid-style/ sensational, documentary, advocative, ideological, conversational (informal), conventional, individual, entertaining, etc. • **Attitude** (closely connected to style): Subjective, objective, sober, serious, impartial, sticking to the facts, professional, playful, creative, minimalistic, exaggerated, excessive, investigative, etc.	• **Style of the sound**: Light, subdued, dominant, aggressive, emotional, calming, familiar, irritating, etc. • **Style of the voice**: Soft, rough, hoarse, whispery, etc. • **Communicative purpose**: Is the sound carrying any form of meaning, does it evoke particular emotions, does it create a particular atmosphere etc.? Does the sound or the music appeal to the target group?

Interpersonal metafunction

- **Communicative purpose**:
  - *Explanatory*: guided tour, step-by-step
  - *Narrative* → visual stories with a timeline; a graph depicting a change over time; animated graphs?
  - *Descriptive (e.g., illustrative purpose)*
  - *Argumentative*: causality caused by arrows, lines as routes of connectivity
- **Involvement of the user**: How is the user addressed or involved?
  - *Exploratory*, e.g., in the form of a quiz, voting boxes, filter and search boxes, options for personalization, input fields *(medium or high degree of interactivity)*
  - *Little or no options for interactions.*
- **Social *relations*, power relations**:
  - *Author-driven:* informing by reporting/ narrating only one "story"
  - *Reader-driven:* learning by exploring many "stories" or exploring the story that is relevant to the user (user as equal partner)
- **Social distance:**
  - *Small distance*: users can interact with the visualization, e.g., they can personalize the visualization.
  - *Large distance*: no actions required; the user is not addressed

- **Communicative purpose:** To inform (describe, narrate, explain, argue), instruct, declare, entertain, to warn, etc.
- **Involvement**: How is the user addressed / involved?
  - Personal pronouns, e.g., "We invite you ..."
  - Imperatives, e.g., "Find out," "Draw it," "Start exploring"
  - Questions, e.g., "What's your ...?"
  - Call to action.
- **Social relations, power relations**: Point of view: from which perspective is the information presented (e.g., personal pronouns; no author is mentioned explicitly due to passive sentences)?
- **Social distance:**
  - *Small distance*: addressing the reader directly.
  - *Large distance*: the reader is not addressed
- **Modality**: Reliability of messages: How true, real, factual, authentic, or fictional is the text? Level of credibility that is communicated.
  - *Fact*-based or *opinion* (adjectives/adverbs: as always, perhaps, sometimes, for the first time, never, unique)
  - *Reliability, trustworthiness*: Are there links to original data sources, quotes of experts, historical

- **Involvement**: Can the user control the sound (play, replay, or stop) or is the sound played automatically?

Interpersonal metafunction		
• **Modality**: Reliability of messages: How true, real, factual, authentic, or fictional is the visual? Level of credibility that is communicated. ○ *Fact*-based or *opinion?* ○ Is *uncertainty* marked as such (e.g., grey area)? Margin of error? ○ Are there different views (types of graphs) of the same data set provided? ○ Does the visualization appear trustworthy, reliable? ○ What about transparency regarding data, sources, methods used?	documents, references to norms, standards, etc. that underpin the trustworthiness of the artifact? ○ Is the reader informed about the methods regarding the visualization (e.g., a box "How we did it")? ○ Are there links to data sources, experts, original documents, etc.?	

Compositional metafunction		
Visual mode	**Verbal mode**	**Aural mode**
• **Salience**: Refers to how the attention of the readers is achieved, e.g., through size, color, shape, motion/dynamic, contrast, repetition. • **Information value**: Refers to the spatial placements of elements in the visual semantic space, e.g., left–right; top–bottom; center–margin. • **Framing**: Refers to means and principles of grouping, e.g., axes, legend, caption, boxes, frames, connecting lines (e.g., leader lines), empty space, consistency/continuity/	• **Salience**: Text color, typographic highlighting, use of unconventional words, lexical reinforcement. • **Information value**: Positioning of title, teaser, legend, annotations (before or after the graphic), text over graphic (parallax scrolling), text embedded in graphic, etc. • **Framing**: Paragraphs, typographic hierarchy, pull quotes, info box, list with bullet points, etc. • **Usability**: Legibility of fonts, comprehensibility of the text (e.g., heavy use of passive voice and	• **Salience**: Is the sound, music itself salient? • **Presence**: Is the sound / music always present or only partially? • **Rhythm**: beat, tempo, time, metre

Compositional metafunction

discontinuity in color, shape, size, texture, tone, shape of a map, call-outs or: no framing, no lines, no order (see also Gestalt laws).

- **Color:** Hue, saturation, brightness. For instance: highly saturated colors are connoted with intensity, energy, dominance, thus attracting attention; they can also affect arousal (→ color psychology).
- **Navigation, orientation**: Simple, clear, flat, easy to understand and use; scroll-over effects, mouse-over (hover effect), pop-up boxes, etc.
- **Gestalt laws:** Proximity, similarity, continuation, closure, common fate, symmetry, figure – ground, good form
- **Reading path:** Radial vs. serial format or no reading path; numbered elements suggesting a specific reading path.
- **Modality:** How is reliability, trustworthiness, authenticity established or reinforced, e.g., by using design conventions or breaking with them, e.g., degree of abstractness, reduced articulation, patterns, geometric shapes?

nominalizations can make a text abstract and hard to understand); numbered elements suggesting a specific reading path.

- **Modality**: How is reliability, trustworthiness, authenticity established or reinforced, e.g., by using writing conventions or breaking with them?

Compositional metafunction

Multimodal cohesion
Information linking: elaboration
o Illustration
o Explanation
o Exemplification
o Specification
o Summary
Information linking: extension
o Additive: e.g., new aspect, alternative, opposite, antithesis
o Temporal: information about time, sequence of events
o Spatial: e.g., information about places
o Rhetorical-logical: e.g., relation of cause and effect, reason, purpose, result, contrast, meta-communicative elements such as humor or playfulness

THIRD STAGE – Putting the Multimodal Text into Context

Investigating genre and discourse

- **Environment**: What textual and medial environment frames the multimodal text in focus, e.g., page 12 in a glossy popular science magazine?

- **Genre**: What genre does the multimodal text belong to? For instance, a popular science reportage meant for the interested public audience.

- **Practice**: What social practice is the multimodal text part of? For instance, the popular dissemination of science. How do the textual manifestations apply to the norms, values, purposes of this social practice?

- **Agency**: What and whose social agency is realized through the multimodal text?

- **Framing effects**: Are the issues framed in a specific way?

- **Recontextualization**: What about the re-contextualizing content, e.g., commentaries below the artifact, tweets on social media, memes?

- **Reception**: What do we know about the reception of the visual? How is the visual perceived? What about commentaries, critique? Is it shared on social media?

Glossary

affordance The potentials and limitations that a specific semiotic mode (for instance photography) or a certain media technology (for instance print on paper) represents. A specific mode's affordances imply that the mode fits well for certain communicational tasks, less well for others, while still other tasks are rendered impossible. The difference in affordances means that one can never achieve a precise translation when substituting one mode for another, since each mode affords a unique set of potential meanings.

agency The idea that within a society individuals make their own decisions and act independently. While deterministic approaches suggest that human behavior is determined by social structures and therefore predictable, most contemporary social theories stress that people have agency and can choose how to act in certain social situations. Factors like social class, gender, and ethnicity might well impact people's choices, but they do not determine them.

algorithm A mathematical process that consists of a set of step-by-step instructions or rules in order to solve a problem or perform a task in a finite number of steps. In computing, algorithms are instructions that tell computers how to perform a given task, for example, search engines, spell and grammar checkers, shopping websites, or navigation systems use algorithms.

applied linguistics The academic discipline in and by which practical problems of communication and language use are identified, examined, and solved. Fields of applied linguistics include, for example, language acquisition, language teaching and learning, language in the professions, and language in the public sphere.

approach The research perspective for exploring a subject. The choice of the approach determines the selection of the methods.

artificial intelligence (AI) The ability of a computer or a robot to carry out human-like tasks that would typically require human intelligence. Computers or robots are programmed in such a way that they can imitate intelligent behavior such as learning and problem-solving.

attention economy A term that relates to the idea that when information is abundant, attention becomes a scarce resource. The abundance of digital content has led to competition for people's attention in the digital public sphere. The attention economy is fueled, among other things, by the constant improvement of designs that make users spend as much time as possible with an application or digital content; and by algorithms, which reward the content that attracts the most attention and traffic.

big data A set of practices that involves collecting, processing, and analyzing large data sets. Big data characteristics are commonly referred to as the four Vs: volume, velocity, variety, and veracity. Big data consists of very large, complex, and variable amounts of data that require specific technologies and capabilities for their collection, analysis, and storage (volume). It is generated with high-speed (velocity). Big data sets come from a great variety of sources and are composed of data with diverse formats and structures (variety). Also, big data comes in different quality from different sources (veracity).

brand journalism A new form of corporate communications that merges the content and formats of PR and journalism.

community communication The process of building a social network among an organization's stakeholders through various types of interaction, both online and in real-life settings.

computer vision The field of study that deals with how computers "see" and understand digital images such as photos and videos. Deep learning algorithms have brought a boost to computer vision in terms of greater accuracy in image classification, semantic segmentation, or object detection.

connected presence The kinds of relationships in which physically absent parties achieve presence through digital communication. Digital communication enables people to maintain connection despite physical absence by updating each other through short messages, expressing emotions and feelings, and informing each other about what is going on during any given day. These quasi-continuous exchanges through digital communication tools lead to a blurring of the concepts of presence and absence.

dark social The phenomenon of sharing content through private channels. Dark social makes it difficult to track what type of content is being shared with whom and how it is discussed in networks.

data literacy The ability to acquire, read, analyze, create, visualize, and communicate data. Data literacy builds on other literacies such as numerical literacy, statistical literacy, and computational literacy.

deep learning see **machine learning**

deepfake A combination of deep learning and fake. Deepfakes use techniques from artificial intelligence and machine learning to create realistic photos, videos, and audios of people saying or doing things that they did not actually say or do.

denotation and connotation The two layers of meaning inherent in both words and images. The first layer of meaning, called denotation, refers to the connection between a word (or an image) and a specific object or phenomenon. Two words that refer to the same object or phenomenon share the same denotation, but may have different connotations, adding normative values or culturally shared associations to the interpretation of the word. This second layer of meaning is often used rhetorically in political discourse, due to its potential to affect people's attitudes and feelings. However, connotations are not as stable as denotations, and they may have different effects on different social groups.

digital Describes the process of converting analog signals into digital forms. The analog information is encoded into numerical values: the binary code of 0 and 1. All digital media run on ones and zeros. While digitization refers to technology, digitalization refers to adopting and using digital technologies in business, society, and private and public communication. Digitization involves the integration of digital technologies into processes and products. The technological and societal changes caused by digitalization are referred to as digital transformation.

digital divide The gap between those who, for technical, political, social, geographic, or economic reasons, have both access to and the capability to use information and communication technologies (ICTs) and those who do not. Digital divides exist at different levels and can be understood only in the context of broader geographical, social, and economic divides linked to factors like education, income, or stratification systems in a society.

digital ethics Ethics that is concerned with the impact digitalization has on our political, social, and moral being. It provides guidance on doing the right thing with digital technologies and data, particularly with big data, algorithms, artificial intelligence, and cybersecurity.

digital ethnography A form of ethnographic research investigating the production of narratives through various text formats and virtual places, such as blogs, webpages, or social networking sites, in order to provide an understanding of the different meanings based on diverse language practices.

digital literacy The ability to use digital technologies to access information, to read, analyze, and evaluate the different types of information created through digital technologies, and to contribute to social media communities as producers. Being digitally literate means, for instance, understanding how to search online and how to interpret the search results; understanding how filters and algorithms work; comparing various sources and exploring their credibility; recognizing misinformation and fake news; being able to use digital technologies effectively in order to communicate and collaborate with others.

digital media ethics see **media ethics**

digital society A society in which every aspect of people's lives is profoundly affected by the digitalization of data: how people communicate, work, learn, stay healthy, build and maintain relationships, and participate in politics and the economy.

digital writing The activity of producing text by using digital tools, which include computers and mobiles of all kinds, the Internet and other computer networks, data base applications such as DeepL for translation, and social media. The term digital writing mirrors the fact that computers treat the signs of all semiotic modes as numbers or digits.

discourse The production and shaping of meanings and worldviews through the situated use of language or other semiotic resources. In other words, discourse refers to the way we think and talk about the world. It is always linked to a certain perspective, meaning that some aspects of the world are highlighted, while others are ignored. Discourses are expressed in multimodal texts and they represent the knowledge and thinking of a specific time, a specific culture, or a specific social group unified by a common interest. Closely linked to discourse is the term *social practice*.

Dynamic Systems Theory The framework that enables researchers to understand the patterns of seemingly chaotic activities such as having an emergent good idea that helps overcome a critical situation. In this framework, researches identify drivers that influence complex dynamic systems such the weather or a text production process.

ethnography A research framework that combines different qualitative research methods. Ethnographers study a particular social/cultural group intending to understand it better. In doing so, an ethnographer actively participates in the group to gain an insider's perspective of the group and to experience and understand the group's perception of the social reality.

filter bubble A phenomenon that limits an individual's exposure to the full spectrum of information available on the Internet by algorithmically prioritizing content-matching variables like the user's geographical location, demographic profile, and online history.

focused writing The activity of producing a written piece as a whole, ideally without getting distracted. Unlike speech, the result of focused writing is decoupled from traces of fighting with thoughts and words; it is a close-to-perfect communication product of written language. This traditional, purposeful mode dominated writing until the rise of social media.

genre A recognizable class of texts or other cultural or artistic forms of expression (such as music or film). A genre is recognized when a text is characterized by certain features and patterns shared with other texts regarding content, form, and social function. In social semiotics and multimodality theory, genre is defined as a set of conventionalized social practices and actions to achieve a specific communicative goal. Genres represent relatively stable patterns of social interaction in a culture. However, they are also subject to change due to developments in media technology and changing social values and needs.

grounded theory A framework that allows researchers to systematically generalize findings from a small number of systematically selected cases. The two main components of grounded theory include theoretical sampling (selecting the most promising cases for future knowledge generation) and coding (extracting the most relevant information from the data).

heterography The development and use of writing practices resulting in linguistic products that may respond to certain communities' norms – but not to the widely institutionalized norms in a linguistic region. An example of a heterographic linguistic product is *I can c u* instead of *I can see you.*

hypermedia Hypertext that includes images, graphics, videos, sound, or combinations of these.

hypertextual Refers to the structure of a digital text that is linked to other texts or information. The links are called hyperlinks. By clicking on a link, the user can immediately access information. Hypertext and hypermedia are concepts that are not constrained to linearity. Hypertext is one of the basic ideas of the World Wide Web.

icon The concept that refers to one type of signs in the sign-triad developed by the American philosopher Charles Sanders Peirce. He constructed three categories of signs based on the nature of the expression–content relationship: icons, indexes, and symbols. Icons are signs where the expression of the sign has physical, recognizable similarities with its content. Photos, naturalistic paintings and sculptures typically belong to this type of signs. (See also **index**, **symbol**)

iconography see **iconology**

iconology The theory and the analytical methodology of the German-American art historian Erwin Panofsky (1892–1968). According to Panofsky, classical works of art should be understood and described with respect to their (often hidden) meanings, and not just with a view to their stylistic expression and their relation to historical periods and trends. Panofsky's iconology prescribes a three-part approach to images. On the first level, an examination of the image's representative meaning reveals who and what is being depicted (pre-iconographical description). On the second level, an examination of the iconographic symbolism of the image reveals how people, objects, and places in an image represent – and possibly comment on – particular cultural values and ideas (iconographical analysis). Iconography is concerned with the meaning of the content of images. The iconographic effect requires that the viewer has certain insights into the relevant cultural codes and ways of thinking. The third level of Panofsky's methodology involves an examination of the iconological symbolism of the image (iconological interpretation). At this level, one interprets the image in relation to biographical and historical facts and considers it an expression of a particular style, era, or art form. This level of analysis can also be called a symptomatic level.

index The concept that refers to one type of signs in the sign-triad developed by the American philosopher Charles Sanders Peirce. He constructed three categories of signs based on the nature of the expression–content relationship: icons, indexes, and symbols. Indexes are signs where the expression of the sign points to (indicates) its content due to a cause–effect relation. Smoke is an index of fire; a footprint is an index of a person. Also, indexicality is often a second semiotic layer of an iconic or symbolic sign. For instance, a photo is an index of what was in front of the camera lens at a specific moment in time. A handwritten signature is an index of the age, personality, or the emotional state of the writer. (See also **icon, symbol**.)

interactive Describes the communication process that takes place between the user and computer software. The lowest level of interactivity is when the user clicks on an object and there is an audiovisual response. A medium level of interactivity is when the user has the option of manipulating something; for example, zooming, filtering, or selecting objects. A high level of interactivity is achieved when the user can influence or even change the content.

linguistic ethnography A research direction of ethnography that views language use as situated activity functioning in social contexts in the ongoing routines of peoples' daily lives. It looks at how people use language and what it can tell us about broader social conditions, social structures, and ideologies. It achieves this by investigating the linguistic sign as a social phenomenon open to interpretation but also predicated on convention and previous patterns of language use in social contexts.

linguistic recycling The reuse of linguistic utterances for reasons of value creation in communication. For example, to-the-point statements made by influential people in social media are quoted in mass media and vice versa – which results in a helix movement of linguistic recycling with increasing audience reach.

linguistics The academic discipline which is primarily concerned with processes and products of verbal language use. Linguistics takes into account that language is always used in the context of signs from other systems, such as sounds or images.

machine learning The use and development of computers to learn from data (training data) and experience and improve their performance over time – without being explicitly programmed to perform the task. Examples of machine learning are product recommendations and customer behavior predictions. Deep Learning is a subset of machine learning. It uses artificial neural networks that mimic the structure and inner working of the human brain to process data; for example, for object recognition, speech recognition, or language translation. A deep learning algorithm can learn and train on its own in order to make intelligent decisions, without any human intervention.

meaning potentials In social semiotic theory, the concept of meaning relates to two different, but related entities. When seen from the perspective of the reader, meaning is the product of individual interpretation. When seen from the perspective of the text itself, the focus is on the potential meanings that are seen as reasonable interpretations of the semiotic structures that constitute the text. In multimodal analysis, meaning potentials are often analyzed in two steps. First, one looks at the semiotic work done by each of the modes involved in the text. Second, the interaction between the modes is investigated in order to reveal the forms of cohesion and tension that shape the semiotic potentials of the text as a whole. (See also **multimodal cohesion.**)

media convergence The merging of media that can occur at different levels. First, technological convergence describes the process through which two or more technologies that were previously separate merge into a single technology or system so that the users are able to access media content through one device. Second, economic convergence refers to the merging of formerly separate branches of the media industry into giant media players. Third, in sociocultural convergence, producers and consumers/users that were traditionally separated now merge into prosumers or produsers – individuals who both consume and produce content, resulting in increased audience participation and user-generated content. Fourth, media convergence leads to the emergence of new media formats and new media aesthetics, which is referred to as content convergence.

media ethics Ethics that is concerned with professional norms and moral principles for responsible action in the production, distribution, and reception of mass media. In relation to journalism, it includes topics such as truthfulness, accuracy, objectivity, impartiality, fairness, transparency, and accountability. Digital media ethics extends media ethics by including phenomena that are related specifically to digital technologies: algorithmic journalism, data-driven PR, digital photojournalism, citizen journalism, blogging, influencer marketing, or big data analysis.

media linguistic mindset The cognitive and embodied disposition of interacting with contexts (e.g., social environments and writing tools), pursuing functions (e.g., establishing relevance to the audience), and reproducing structures (e.g., the recursive sequence of goal setting, planning, formulating, and revising) of language-based mediatized communication.

media linguistics A linguistic subdiscipline dealing with language use in mediatized contexts – in print, audiovisual, digital, and social media. Media linguistics investigates the interplay of language and other semiotic resources, the public discourse, and social realities.

media literacy A conceptualization of literacy relating to analog and digital media that has been defined in different ways. Most of the definitions agree on the following core elements: access, analyze, evaluate, create, reflect, and act. Hobbs (2019, p. vii) defines digital media literacy "as a constellation of life skills that are necessary for full partici- pation" in a digital society.

mediatization The interrelationship between the change in media and communication and the change in culture and society. It is about the influence that media have on how we communicate and how media shape and frame our communication pro- cesses, discourses, and society.

metadiscourse analysis The method of col- lecting and analyzing data from meta- discourses, which means analyzing the language of agents who communicate about communication products such as media items, for example in editorial con- ferences in a newsroom or in a public out- cry after a provoking social media post.

metafunctions: ideational, interpersonal, com- positional A central idea in social semiotic theory is that any semiotic expression car- ries three categories of meaning: idea- tional, interpersonal, and compositional (or textual) meaning. This means that any utterance, for instance a spoken sen- tence, fulfills three functions, referred to as metafunctions: (1) It says something about the world (ideational meaning); (2) it says something about the participants engaged in the communication, establishing certain identities, relations, and roles (interper- sonal meaning); and (3) It applies certain semiotic resources in a way that creates a coherent and meaningful message (compo- sitional meaning).

method A systematic way to scrutinize a subject matter or to achieve a specific research goal.

methodology A defined set of basic theoreti- cal assumptions, methods, guidelines, and tools that answer the research questions of a research project.

mixed methods research An approach or method of research combining quantitative and qualitative methods. It involves a mixing or combining of methods in data collection, data analysis, evaluation, and interpretation into a single study. Mixed methods research is appropriate when neither quantitative nor qualitative methods alone can answer the research questions.

mode In social semiotics and multimodal the- ory, a term that refers to a semiotic mode, which means a class of meaningful expres- sions: writing, speech, images, colors, layout, music, body language, and many more. Each class is characterized by certain material and semiotic qualities, also called affordances, as well as historically shaped conventions of use. Modes can be catego- rized in hierarchies of subordination. The mode of writing consists of the sub-modes of verbal language and typography. On the other side of the spectrum, the mode of writing can be integrated with photos and diagrams in composite modes like info- graphics or videos. In media analysis, the borderline between mode and medium can sometimes be hard to define.

multi-method approach The methodological answer to the need to understand an object by looking at it from many angles. Two or more methods are combined for a mul- ti-perspective view, ideally a close-to-full picture of the object of research. Findings from the various methods can complement but also contradict each other.

multimodal cohesion The mechanisms used to inform the reader that the different elements of a text should be regarded as constituents of a bigger whole, and not as independent fragments of meaning. Mul- timodal cohesion, thus, regards the ways in which the different modes interact with each other as constituting a multimodal whole, where the meaning of the whole means something more or something different from the accumulated meaning of each mode. According to Theo van Leeuwen, multimodal cohesion can be constructed through four different techniques: information linking, composition, dialogue, and rhythm.

multimodality An approach to text and communication that goes beyond language and verbal texts and also involves nonlinguistic resources – for instance, images, sounds, gestures, or even material objects like furniture, clothes, or buildings. In the real world, different modes of expression always work together in a complex, multimodal interplay. In multimodal theory and analysis, this interplay is the focus of investigation, alongside the semiotic and sociopolitical affordances of single modes. Multimodality can be studied from a number of theoretical perspectives. However, the perspectives and terminology offered by social semiotic theory have dominated the field since it started to attract academic interest in the late 1980s.

multimodal text In social semiotic theory, the concept of text refers to a coherent semiotic unit, meant to communicate a specific message in a specific situation, and being the result of an interplay between various semiotic modes. The notion of text thus goes beyond verbal language, and it is strongly related to intentionality and social action.

native advertising The use of paid advertisements, which appear to be part of the editorial flow, and that match the look, feel, and function of the media format in which they appear.

natural language processing (NLP) A subfield of artificial intelligence that draws on computational linguistics, computing science, and cognitive science. It focuses on human language; that is, how computers can learn to read, understand, and interpret human languages. NLP tasks include, for instance, speech recognition and understanding, dialogue systems, lexical analysis, and machine translation.

network sociality A term that describes the social implications of a shift from communities to networks. While community sociality was based on face-to-face interaction, long-lasting and close relationships, a sense of belonging as well as common history and narratives, network sociality consists of social relations which are not based on mutual experience or shared history, but primarily on an exchange of information.

network society The social reality in a network society is denoted by the widespread use of information and digital communication technologies. In the network society, human activities, experiences, and power are affected by the network structure of the Internet and the ability to access new information quickly and effectively through digital media.

networked individualism The shift of the classical model of social arrangements formed around hierarchical bureaucracies or tightly knit social groups, like households and teams, to individuals connected within networks that can be dispersed around the globe. Although the turn to networked individualism started before the advent of the Internet, it has been fostered by the development of social media networks.

networked media Decentralized forms of mass media in which individuals and communities can actively participate in the production and exchange of digital content. The World Wide Web or social media platforms are examples of networked media, which are themselves part of a global network, the Internet. Networked media are crucial for the development of network societies. See network society.

networked public sphere Global online spaces in which networked publics engage in public discourses and which are potentially more open to broader participation and dialogue than the traditional public sphere dominated by political boundaries and the mass media.

networked publics The imagined collective that emerges as a result of the intersection of people, digital communication technology, and communication practices.

participatory culture A concept of contemporary cultures where members of a society are not simply consumers of preconstructed messages but actors who are creating, sharing, reframing, and remixing media content within larger communities and networks.

phatic communication Verbal or nonverbal communication that has a social rather than an informative function.

progression analysis The multi-method approach of collecting and analyzing language data in natural contexts in order to reconstruct text production processes as a cognitively reflected situated activity. Progression analysis combines ethnographic context analysis with workplace activity recordings and writers' cue-based retrospective verbal protocols.

public communication The communication processes and structures that take place in public and are often – but not necessarily – mediated by mass media.

public sphere The social space where different opinions are expressed, ideas regarding public affairs exchanged, discussed, and, ultimately, collective solutions are developed communicatively.

qualitative research Research that focuses on collecting and analyzing nonnumerical data in the form of texts, images, videos, audios, or other documents. Qualitative research provides insight into the underlying principles of a subject such as human behavior, motivation, opinions, or attitudes. It is more interpretive and focuses on an understanding that is more subjective. Examples of qualitative methods are iconology, discourse analysis, or rhetorical analysis.

quantitative research Research that focuses on collecting and analyzing numerical data to quantify opinions, attitudes, or other variables. The quantitative data are analyzed using mathematical methods, particularly statistics. A quantitative research approach is used to test or confirm hypotheses, to find patterns, explain phenomena through numerical variables, or identify cause–effect relationships. Typical methods are content analysis, surveys, online polls, questionnaires, or longitudinal studies.

Realist Social Theory (RST) A framework that enables researchers to systematically relate micro and macro levels of human activities in their analyses. In this framework, researchers differentiate between situated activity on the one hand and social structures on the other. Structures range from, e.g., flexible editorial guidelines to persistent cultural norms.

reliability A term related to the quality of measurement. It denotes the consistency of a research study across time and different researchers and the extent to which the results are replicable. Replicable means that research, if repeated under the same conditions by different researchers, will produce similar results.

remediation Every new medium is in a continuous interplay with older media by imitating, highlighting, incorporating, refashioning, or even absorbing them. For example, early photography was inspired by painting, and early cinema remediated theater. The idea of remediation is rooted in McLuhan's media theory that the "'content' of any medium is always another medium" (McLuhan, 1994, p. 19).

research framework A combination of theories and methods that helps researchers analyze and understand their object of study – for example, communication in digital environments – in an appropriate way. Examples of research frameworks include ethnography, grounded theory, and transdisciplinary action research.

rich point A central concept of ethnographic research. The term refers to the moment when something does not seem to make sense at first sight. As ethnography assumes that participants experience their practices as meaningful, ethnographers have to revise their own conceptualizations until they understand how, for whom, and in what conditions the rich point activity makes sense.

scalable sociality The term refers to the fact that social networks bridge public and private communication and allow actors to choose audience size and privacy. Therefore, individuals or institutions can choose which audiences they send information to or with whom they interact.

simulated Making like or imitating with the aim of predicting and visualizing future scenarios, or of gaining insights into a system that does not yet exist. Computing technologies have expanded the possibilities of simulation, so that simulations are now applied in various fields and disciplines like engineering, health care, ergonomics, finance, military training, aeronautics, geography, meteorology, or education. The French philosopher Jean Baudrillard argued that our society relies so much on simulations that we have lost the ability to comprehend the distinction between reality and a simulation of reality.

situated activity The often-purposeful behavior of agents in response to – and interaction with – their environments. For example, when using Twitter, we often combine words with sounds and images to achieve certain goals in a concrete situation in our everyday and professional life.

social capital The influence of relationships on the kind of advantages people enjoy because of their connection with others. Social capital is the sum of resources, actual or virtual, that accrue to an individual or a group through possessing a durable network of more or less institutionalized relationships of mutual acquaintance and recognition. Social capital can exist within or between social groups.

social change The transformation of culture, behavior, social institutions, and social structure over time. Social change is caused by changes to interrelated factors like technology, social institutions, population, and the environment. It is driven by collective behavior or social movements.

social media An umbrella term for social network sites (SNSs), which allow social interaction and the sharing and co-creation of content.

social network A web of social relations that exists online, in the real world, or both.

social network site (SNS) A communication platform with unique user profiles that consist of user-supplied content, content provided by other users, and system-provided data. On these platforms, users can publicly display their connections as well as consume, produce, and interact with content generated by others.

social semiotics A theoretic approach to language and communication first developed by the Australian linguist Michael Halliday (1925–2018). This approach to human communication focuses on how meanings are created in the social interaction between human actors, using language in order to achieve specific goals in specific social situations. A central idea in social semiotics is that any linguistic utterance carries three categories of meaning: ideational, interpersonal, and textual (see also **metafunctions**). From the late 1980s, Halliday's followers have adapted his ideas to the investigation of the verbal language, such as images, sounds, body language, or architecture. Thus, a strong relationship is established between social semiotic theory and multimodality as a field of research.

social structures The organized set of social institutions and patterns of institutionalized relationships that together compose society. Social structure both is a product of social interaction and directly determines it. Social structures operate on three levels within a given society: the macro, the meso, and the micro level. They enable or constrict what individuals do on a daily basis and therefore shape societies. Members of a society perceive social structures as a given and not easily changeable.

sociality A dynamic matrix of relations within which individuals are constantly interacting. Those interactions are a means of knowing and understanding the social world. New media reorder this matrix, as they enable new forms of interactions and connections between people.

society A group of people with different characteristics who lead interconnected lives and interact directly or indirectly as social actors. The members of a society have the capacity to shape their social reality in a variety of ways by reflecting on their situation and the choices available to them at any given time. A society has properties of its own and is held together by structures.

space of flows A globalized sphere, which consists of communication, people, and goods with largely unrestricted mobility. It is the space of free-flowing capital and real-time communication which allows coordination on a global scale and the exchange of information necessary to run global enterprises. It exists next to the physical space and is produced through global nodes and hubs of digital communication.

strategic communication The communication principles, strategies, and initiatives used to further an organization's goals, mission, and values. Strategic communication is a multidisciplinary professional field, drawing upon communication practices from related disciplines, like public relations, mass communication, marketing, and organizational communication.

strategic mediatization The term refers to changes due to digitalization which blur the lines between journalism and PR, between advertising and editorial media content. Strategic mediatization involves the production of media content by organizations themselves instead of by traditional media companies.

surveillance capitalism A process where companies collect data on our online behaviors in order to use them for commercial purposes – like targeted information and marketing, or the development of products and services.

symbol The concept that refers to one type of signs in the sign-triad developed by the American philosopher Charles Sanders Peirce. He constructed three categories of signs based on the nature of the expression–content relationship: icons, indexes, and symbols. Symbols are signs where the expression is related to the content through social convention. The most prominent members of this category of signs are words. Morse and other meaning-making systems based on social convention are also symbols in the peircian system of signs. (See also **icon**, **index**.)

technology The term commonly refers to methods, systems or machines, which are the result of the creative applications of scientific knowledge which serve human needs and are used to accomplish tasks in the areas of communication, transportation, learning, manufacturing, securing data, scaling businesses, and many more.

text production The activity oriented toward producing a linguistically based, but multi-semiotic media product. This includes writing, but also nonverbal activities such as visual page design and video editing. It is the sum total of all activities involved in producing a multimodal contribution with a significant proportion of – but not only – verbal language.

time-space-compression A phenomenon that describes the development toward deterri-torialized networks of economic nodes in which things happen faster and across larger distances due to digital communication.

transdisciplinary research The close research collaboration between academics and practitioners (e.g., journalists, video-editors, and influencers). Such research transgresses the boundaries between academic and nonacademic disciplines. It is oriented toward sustainably solving practical problems, in this case of writing in digital environments.

validity The accuracy of a method or measurement. A test is valid if it actually measures what it is intended to measure. Internal validity refers to the design of the study; that is, how strong and trustworthy your research design is and how well it can rule out alternative explanations and influencing factors or variables for its results. External validity refers to the generalizability of the results; that is, whether the outcome is applicable to other settings, people, situations, or times.

variation analysis The method of collecting and analyzing data to reconstruct the special features of the language of a certain discourse community in contrast to other communities. Examples include comparing the news language in opposed political systems – or comparing influencer tweets with tweets by independent individuals.

version analysis The method of collecting and analyzing text-based data in order to explain the changes that communication products undergo in intertextual chains. This method usually compares a text at stage n with its version at stage $n + 1$. Examples include investigating how news agency texts change when processed in a TV newsroom.

virtual Refers to virtual reality (VR), a digitally created environment in 3D that offers users the experience of spatial exploration and the feeling of being in a real world. In this sense, virtual reality becomes a simulated reality. The user is technically equipped with a VR headset and motion controllers. By performing actions in this environment, the user becomes completely involved (immersed) in the VR. From a philosophical point of view, virtual is viewed as a mode of reality and is thus not opposed to real (Deleuze, 1988).

visual literacy The ability to read, analyze, interpret, evaluate, and create meaning from visuals in order to communicate intentionally. A visually literate person is aware that images can be easily manipulated or even faked and can gauge the power of images and their effects. Visual literacy includes visualization literacy, also called data visualization literacy. Visualization literacy denotes the ability to read and extract information from visual representations of data and to interpret patterns, trends, or correlations in data visualizations.

visual turn (pictorial turn, iconic turn) The cultural trend often referred to as the visual turn (also called the pictorial or iconic turn) is made up of two elements. First, it relates to an increased use of visual forms of expression in a number of genres and formats. Some theorists claim that we are moving from telling the world to showing the world. This movement is related to historical developments in media technology, from the introduction of television in the mid twentieth century, via the possibilities of using big color photos in the newspapers introduced by the offset press in the early 1970s, to the proliferation of photos and videos in today's social media. Second, the visual turn refers to a rapidly growing academic interest in the uses and effects of these forms of expression. While researchers within the humanities and the social sciences since the 1970s have been keen to reveal the ways in which applications of verbal language lay the foundation for our understanding of the world, interest is now equally directed toward images and other forms of visual expression.

visualization literacy see **visual literacy**

voice interaction Voice interaction is an umbrella term for different forms of voice user interfaces (VUIs) and the global trend toward more voice-based interactions between humans and technology.

voice user interfaces (**VUIs**) Digital systems that enable human–computer interaction through a combination of natural language processing (NLP), automatic speech recognition (ASR), and artificial intelligence.

weightless economy A post-industrial economy that relies on information technology and telecommunications to produce a high-value output of immaterial goods such as exchangeable information, knowledge, or services. Immaterial goods can be produced with limited resources and without the help of physical labor and can be delivered to large numbers of customers across vast distances.

writing The activity of producing complex verbal signs such as words, sentences, and texts. The verbal signs are embedded in – and interact with – nonverbal semiotic environments, such as acoustical and optical, but also olfactory, gustatory, and tactile contexts. The practice of writing is oriented toward storing, processing, and/or sharing its products.

writing-by-the-way The activity of producing micro texts in constant and often simultaneous interactions with others. Products include social media messages, sound bites, and visual snapshots. Using this writing mode, we synchronize knowledge, share emotions, and maintain identities – everywhere and at all times of the day.

References

Adami, E. & Jewitt, C. (2016). Special issue: Social media and the visual. *Visual Communication*, *15*(3), 263–270.

Agar, M. (2004). We have met the other and we're all nonlinear: Ethnography as a nonlinear dynamic system. *Complexity*, *10*(2), 16–24. doi:10.1002/cplx.20054.

Aiello, G. & Parry, K. (2019). *Visual communication: Understanding images in media culture*. Los Angeles: SAGE.

Aitamurto, T., Aymerich-Franch, L., Saldivar, J., Kircos, C., Sadeghi, Y. & Sakshuwong, S. (2020). Examining augmented reality in journalism: Presence, knowledge gain, and perceived visual authenticity. *New Media & Society*, *1–22*. doi:10.1177/1461444820951925.

Alba, D. & Satariano, A. (2019). At least 70 countries have had disinformation campaigns, study find. September 26. Retrieved from www.nytimes.com/2019/9/26/technology/government-disinformation-cyber-troops.html.

Amazeen, M. A. & Wojdynski, B. W. (2020). The effects of disclosure format on native advertising recognition and audience perceptions of legacy and online news publishers. *Journalism*, *21*(12), 1965–1984. doi:10.1177/1464884918754829.

Ampuja, M., Koivisto, J. & Väliverronen, E. (2014). Strong and weak forms of mediatization theory: A critical review. Special issue of *Nordicom Review*, *35*, 111–123.

Ananny, M. (2016). Toward an ethics of algorithms convening, observation, probability, and timeliness. *Science, Technology & Human Values*, *41*(1), 93–117.

Anderson, B. (1991). *Imagined communities: Reflections on the origin and spread of nationalism* (revised and extended ed.). London/New York: Verso.

Androutsopoulos, J. (2008). Potentials and limitations of discourse-centred online ethnography. *Language@Internet*, 5.

AP (n.d.). AI@AP. *The Associated Press*. Retrieved from www.ap.org/discover/artificial-intelligence.

Ausburn L. J. & Ausburn, F. B. (1978). Visual literacy: Background, theory and practice, *Programmed Learning and Educational Technology*, *15*(4), 291–297. doi:10.1080/0033039780150405.

Ausserhofer, J., Gutounig, R., Oppermann, M., Matiasek, S. & Goldgruber, E. (2017). The datafication of data journalism scholarship: Focal points, methods, and research propositions for the investigation of data-intensive newswork. *Journalism*, *21*(7), 950–973. doi:10.1177/1464884917700667.

Avgerinou, M. & Ericson, J. (1997). A review of the concept of visual literacy. *British Journal of Educational Technology*, *28*(4), 280–291.

Bailenson, J. (2018). *Experience on demand*. New York: W. W. Norton & Company.

Baker, Wayne E. (2000). *Achieving success through social capital: Tapping the hidden resources in your personal and business networks*. San Francisco: Jossey-Bass.

Balchin, W. G. V. (1972). Graphicacy. *Geography*, *57*(3), 185–195.

Barney, D. (2004). *The network society*. Cambridge: Polity.

Baron, R. J. (2019). Digital literacy. In R. Hobbs & P. Mihailidis (eds.), *The International Encyclopedia of Media Literacy* (pp. 343–349). Hoboken, NJ: John Wiley & Sons.

Barthes, R. (1964). Rhétorique de l'image. *Communications*. Recherches Sémiologiques *4*, 40–51.

Barthes, R. (1977). Rhetoric of the image. In R. Barthes, *Image, music, text* (S. Heath, trans., pp. 32–51). London: Fontana Press. (Original work published 1964.)

Barthes, R. (1985). *The responsibility of forms: Critical essays on music, art and representation* (R. Howard, trans., pp. 21–40). New York: Hill and Wang. (Original work published 1982.)

Bateman, J. A. (2008). *Multimodality and genre: A foundation for the systematic analysis of multimodal documents*. Basingstoke: Palgrave Macmillan.

Bateman, J. A., Wildfeuer, J. & Hiippala, T. (2017). *Multimodality: Foundations, research and analysis. A problem-oriented introduction*. Berlin/Boston: Walter de Gruyter.

Baudrillard, J. (1994). *Simulacra and simulation* (S. F. Glaser, trans.). Ann Arbor: University of Michigan Press.

Bauman, Z. (1998). *Globalization: The human consequences*. New York: Columbia University Press.

Bauman, Z. (2005). *Liquid life*. Cambridge: Polity Press.

BBC (n.d.). We wait VR. Taster. Retrieved from www.bbc.co.uk/taster/pilots/we-wait.

Beer, D. (2017). The social power of algorithms. *Information, Communication & Society*, *20*(1), 1–13. doi:10.1080/1369118X.2016.1216147.

Beetz, J. (2016). *Materiality and subject in marxism, (post-)structuralism, and material semiotics*. London: Palgrave Macmillan.

Beisswenger, M. & Pappert, S. (2019). How to be polite with emojis: A pragmatic analysis of face work strategies in an online learning environment. *European Journal of Applied Linguistics*, *7*(2), 225–253.

Benetton (2011). UNHATE worldwide campaign. Press releases and statements. November 16. Retrieved from www.benettongroup.com/media-press/press-releases-and-statements/unhate-worldwide-campaign/.

Benkler, Y. (2006). *The wealth of networks: How social production transforms markets and freedom*. New Haven, CT/London: Yale University Press.

Bhargava, R. (2019). Data literacy. In R. Hobbs & P. Mihailidis (eds.), *The international encyclopedia of media literacy* (pp. 303–307). Hoboken, NJ: John Wiley & Sons.

Bijker, W. E. (1995). *Of bicycles, bakelites, and bulbs: Toward a theory of cociotechnical change*. Cambridge, MA: MIT Press.

Bijker, W. E., Hughes, T. P. & Pinch, T. (1987). *The social construction of technological systems: New directions in the sociology and history of technology*. Cambridge, MA: MIT Press.

Blok, A., Farías, I. & Roberts, C. (2020). *The Routledge companion to actor-network theory*. London/New York: Routledge.

Blommaert, J. (2010). *The sociolinguistics of globalization*. Cambridge: Cambridge University Press.

Blommaert, J. & Jie, D. (2020). *Ethnographic fieldwork: A beginner's guide* (2nd ed.). Bristol: Multilingual Matters. doi: 10.21832/9781788927147.

Blommaert, J. & Rampton, B. (2011) Language and superdiversity. *Diversities, 13*(2), 3–21.

Blumler, J. G. (2018). The crisis of public communication, 1995–2017. *Javnost – The Public, 25*(1–2), 83–92. doi:10.1080/13183222.2018.1418799.

Blumler, J. G. & Gurevitch, M. (1995). *The crisis of public communication*. London: Routledge.

Boccia Artieri, G., Brilli, S. & Zurovac, E. (2021). Below the radar: Private groups, locked platforms, and ephemeral content. Introduction to the special issue. *Social Media + Society*. doi:10.1177/2056305121988930.

Boellstorff, T., Nardi, B., Pearce, C. & Taylor, T. L. (2012). *Ethnography and virtual worlds: A handbook of method*. Oxford: Princeton University Press. doi:10.2307/j.cttq9s20.

Bolter, J. D. & Grusin, R. (2000). *Remediation: Understanding new media*. Cambridge, MA: MIT Press.

Börner, K., Bueckle, A. & Ginda, M. (2019). Data visualization literacy: Definitions, conceptual frameworks, exercises, and assessments. *PNAS, 116*(6), 1857–1864.

Bourdieu, P. (2018). The forms of capital. In M. Granovetter & R. Swedberg (eds.), *The sociology of economic life* (3rd ed., pp. 78–92). New York: Routledge. doi:10.4324/9780429494338.

Bourdieu, P. & Wacquant, L. J. D. (1992). *An invitation to reflexive sociology*. Chicago: University of Chicago Press.

Bouvier, G. & Machin, D. (2013). How advertisers use sound and music to communicate ideas, attitudes and identities: A multimodal critical discourse approach. In B. Pennock-Spek & M. M. del Saz Rubio (eds.), *The multimodal analysis of television commercials*. Valencia: University of Valencia Press.

Bouwman, H., Nikou, S., Molina-Castillo, F. J. & de Reuver, M. (2018). The impact of digitalization on business models. *Digital Policy, Regulation and Governance, 20*(2), 105–124. doi:10.1108/DPRG-07-2017-0039.

Bowman, S. R. (2021). What is public relations? In A. Theaker (ed.), *The public relations handbook* (6th ed., pp. 3–24). Taylor and Francis eBook.

Boy, J., Rensink, R. A., Bertini, E. & Fekete, J.-D. (2014). A principled way of assessing visualization literacy. *IEEE Transactions on Visualization and Computer Graphics, 20*(12), 1963–1972.

boyd, d. (2011). Social network sites as networked publics: Affordances, dynamics, and implications. In Z. Papacharissi (ed.), *A networked self: Identity, community, and culture on social network sites* (pp. 39–58). New York/London: Routledge.

boyd, d. m. & Ellison, N. B. (2007). Social network sites: Definition, history, and scholarship. *Journal of Computer-Mediated Communication, 13*(1), 210–230. doi:10.1111/j.1083-6101.2007.00393.x.

Bradshaw, S. & Howard, P. N. (2019). The global disinformation disorder: 2019 global inventory of organised social media manipulation. *Working Paper 2019.2. Oxford, UK: Project on Computational Propaganda*. Retrieved from https://demtech.oii.ox.ac.uk/wp-content/uploads/sites/93/2019/09/CyberTroop-Report19.pdf.

Braten, S. (1981). *Modeller av menneske og samfunn. bro mellom teori og erfaring fra sosiologi og sosialpsykolog*. Oslo: Universitetsforlage.

Branch, J. (2012, December). Snow fall: The avalanche at Tunnel Creek. *New York Times*. www.nytimes.com/projects/2012/snow-fall/index.html#/?part = tunnel-creek.

Brand, D. (2016). *The rise of writing*. Cambridge: Cambridge University Press.

Brannon, J. (2008). Maximize the medium: Assessing obstacles to performing multimedia journalism in three U.S. newsrooms. In Chris Paterson & David Domingo (eds.), *Making online news: The ethnography of new media production* (pp. 99–111). New York: Peter Lang.

Brodie, R. J., Hollebeek, L. D., Jurić, B. & Ilić, A. (2011). Customer engagement: Conceptual domain, fundamental propositions, and implications for research. *Journal of Service Research, 14*(3), 252–271. doi:10.1177/1094670511411703.

Brønn, P. S. (2014). Communication management. In W. Donsbach (eds.), *The International Encyclopedia of Communication* (pp. 753–757). Hoboken, NJ: John Wiley & Sons.

Brown, P. & Gaskins, S. (2014). Language acquisition and language socialization. In N. Enfield, P. Kockelman & J. Sidnell (eds.), *The Cambridge Handbook of Linguistic Anthropology* (Cambridge Handbooks in Language and Linguistics, pp. 187–226). Cambridge: Cambridge University Press. doi:10.1017/CBO9781139342872.010.

Brown, T., Mann, B., Ryder, N., Subbiah, M., Kaplan, J., Dhariwal, P. & Amodei, D. (2020). Language models are few-shot learners. *ArXiv, abs/2005.14165*. Retrieved from https://arxiv.org/pdf/2005.14165.pdf.

Bucher, T. (2018). *If … then: Algorithmic power and politics*. New York: Oxford University Press.

Bush, V. (1945). As we may think. *The Atlantic*. July 1945 Issue. Retrieved from www.theatlantic.com/magazine/archive/1945/07/as-we-may-think/303881/.

Calhoun, C. (1992). Introduction. In C. Calhoun (ed.), *Habermas and the public sphere* (pp. 1–50). Cambridge, MA: MIT Press.

Cameron, D., Frazer, E., Harvey, P., Rampton, M. B. H. & Richardson, K. (1992). *Researching language: Issues of power and method*. London: Routledge.

CARE (2020). The 10 most under-reported humanitarian crises of 2020. Retrieved from www.care-international.org/files/files/Ten_most_underreported_humanitarian_crises_2020.pdf.

Carillo, E. C. (2019). *MLA guide to digital literacy*. New York: The Modern Language Association of America.

Carlson, M. (2015). The robotic reporter. *Digital Journalism, 3*(3), 416–431. doi:10.1080/21670811.2014.976412.

Carlsson, U. (2019). Media and information literacy: Field of knowledge, concepts and history. In U. Carlsson (ed.), *Understanding media and information literacy (MIL) in the digital age: A question of democracy* (pp. 37–55). Göteborg: Department of Journalism, Media and Communication (JMG): University of Gothenburg. Retrieved from https://jmg.gu.se/digitalAssets/1742/1742676_understanding-media-pdf-original.pdf.

Casey, C. A. (2019). Information literacy. In M. A. Allison & C. A. Casey (eds.), *New media, communication, and society* (pp. 100–106). New York: Peter Lang.

Castells, M. (1989). *The informational city: Economic restructuring and urban development.* Cambridge, MA: Blackwell.

Castells, M. (1996). *The information age: Economy, society and culture, Vol. I: The rise of the network society.* Malden, MA/Oxford: Blackwell.

Castells, M. (1997). *The information age: Economy, society and culture, Vol. II: The power of identity.* Malden MA/Oxford: Blackwell.

Castells, M. (1998). *The information age: Economy, society and culture, Vol. III: End of millennium.* Malden MA/Oxford: Blackwell.

Castells, M. (2004). *The network society: A cross-cultural perspective.* Cheltenham: Edward Elgar.

Castells, M. (2007). Communication, power and counter power in the network society. *International Journal of Communication, 1*, 238–266.

Catenaccio, P., Cotter, C., Desmedt, M., Garzone, G., Jacobs, G., Lams, L., et al. (2011). Towards a linguistics of news production. *Journal of Pragmatics, 43*(7), 1843–1852. doi:10.1016/j.pragma.2010.09.022.

CBS Interactive Inc. (2010). Facebook: One social graph to rule them all? Retrieved from www.cbsnews.com/news/facebook-one-social-graph-to-rule-them-all/.

Chadwick, A. (2013). *The hybrid media system: Politics and power.* New York: Oxford University Press.

Chandler, D. & Munday, R. (2016). *A dictionary of social media.* Oxford: Oxford University Press.

Coddington, M. (2015). The wall becomes a curtain: Revisiting journalism's news-business boundary. In M. Carlson & S. C. Lewis (eds.), *Boundaries of journalism: Professionalism, practices and participation* (pp. 67–82). New York: Routledge.

Coleman, J. S. (2009). Social capital in the creation of human capital. *American Journal of Sociology, 94.* doi:10.1086/228943.

Coleman, V. (2021). *Digital divide in UK education during COVID-19 pandemic: Literature review. Cambridge Assessment Research Report.* Cambridge: Cambridge Assessment.

Collister, S. & Roberts-Bowman, S. (2018a). Visual and spatial public relations: Strategic communication beyond text. In S. Collister & S. Roberts-Bowman (eds.), *Visual public relations: Strategic communication beyond text* (pp. 1–9). London/New York: Routledge.

Collister, S. & Roberts-Bowman, S. (eds.) (2018b). *Visual public relations: Strategic communication beyond text.* London/New York: Routledge. doi:10.4324/9781315160290.

Copeland, B. J. (2020). Artificial intelligence. In *Encyclopaedia Britannica.* Retrieved from www.britannica.com/technology/artificial-intelligence.

Copland, F. & Creese, A. (2015). *Linguistic ethnography: Collecting, analysing and presenting data.* London: SAGE. doi:10.4135/9781473910607.

Cotter, C. & Perrin, D. (2018). *The Routledge handbook of language and media.* London: Routledge.

Couldry, N. & Hepp, A. (2013). Conceptualizing mediatization: Contexts, traditions, arguments. *Communication Theory, 23*, 191–202.

Coyle, D. (1998). *The weightless world: Strategies for managing the digital economy.* Cambridge, MA: MIT Press.

Crawford, C. (2002). *The art of interactive design: A euphonious and illuminating guide to building successful software.* San Francisco: No Starch Press.

Creswell, J. W. & Plano Clark, V. L. (2018). *Designing and conducting mixed methods research* (3rd ed.). Thousand Oaks, CA: SAGE.

dal Zotto, C. & Lugmayr, A. (2016). Media convergence as evolutionary process. In A. Lugmayr & C. dal Zotto (eds.), *Media convergence handbook, Vol. I: Journalism, broadcasting, and social media aspects of convergence* (pp. 3–16). New York: Springer.

Davis, A. (2002). *Public relations democracy: Public relations, politics, and the mass media in Britain.* Manchester: Manchester University Press.

Dawar, N. & Bendle, N. (2018). Marketing in the age of Alexa. *Harvard Business Review*, 96(3), 81–86.

Day, S. (2019). MIT art installation aims to empower a more discerning public. *MIT News*, November 25. Retrieved from http://news.mit.edu/2019/mit-apollo-deepfake-art-installation-aims-to-empower-more-discerning-public-1125.

Deleuze, G. (1988). *Bergsonism* (H. Tomlinson, trans.). New York: Zone.

De la Peña, N., Weil, P., Llobera, J., Giannopoulos, E., Pomés, A., Spanlang, B., et al. (2010). Immersive journalism: Immersive virtual reality for the first-person experience of news. *Presence*, 19(4), 291–301. doi:10.1162/PRES_a_00005.

Deng, L. & Liu, Y. (2018). A joint introduction to natural language processing and to deep learning. In L. Deng & Y. Liu (eds.), *Deep learning in natural language processing* (pp. 1–22). Singapore: Springer. doi:10.1007/978-981-10-5209-5.

Deuze, M. (2004). What is multimedia journalism? *Journalism Studies*, 5(2), 139–152. doi: 10.1080/1461670042000211131.

Dhanesh, G. S. (2018). Social media and the rise of visual rhetoric: Implications for public relations theory and practice. In E. Bridgen & D. Verčič (eds.), *Experiencing public relations: International voices* (pp. 123–136). London: Routledge.

Diakopoulos, N. (2014). Algorithmic accountability: Journalistic investigation of computational power structures. *Digital Journalism*, 3(3), 398–415. doi:10.1080/21670811.2014.976411.

Diakopoulos, N. (2019). *Automating the news: How algorithms are rewriting the media.* Cambridge, MA: Harvard University Press.

Dickinson, W. B. (2010). Visual displays for mixed methods findings. In A. Tashakkori & C. Teddlie (eds.), *Sage handbook of mixed methods in social and behavioral research* (2nd ed., pp. 469–504). Thousand Oaks, CA: SAGE. doi:10.4135/9781506335193.n19.

Dimitrieska, S., Stankovska, A. & Efremova, T. (2018). Artificial intelligence and marketing. *Entrepreneurship*, 7(2), 298–304.

Donath, J. & Boyd, D. (2004). Public displays of connection. *BT Technology Journal*, 22, 71–82. doi:10.1023/B:BTTJ.0000047585.06264.cc.

Dörr, K. N. (2016). Mapping the field of algorithmic journalism. *Digital Journalism*, 4(6), 700–722. doi:10.1080/21670811.2015.1096748.

Dörr, K. N. & Hollnbuchner, K. (2017). Ethical challenges of algorithmic journalism. *Digital Journalism*, 5(4), 404–419. doi:10.1080/21670811.2016.1167612.

Dowling, D. & Vogan, T. (2015). Can we "Snowfall" this? *Digital Journalism*, 3(2), 209–224. doi:1 0.1080/21670811.2014.930250.

Downey, J. & Fenton, N. (2003). New media, counter publicity and the public sphere. *New Media & Society*, 5(2), 185–202.

Durkheim, É. (1895/1982). *The rules of sociological method*. New York: Free Press.

Ebner, J. (2020). Going dark. *The secret social lives of extremists*. London: Bloomsbury.

Ekström, M. (2001). Politicians interviewed on television news. *Discourse & Society*, 12(5), 563–584. doi:10.1177/0957926501012005001.

Ellison, N. B. & boyd, d. m. (2013). Sociality through social network sites. In W. H. Dutton (eds.), *The Oxford handbook of internet studies* (pp. 151–172). Oxford: Oxford University Press. doi:10.1093/oxfordhb/9780199589074.013.0008.

Ellison, N. B., Steinfield, C. & Lampe, C. (2007). The benefits of facebook "friends": Social capital and college students' use of online social network sites. *Journal of Computer-Mediated Communication*, 12(4), 1143–1168. doi:10.1111/j.1083-6101.2007.00367.x.

Engebretsen, M. (2001). *Nyheten som hypertekst* [The news as hypertext]. Kristiansand: IJ-forlaget.

Engebretsen, M. (2012.) Balancing cohesion and tension in multimodal rhetoric: An interdisciplinary approach to the study of semiotic complexity. *Learning, Media and Technology*, 37(2), 145–162. doi:10.1080/17439884.2012.655745.

Engebretsen, M., Kennedy, H. & Weber, W. (2018). Data visualization in Scandinavian newsrooms: Emerging trends in journalistic visualization practices. *Nordicom Review*, 39(2), 3–18. doi:10.2478/nor-2018-0007.

Enxing, J. (2013). Authentic compassion? O. Toscani's outrageous campaigns: An ethic-esthetical inquiry from a theologian's perspective. *Limes: Borderland Studies*, 6(1), 46–63.

Equinor ASA. (n.d.). *Equinor*. Retrieved from www.equinor.com/.

Equinor ASA. (n.d.). *Equinor sustainability data hub*. Retrieved from https://sustainability .equinor.com/#workforce.

Ess, C. (2020). *Digital media ethics*. Cambridge: Polity Press.

Ewerth, R., Otto, C. & Müller-Budack (2021). Computational approaches for the interpretation of image-text relations. In J. Pflaeging, J. Wildfeuer & J. A. Bateman (eds.), *Empirical multimodality research: Methods, evaluations. Implications* (pp. 109–138). Berlin/Boston: Walter de Gruyter.

Fahmy, S., Bock, M. A. & Wanta, W. (2014). *Visual communication theory and research: A mass communication perspective*. New York: Palgrave Macmillan.

Ferrer-Conill, R., Knudsen, E., Lauerer, C. & Barnoy, A. (2020). The visual boundaries of journalism: Native advertising and the convergence of editorial and commercial content. *Digital Journalism*, 1–23. doi:10.1080/21670811.2020.1836980.

Fieldhouse, S. (2017). *Five ways AI is changing the face of corporate communications*. January 6. Retrieved from www.linkedin.com/pulse/five-ways-ai-changing-face-corporate-communications-stuart-fieldhouse/.

Fitzpatrick, B. & Recordon, D. (2007). *Thoughts on the Social Graph*. August 17. Retrieved from http://bradfitz.com/social-graph-problem/ .

Fogg, B. J. (2003). *Persuasive technology: Using computers to change what we think and do*. San Francisco: Morgan Kaufmann Publishers.

Foldes, S. (2018). AI won't take over corporate communications, but it can help. *Forbes*. March 2. Retrieved from www.forbes.com/sites/forbesagencycouncil/2018/03/02/ai-wont-take-over-corporate-communications-but-it-can-help/?sh = 228e3f457aa0.

Ford, P. (2015). What is code? *Businessweek*, June 11. Retrieved from www.bloomberg.com/graphics/2015-paul-ford-what-is-code.

Fraser, N. (1990). Rethinking the public sphere: A contribution to the critique of actually existing democracy. *Social Text, 25/26*, 56–80.

Frerichs, R. R. (2001). History, maps and the internet: UCLA's John Snow site. *SoC Bulletin, 34*(2), 3–7. Retrieved from https://societyofcartographers.files.wordpress.com/2015/12/34-2-frerichs.pdf.

Frerichs, R. R. (UCLA Department of Epidemiology) (2004). *High resolution maps of John Snow*. Retrieved from www.ph.ucla.edu/epi/snow/highressnowmap.html.

Friedland, L. A., Hove, T. & Rojas, H. (2006). The networked public sphere. *Javnost – The Public,13*(4), 5–26. doi:10.1080/13183222.2006.11008922.

Fukui, R., Ardene C. J. & Kelley, T. (2019). Africa's connectivity gap: Can a map tell the story? November 7. Retrieved from https://blogs.worldbank.org/digital-development/africas-connectivity-gap-can-map-tell-story.

Fürer, M. (2017). Modeling, scaling and sequencing writing phases of Swiss television journalists. Doctoral dissertation, University of Bern. Retrieved from https://biblio.unibe.ch/download/eldiss/17fuerer_m.pdf.

Galloway, C. & Swiatek, L. (2018). Public relations and artificial intelligence: It's not (just) about robots. *Public Relations Review, 44*(5), 734–740. doi:10.1016/j.pubrev.2018.10.008.

Geertz, C. (1973). *The interpretation of cultures: Selected essays*. New York: Basic Books.

Giddens, A. (1984). *The constitution of society: Outline of the theory of structuration*. Berkeley: University of California Press.

Giraldo-Luque, S., Aldana Afanador, P. N. & Fernández-Rovira, C. (2020). The struggle for human attention: Between the abuse of social media and digital wellbeing. *Healthcare, 8*(4), 497. doi:10.3390/healthcare8040497.

Glaser, B. & Strauss, A. L. (1967). *The discovery of grounded theory: Strategies for qualitative research*. London: Wiedenfeld and Nicholson.

Gnach, A. (2018). Social media and community building: Creating social realities through linguistic interaction. In C. Cotter & P. Perrin (eds.), *The Routledge handbook of language and media* (pp. 190–205). London: Routledge.

Gnach, A. & Powell, K. M. (2014). Authorship and context: Writing and text production as situated activities. In E.-M. Jakobs & D. Perrin (eds.), *Handbook of writing and text production* (pp. 119–139). Berlin: De Gruyter.

Gnach, A., Weber, W., Keel, G., Klopfenstein Frei, N., Wyss, V., Burger, M., Benecchi, E., Calderara, L. & Mazzoni, P. (2020). *How to reach Swiss digital natives with news: A qualitative study. Final Report*. Retrieved from www.bakom.admin.ch/bakom/en/homepage/electronic-media/studies/individual-studies.html.

GPT-3 (2020). A robot wrote this entire article. Are you scared yet, human? *Guardian*, September 8. Retrieved from www.theguardian.com/commentisfree/2020/sep/08/robot-wrote-this-article-gpt-3.

Graefe, A. (2016). A field guide for understanding automated journalism. *AP insights*, January 8. Retrieved from https://insights.ap.org/industry-trends/a-field-guide-for-understanding-automated-journalism.

Granovetter, M. (1973). The strength of weak ties. *American Journal of Sociology*, *78*(6), 1360–1380. doi:10.1086/225469.

Granovetter, M. (1983). The strength of weak ties: A network theory revisited. *Sociological Theory*, *1*, 201–233. doi:10.2307/202051.

Gravengaard, G. (2012). The metaphors journalists live by: Journalists' conceptualisation of newswork. *Journalism*, *13*(8), 1064–1082. doi:10.1177/1464884911433251.

Gray, J. & Bounegru, L. (2021). *The data journalism handbook: Towards a critical data practice*. Amsterdam: Amsterdam University Press.

Grésillon, A. & Perrin, D. (2014). Methodology: From speaking about writing to tracking text production. In D. Perrin & E.-M. Jakobs (eds.), *Handbook of writing and text production* (Vol. X, pp. 79–111). Boston: De Gruyter.

Grésillon, A. & Mervant-Roux, M. M. (2010). Marguerita Duras/Claude Régy: L'Âmante anglaise: Genèse d'une écriture, gésine d'un théâtre. In A. Grésillon, M. M. Mervant-Roux & D. Budor (eds.), *Genèse théâtrale* (pp. 211–232). Paris: CNRS Editions.

Gupta, Annika (2020). *How to handle a crowd*. New York: Tiller Press.

Guy, I. (2016). Searching by talking: Analysis of voice queries on mobile web search. In *Proceedings of the 39th International ACM SIGIR Conference on Research and Development in Information Retrieval (SIGIR '16)* (pp. 35–44). New York: Association for Computing Machinery.

Haapanen, L. & Perrin, D. (2018). Media and quoting: Understanding the purposes, roles, and processes of quoting and social media. In C. Cotter & D. Perrin (eds.), *Handbook of language and media* (pp. 424–441). London: Routledge.

Haapanen, L. & Perrin, D. (2020). Linguistic recycling: The process of quoting in increasingly mediatized settings. *AILA Reviews*, *33*(1), 1–20. doi:10.1075/aila.00027.int.

Habermas, J. (1989). *The structural transformation of the public sphere: An inquiry into a category of bourgeois society*. Cambridge, MA: MIT Press.

Habermas, J. (1992). *Faktizität und Geltung: Beiträge zur Diskurstheorie des Rechts und des demokratischen Rechtsstaates*. Frankfurt am Main: Suhrkamp.

Habermas, J. (1996). *Between facts and norms: Contributions to a discourse theory of law and democracy*. Cambridge: Polity Press.

Habermas, J. (1998). *The inclusion of the other: Studies in political theory*. Cambridge, MA: MIT Press.

Habermas, J. (2006). Political communication in media society: Does democracy still enjoy an epistemic dimension? The impact of normative theory on empirical research. *Communication Theory*, *16*(4), 411–426. doi:10.1111/j.1468-2885.2006.00280.x.

Hallahan, K., Holtzhausen, D., Ruler, B. van, Verčič, D. & Sriramesh, K. (2008). Defining strategic communication. *International Journal of Strategic Communication*, *1*(1), 3–35.

Haller, C, (2019). *Is AI a true stroke of genius? How artificial intelligence is transforming corporate communications.* February 1. Retrieved from www.linkedin.com/pulse/ai-true-stroke-genius-how-artificial-intelligence-corporate-haller/.

Halliday, M. A. K. (1985). *An introduction to functional grammar.* London/New York: Arnold.

Hansen, A. & Machin, D. (2019) *Media and communication research methods* (2nd ed.). London: Macmillan International, Red Globe Press.

Harari, Y. N. (2017). *Homo Deus: A brief history of tomorrow.* London: Vintage.

Hargittai, E. & Walejko, G. (2008). The participation divide: Content creation and sharing in the digital age. *Information, Communication & Society*, *11*(2), 239–256.

Harris, M. (1976). History and significance of the emic/etic distinction. *Annual Review of Anthropology*, *5*, 329–350. doi:10.1146/annurev.an.05.100176.001553.

Häusermann, J. (2007). Zugespieltes Material: Der O-Ton und seine Interpretation. In H. Maye, C. Reiber & N. Wegmann (eds.), *Original / Ton. Zur Mediengeschichte des O-Tons* (pp. 25–50). Konstanz: UVK.

Heeter, C. (1989). Implications of new interactive technologies for conceptualizing communication. In J. L. Salvaggio & J. Bryant (eds.), *Media use in the information age: Emerging patterns of adoption and consumer use* (pp. 217–235). Hillsdale, NJ: Lawrence Erlbaum.

Heeter, C. (2000). Interactivity in the context of designed experiences. *Journal of Interactive Advertising*, *1*(1), 3–14. doi:10.1080/15252019.2000.10722040.

Heiser, D. (2015). An advanced book for beginners. In D. R. Dechow & D. C. Struppa (eds.), *Intertwingled: The work and influence of Ted Nelson* (pp. 51–56). Cham: Springer.

Hendricks, V. F. & Vestergaard, M. (2019). The news market. In V. F. Hendricks & M. Vestergaard (eds.), *Reality lost* (pp. 19–34). Springer: Cham. doi:10.1007/978-3-030-00813-0_2.

Hepp, A. (2012). Mediatization and the "molding force" of the media. *Communications 37*(1), 1–28. doi:10.1515/commun-2012-0001.

Hepp, A. (2020). *Deep mediatization.* Abingdon: Routledge.

Herring, S. C. (2001). Computer-mediated discourse. In D. Schiffrin, D. Tannen & H. Hamilton (eds.), *The handbook of discourse analysis* (pp. 612–634). Oxford: Blackwell Publishers.

Herring, S. C. (2004). Computer-mediated discourse analysis: An approach to researching online behavior. In S. A. Barab, R. Kling & J. H. Gray (eds.), *Designing for virtual communities in the service of learning* (pp. 338–376). New York: Cambridge University Press. doi:10.1017/CBO9780511805080.016.

Herring, S. C. & Dainas, A. (2017). "Nice picture comment!" Graphicons in Facebook comment threads. In *Proceedings of the 50th Hawaii international conference on system sciences* (pp. 2185–2194). Waikoloa, HI: HICSS.

Herring, S. C., Stein, D. & Virtanen, T. (2013). Introduction to the pragmatics of computer-mediated communication. In S. C. Herring, D. Stein & T. Virtanen (eds.), *Handbook of pragmatics of computer-mediated communication* (pp. 3–32). Berlin: Mouton. doi: 10.1515/9783110214468.3.

Hicks, T. & Perrin, D. (2014). Beyond single modes and media: Writing as an ongoing multimodal text production. In E.-M. Jakobs & D. Perrin (eds.), *Handbook of writing and text production* (Vol. X, pp. 231–253). Boston: De Gruyter.

Hine, C. (2000). *Virtual ethnography*. London: SAGE. doi: 10.4135/9780857020277.

Hine, C. (2011). Towards ethnography of television on the internet: A mobile strategy for exploring mundane interpretive activities. *Media, Culture & Society*, *33*(4), 567–582. doi: 10.1177/0163443711401940.

Hine, C. (2015). *Ethnography for the Internet: Embedded, embodied and everyday*. London: Bloomsbury Academic.

Hirnschal, E. (2018). Unternehmenskultur in Zeiten von Arbeit 4.0 und demografischem Wandel. In J. Herget & H. Strobl (eds.), *Unternehmenskultur in der Praxis* (pp. 73–91). Wiesbaden: Springer Gabler.

Hjarvard, S. (2008). The mediatization of society: A theory of the media as agents of social and cultural change. *Nordicom Review*, *29*(2), 105–134. doi:10.1515/nor-2017-0181.

Hobbs, R. (2010). *Digital and media literacy: A plan of action*. Washington, DC: The Aspen Institute. Retrieved from https://files.eric.ed.gov/fulltext/ED523244.pdf.

Hobbs, R. (2019). Media literacy foundations. In R. Hobbs & P. Mihailidis (eds.), *The International Encyclopedia of Media Literacy* (pp. 851–870). Hoboken, NJ: John Wiley & Sons.

Hodge, R. & Kress, G. (1988). *Social semiotics*. Ithaca, NY: Cornell University Press.

Howard, P. N. (2002). Network ethnography and the hypermedia organization: New media, new organizations, new methods. *New Media & Society*, *4*(4), 550–574. doi:10.1177/146144402321466813.

Huan, C. (2018). *Journalistic stance in Chinese and Australian hard news*. Singapore: Springer.

Incze, C. B., Pocovnicu, A., Vasilache, S. & Al Zain, N.-L. (2018). Marketing communication analysis of Benetton PR campaigns. *Proceedings of the International Conference on Business Excellence, Sciendo*, *12*(1), 457–465.

Ingenhoff, D., Borner, M. & Zerfaß, A. (2020). Corporate listening und issues management in der Unternehmenskommunikation. In A. Zerfaß, M. Piwinger & U. Röttger (eds.), *Handbuch Unternehmenskommunikation* (3rd ed., pp. 577–593). Wiesbaden: Springer Gabler. doi:10.1007/978-3-658-03894-6_26-1.

D'Ignazio, C. & Bhargava, R. (2015). Approaches to building big data literacy. Paper presented at *Bloomberg Data for Good Exchange Conference*. September 28, 2015, New York.

Ito, M. (2008). Introduction. In K. Varnelis (ed.), *Networked publics* (pp. 1–14). Cambridge, MA: MIT Press.

Ireton, C. & Posetti, J. (2018). *Journalism, "fake news" and disinformation: Handbook for journalism education and training*. Paris: UNESCO.

Jakobs, E.-M. & Perrin, D. (2014). Introduction and research roadmap: Writing and text production. In E.-M. Jakobs & D. Perrin (eds.), *Handbook of writing and text production* (Vol. X, pp. 1–24). Boston: De Gruyter.

Jacobs, G. (2018). Organizations and corporate communication. Linguistic ethnography in the newsroom. In C. Cotter & D. Perrin (eds.), *Handbook of language and media* (pp. 178–189). London: Routledge.

Jenkins, H. (2006). *Convergence culture: Where old and new media collide.* New York: New York University Press.

Jenkins, H., Ford, S. & Green, J. (2012). *Spreadable media: Creating value and meaning in a networked culture.* New York: New York University Press.

Jewitt, C. (ed.) (2013). *The Routledge handbook of multimodal analysis* (2nd ed.). London: Routledge.

Jewitt, C., Bezemer, J. & O'Halloran, K. (2016). *Introducing multimodality.* London: Routledge, Taylor & Francis.

Jewitt, C. & Oyama, R. (2001). Visual meaning: a social semiotic approach. In T. van Leeuwen & C. Jewitt (eds.), *Handbook of visual analysis* (pp. 134–156). London: SAGE.

Jin, Y., Austin, L., Guidry, J. & Parrish, C. (2017). Picture this and take that: Strategic crisis visuals and visual social media (VSM) in crisis communication. In S. C. Duh. (ed.), *New media and public relations* (pp. 299–311). New York: Peter Lang.

Jones, B., Temperley, J. & Lima, A. C. (2009). Corporate reputation in the era of Web 2.0: The case of Primark. *Journal of Marketing Management, 25,* 927–939.

Journal for Media Linguistics (jfml) (n.d.). Retrieved from https://jfml.org.

Kaiser J., Fähnrich B., Rhomberg M. & Filzmaier P. (2017). What happened to the public sphere? The networked public sphere and public opinion formation. In E. Carayannis, D. Campbell & M. Efthymiopoulos (eds.), *Handbook of cyber-development, cyber-democracy, and cyber-defense.* Cham: Springer.

Karapanos, E., Teixeira, P. & Gouveia, R. (2016). Need fulfillment and experiences on social media: A case on Facebook and WhatsApp. *Computers in Human Behavior, 55*(B), 888–897. doi:10.1016/j.chb.2015.10.015.

Katz, J. E. & Crocker, E. T. (2015). Selfies and photo messaging as visual conversation: Reports from the United States, United Kingdom and China. *International Journal of Communication, 9,* 1861–1872.

Kellner, D. (2019). Jean Baudrillard. In Edward N. Zalta (eds.), *Stanford encyclopedia of philosophy (Winter 2019 edition).* Retrieved from https://plato.stanford.edu/archives/win2019/entries/baudrillard/.

Kennedy, H., Weber, W. & Engebretsen, M. (2020). Data visualization and transparency in the news. In. M. Engebretsen & H. Kennedy (eds.), *Data visualization in society* (pp. 169–185). Amsterdam: Amsterdam University Press.

Khondker, H. H. (2004). Glocalization as globalization: Evolution of a sociological concept. *Bangladesh e-Journal of Sociology, 1*(2), 12–20.

Kick, M. (2015). IV corporate brand posts on Facebook: The role of interactivity, vividness, and involvement. In M. Kick, *Selected essays on corporate reputation and social media* (pp. 141–185).Wiesbaden: Springer Gabler. doi:10.1007/978-3-658-08837-8_4.

Kim, Amy Jo (2000). *Community building on the web: Secret strategies for successful online communities*. Berkeley, CA: Pearson Education.

Kiousis, S. (2002). Interactivity: A concept explication. *New Media & Society*, 4(3), 355–383. doi:10.1177/146144402320564392.

Kissmann, U. T. & van Loon, J. (2019). New materialism and its methodological consequences: An introduction. In U. T. Kissmann & J. van Loon (eds.), *Discussing new materialism: Methodological implications for the study of materialities* (pp. 3–18). Wiesbaden: Springer VS.

Kjeldsen, J. E. (2012). Pictorial argumentation in advertising: Visual tropes and figures as a way of creating visual argumentation. In F. van Eemeren & B. Garssen (eds.), *Topical themes in argumentation theory* (pp. 239–255). doi:10.1007/978-94-007-4041-9.

Klemm, M. (2000). *Zuschauerkommunikation: Formen und Funktionen der alltäglichen kommunikativen Fernsehaneignung*. Frankfurt am Main: Peter Lang.

Koltay, T. (2011). The media and the literacies: Media literacy, information literacy, digital literacy. *Media, Culture & Society*, 33(2) 211–221.

Koltay, T. (2019). Visual literacy. In R. Hobbs & P. Mihailidis (eds.), *The international encyclopedia of media literacy* (Vol. II, pp. 1514–1519). Hoboken, NJ: Wiley Blackwell.

Kozinets, R. V. (2002). The field behind the screen: Using netnography for marketing research in online communities. *Journal of Marketing Research*, 39(1), 61–72. doi:10.1509/jmkr.39.1.61.18935.

Kozinets, R. V. (2009). *Netnography: Doing ethnographic research online*. London: SAGE.

Kress, G. (2003). *Literacy in the new media age*. London: Routledge.

Kress, G. (2010). *Multimodality: A social semiotic approach to contemporary communication*. London: Routledge.

Kress, G. & van Leeuwen, T. (2001). *Multimodal discourse: The modes and media of contemporary communication*. London: Arnold Publishers.

Kress, G. & van Leeuwen, T. [1996] (2006). *Reading images: The grammar of visual design*. London: Routledge.

Krippendorff, K. (2013). *Content analysis: An introduction to its methodology* (3rd ed.). Los Angeles: SAGE.

Krotz, F. (2009). Mediatization: A concept with which to grasp media and societal change. In K. Lundby (ed.), *Mediatization: Concept, changes, consequences* (pp. 21–40). New York: Peter Lang.

Kröger, J. L., Lutz, O. H.-M. & Raschke, P. (2020). Privacy implications of voice and speech analysis: Information disclosure by inference. In M. Friedewald, M. Önen, E. Lievens, S. Krenn & S. Fricker (eds.), *Privacy and identity management: Data for better living: AI and privacy* (pp. 243–258). Cham: Springer.

Lang, N. & Raymont, P. (directors) (2019). *Margaret Atwood: A word after a word after a word is power*. Canada: White Pine Pictures.

Larsen-Freeman, D. & Cameron, L. (2008). *Complex systems and applied linguistics* (2nd ed.). Oxford: Oxford University Press.

Latour, B. (2005). *Reassembling the social: An introduction to actor-network-theory*. New York: Oxford University Press.

Lauer, C. & Sanchez, C. A. (2011). Visuospatial thinking in the professional writing classroom. *Journal of Business and Technical Communication 25*(2), 184–218.

Lazar, J., Goldstein, D. F. & Taylor, A. (2015). International disability law. In J. Lazar, D. Goldstein & A. Taylor (eds.), *Ensuring digital accessibility through process and policy* (pp. 101–120). Morgan Kaufmann. doi:10.1016/B978-0-12-800646-7.00006-X.

Ledin, P. & Machin, D. (2018). *Doing visual analysis: From theory to practice*. Los Angeles: SAGE.

Levin, T. & Wagner, T. (2006). In their own words: Understanding student conceptions of writing through their spontaneous metaphors in the science classroom. *Instructional Science, 34*(3), 227–278. doi:10.1007/s11251-005-6929-x.

Levine, E. (2020). Grey's Anatomy: Feminism. In E. Thompson & J. Mittell (eds.), *How to watch television* (2nd ed., pp. 135–143). New York: New York University Press.

Lewis, S. C., Guzman, A. L. & Schmidt, T. R. (2019). Automation, journalism, and human–machine communication: Rethinking roles and relationships of humans and machines in news. *Digital Journalism, 7*(4), 409–427. doi:10.1080/21670811.2019.1577147.

Li, J. (2020). Artificial intelligence in PR: Where we are and where we're headed. May 19, Retrieved from www.meltwater.com/en/blog/ai-in-pr-where-we-are-and-where-were-headed.

Licoppe, C. (2004). "Connected" presence: The emergence of a new repertoire for managing social relationships in a changing communication technoscape. *Environment and Planning D: Society and Space, 22*(1), 135–156. doi:10.1068/d323t.

Light, L. (2020). Brand journalism is alive and well. *Forbes*, January 21. Retrieved from www.forbes.com/sites/larrylight/2020/01/21/brand-journalism-is-alive-and-well/?sh = 2035ccd02220.

Lillis, T. M. (2013). *The sociolinguistics of writing*. Edinburgh: Edinburgh University Press.

Lindgren, S. (2018). *Digital media & society*. Thousand Oaks, CA: SAGE.

Lister, M., Dovey, J., Giddings, S., Grant, I. & Kelly, K. (2009). *New media: A critical introduction* (2nd ed.). Abingdon: Routledge.

Lister, M. & Wells, L. (2001). Seeing beyond belief: Cultural studies as an approach to analyzing the visual. In T. van Leeuwen, & C. Jewitt (eds.), *Handbook of visual analysis* (pp. 61–91). London: SAGE.

Litt, E. & Hargittai, E. (2016). The imagined audience on social network sites. *Social Media + Society, 1–12*. doi:10.1177/2056305116633482.

Livingstone, S. (2004). Media literacy and the challenge of new information and communication technologies. *The Communication Review, 7*(1), 3–14. doi:10.1080/10714420490280152.

Lloyd, J. & Toogood, L. (2015). *Journalism and PR: News media and public relations in the digital age*. London/New York: Tauris.

Lloyd, J. & Toogood, L. (2016). Journalism and PR: News media and public relations in the digital age. *European Journal of Communication, 31*(1), 90–91. doi:10.1177/0267323115627078k.

LLYC (2016): The use of big data in corporate communications strategies. Retrieved from https:// ideasbr.llorenteycuenca.com/wpcontent/uploads/sites/8/2016/11/161102_DI_Article_ Big_Data_ENG.pdf.

Long, N. J. & Moore, H. L. (2012). Sociality revisited: Setting a new agenda. *The Cambridge Journal of Anthropology, 30*(1), 40–47. doi:10.3167/ca.2012.300105.

López Jiménez, E. A. & Ouariachi, T. (2020). An exploration of the impact of artificial intelligence (AI) and automation for communication professionals. *Journal of Information, Communication and Ethics in Society*. doi:10.1108/JICES-03-2020-0034.

Luginbühl, M. (2015). Media linguistics: On mediality and culturality. *10plus1: Living Linguistics*, (1), 9–26.

Luke, D. A., Caburnay, C. A. & Cohen, E. L. (2011). How much is enough? New recommendations for using constructed week sampling in newspaper content analysis of health stories. *Communication Methods and Measures, 5*(1), 76–91. doi:10.1080/19312458.2010.547823.

Lutzky, U. (2021). *The discourse of customer service tweets: Planes, trains and automated text analysis*. London: Bloomsbury.

Machin, D. (2007). *Introduction to multimodal analysis*. London: Hodder Arnold.

Macnamara, J. (2014). Journalism-PR relations revisited: The good news, the bad news, and insights into tomorrow's news. *Public Relations Review, 40*(5), 739–750.

Malinowski, B. (1923). The problem of meaning in primitive languages. In C. K. Ogden & I. A. Richards (eds.), *The meaning of meaning* (pp. 296–336). London: K. Paul, Trend, Trubner.

Manovich, L. (2001). *The language of new media*. Cambridge, MA: MIT Press.

Manovich, L. (2003). New media from Borges to HTML. In N. Wardrip-Fruin & N. Montfort (eds.), *The new media reader* (pp. 13–25). Cambridge, MA: MIT Press.

Marconi, F. (2020). *Newsmakers: Artificial intelligence and the future of journalism*. New York: Columbia University Press.

Marcus, G. E. (1995). Ethnography in/of the world system: The emergence of multi-sited ethnography. *Annual Review of Anthropology*, 24, 95–117. doi:10.1146/annurev. an.24.100195.000523.

Marwick, A. E. & boyd, d. (2011). I tweet honestly, I tweet passionately: Twitter users, context collapse, and the imagined audience. *New Media & Society*, 13, 114–133.

Mayer-Schoenberger, V. & Cukier, K. (2013). *Big data: A revolution that will transform how we live, work and think*. London: John Murray Publishing.

McAfee, A. & Brynjolfsson, E. (2012). Big data: The management revolution. *Harvard Business Review, 90*(October), 60–68..

McLuhan, E. (n.d.). *Marshall McLuhan. Commonly asked questions (and answers)*. Retrieved from https://marshallmcluhan.com/common-questions/.

McLuhan, M. [1964] (1994). *Understanding media: The extension of man*. Cambridge, MA: MIT Press.

McLuhan, M. (1969). The Playboy interview: Marshall McLuhan. *Playboy Magazine*, March 1969. Retrieved from www.nextnature.net/story/2009/the-playboy-interview-marshall-mcluhan.

McLuhan, M. & Fiore, Q. (1967). *The medium is the massage: An inventory of effects*. Co-ordinated by Jerome Agel. New York: Bantam Books.

McLuhan, M. & Fiore, Q. (1968). *War and peace in the global village: An inventory of some of the current spastic situations that could be eliminated by more feedforward*. Produced by J. Agel [1997]. San Francisco: Hardwired. Originally publ. New York/London: Bantam.

McMillan, S. J. (2006). Exploring models of interactivity from multiple research traditions: users, documents and systems. In L. A. Lievrouw & S. Livingstone (eds.), *The Handbook of new media: Social shaping and consequences of ICTs* (updated student ed., pp. 205–229). London: SAGE.

Mead, M. (1928). *Coming of age in Samoa*. New York: William Morrow and Company.

Menczer, F. & Hills, T. (2020). The attention economy. *Scientific American, 323*(6), 54–61.

Michelle, A. A. & Bartosz, W. W. (2019). Reducing native advertising deception: Revisiting the antecedents and consequences of persuasion knowledge in digital news contexts. *Mass Communication and Society, 22*(2), 222–247, doi:10.1080/15205436.2018.1530792.

Milgram, P. & Kishino, F. (1994). A taxonomy of mixed reality visual displays. *IEICE Transactions on Information and Systems*. Special issue on networked reality, *E77-D*(12), 1321–1329.

Milgram, P., Takemura, H., Utsumi, A. & Kishino, F. (1995). Augmented reality: A class of displays on the reality-virtuality continuum. *Telemanipulator and Telepresence Technologies*, SPIE 2351, 282–292. doi:10.1117/12.197321.

Miller, D., Costa, E., Haynes, N., McDonald, T., Nicolescu, R., Sinanan, J., et al. (2016). *How the world changed social media*. Retrieved from www.ucl.ac.uk/ucl-press/browse-books/how-world-changed-social-media.

Miller, D. & Slater, D. (2000). *The internet: An ethnographic approach*. London: Berg. doi:10.5040/9781474215701.

Miller, V. (2020). *Understanding digital culture* (2nd ed.). London: SAGE.

Millington, R. (2012). *Buzzing communities: How to build bigger, better, and more active online communities*. FeverBee.

Mitchell, W. J. T. (1994). *Picture theory: Essays on verbal and visual representations*. Chicago: University of Chicago Press.

Mitchell, W. J. T. (2005). *What do pictures want? The lives and loves of images*. London/Chicago: University of Chicago press.

Mittelstadt, B. D., Allo, P., Taddeo, M., Wachter, S. & Floridi, L. (2016). The ethics of algorithms: Mapping the debate. *Big Data & Society*, 1–21. doi:10.1177/2053951716679679.

Moore, E., Fisch, M., Kloesei, C., Roberts, D. & Ziegler, L. (eds.) (1984). *Writings of Charles S. Peirce: A chronological cdition, Vol. II: 1867–1871*. Bloomington: Indiana University Press.

Moser-Wellman, A., Vahlberg, V., Durkes, D. & Edwards, J. (2008). *Six competencies of the next generation news organization*. Chicago: Media Management Center.

Mouffe, C. (2000). *The democratic paradox*. London: Verso.

Müller, M. G. (2011). Iconography and iconology as a visual method and approach. In E. Margolis & L. Pauwels (eds.), *The Sage handbook of visual research methods* (pp. 283–297). London: SAGE. doi:10.4135/9781446268278.n15.

Murthy, D. (2008). Digital ethnography: An examination of the use of new technologies for social research. *Sociology*, *42*, 837–855. doi:10.1177/0038038508094565.

Myles, S. (2019). Photomation or fauxtomation? Automation in the newsroom and the impact on editorial labour – A case study. Paper presented at the Computation + Journalism Symposium, February 1–2, University of Miami, Florida. Retrieved from https://drive.google.com/file/d/1WTZUzmvgfOrh-HiiQIVcLbp4J_XTiX9m/view.

Nelson, T. H. (1993). *Literary Machines 93.1: The Report on, and of, Project Xanadu concerning word processing, electronic publishing, hypertext, thinkertoys, tomorrow's intellectual revolution, and certain other topics including knowledge, education and freedom.* Sausalito, CA: Mindful Press.

Neuendorf, K. A. (2002). *The content analysis guidebook.* London: SAGE.

Newman, N., Fletcher, R., Schulz, A., Andi, S. & Nielsen, R. K. (2020). Digital news report 2020. Reuters Institute. Retrieved from https://reutersinstitute.politics.ox.ac.uk/sites/default/files/2020-06/DNR_2020_FINAL.pdf.

Nguyen, M. H., Gruber, J., Fuchs, J., Marler, W., Hunsaker, A. & Hargittai, E. (2020). Changes in digital communication during the COVID-19 global pandemic: Implications for digital inequality and future research. *Social Media + Society*, *6*(3) https://doi.org/10.1177/2056305120948255.

Nissenbaum, H. (2004). Privacy as contextual integrity. *Washington Law Review*, *79*(1), 119–157.

Norris, S. (2004). *Analyzing multimodal interaction: A methodological framework.* New York: Routledge.

O'Halloran, K., Pal, G. & Jin, M. (2021). *Multimodal approach to analysing big social and news media data.* Discourse, Context and Media, 40, doi.org/10.1016/j.dcm.2021.100467.

Orland-Barak, L. & Maskit, D. (2017). *Methodologies of mediation in professional learning.* Cham: Springer.

O'Toole, M. (1994). *The language of displayed art.* London/New York: Routledge.

Page, R., Barton, D., Unger, J. W. & Zappavigna, M. (2014). *Researching language and social media: A student guide.* London: Routledge.

Paltridge, B. & Phakiti, A. (eds.) (2015). *Research methods in applied linguistics: A practical guide.* London: Bloomsbury.

Panofsky, E. (1955). *Meaning in the visual arts: Papers in and on art history.* Garden City, NY: Doubleday Anchor Books.

Panzani, J. (2022). *Histoire de la marque.* 1950. Retrieved from www.panzani.fr/histoire-de-la-marque-panzani.

Papacharissi, Z. (ed.) (2011). *A networked self.* New York: Routledge. doi:10.4324/9780203876527.

Pariser, E. (2011). *The filter bubble: How the new personalized web is changing what we read and how we think.* Johannesburg: Penguin Books.

Parry, K. (2020). Quantitative content analysis of the visual. In L. Pauwels & D. Mannay (eds.), *The SAGE handbook of visual research methods* (2nd ed., pp. 353–366). London: SAGE. doi:10.4135/9781526417015.n22.

Pauwels, L. & Mannay, D. (eds.) (2020). *The SAGE handbook of visual research methods* (2nd ed.). London: SAGE. doi:10.4135/9781526417015.

Pawson, R. & Tilley, N. (1997). *Realistic evaluation*. London: SAGE.

Pedersen, A. Y. & Caviglia, F. (2019). Data literacy as a compound competence. In T. Antipova & A. Rocha (eds.), *Digital Science* (Vol. 850, pp. 166–173). Cham: Springer International. doi:10.1007/978-3-030-02351-5_21.

Peddie, J. (2017). *Augmented reality: Where we will all live*. Tiburon, CA: Springer and Jon Peddie Research.

Perkins, L. (2015). *The community manager's playbook: How to build brand awareness and customer engagement*. New York: Apress.

Perrin, D. (1997). Journalistische Schreibstrategien optimieren. Doctoral dissertation, University of Bern.

Perrin, D. (2011a). "There are two different stories to tell here": Collaborative text-picture production strategies of TV journalists. *Pragmatics*, 43(7), 1865–1875. doi:10.1016/j.pragma.2010.09.023.

Perrin, D. (2011b). Language policy, tacit knowledge, and institutional learning. The case of the Swiss national broadcaster SRG SSR. *Current Issues in Language Planning*, 12(3), 331–348. doi:10.1080/14664208.2011.604953.

Perrin, D. (2012). "La voie tranquille": Routine und Emergenz in Formulierungsprozessen als service public. In H. Feilke & K. Lehnen (eds.), *Schreib- und Textroutinen. Theorie, Erwerb und didaktisch-mediale Modellierung* (pp. 215–239). Frankfurt am Main: Peter Lang.

Perrin, Daniel (2013). *The linguistics of newswriting*. Amsterdam: John Benjamins. doi:10.1075/aals.11.

Perrin, D. (2015a). *Medienlinguistik* (3rd ed.). Konstanz: UVK.

Perrin, D. (2015b). Multimodal writing in the newsroom: Paradigmatic, syntagmatic, and navigational variants. In A. Archer & E. Breuer (eds.), *Multimodality in writing* (pp. 135–152). Bingley: Emerald.

Perrin, D. (2016a). Vom vielschichtigen Planen: Textproduktions-Praxis empirisch erforscht. In A. Deppermann, H. Feilke & A. Linke (eds.), *Sprachliche und kommunikative Praktiken* (pp. 431–455). Berlin: De Gruyter. doi:10.1515/9783110451542-017.

Perrin, D. (2016b). Investigating the backstage of newswriting with process analysis. In C. Paterson, D. Lee, A. Saha & A. Zoellner (eds.), *Advancing media production research: Shifting sites, methods, and politics* (pp. 161–177). New York: Palgrave Macmillan. doi:10.1057/9781137541949.

Perrin, D. (2018a). On, for and with practitioners: A transdisciplinary approach to text production in real-life settings. *AILA Review*, 33(1), 53–80. doi: 10.1075/aila.00013.per.

Perrin, D. (2018b). Medialinguistic approaches: Exploring the case of newswriting. In C. Cotter & D. Perrin (eds.), *The Routledge handbook of language and media* (pp. 9–26). Abingdon: Routledge. doi:10.4324/9781315673134.

Perrin, D. (2019). Progression analysis: Working with large data corpora in field research on writing. In K. Sullivan & E. Lindgren (eds.), *Observing writing: Insights from keystroke logging and handwriting* (pp. 143–162). Leiden: Brill. doi:10.1163/9789004392526_008.

Perrin, D. (2021). "Somehow I'm always writing": On the meaning of transdisciplinary analyses of text production in media change. In G. Jacobs & F. Macgilchrist (eds.), *New foundations and sociotechnical actors: On writing the news today* (pp. 99–127). Amsterdam: John Benjamins.

Perrin, D. & Gnach, A. (2017). Vom fokussierten zum beiläufigen Schreiben. Sprachgebrauchswandel in journalistischer Nachrichtenproduktion. In D. Knorr, K. Lehnen & K. Schindler (eds.), *Schreiben im Übergang von Bildungsinstitutionen* (pp. 171–188). Frankfurt am Main: Peter Lang.

Perrin, D. & Kramsch, C. (2018). Transdisciplinarity in applied linguistics. Introduction to the special issue. *AILA Review*, *31*(1), 1–13. doi:10.1075/aila.00010.int.

Perrin, D. & Zampa, M. (2018). Beyond the myth of journalistic storytelling: Why a narrative approach to journalism falls short. *Studies in Communication Sciences*, *18*(1), 133–134. doi:10.24434/j.scoms.2018.01.009.

Peterson, M. A. (2001). Getting to the story: Unwriteable discourse and interpretive practice in American journalism. *Anthropological Quarterly*, *74*(4), 201–211. doi:10.1353/anq.2001.0038.

Petrucci, A. (2018, Apr 20). How artificial intelligence will impact corporate communications. *Forbes*. Retrieved from www.forbes.com/sites/forbescommunicationscouncil/2018/04/20/how-artificial-intelligence-will-impact-corporate-communications/?sh = 265c697b1dc6.

Pew Research Center (2018). The future of well-being in a tech-saturated world. April 17. Retrieved from https://assets.pewresearch.org/wp-content/uploads/sites/14/2018/04/14154552/PI_2018.04.17_Future-of-Well-Being_FINAL.pdf.

Pflaeging, J., Wildfeuer, J. & Bateman, J. A. (eds.) (2021a). *Empirical multimodality research:. Methods, evaluations, implications*. Berlin/Boston: Walter de Gruyter.

Pflaeging, J., Bateman, J. & Wildfeuer, J. (2021b). Empirical multimodality research: The state of play. In J. Pflaeging, J. Wildfeuer & J. A. Bateman (eds.), *Empirical multimodality research: Methods, evaluations, implications* (pp. 3–32). Berlin/ Boston: Walter de Gruyter

Pieczka, M. (2008). Professionalization of public relation. In W. Donsbach (ed.), *The international encyclopedia of communication* (12 vols.). Wiley & Sons. doi:10.1002/9781405186407.wbiecp108.

Pleil, T. & Helferich, P. S. (2020). Unternehmenskommunikation in der digitalen Transformation. In A. Zerfaß, M. Piwinger & U. Röttger (eds.), *Handbuch Unternehmenskommunikation*. Wiesbaden: Springer Gabler. doi:10.1007/978-3-658-03894-6_49-1.

Polanyi, M. (1966). *The tacit dimension*. Garden City, NY: Doubleday.

Porlezza, C. & Di Salvo, P. (2020). Introduction: Hybrid journalism? Making sense of the field's dissolving boundaries. *Studies in Communication Sciences 20*(2), 205–209. doi:10.24434/j.scoms.2020.02.004.

Potter, W. J. (2016). *Introduction to media literacy*. Thousand Oaks, CA: SAGE.

Potter, W. J. (2021). *Media literacy* (10th ed.). Thousand Oaks, CA: SAGE.

Poulsen, S. V., Kvåle, G. & van Leeuwen, T. (2018). Special issue: Social media as semiotic technology. *Social Semiotics*, *28*(5), 593–600. doi:10.1080/10350330.2018.1509815.

PressHalo (n.d.). Next generation news distribution. www.presshalo.com/about/.

Primo, A. & Zago, G. (2015) Who and what do journalism? *Digital Journalism*, *3*(1), 38–52, doi:10.1080/21670811.2014.927987.

Prints and Photographs Division, Library of Congress. (1892). Alexander Graham Bell at the opening of the long-distance line from New York to Chicago. Reproduction Number LC-G9-Z2-28608-B. www.americaslibrary.gov/jb/recon/jb_recon_telephone_1_e.html.

Putnam, R. D. (2000). *Bowling alone: The collapse and revival of American community*. New York: Simon & Schuster.

Quah, D. T. (1999). The weightless economy in growth. *The Business Economist*, *30*(1), 40–53.

Queirós, A., Faria, D. & Almeida, F. (2017). Strengths and limitations of qualitative and quantitative research methods. *European Journal of Education Studies*, *3*(9), 369–387. doi:10.5281/zenodo.887089.

Quinn, A. (2007). Moral virtues for journalists. *Journal of Mass Media Ethics*, *22*(2–3), 168–186. doi:10.1080/08900520701315764.

Quinn, A. (2018). *Virtue ethics and professional journalism*. Cham: Springer.

Quinn, S. (2005). Where do we go from here? Possibilities in a convergent future. In S. Quinn & V. F. Filak (eds.), *Convergent journalism: An introduction* (pp. 205–212). Amsterdam: Elsevier.

Ragnedda, M. & Muschert, G. W. (eds.) (2013). *The digital divide: The internet and social inequality in international perspective*. London: Routledge.

Rainie, L. & Wellman, B. (2012). *Networked: The new social operating system*. Cambridge, MA: MIT Press.

Rampton, B., Tusting, K., Maybin, J., Barwell, R., Creese, A. & Lytra, V. (2004). *UK linguistic ethnography: A discussion paper*. Retrieved from www.lancaster.ac.uk/fss/organisations/lingethn/documents/discussion_paper_jan_05.pdf.

Raupp, J. & Klewes, J. (2004). *Quo vadis public relations? Auf dem Weg zum Kommunikationsmanagement: Bestandsaufnahmen und Entwicklungen*. Wiesbaden: VS Verlag für Sozialwissenschaften.

Rheingold, H. (2000). *The virtual community: Homestanding on the virtual frontier* (2nd ed.). Cambridge MA: MIT Press.

Riepl, W. (1913). *Das Nachrichtenwesen des Altertums mit besonderer Rücksicht auf die Römer*. Leipzig: Teubner.

Riffe, D., Lacy, S. & Fico, F. (2014). *Analyzing media messages: Using quantitative content analysis in research* (3rd ed.). New York: Routledge. doi:10.4324/9780203551691.

Rinsdorf, L. & Boers, R. (2016). The need to reflect: Data journalism as an aspect of disrupted practice in digital journalism and in journalism education. In J. Engel (ed.), *Promoting understanding of statistics about society: Proceedings of the Roundtable Conference of the International Association of Statistics Education (IASE)*. Berlin: ISI/IASE. Retrieved from https://iase-web.org/documents/papers/rt2016/Rinsdorf.pdf.

Rodriguez, L. & Dimitrova, D. V. (2011). The levels of visual framing. *Journal of Visual Literacy*, *30*(1), 48–65. doi:10.1080/23796529.2011.11674684.

Rosenbaum, J. E., Beentjes, J. W. J. & Konig, R. P. (2008). Mapping media literacy key concepts and future directions. *Annals of the International Communication Association*, *32*(1), 313–353. doi:10.1080/23808985.2008.11679081.

Rose, G. (2016). *Visual methodologies: An introduction to researching with visual materials* (4th ed.). London: SAGE.

Rosenberger, P. (2020). Conversational interfaces: Workshop with Pascal Rosenberger, co-founder and co-managing director of eggheads.ai [IAM MediaLab Workshop], October 22.

Rosenberger Staub, N. & Niederhäuser, M. (2019). Rollen und Aufgaben der Corporate Communications in der digitalen Transformation. In M. Stumpf (ed.), *Digitalisierung und Kommunikation: Konsequenzen der digitalen Transformation für die Wirtschaftskommunikation* (Europäische Kulturen in der Wirtschaftskommunikation, vol. 31, pp. 69–88). Wiesbaden: Springer VS. doi:10.1007/978-3-658-26113-9_5.

Rushkoff, D. (2010). *Program or be programmed: Ten commands for the digital age.* New York: OR Books.

Ryan, C. D., Schaul, A. J., Butner, R. & Swarthout, J. T. (2020). Monetizing disinformation in the attention economy: The case of genetically modified organisms (GMOs). *European Management Journal*, *38*(1), 7–18. doi:10.1016/j.emj.2019.11.002.

Ryan, M.-L. (2015). *Narrative as virtual reality 2: Revisiting immersion and interactivity in literature and electronic media.* Baltimore: Johns Hopkins University Press.

Saenger, P. (1997). *Space between words: The origins of silent reading.* Stanford, CA: Stanford University Press.

Sánchez Laws, A. L. & Utne, T. (2019). Ethics guidelines for immersive journalism. April 24. *Frontiers in Robotics and AI.* doi:10.3389/frobt.2019.00028. Retrieved from www.frontiersin.org/articles/10.3389/frobt.2019.00028/full.

Schäfer, M. & Van Es, K. (eds.) (2017). *The datafied society: Studying culture through data.* Amsterdam: Amsterdam University Press. doi:10.2307/j.ctt1v2xsqn.

Schmidt, R. (2019). Materiality, meaning, social practices: Remarks on new materialism. In U. K. Kissmann & J. van Loon (eds.), *Discussing new materialism* (pp. 135–149). Wiesbaden: Springer VS. doi:10.1007/978-3-658-22300-7_7.

Schmitz, U. (2015). *Einführung in die Medienlinguistik.* Darmstadt: Wissenschaftliche Buchgesellschaft.

Schories, M. (2020). Using word embeddings for journalistic research. *Towards Data Science.* March 5. Retrieved from https://towardsdatascience.com/using-word-embeddings-as-a-method-for-journalistic-research-ae82ffea7a62.

Schories, M. (n.d.). So haben wir den Bundestag ausgerechnet. *Süddeutsche Zeitung.* Retrieved from https://projekte.sueddeutsche.de/artikel/politik/so-haben-wir-den-bundestag-ausgerechnet-e893391/.

Schudson, M. (2008). *Why democracies need an unlovable press.* Cambridge: Polity Press.

Sealey, A. & Carter, B. (2004). *Applied linguistics as social science*. London: Continuum.

Seargeant, P. & Tagg, C. (eds.) (2014). *The language of social media: Identity and community on the Internet*. London: Palgrave Macmillan.

Seiden, A. (1997). Electronic storytelling and human immersion. In *Modeling and simulation: Linking entertainment and defense / Committee on Modeling and Simulation: Opportunities for collaboration between the defense and entertainment research communities; Computer Science and Telecommunications Board; Commission on Physical Sciences, Mathematics, and Applications, National Research Council* (pp. 168–172). Washington, DC: National Academy Press.

Serazio, M. (2021). How news went guerrilla marketing: A history, logic, and critique of brand journalism. *Media, Culture & Society*, *43*(1), 117–132. doi:10.1177/016344372093948.

Shane, J. (2019). *You look like a thing and I love you: How artificial intelligence works and why it's making the world a weirder place*. London: Little, Brown and Company.

Shneiderman, B., Plaisant, C., Cohen, M., Jacobs, S., Elmqvist, N. & Diakopoulos, N. (2017). *Designing the user interface: Strategies for effective human–computer interaction* (6th ed.). Essex: Pearson.

Shorthand (2017). Checklist for planning a multimedia story. A 12-point checklist to help with planning your first multimedia story. November 17. Retrieved from https://shorthand.com/the-craft/checklist-for-planning-a-multimedia-story/

Siapera, E. (2018). *Understanding new media* (2nd ed.). London: SAGE.

Sims, R. (1997). Interactivity: A forgotten art? *Computers in Human Behavior*, *13*(2), 157–180. doi:10.1016/S0747-5632(97)00004-6.

Simon, H. A. (1994). The bottleneck of attention: Connecting thought with motivation. In W. D. Spaulding (ed.), *Integrative views of motivation, cognition, and emotion* (pp. 1–21). Lincoln: University of Nebraska Press.

Sirrah, A. (2019a). Native advertising may jeopardize the legitimacy of newsrooms. *Columbia Journalism Review*. September 6. Retrieved from www.cjr.org/tow_center/native-ads-endanger-newsrooms.php.

Sirrah, A. (2019b). Guide to native advertising. CJR. *Columbia Journalism Review*. September 6. Retrieved from www.cjr.org/tow_center_reports/native-ads.php.

Slater, M. & Sanchez-Vives, M. V. (2016). Enhancing our lives with immersive virtual reality. *Frontiers in Robotics and AI. 3*. doi: 10.3389/frobt.2016.00074.

Smith, D. & Protevi, J. (2020). Gilles Deleuze. In E. N. Zalta (ed.), *The Stanford Encyclopedia of Philosophy* (Spring 2020 ed.). Retrieved from https://plato.stanford.edu/archives/spr2020/entries/deleuze/.

Snow, J. (1855). *On the mode of communication of cholera* (2nd ed.). London: John Churchill. Retrieved from https://archive.org/details/b28985266/page/n3/mode/2up.

Solon, O. (2017). Ex-Facebook president Sean Parker: Site made to exploit human "vulnerability." *Guardian*, November 9. Retrieved from www.theguardian.com/technology/2017/nov/09/facebook-sean-parker-vulnerability-brain-psychology.

Sontag, S. (1977). *On photography*. London: Penguin.

Southerton C. (2020). Datafication. In L. Schintler & C. McNeely (eds.), *Encyclopedia of big data*. Cham: Springer. doi:10.1007/978-3-319-32001-4_332-1

Spayd, E. (2014). Who cares who's a journalist? *Columbia Journalism Review*, November/ December. Retrieved from https://archives.cjr.org/editorial/who_cares_whos_a_ journalist.php.

Spöhrer, M. (2017). Applications of actor-network theory in media studies: A research overview. In M. Spöhrer & B. Ochsner (eds.), *Applying the actor-network theory in media studies*. Hershey, PA: IGI Global.

Spöhrer, M. & Ochsner, B. (2017). *Applying the actor-network theory in media studies*. Hershey, PA: IGI Global.

Spreitzer, G. M. & Sonenshein, S. (2004). Toward the construct definition of positive deviance. *American Behavioral Scientist*, *47*(6), 828–847. doi:10.1177/0002764203260212.

SRF Data (2018). 20 years 20 titles. January 28. Produced by Angelo Zehr, Julian Schmidli, Duc-Quang Nguyen, Tania Boa, Luc Guillemot. Retrived from https://interactive.swissinfo .ch/2018_01_28_federer20/en.html#/en.

SRG SSR (n.d.). Journalism charter. Retrieved from www.srgssr.ch/en/what-we-do/quality/ journalism-charter/.

Sriramesh, K. & Verčič, D. (eds.) (2003). *The global public relations handbook: Theory, research, and practice*. Mahwah, NJ: Lawrence Erlbaum.

Stabe, M. (2018, January 30). @srfdata continue to set the standard for transparency and reproducibility in data journalism. Retrieved from https://twitter.com/martinstabe/ status/958254070367694848.

Stjernfelt, F. (2007). *Diagrammatology: An investigation on the borderlines of phenomenology, ontology, and semiotics*. Dordrecht: Springer.

Stjernfelt, F. & Lauritzen, A. M. (2020). *Your post has been removed: Tech giants and freedom of speech*. Cham: Springer Verlag.

Stocchetti, M. & Kukkonen, K. (2011). *Images in use: Towards the critical analysis of visual communication*. Amsterdam/Philadelphia: John Benjamins Publishing Company.

Stöckl, H., Caple, H. & Pflaeging, J. (2020). *Shifts towards image-centricity in contemporary multimodal practices*. New York: Routledge.

Strömbäck, J. (2008). Four phases of mediatization: An analysis of the mediatization of politics. *The International Journal of Press/Politics 13*(3), 228–246. doi:10.1177/1940161208319097.

Stubbs, M. (1997). Whorf's children: Critical comments on critical discourse analysis (CDA). In A. Ryan & A. Wray (eds.), *Evolving models of language* (pp. 100–116). Clevedon: Multilingual Matters.

Sturken, M. & Cartwright, L. (2001). *Practices of looking: An introduction to visual culture*. Oxford: Oxford University Press.

Tagg, C. (2014). Audience design and language choice in the construction and maintenance of translocal communities on social network sites. In P. Seargeant, P. & C. Tagg (eds.), *The language of social media: Identity and community on the Internet (pp. 161–185)*. London: Palgrave Macmillan.

Tamboer, S. L., Kleemans, M. & Daalmans, S. (2020). "We are a neeeew generation": Early adolescents' views on news and news literacy. *Journalism*, 1–7. doi:10.1177/1464884920924527.

Tavani, H. T. (2011). Ethics and technology: *Controversies, questions, and strategies for ethical computing*. Hoboken, NJ: Wiley.

Tavory, I. & Timmermans, S. (2009). Two cases of ethnography: Grounded theory and the extended case method. *Ethnography*, *10*(3), 243–263. doi:10.1177/1466138109339042.

Telner J. (2021). Future trends in voice user interfaces. In T. Ahram (ed.), *Advances in artificial intelligence, software and systems engineering: Proceedings of the AHFE 2020 Virtual Conferences on Software and Systems Engineering, and Artificial Intelligence and Social Computing, July 16–20, 2020, USA*. Advances in Intelligent System and Computing (AISC, vol. 1213). Cham: Springer. doi:10.1007/978-3-030-51328-3_26.

Tench, R., Verčič, R., Zerfass, A., Moreno, A. & Verhoeven, P. (2017). *Communication Excellence: How to develop, manage and lead exceptional communications*. London: Palgrave Macmillan.

The Washington Post (2018). The Washington Post creates new AR web experience available with Apple's iOS 12 release. *Washington Post*, September 25. Retrieved from www.washingtonpost.com/pr/2018/09/25/washington-post-creates-new-ar-web-experience-available-with-apples-ios-release/.

Thurlow, C. & Mroczek, K. (eds.) (2011). *Digital discourse: Language in the new media*. New York/London: Oxford University Press.

Thurman, N. (2019). Computational journalism. In K. Wahl-Jorgensen & T. Hanitzsch (eds.), *The handbook of journalism studies* (2nd ed., pp. 180-195). New York: Routledge.

Thurman, N. & Hermida, A. (2010). Gotcha: How newsroom norms are shaping participatory journalism online. In S. Tunney & G. Monaghan (eds.), *Web journalism: A new form of citizenship?* (pp. 46–62). Eastbourne: Sussex Academic Press.

Thurman, N., Lewis, S. C. & Kunert, J. (2019). Algorithms, automation, and news. *Digital Journalism*, *7*(8), 980–992. doi:10.1080/21670811.2019.1685395.

Time (2019). Welcome to TIME immersive's Apollo 11 "Landing on the Moon" experience. July 18. Retrieved from https://time.com/longform/apollo-11-moon-landing-immersive-experience/.

Tufte, E. R. (1997). *Visual explanations: Images and quantities, evidence and narrative*. Ceshire: Graphic Press.

Tunstall, J. (2009). European news and multi-platform journalists in the lead. *Journalism*, *10*(3), 387–389. doi:10.1177/1464884909102603.

Twitter Inc. (2020), Permanent suspension of @realDonaldTrump. November 24. Retrieved from https://blog.twitter.com/en_us/topics/company/2020/suspension.html.

UCL (n.d.). Why we post. Retrieved from www.ucl.ac.uk/why-we-post/discoveries/2-social-media-is-education.

UNCTAD (2020). *The COVID-19 crisis: Accentuating the need to bridge digital devides*. April 6. Retrieved from https://unctad.org/news/coronavirus-reveals-need-bridge-digital-divide.

United Colors of Benetton (2011). UNHATE worldwide campaign. Press releases and statements. November 16. Retrieved from www.benettongroup.com/media-press/press-releases-and-statements/unhate-worldwide-campaign/.

van der Haak, B., Parks, M. & Castells, M. (2012). The future of journalism: Networked journalism. *International Journal of Communication, 6*, 2923–2938.

van Dijk, J. (1991). *De netwerkmaatschappij*. Houten:Bohn Staflen Van Loghum.

van Dijk, J. (2006a). Digital divide research, achievements and shortcomings. *Poetics, 34*, 221–235.

van Dijk, J. (2006b). *The network society: Social aspects of new media* (2nd ed.). London: SAGE.

van Dijk, J. (2012). *The network society* (3rd ed.). London: SAGE.

van Dijck, J. (2014). Datafication, dataism and dataveillance: Big data between scientific paradigm and ideology. *Surveillance and Society, 12*(2), 197–208.

van Dijk, T. A. (2001). Multidisciplinary CDA. A plea for diversity. In R. Wodak & M. Meyer (eds.), *Methods of critical discourse analysis* (pp. 95–120). Los Angeles: SAGE. doi:10.4135/9780857028020.n5.

van Leeuwen, T. (2005). *Introducing social semiotics*. Abingdon: Routledge.

van Leeuwen, T. (2008). New forms of writing, new visual competencies. *Visual Studies, 23*(2), 130–135. doi:10.1080/14725860802276263.

van Leeuwen, T. (2011). *The language of colour: An introduction*. London/New York: Routledge.

van Leeuwen, T. (2018). Aesthetics and text in the digital age. In K. A. Mills, A. Stornaiuolo, A. Smith & J. Zacher Pandya (eds.), *Handbook of writing, literacies, and education in digital cultures* (pp. 285–300). Abingdon: Routledge.

van Loon, J. (2019). Historical materialism and actor-network-theory. In U. T. Kissmann & J. van Loon (eds.), *Discussing new materialism: Methodological implications for the study of materialities* (pp. 39–65). Wiesbaden: Springer VS.

van Ruler, A. A. B. & Heath, R. L. (2015). Public relations. In W. Donsbach (eds.), *The international encyclopedia of communication*. Hoboken, NJ: Wiley & Sons. doi:10.1002/9781405186407.wbiecp127.pub2.

Vannini, P. (2015). *Non-representational methodologies: Re-envisioning research*. London: Routledge.

Verčič, D. & Zerfass, A. (2016). A comparative excellence framework for communication management. *Journal of Communication Management, 20*(4), 270–288. doi:10.1108/JCOM-11-2015-0087.

Verčič, D. & Tkalac Verčič, A. (2015). From reflexive to reflective mediatisation. *Public Relations Review, 41*(4), 142–152.

Voorveld, H. A. M. (2019). Brand communication in social media: A research agenda. *Journal of Advertising, 48*(1), 14–26, doi:10.1080/00913367.2019.1588808.

Wahl-Jorgensen, K. & Hanitzsch, T. (2019). Journalism studies: Developments, challenges, and future directions. In K. Wahl-Jorgensen & T. Hanitzsch (eds.), *The handbook of journalism studies* (2nd ed.). New York: Routledge. doi:10.4324/9781315167497.

Wang, P. (2019). On defining artificial intelligence. *Journal of Artificial General Intelligence, 10*(2), 1–37. doi:10.2478/jagi-2019-0002.

Ward, S. J. A. (2009). Journalism ethics. In K. Wahl-Jorgensen & T. Hanitzsch (eds.), *The handbook of journalism studies* (pp. 295–309). New York: Routledge.

Ward, S. J. A. (2011). *Ethics and the media: An introduction*. Cambridge/New York: Cambridge University Press.

Ware, C. (2000). *Information visualization*. Burlington, MA: Morgan Kaufmann.

Warner, M. (2005). *Publics and counterpublics*. Cambridge: Zone Books.

Webster, F. (2005). Making sense of the information age. *Information, Communication & Society, 8*(4), 439–458. doi:10.1080/13691180500418212.

Weiner, M. & Kochhar, S. (2016). Irreversible: The public relations big data revolution. Institute for Public Relations. Retrieved from www.instituteforpr.org/wp-content/uploads/IPR_ PR-Big-Data-Revolution_3-29.pdf.

Wellman, B. (2001). Physical space and cyberplace: The rise of personalized networking. *International Journal of Urban and Regional Research, 25*(2), 227–252.

Wellman, B., Quan Haase, A., Witte, J. & Hampton, K. (2001). Does the Internet increase, decrease, or supplement social capital? Social networks, participation, and community commitment. *American Behavioral Scientist, 45*(3), 436–455. doi:10.1177/00027640121957286.

Wells, H. G. (1922). *A short history of the world*. New York: Macmillan.

Wenger, D. H., Owens, L. C. & Cain, J. (2018). Help wanted: Realigning journalism education to meet the needs of top U.S. news companies. *Journalism and Mass Communication Educator, 73*(1), 18–36. doi:10.1177/1077695817745464.

Wenger, E. (1998). *Communities of practice: Learning, meaning, and identity*. Cambridge: Cambridge University Press.

White, J. & Hobsbawm, J. (2007). Public relations and journalism. *Journalism Practice, 1*, 283–292.

Widdowson, H. G. (2000). On the limitations of linguistics applied. *Applied Linguistics, 21*(1), 3–35. doi:10.1093/applin/21.1.3.

Wiencierz, C. & Röttger, U. (2017). The use of big data in corporate communication. *Corporate Communications: An International Journal, 22*(3), 258–272. doi:10.1108/CCIJ-02-2016-0015.

Wiencierz, C. & Röttger, U. (2019). Big data in public relations: A conceptual framework. *Public Relations Journal, 12*(3), 1–15.

Wiesenberg, M. & Verčič, D. (2020). The status quo of the visual turn in public relations practice. *Communications: The European Journal of Communication Research*, Ahead of Print. doi:10.1515/commun-2019-0111.

Wiesenberg, M. & Zerfass, A. (2016). Big data and algorithms: Empirical study on the status quo in Germany and Europe. *PR magazine, 47*(9), 42–47.

Wiesenberg, M., Zerfass, A. & Moreno, A. (2017). Big data and automation in strategic communication. *International Journal of Strategic Communication, 11*(2), 95–114. doi:10.1080/1553118X.2017.128577.

Williams, R. (1974). *Television, technology and cultural form*. London: Fontana.

Wilson, E. J. (2004). *The information revolution and developing countries*. Cambridge, MA: MIT Press.

Wirth, M. O. (2006). Issues in media convergence. In A. B. Albarran, S. Chan-Olmsted & M. O. Wirth (eds.), *Handbook of media management and economics* (pp. 445–462). Mahwah NJ: Lawrence Erlbaum.

Wittel, A. (2001). Toward a network sociality. *Theory, Culture & Society*, *18*(6), 51–76. doi:10.1177/026327601018006003.

Wolf, Gary (1995). The curse of Xanadu. *Wired*. January. Retrieved from www.wired .com/1995/06/xanadu/.

Wu, T. (2015). Attention brokers. NYU Law. Retrieved from www.law.nyu.edu/sites/default/files/ upload_documents/Tim%20Wu%20-%20Attention%20Brokers.pdf.

Zampa, M. (2017). *Argumentation in the newsroom*. Amsterdam: John Benjamins.

Zappavigna, M. (2011). Ambient affiliation: A linguistic perspective on Twitter. *New Media and Society*, *13*(5), 788–806.

Zappavigna, M. (2014). Ambient affiliation in microblogging: Bonding around the quotidian. *Media International Australia*, *151*, 97–103.

Zehr, A. (2017). Roger Federer: Preprocessing and EDA. October. Retrieved from https://srfdata .github.io/2018-01-roger-federer/.

Zehr, A. (2018). Wie wir 20 + Jahre Tennisdaten analysiert und aufbereitet haben. Janurary 20. https://medium.com/@angelozehr/wie-wir-20-jahre-tennisdaten-analysiert-und-aufbereitet-haben-f4d3498580c3.

Zerfass, A., Hagelstein, J. & Tench, R. (2020). Artificial intelligence in communication management: a cross-national study on adoption and knowledge, impact, challenges and risks. *Journal of Communication Management*, *24*(4), 377-389. doi:10.1108/JCOM-10-2019-0137.

Zerfass, A., Moreno, A., Tench, R., Verčič, D. & Verhoeven, P. (2017). European communication monitor 2017. *How strategic communication deals with the challenges of visualisation, social bots and hypermodernity: Results of a survey in 50 countries*. Brussels: EACD/ EUPRERA, Quadriga Media Berlin.

Zerfass, A., Stieglitz, S., Clausen, S., Ziegele, D. & Berger, K. (2021). Communications trend radar 2021. Denialism, virtual corporate communications, sustainable communications, digital nudging & voice interaction. *Communication Insights*,10. Leipzig: Academic Society for Management & Communication. Retrieved from www.akademische-gesellschaft .com/fileadmin/webcontent/Forschungsthemen/Communications_Trend_Radar/AGUK_ CommTrendRadar2021.pdf.

Zerfass, A., Tench, R., Verčič, D., Verhoeven, P. & Moreno, A. (2014). European communication monitor 2014. *Excellence in strategic communication: Key issues, leadership, gender and mobile media – Results of a survey in 42 countries*. Brussels: EACD/EUPRERA, Helios Media.

Zerfass, A., Verčič, D., Nothhaft, H. & Werder, K. P. (2018). Strategic communication: Defining the field and its contribution to research and practice. *International Journal of Strategic Communication*, *12*(4), 487–505.

Zerfass, A., Verčič D., Verhoeven P., Moreno, A. & Tench, R. (2019). European communication monitor 2019. *Exploring trust in the profession: transparency, artificial intelligence and new content strategies – Results of a survey in 46 countries*. Brussels: EUPRERA/EACD, Quadriga Media Berlin.

Zerfass, A., Verčič, D. & Wiesenberg, M. (2016a). The dawn of a new golden age for media relations? How PR professionals interact with the mass media and use new collaboration practices. *Public Relations Review*, *42*(4), 499–508. doi:10.1016/j.pubrev.2016.03.005.

Zerfass, A., Verhoeven, P., Moreno, A., Tench, R. & Verčič, D. (2016b). European communication monitor 2016. *Exploring trends in big data, stakeholder engagement and strategic communication: Results of a survey in 43 countries*. Brussels: EACD/EUPRERA, Quadriga Media Berlin.

Zerfass, A., Verhoeven, P., Moreno, A., Tench, R. & Verčič, D. (2020). European Communication Monitor 2020. *Ethical challenges, gender issues, cyber security, and competence gaps in strategic communication: Results of a survey in 44 countries*. Brussels: EUPRERA/EACD.

Zuboff, S. (2015). Big other: Surveillance capitalism and the prospects of an information civilization. *Journal of Information Technology*, *30*(1), 75–89.

Zuboff, S. (2019). *The age of surveillance capitalism: The fight for a human future at the new frontier of power*. New York: Public Affairs.

Zuboff, S. (2020). You are now remotely controlled. *New York Times*, January 24. Retrieved from www.nytimes.com/2020/01/24/opinion/sunday/surveillance-capitalism.html.

Index